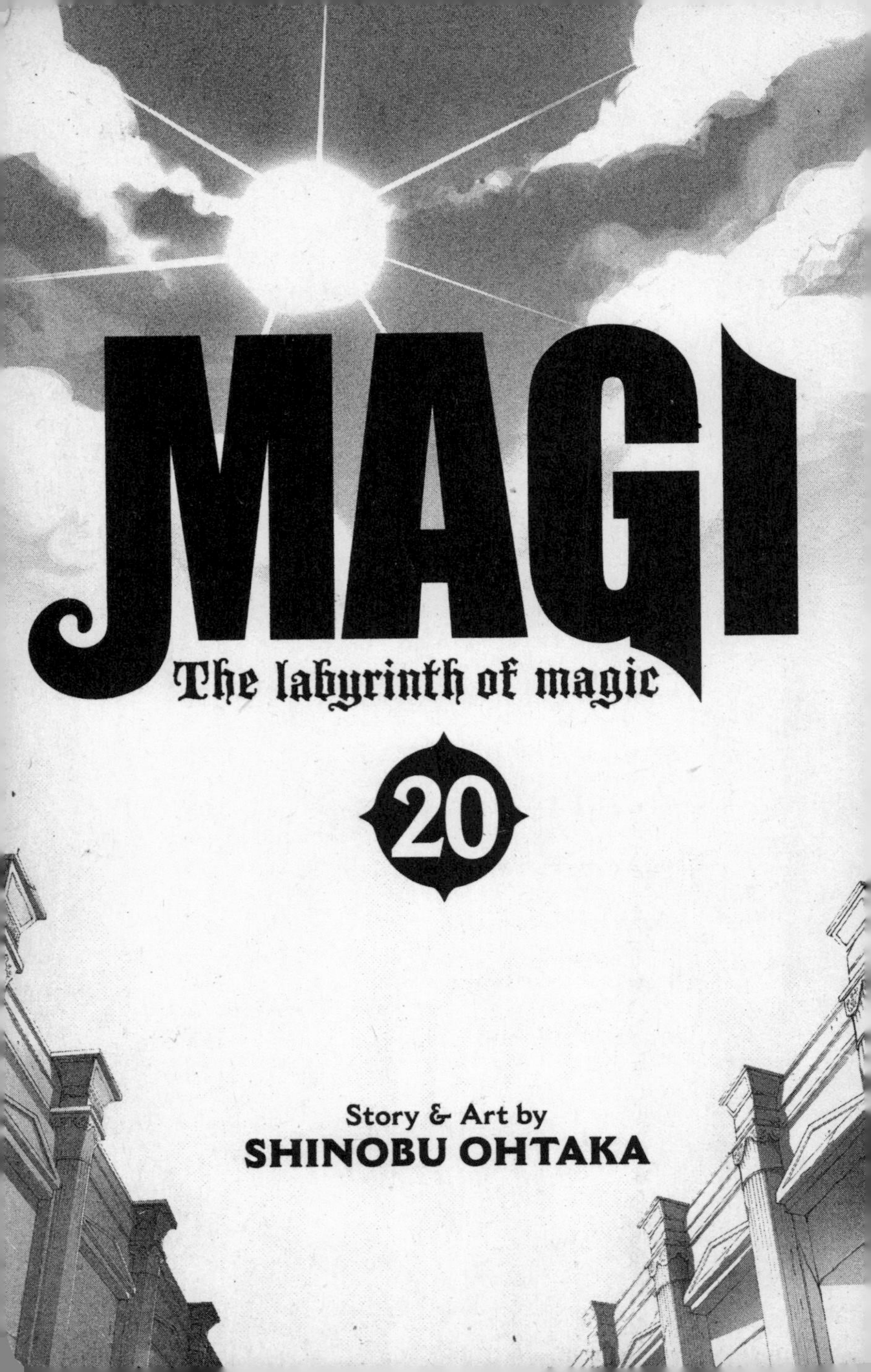
MAGI
The labyrinth of magic
20
Story & Art by
SHINOBU OHTAKA

MAGI
The labyrinth of magic
20

CONTENTS

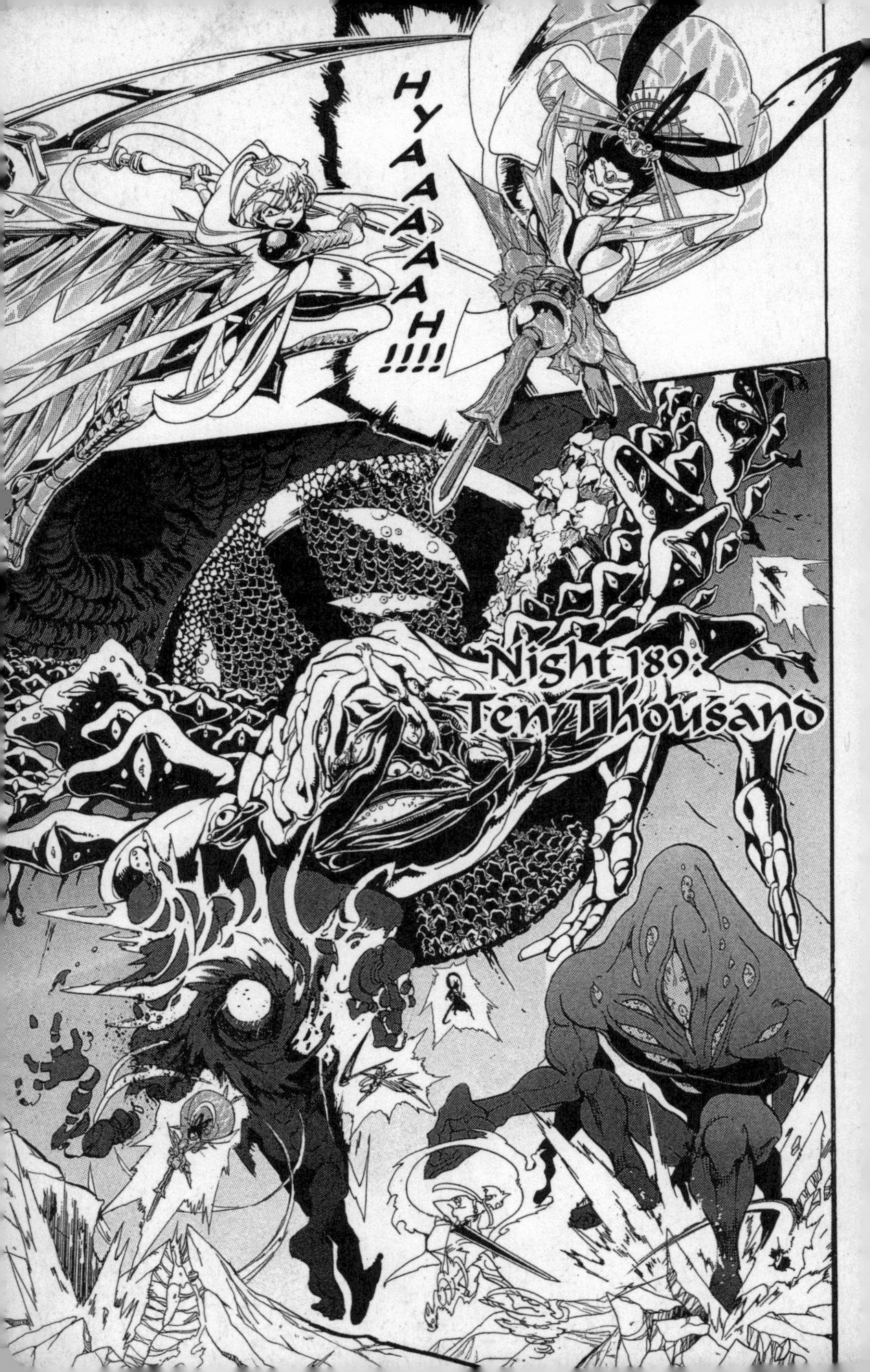
HYAAAAH!!!!
Night 189: Ten Thousand

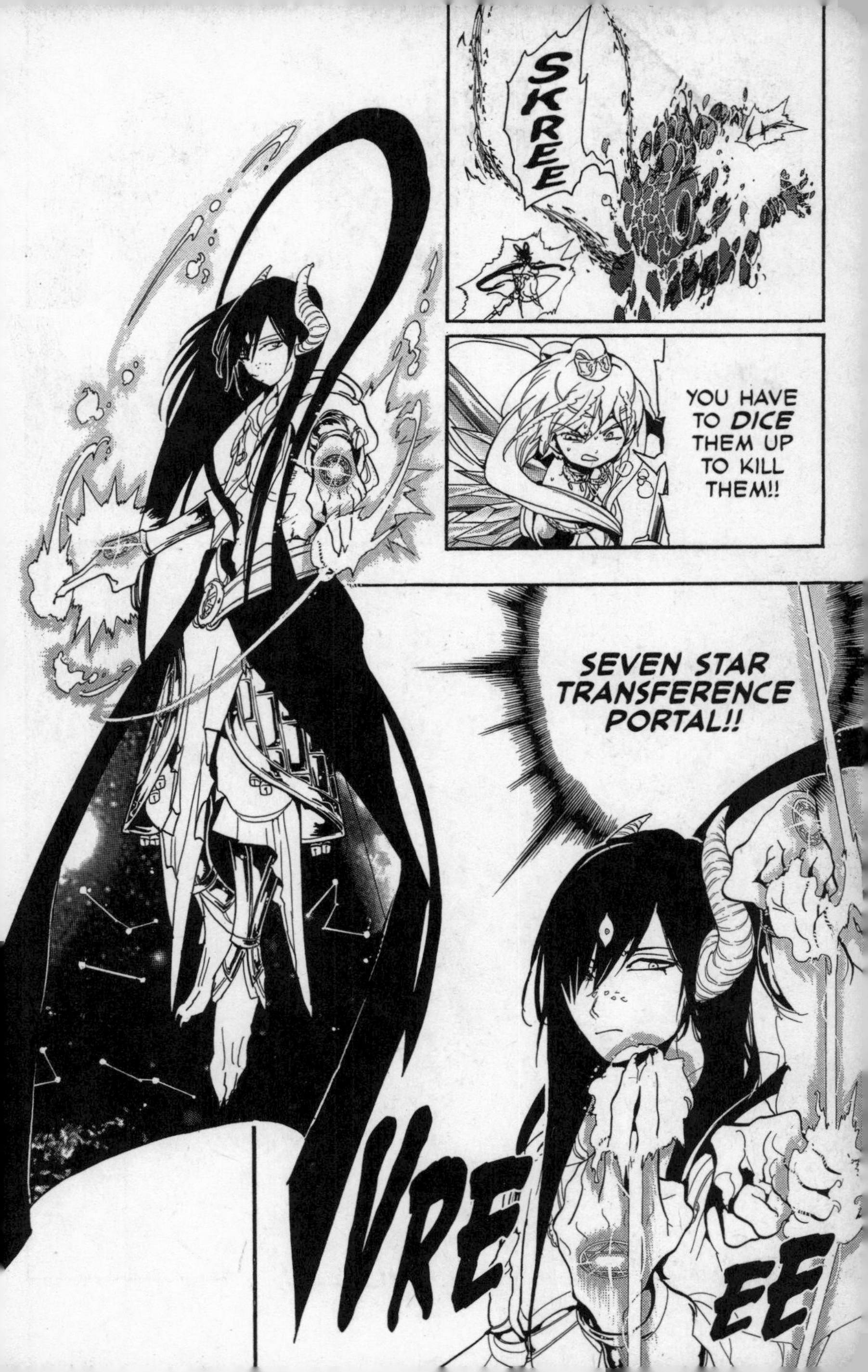
SKREE
YOU HAVE TO *DICE* THEM UP TO KILL THEM!!
SEVEN STAR TRANSFERENCE PORTAL!!
VRE
EE

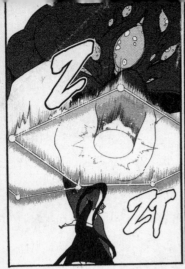

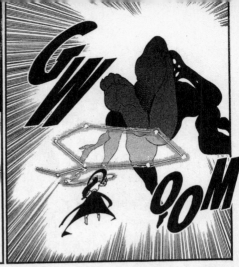

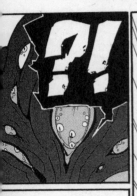

THIS IS TIRING.
MY DJINN
ISN'T GEARED
TOWARD
COMBAT!

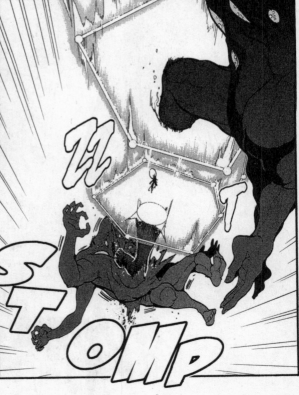

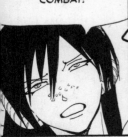

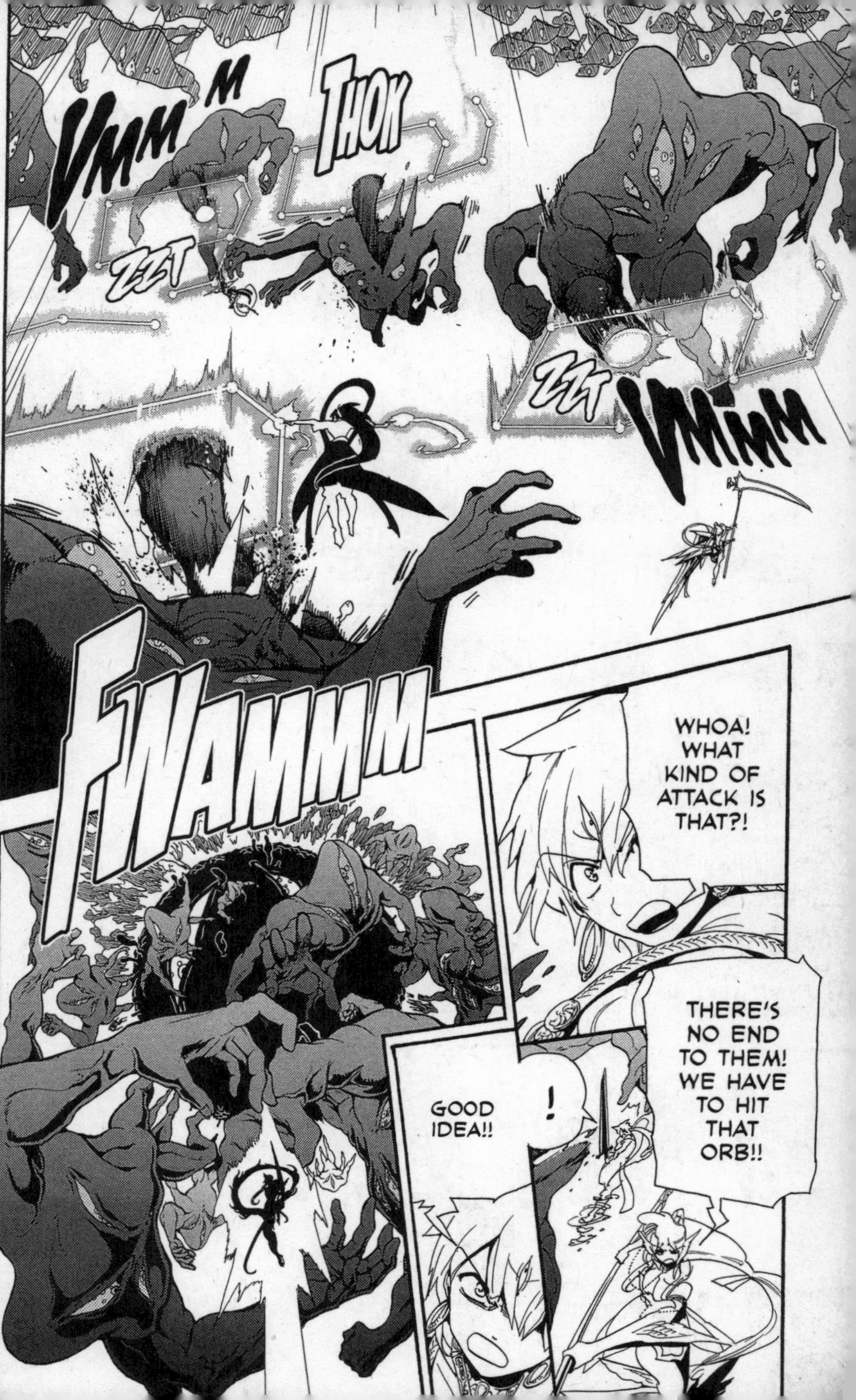
THOK
VMMM
ZZT
ZZT
VMMM
WHOA! WHAT KIND OF ATTACK IS THAT?!
FWAMMM
THERE'S NO END TO THEM! WE HAVE TO HIT THAT ORB!!
!
GOOD IDEA!!

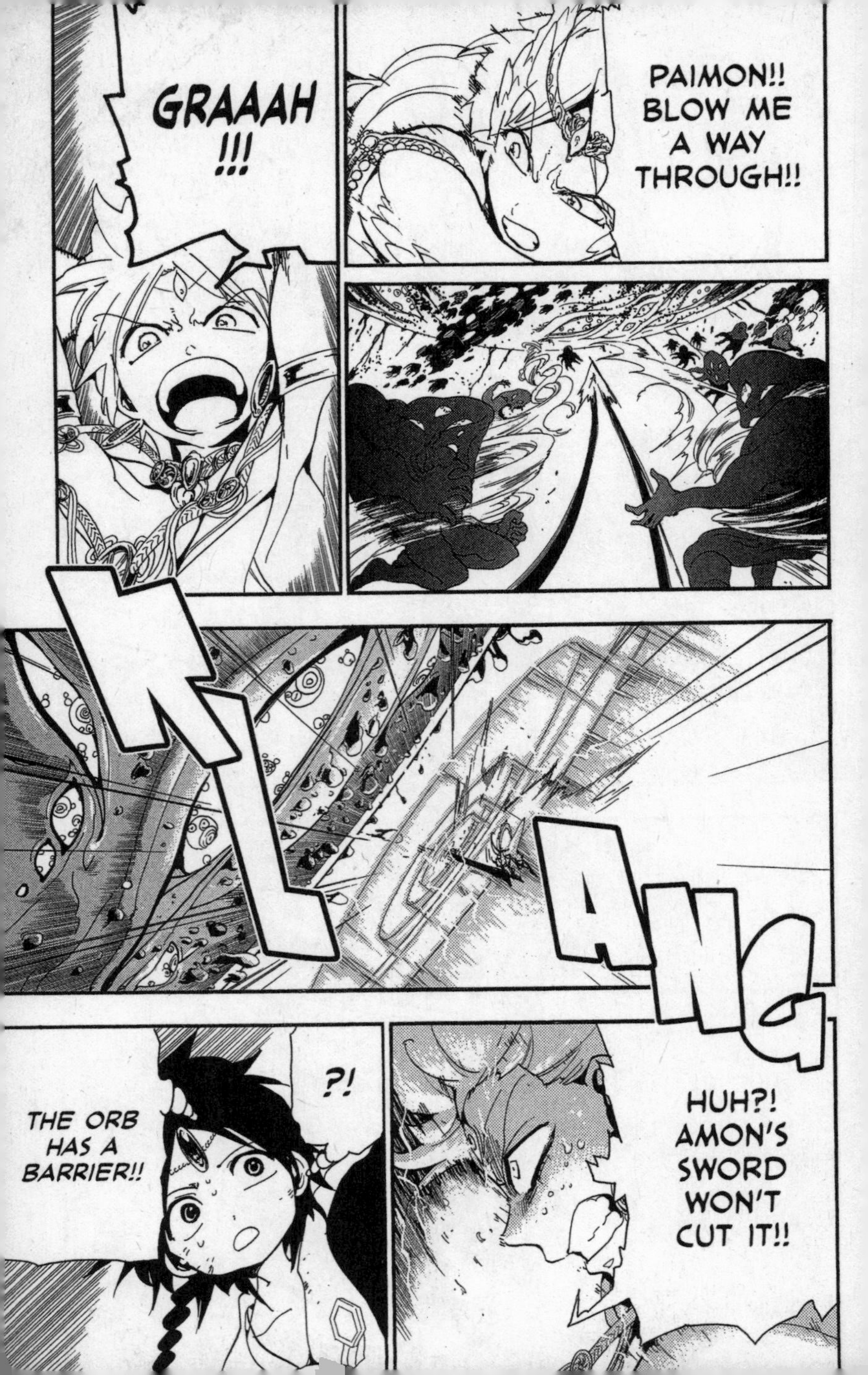
PAIMON!! BLOW ME A WAY THROUGH!!
GRAAAH !!!
KLANG
HUH?! AMON'S SWORD WON'T CUT IT!!
?!
THE ORB HAS A BARRIER!!

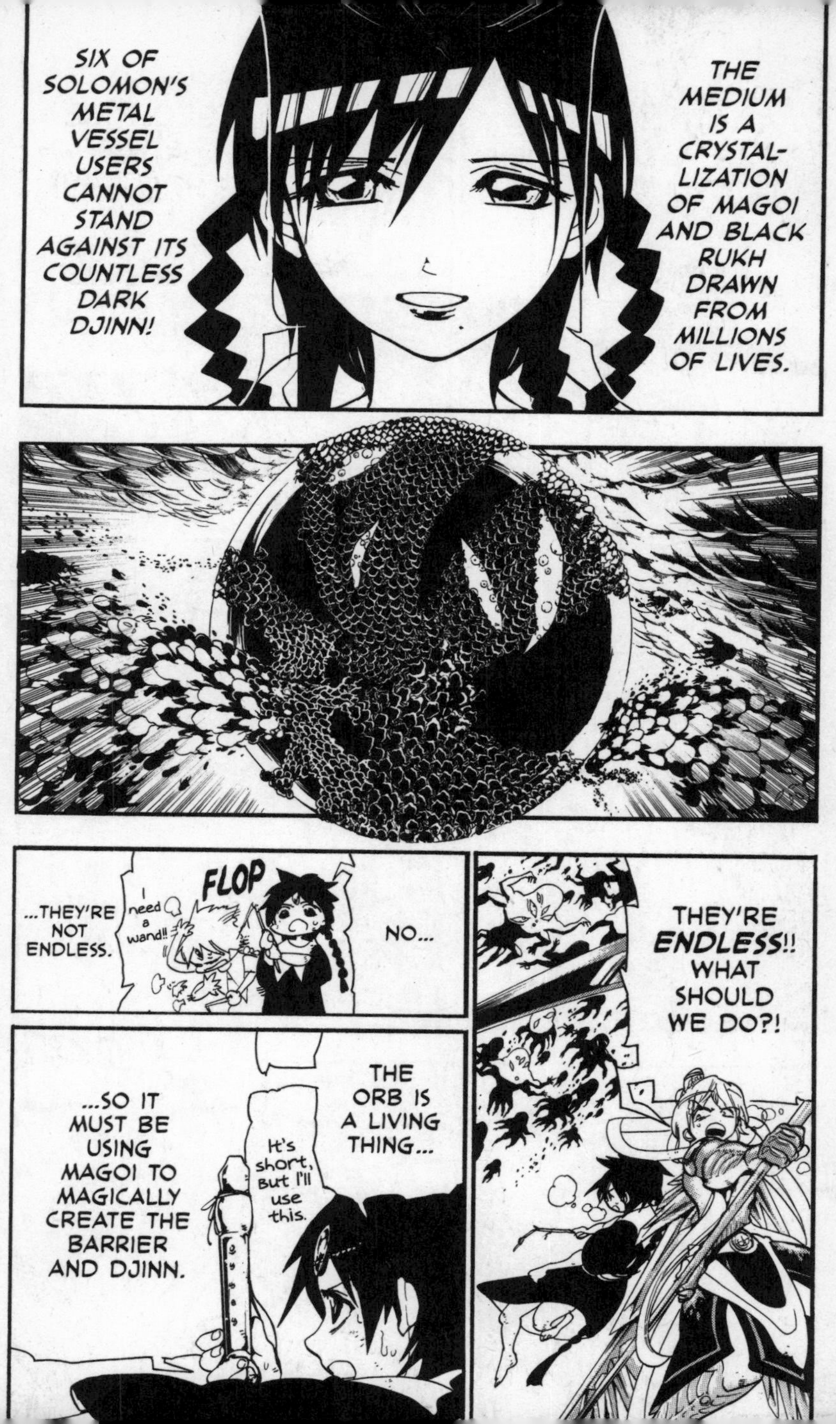
THE MEDIUM IS A CRYSTAL-LIZATION OF MAGOI AND BLACK RUKH DRAWN FROM MILLIONS OF LIVES.
SIX OF SOLOMON'S METAL VESSEL USERS CANNOT STAND AGAINST ITS COUNTLESS DARK DJINN!
THEY'RE ENDLESS!! WHAT SHOULD WE DO?!
NO...
FLOP
I need a wand!!
...THEY'RE NOT ENDLESS.
THE ORB IS A LIVING THING...
It's short, but I'll use this.
...SO IT MUST BE USING MAGOI TO MAGICALLY CREATE THE BARRIER AND DJINN.

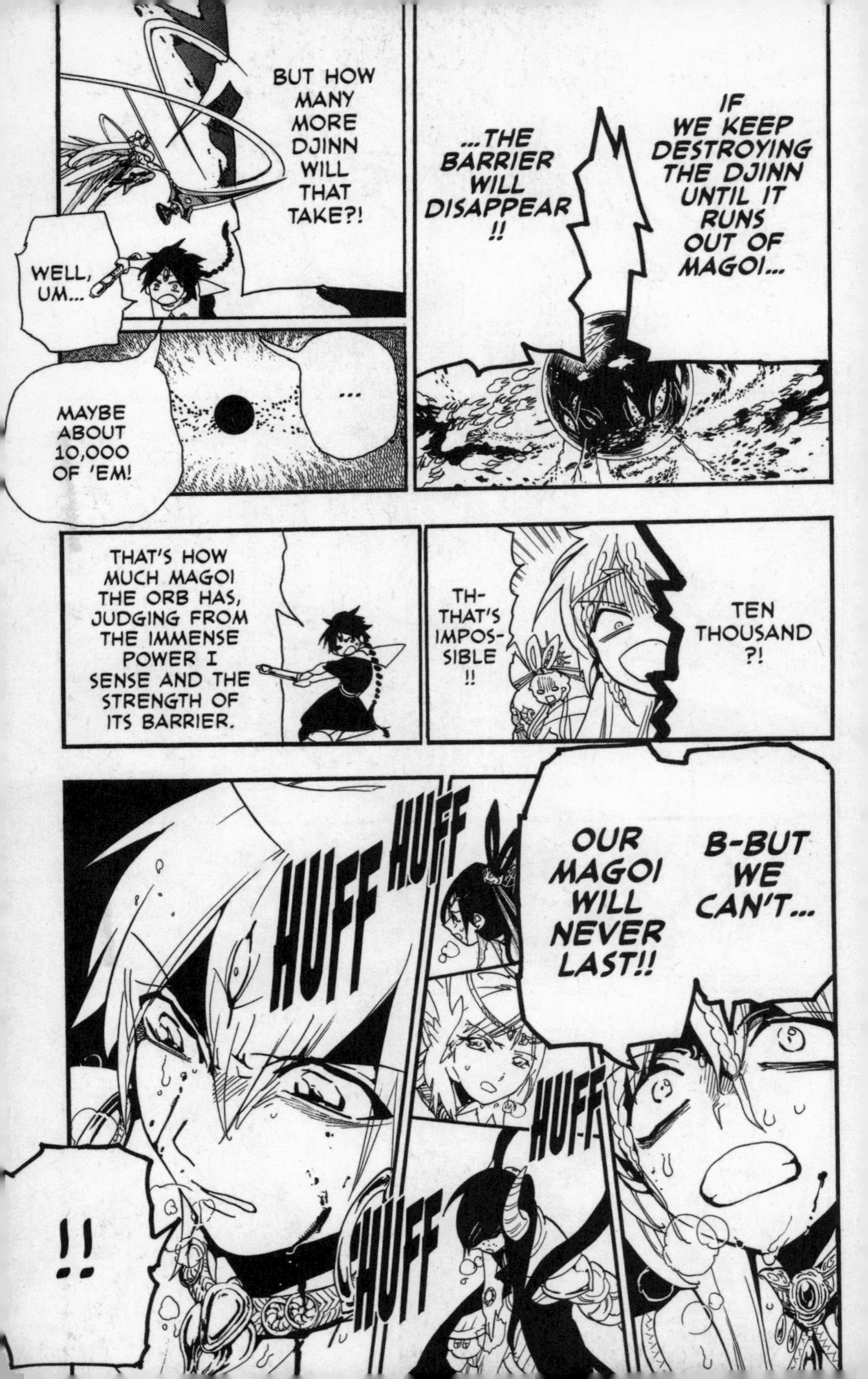
IF WE KEEP DESTROYING THE DJINN UNTIL IT RUNS OUT OF MAGOI...
...THE BARRIER WILL DISAPPEAR!!
BUT HOW MANY MORE DJINN WILL THAT TAKE?!
WELL, UM...
...
MAYBE ABOUT 10,000 OF 'EM!
TEN THOUSAND?!
TH-THAT'S IMPOSSIBLE!!
THAT'S HOW MUCH MAGOI THE ORB HAS, JUDGING FROM THE IMMENSE POWER I SENSE AND THE STRENGTH OF ITS BARRIER.
B-BUT WE CAN'T...
OUR MAGOI WILL NEVER LAST!!
HUFF HUFF
HUFF
HUFF
HUFF
!!

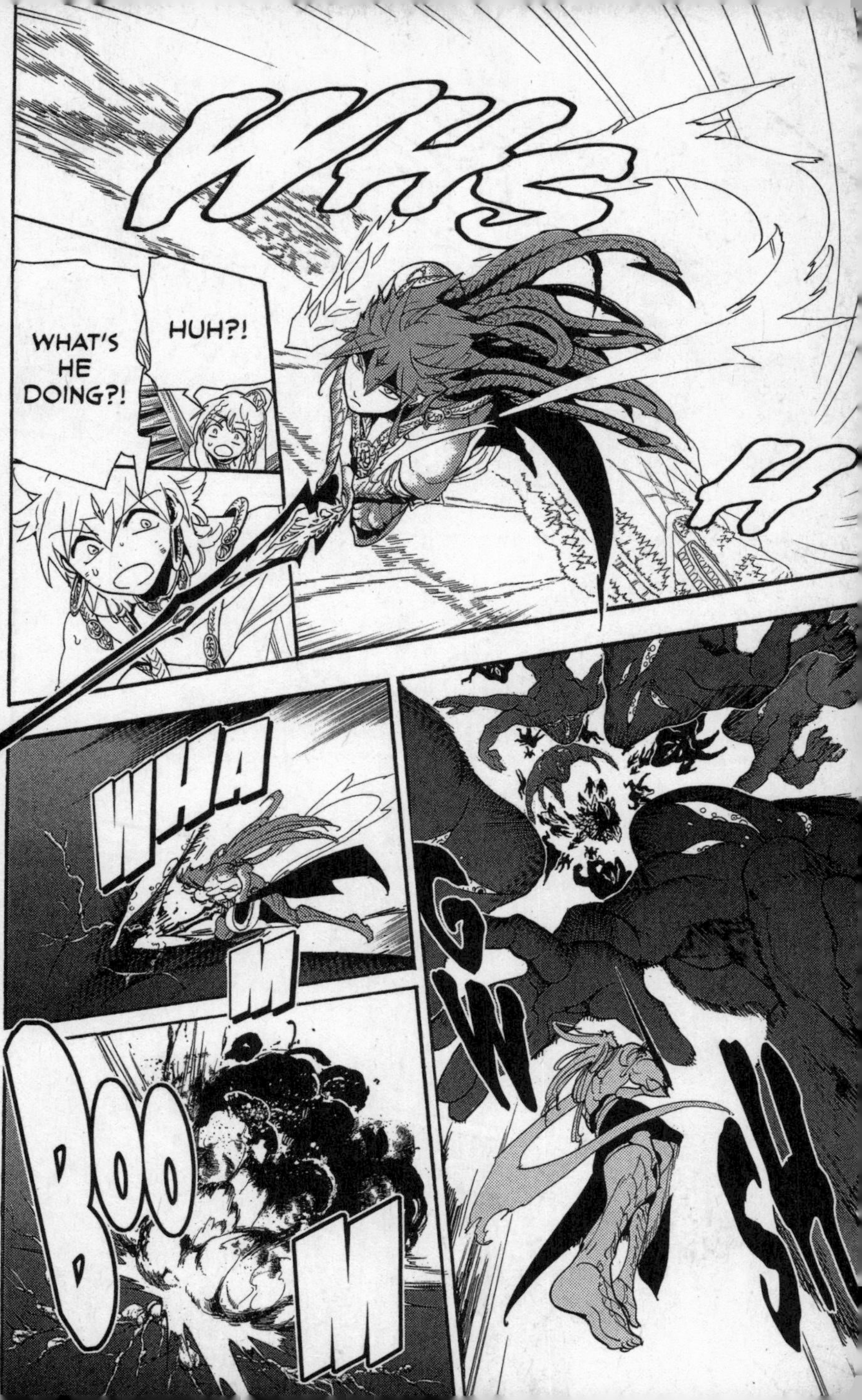
HUH?!
WHAT'S HE DOING?!
WHAM
BOOM

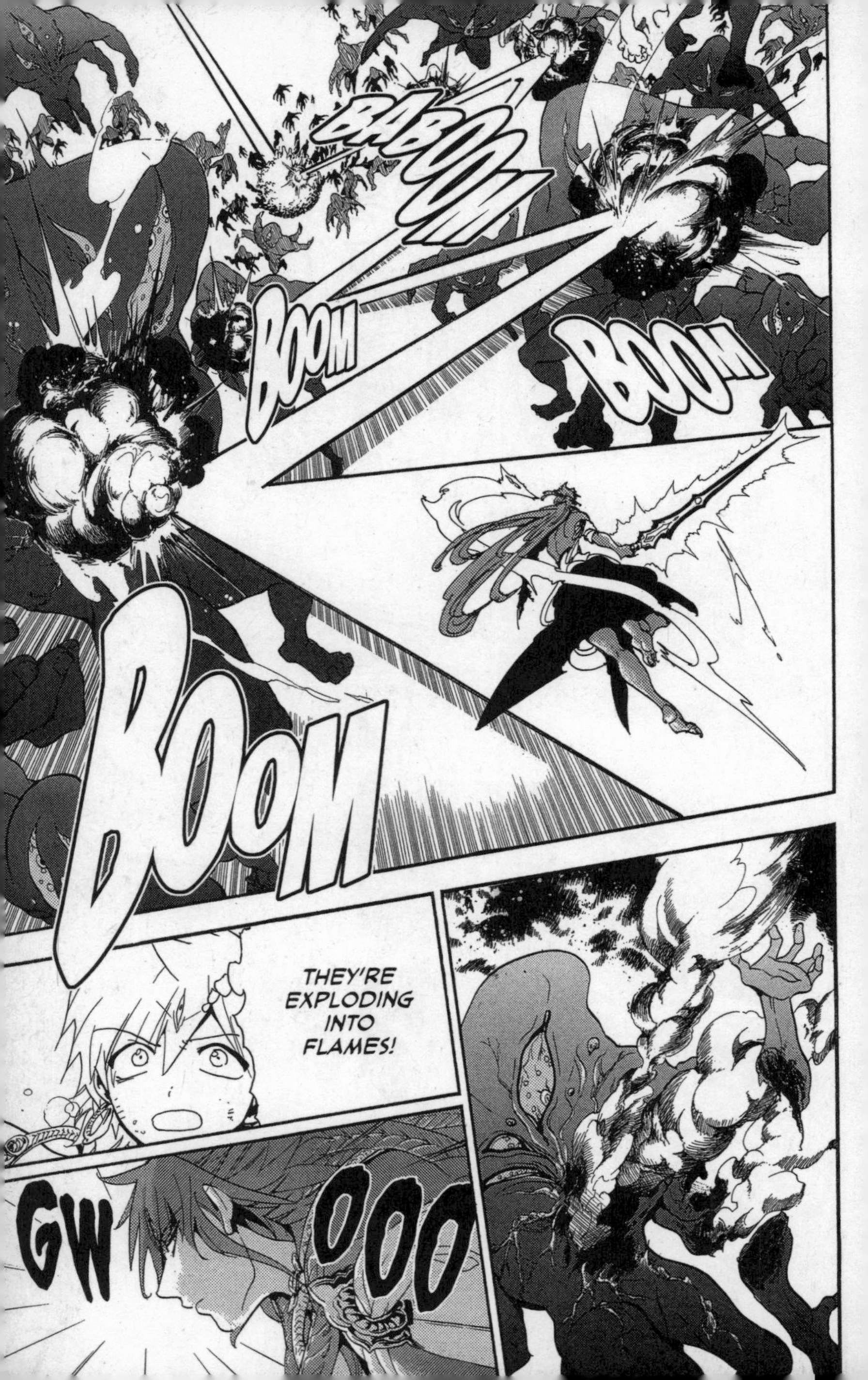
BABOOM
BOOM
BOOM
BOOM
THEY'RE EXPLODING INTO FLAMES!
GWOOOO

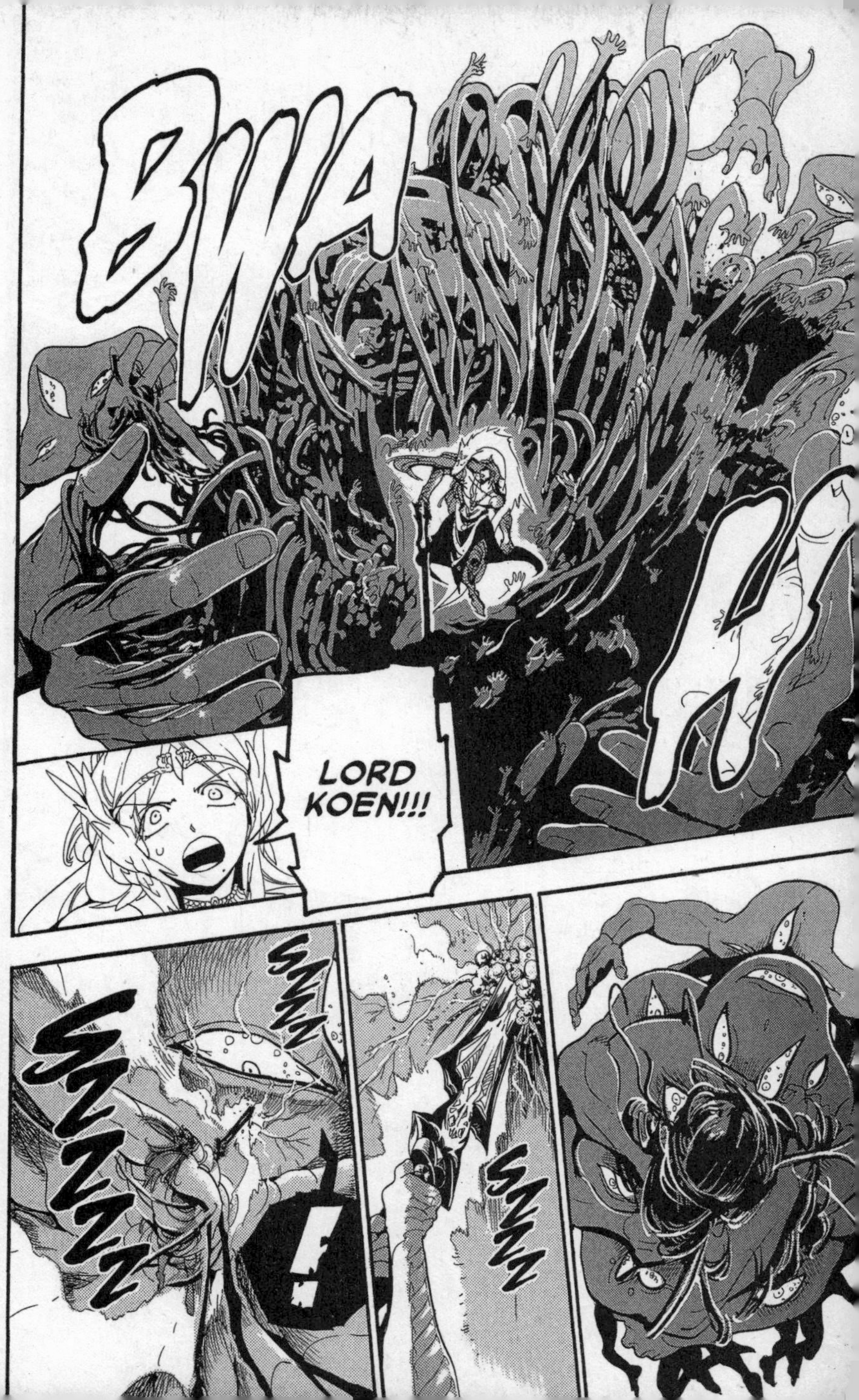
BWA
LORD KOEN!!!
SZZZ
SZZZ
!
SZZZZZ

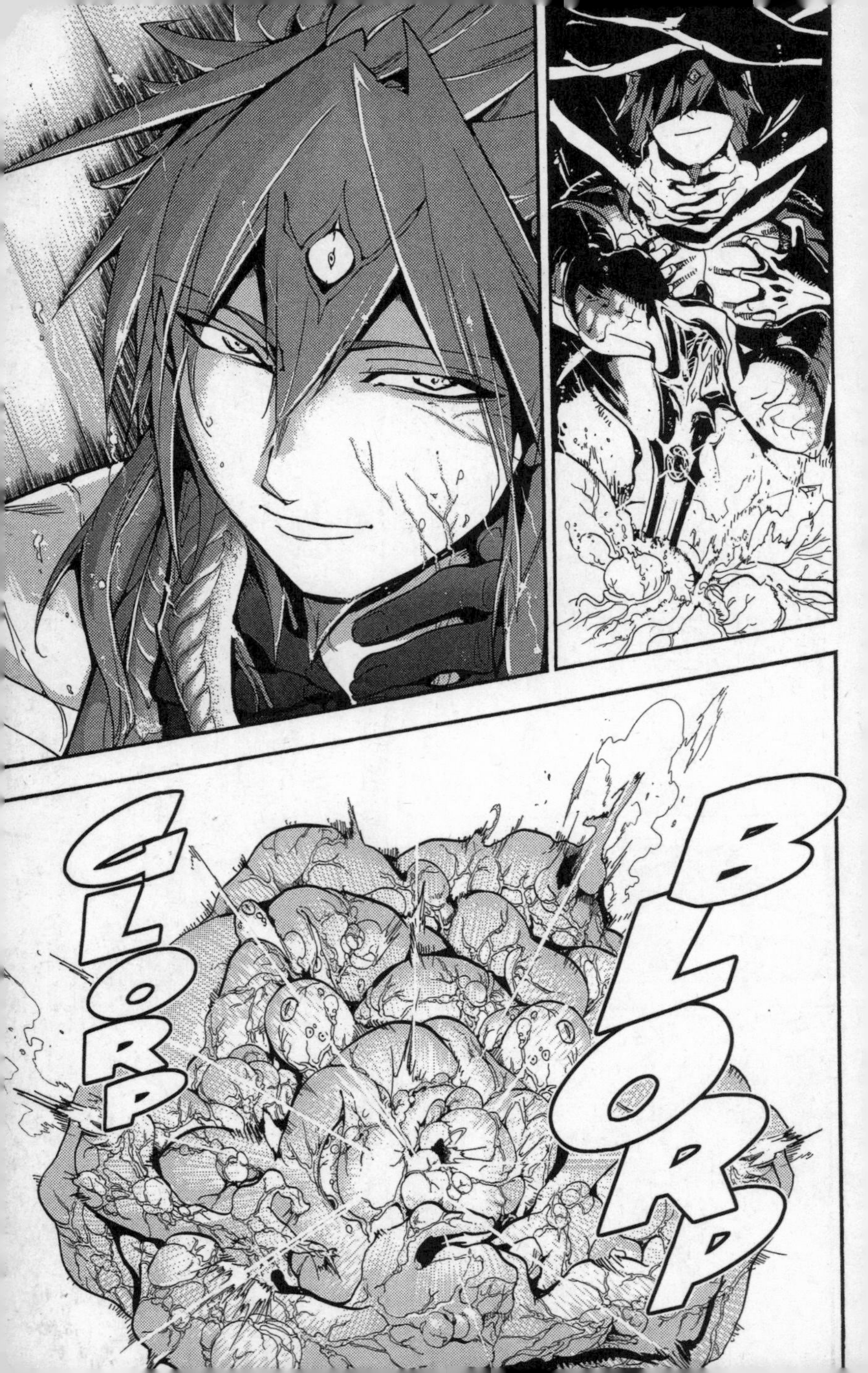
BLORP
GLORP

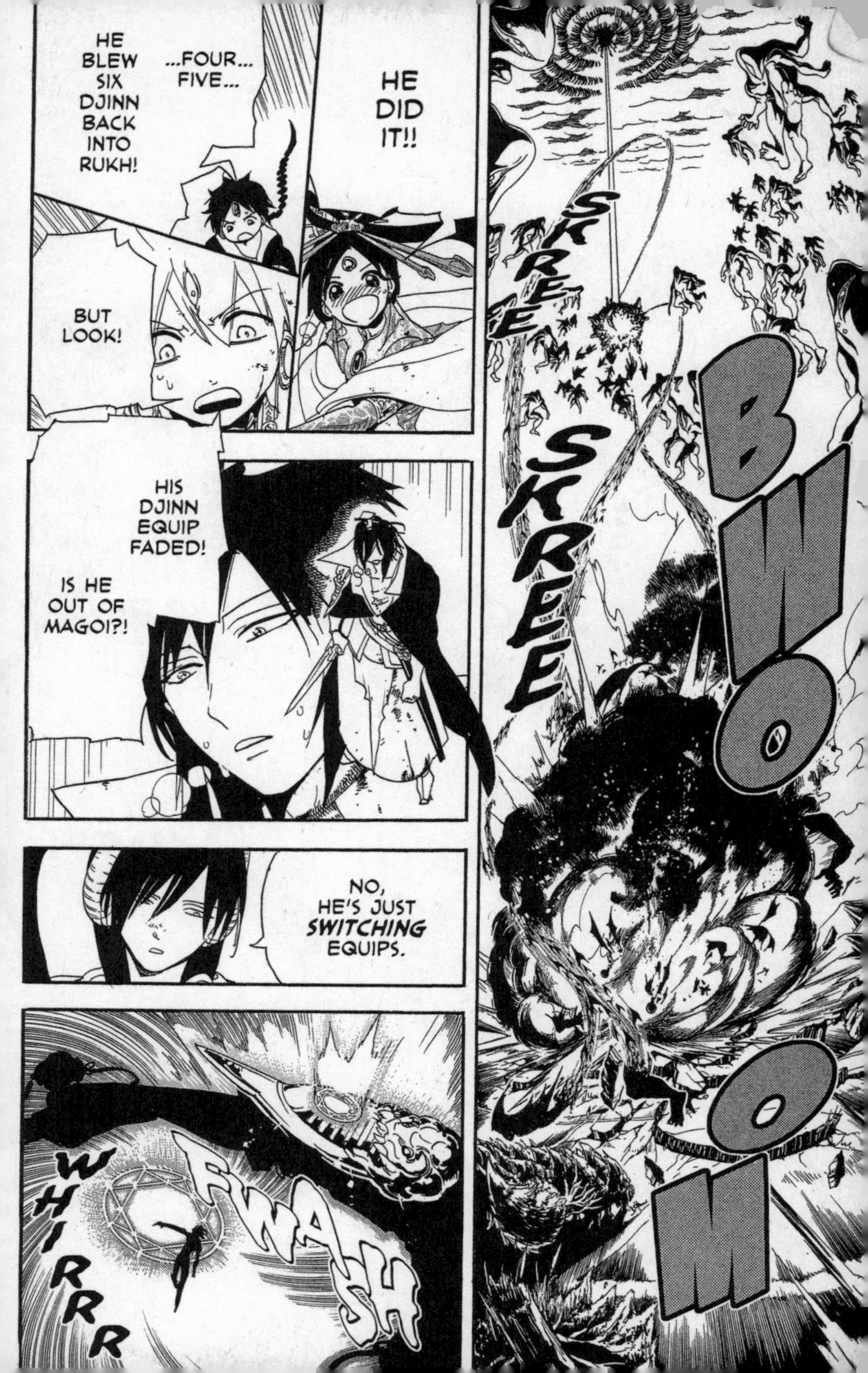
SKREE
SKREE
BWOOOM
HE DID IT!!
...FOUR... FIVE...
HE BLEW SIX DJINN BACK INTO RUKH!
BUT LOOK!
HIS DJINN EQUIP FADED!
IS HE OUT OF MAGOI?!
NO, HE'S JUST *SWITCHING* EQUIPS.
FWASH
WHIRRR

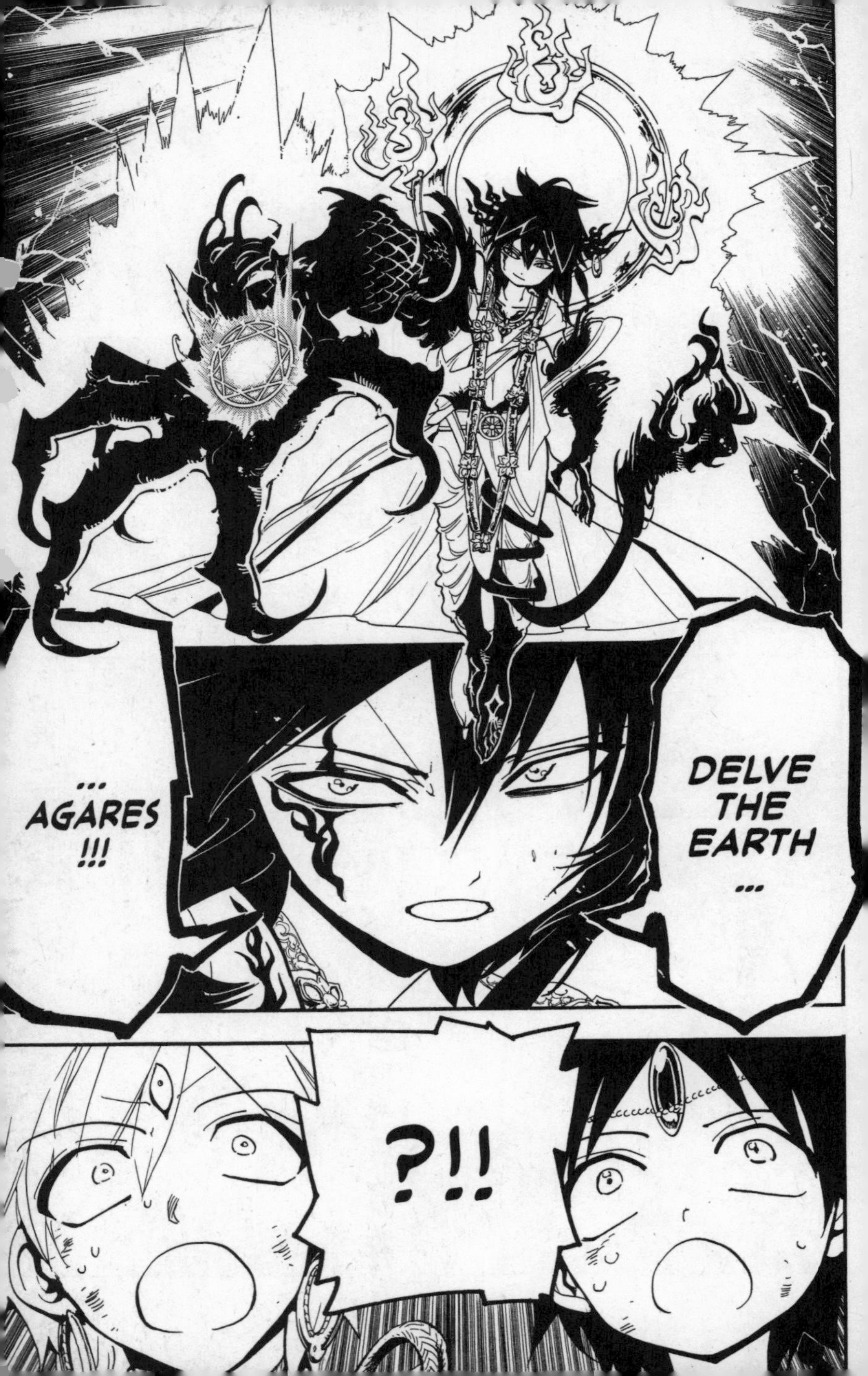
DELVE THE EARTH ...
... AGARES !!!
?!!

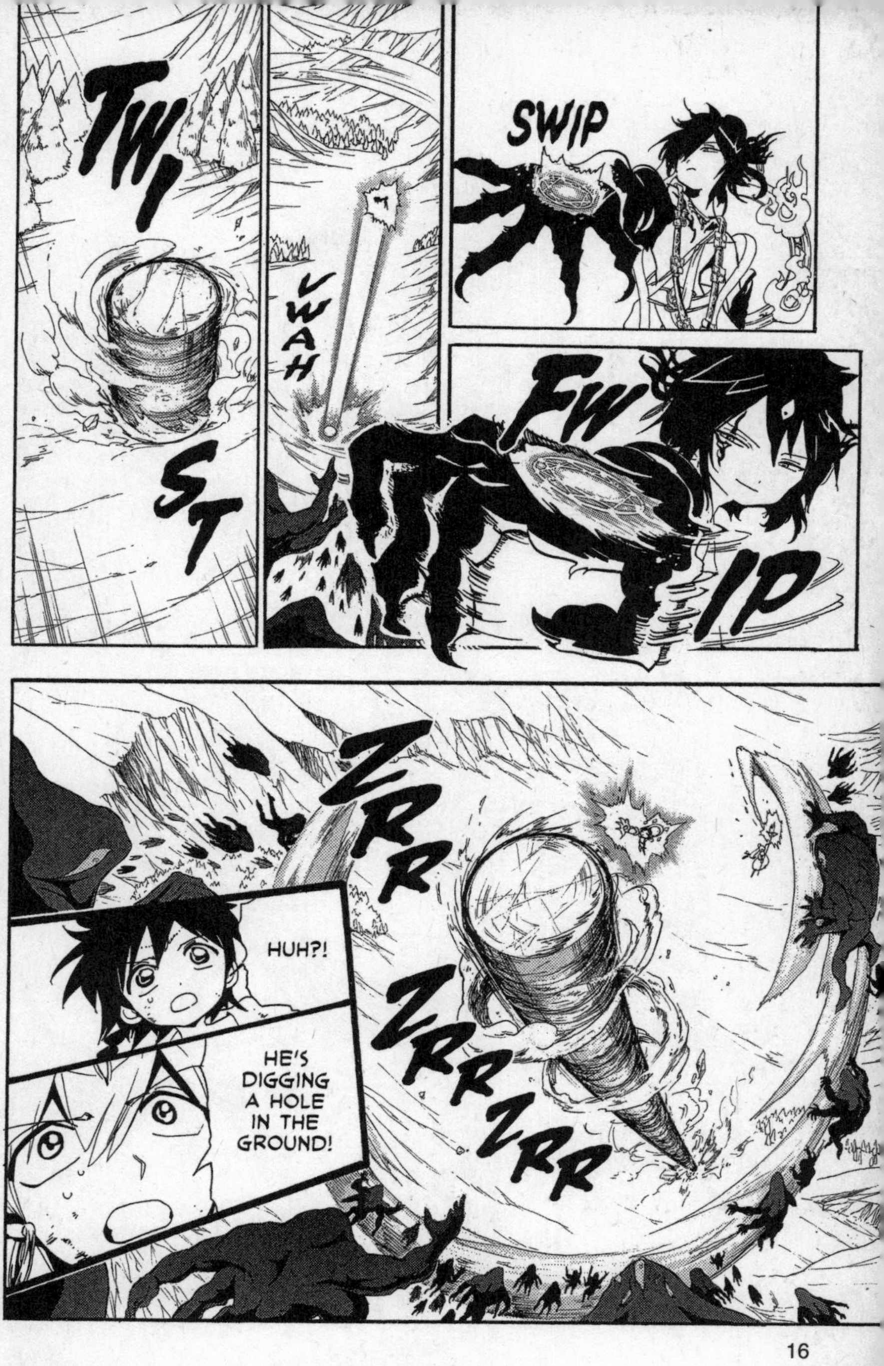
SWIP
FWIP
UWAH
TWIST
ZRR ZRR ZRR
HUH?!
HE'S DIGGING A HOLE IN THE GROUND!

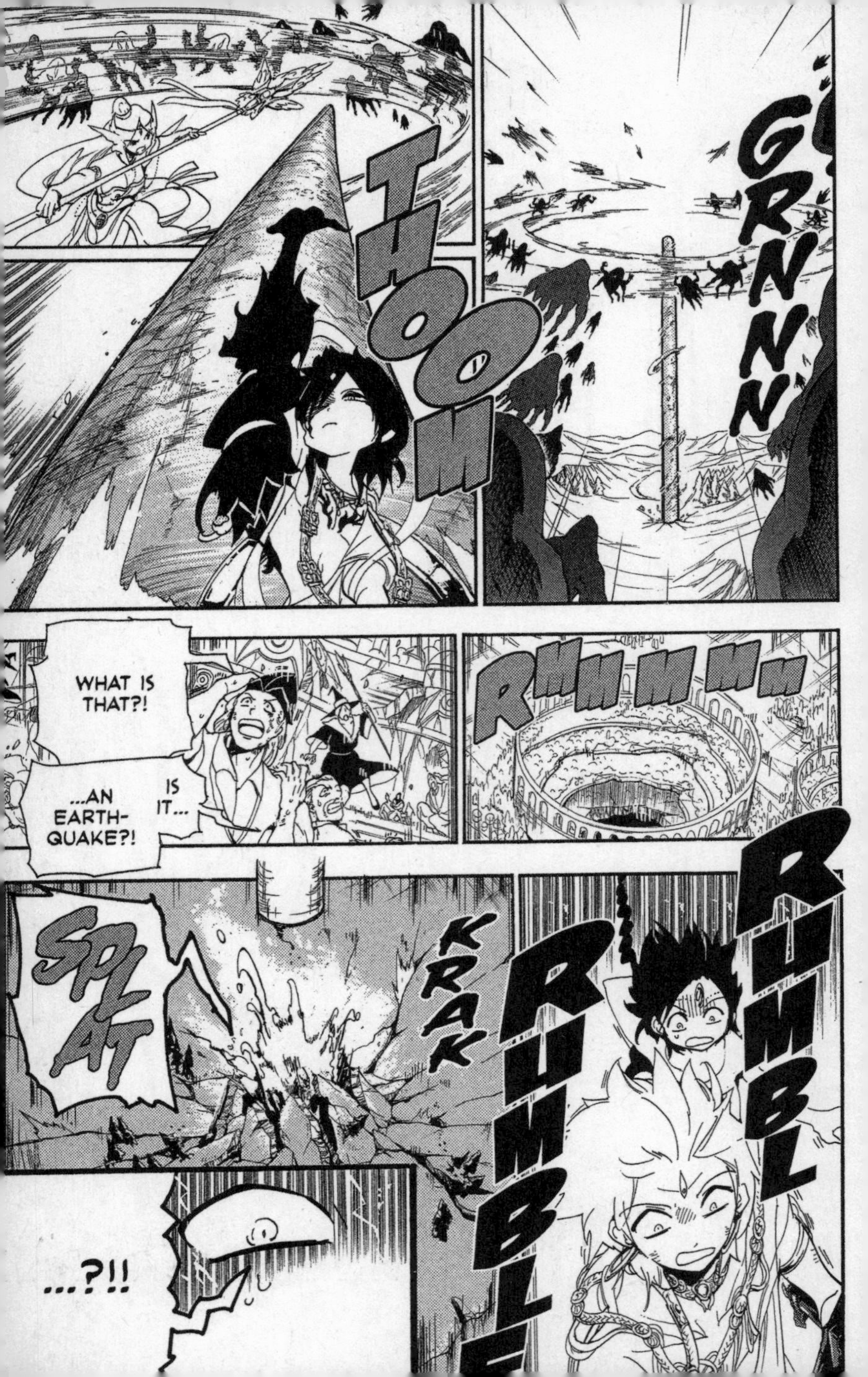
GRNNN
THOOOM
RMMMMMM
WHAT IS THAT?!
IS IT...
...AN EARTHQUAKE?!
RUMBL
RUMBLE
KRAK
SPLAT
...?!!

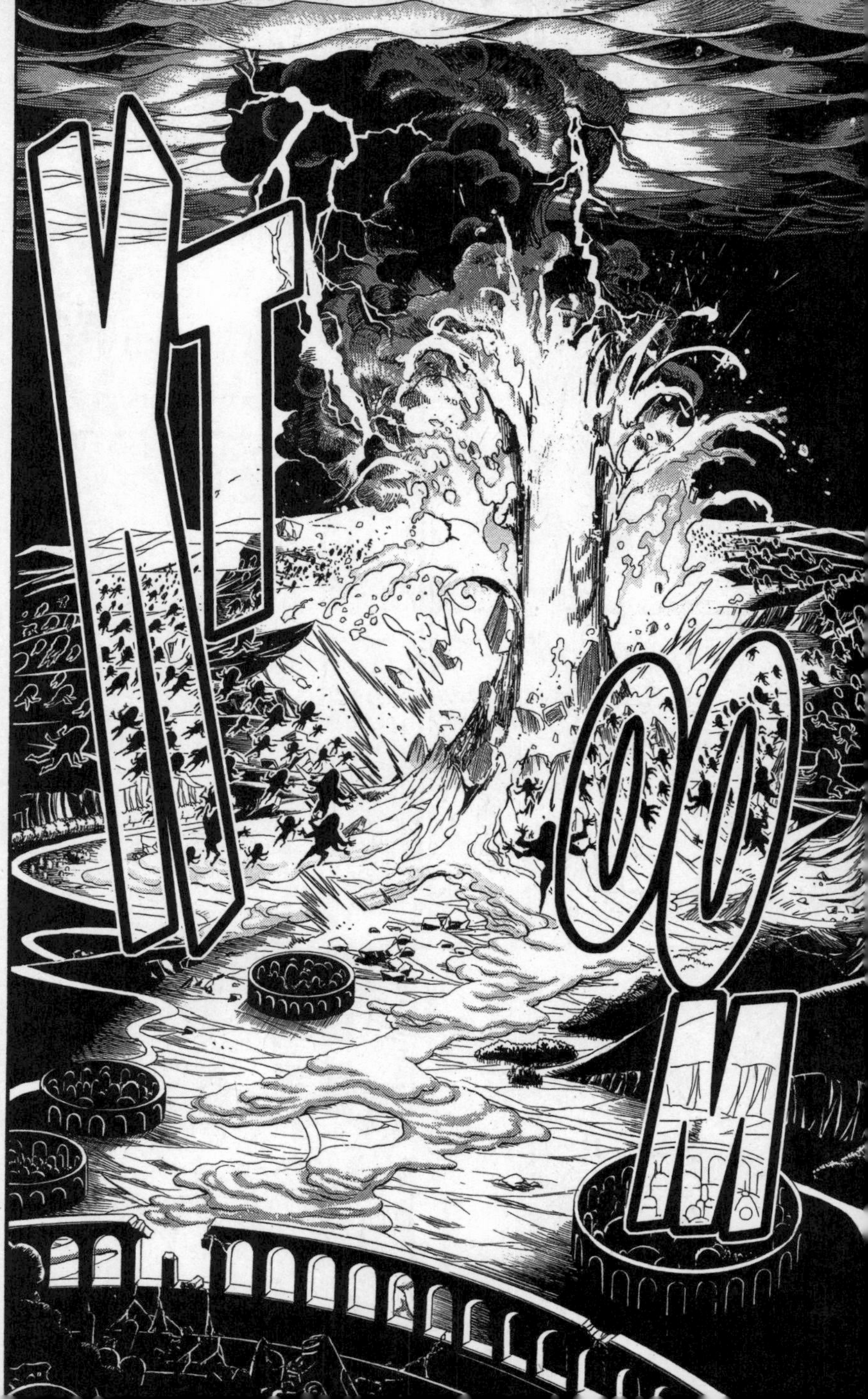
VTOOM

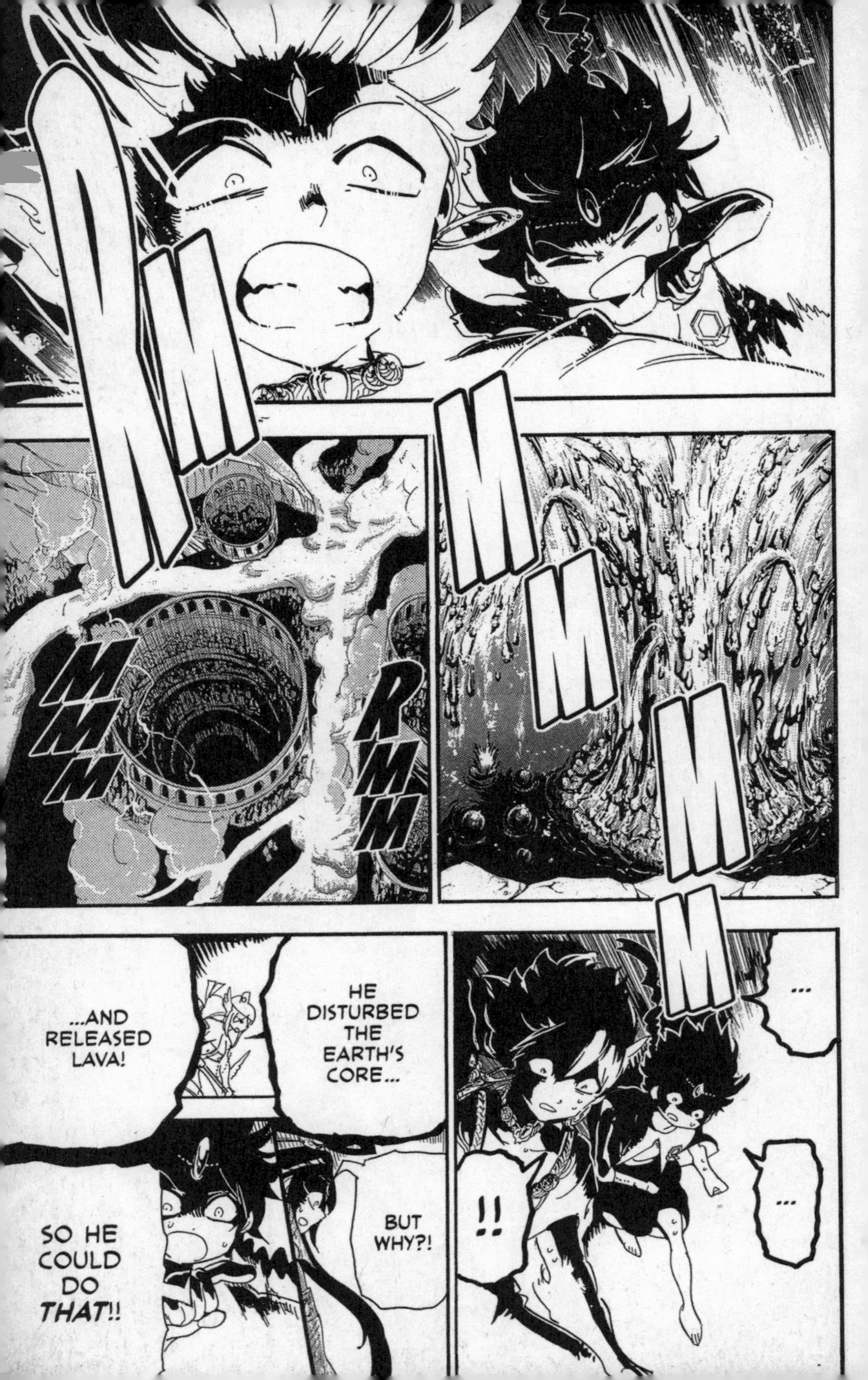
DNMMMMM
RMMM
MMM
...
...
!!
HE DISTURBED THE EARTH'S CORE...
...AND RELEASED LAVA!
BUT WHY?!
SO HE COULD DO *THAT*!!

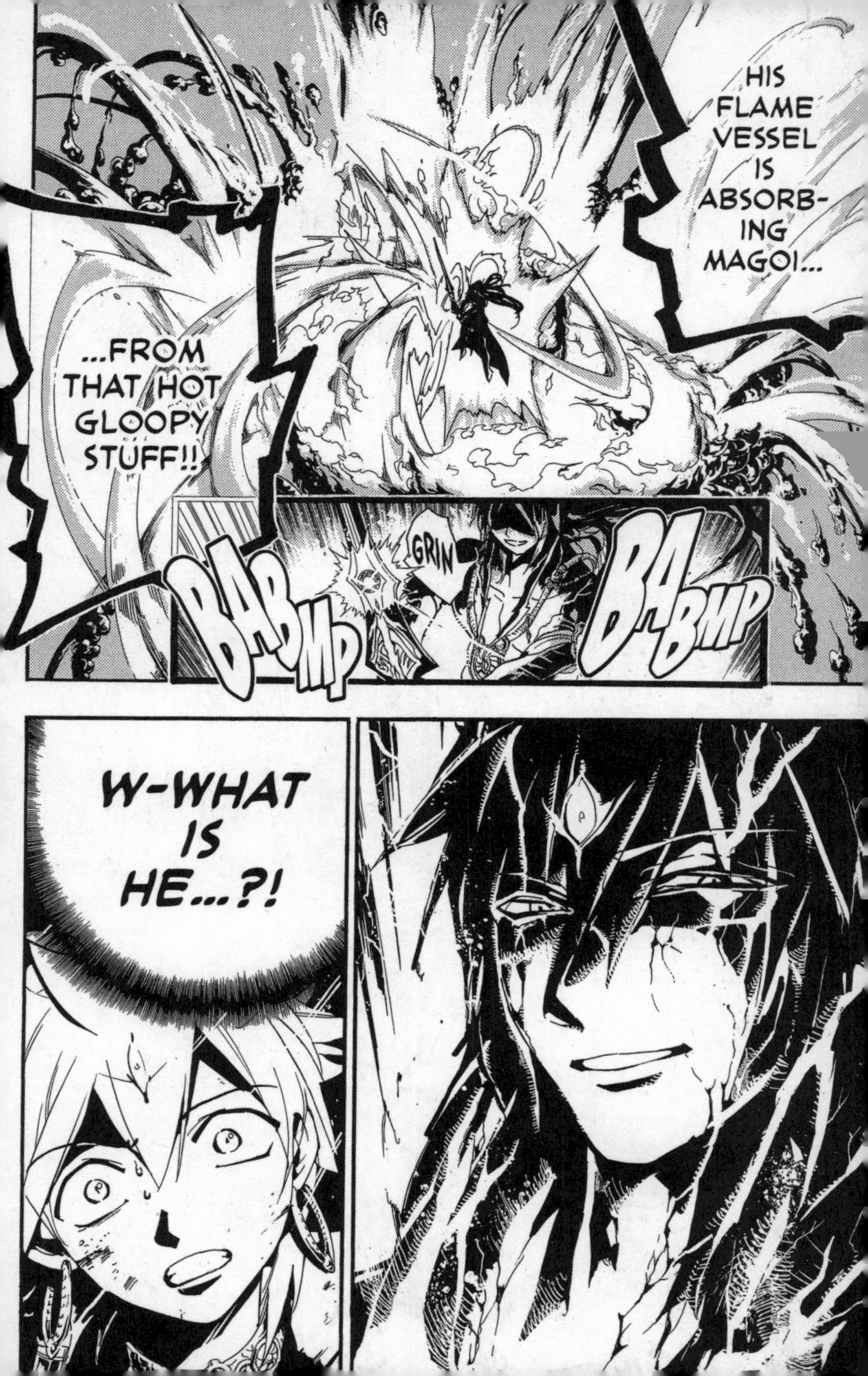
HIS FLAME VESSEL IS ABSORB-ING MAGOI...
...FROM THAT HOT GLOOPY STUFF!!
BABMP
GRIN
BABMP
W-WHAT IS HE...?!

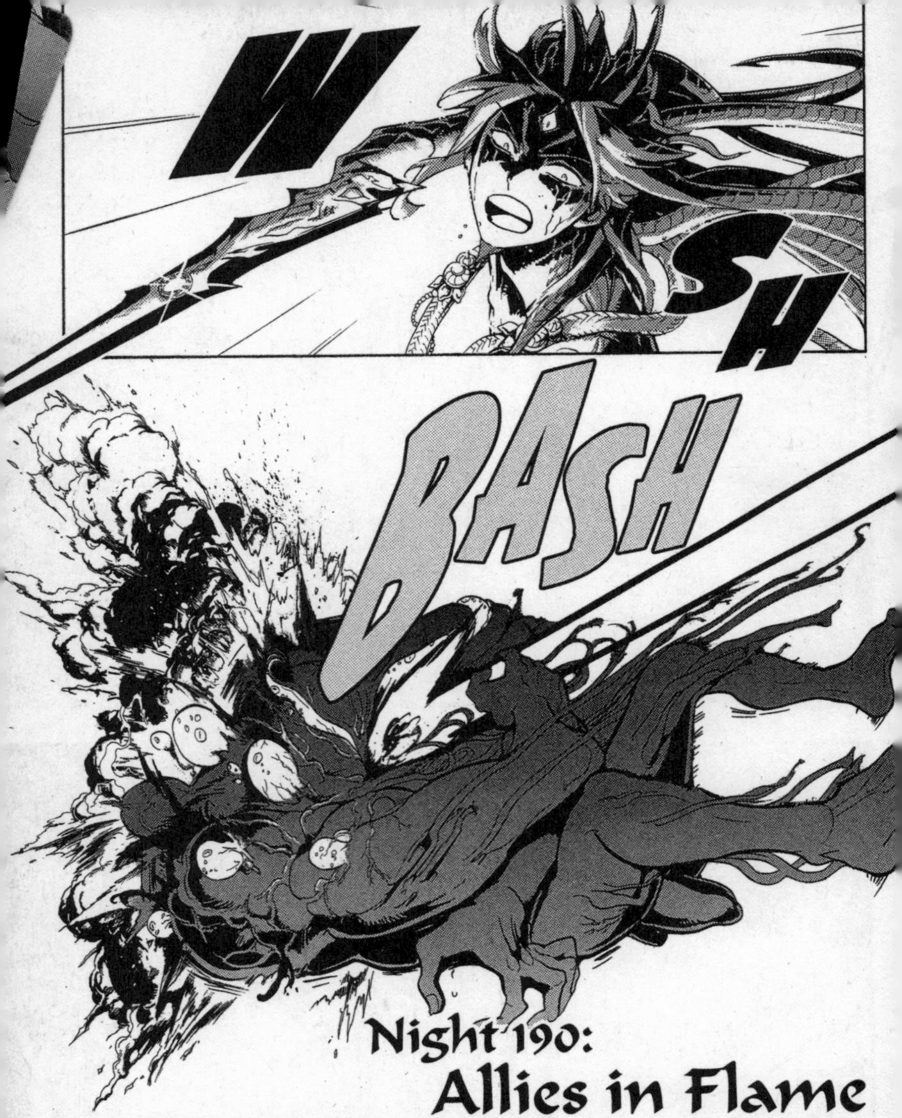
W
SH
BASH

Night 190: Allies in Flame

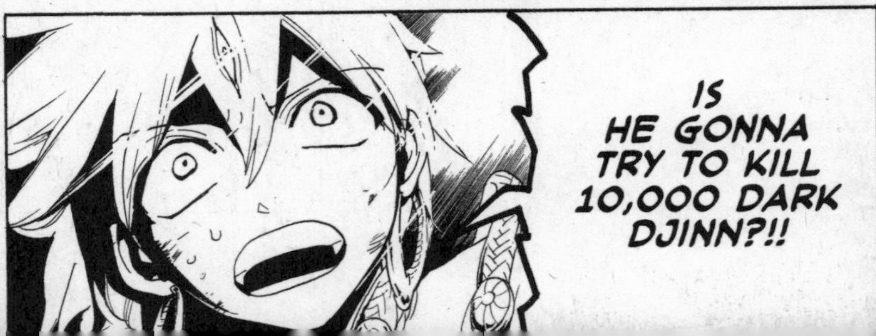
IS HE GONNA TRY TO KILL 10,000 DARK DJINN?!!

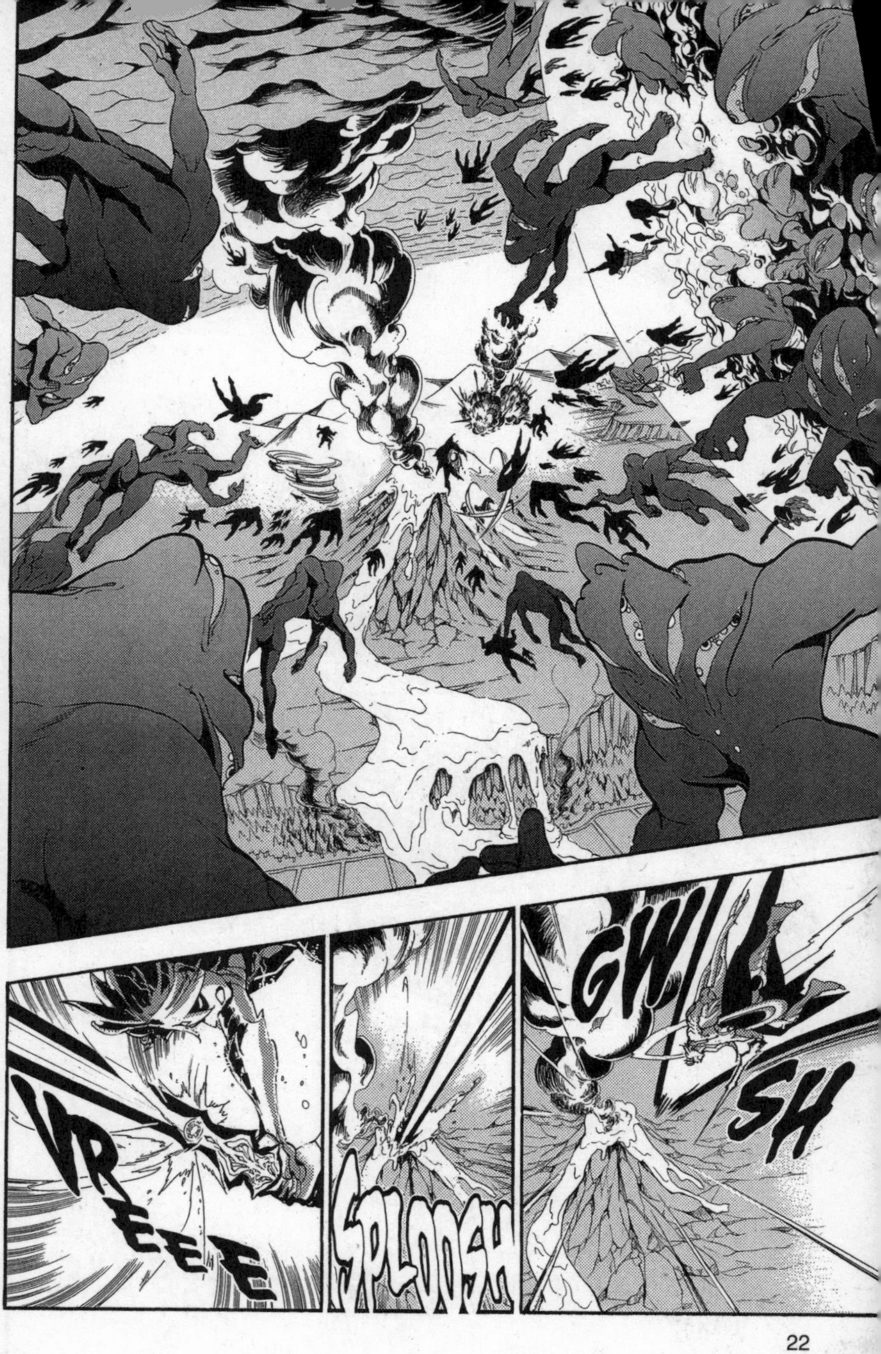
GW
SH
SPLOOSH
VREEEE

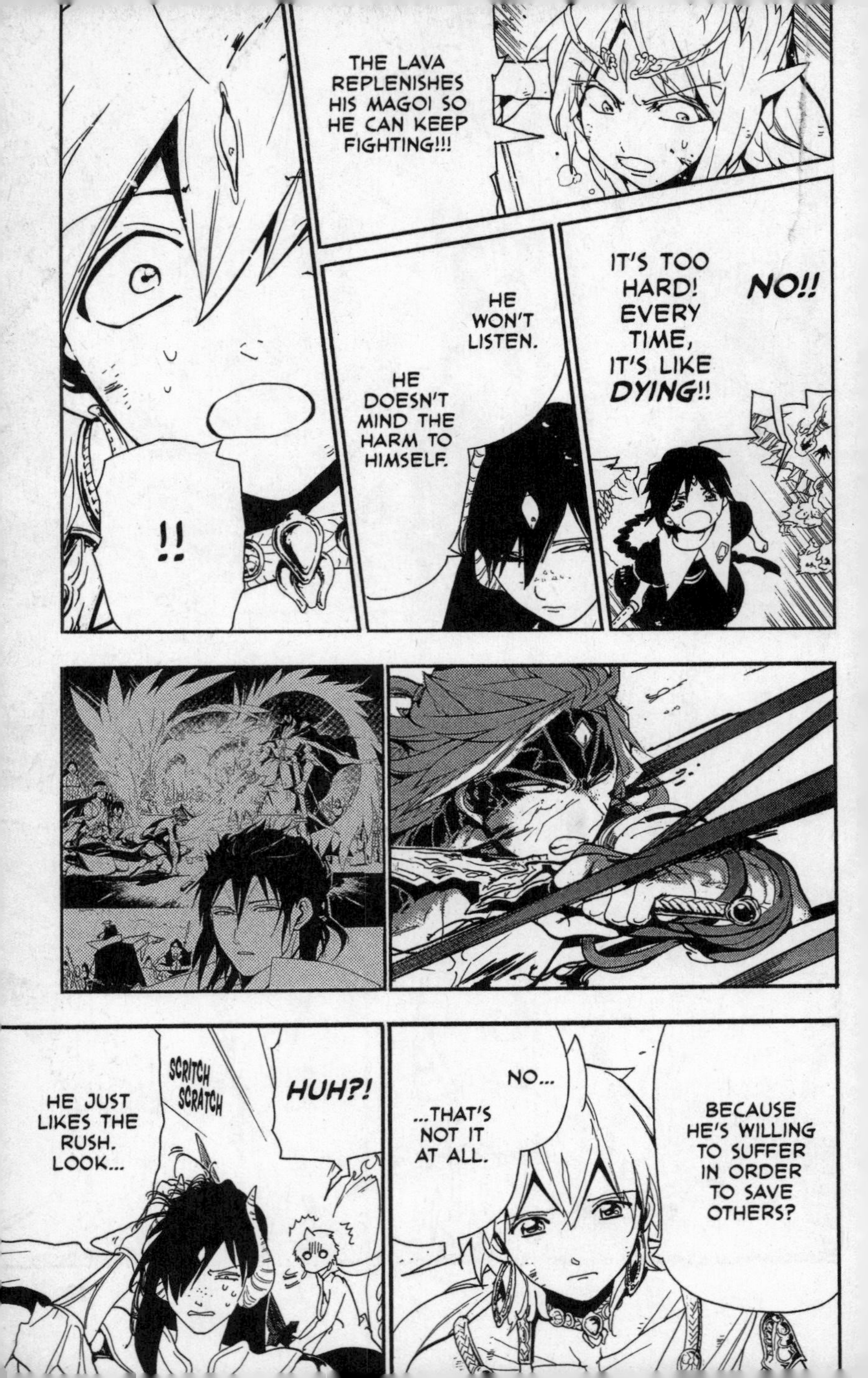
THE LAVA REPLENISHES HIS MAGOI SO HE CAN KEEP FIGHTING!!!
NO!!
IT'S TOO HARD! EVERY TIME, IT'S LIKE DYING!!
HE WON'T LISTEN.
HE DOESN'T MIND THE HARM TO HIMSELF.
!!
BECAUSE HE'S WILLING TO SUFFER IN ORDER TO SAVE OTHERS?
NO...
...THAT'S NOT IT AT ALL.
HUH?!
SCRITCH SCRATCH
HE JUST LIKES THE RUSH. LOOK...

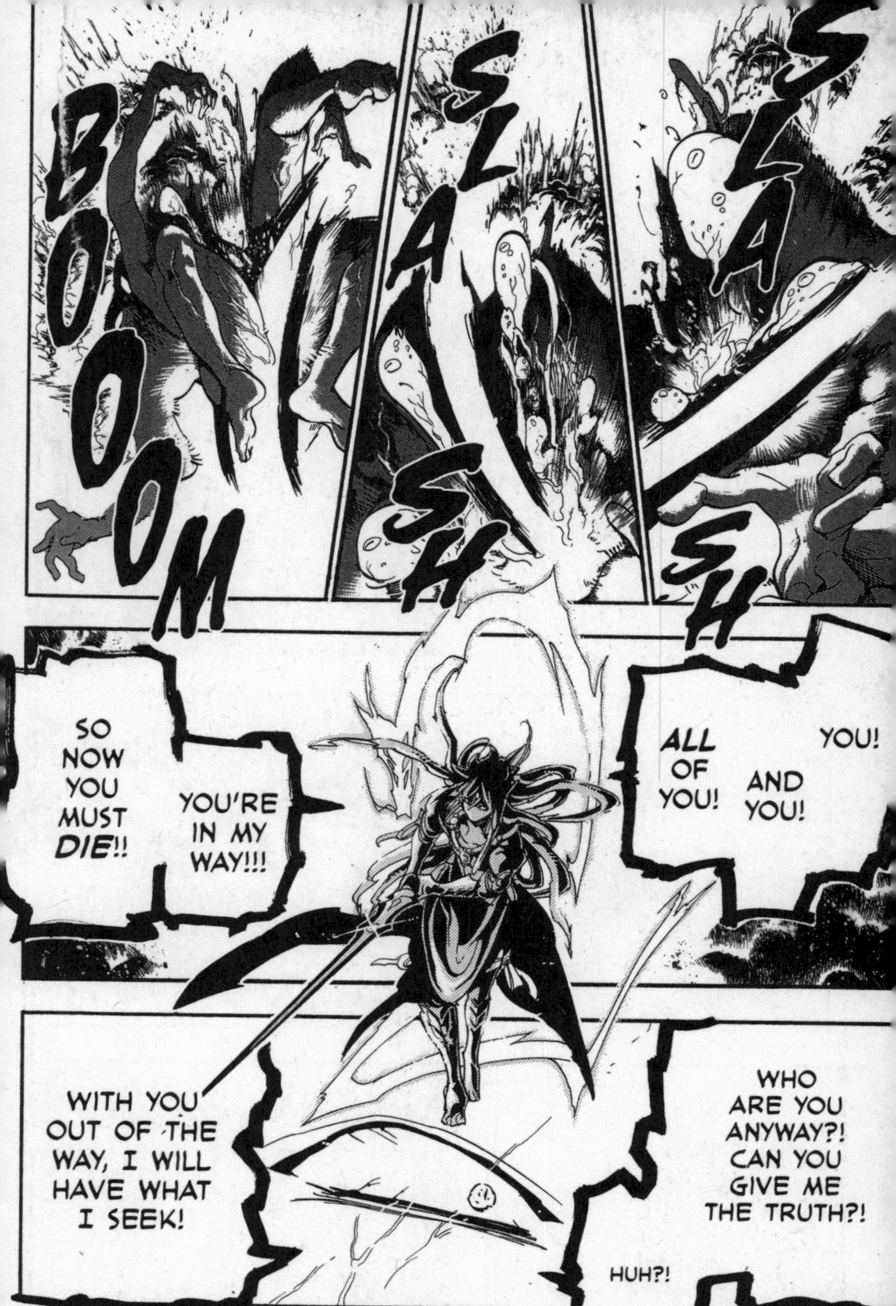
SLASH
SLASH
BOOM
YOU! AND YOU! ALL OF YOU!
YOU'RE IN MY WAY!!!
SO NOW YOU MUST *DIE*!!
WHO ARE YOU ANYWAY?! CAN YOU GIVE ME THE TRUTH?!
WITH YOU OUT OF THE WAY, I WILL HAVE WHAT I SEEK!
HUH?!

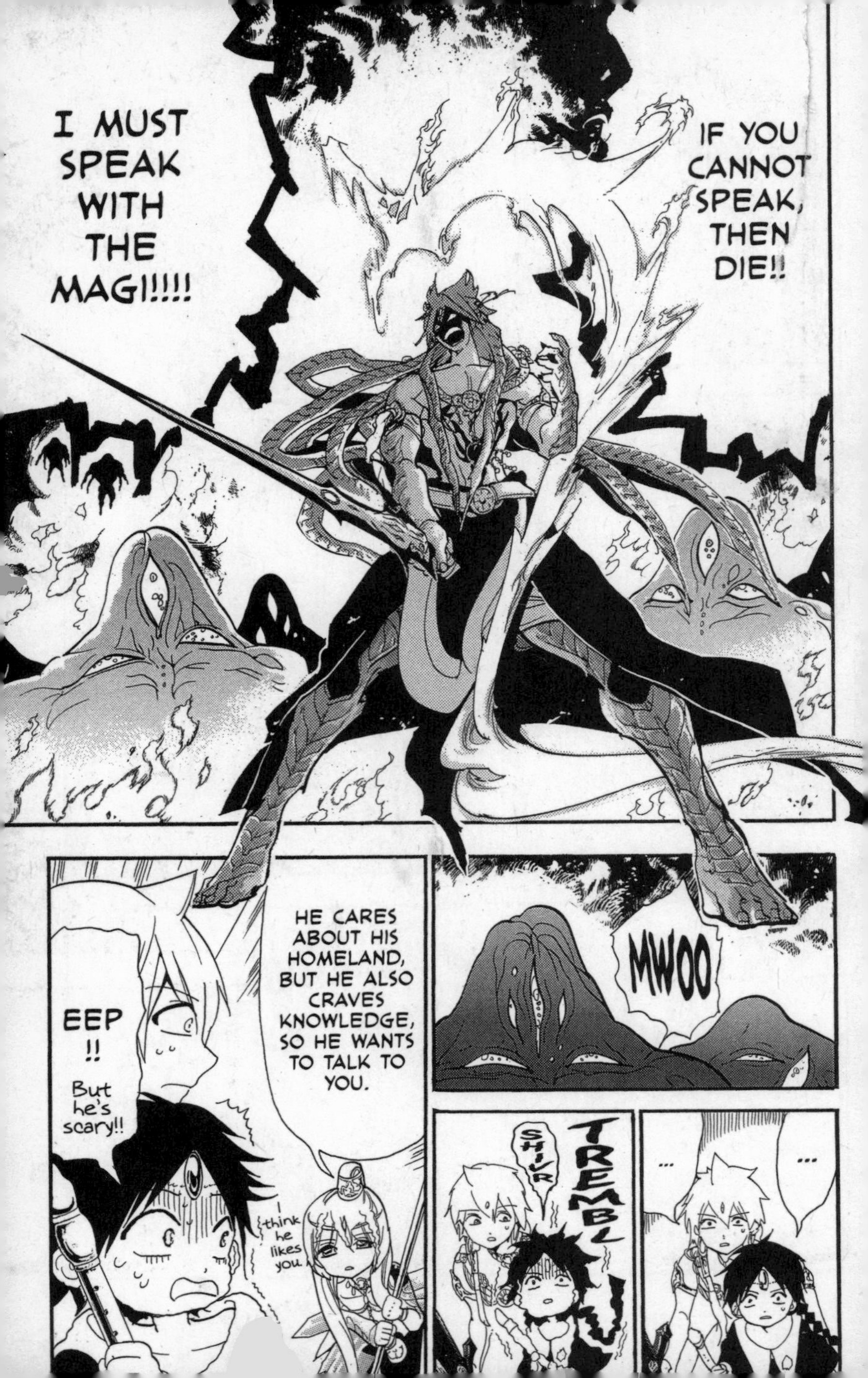
IF YOU CANNOT SPEAK, THEN DIE!!
I MUST SPEAK WITH THE MAGI!!!!!
MWOO
...
...
TREMBL
SHIVR
HE CARES ABOUT HIS HOMELAND, BUT HE ALSO CRAVES KNOWLEDGE, SO HE WANTS TO TALK TO YOU.
I think he likes you.
EEP!!
But he's scary!!

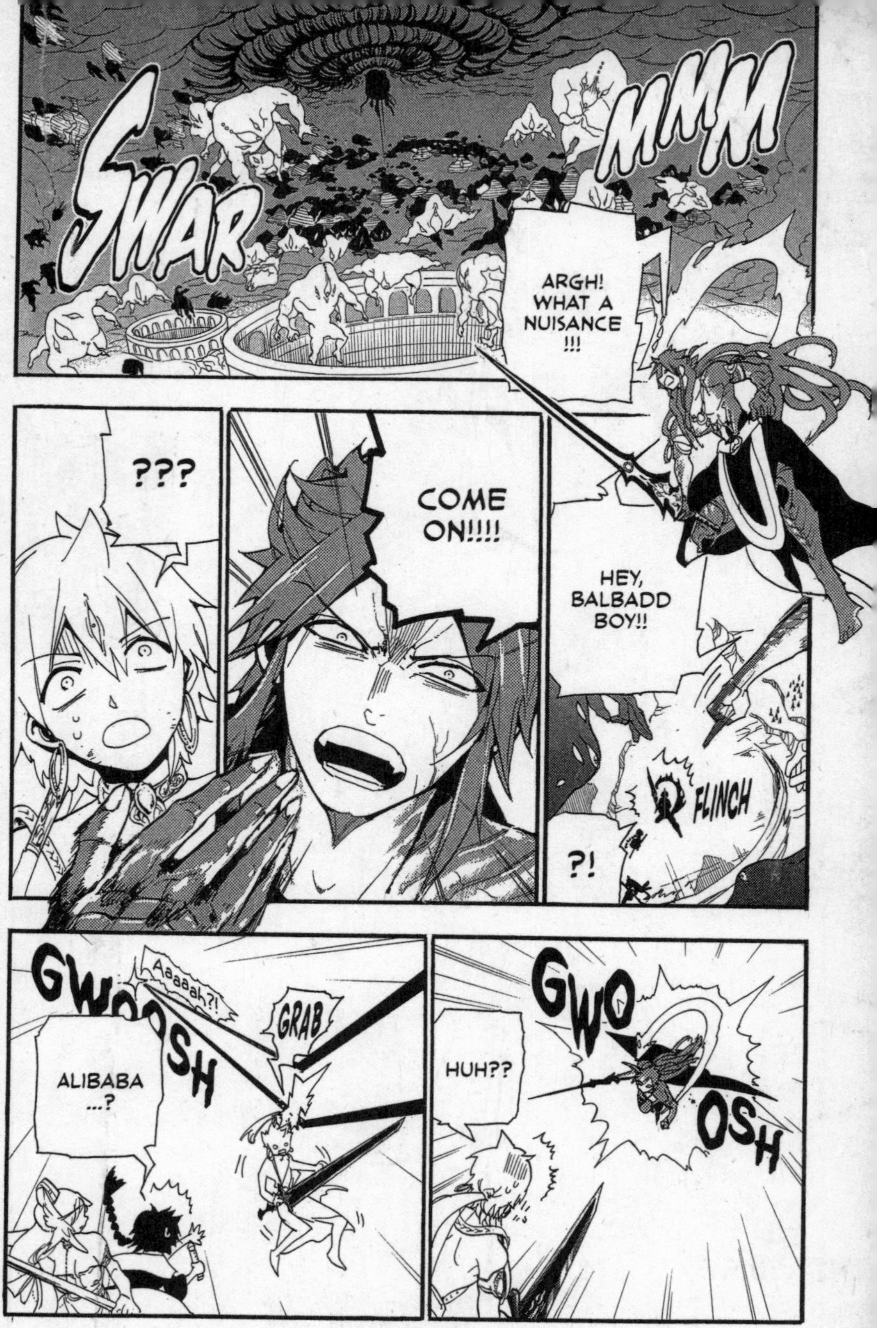
MMMM
SWAR
ARGH! WHAT A NUISANCE!!!
HEY, BALBADD BOY!!
FLINCH
?!
COME ON!!!!
???
GWOOSH
HUH??
GWOOSH
Aaaaah?!
GRAB
ALIBABA ...?

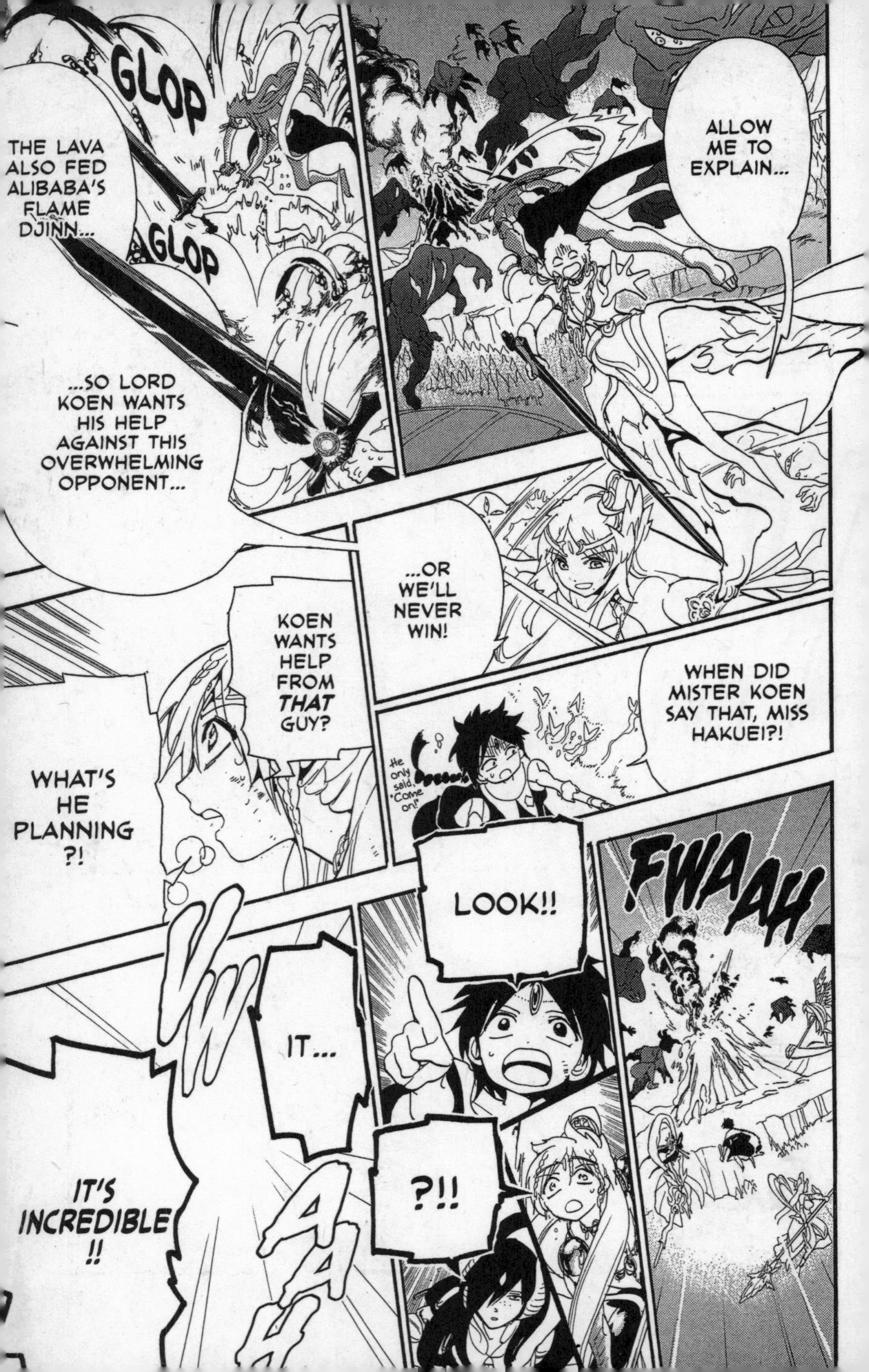
ALLOW ME TO EXPLAIN...
GLOP
THE LAVA ALSO FED ALIBABA'S FLAME DJINN...
GLOP
...SO LORD KOEN WANTS HIS HELP AGAINST THIS OVERWHELMING OPPONENT...
...OR WE'LL NEVER WIN!
WHEN DID MISTER KOEN SAY THAT, MISS HAKUEI?!
He only said, "Come on!"
KOEN WANTS HELP FROM *THAT* GUY?
WHAT'S HE PLANNING ?!
FWAAH
LOOK!!
?!!
IT...
IT'S INCREDIBLE !!

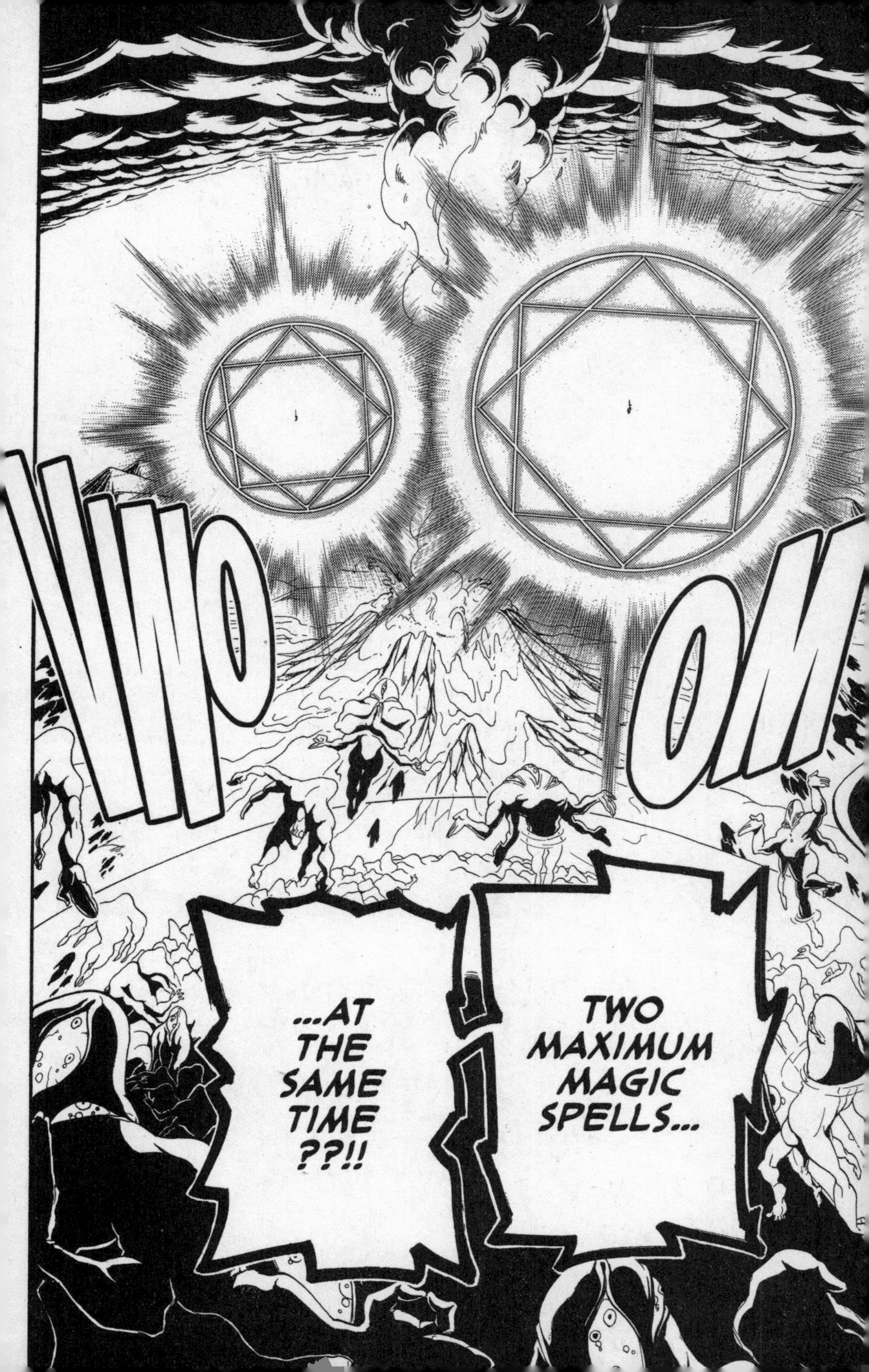
TWO MAXIMUM MAGIC SPELLS...
...AT THE SAME TIME??!!

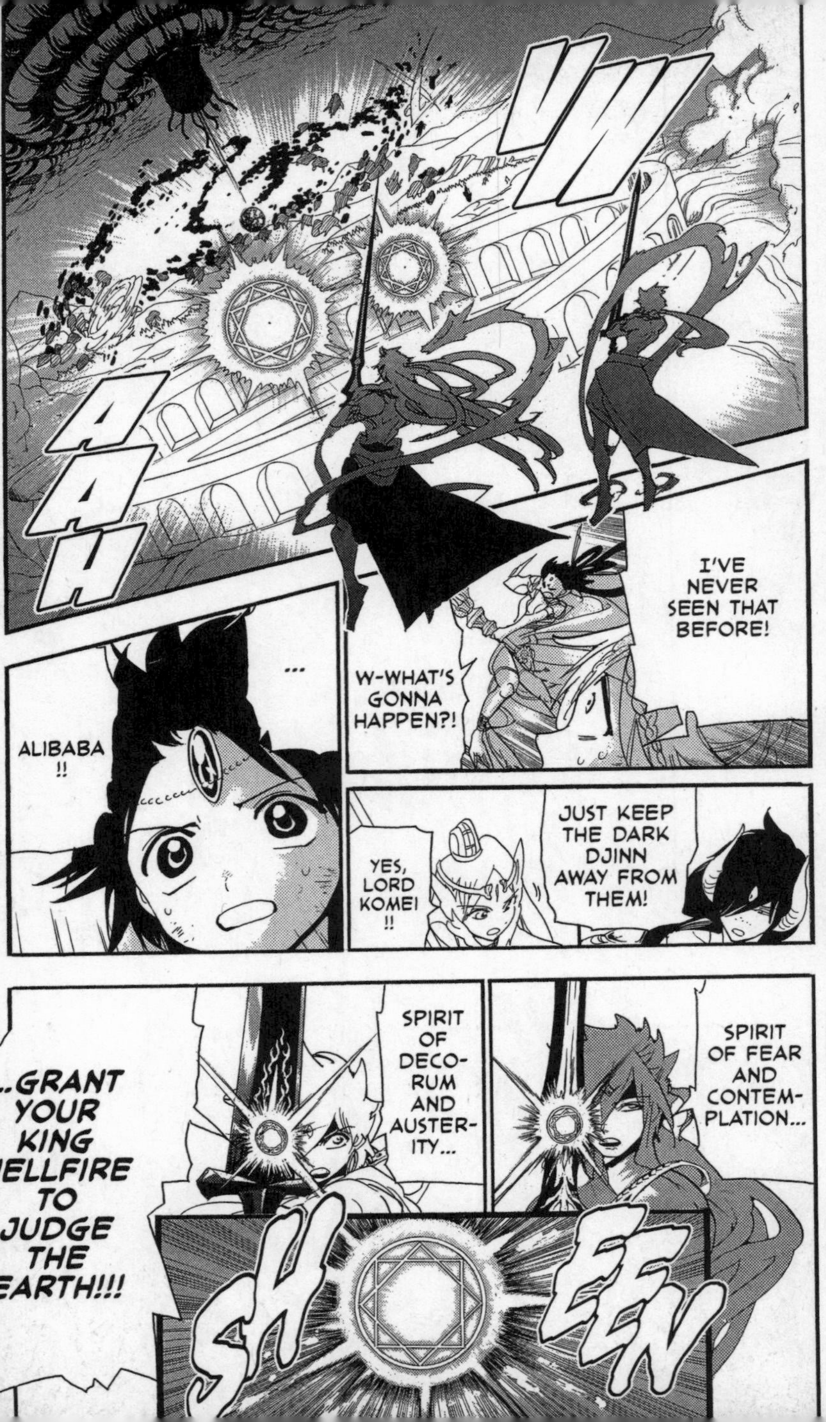
VVN
AAAH
I'VE NEVER SEEN THAT BEFORE!
W-WHAT'S GONNA HAPPEN?!
JUST KEEP THE DARK DJINN AWAY FROM THEM!
YES, LORD KOMEI !!
...
ALIBABA !!
SPIRIT OF FEAR AND CONTEM-PLATION...
SPIRIT OF DECO-RUM AND AUSTER-ITY...
...GRANT YOUR KING HELLFIRE TO JUDGE THE EARTH!!!
SHEEN

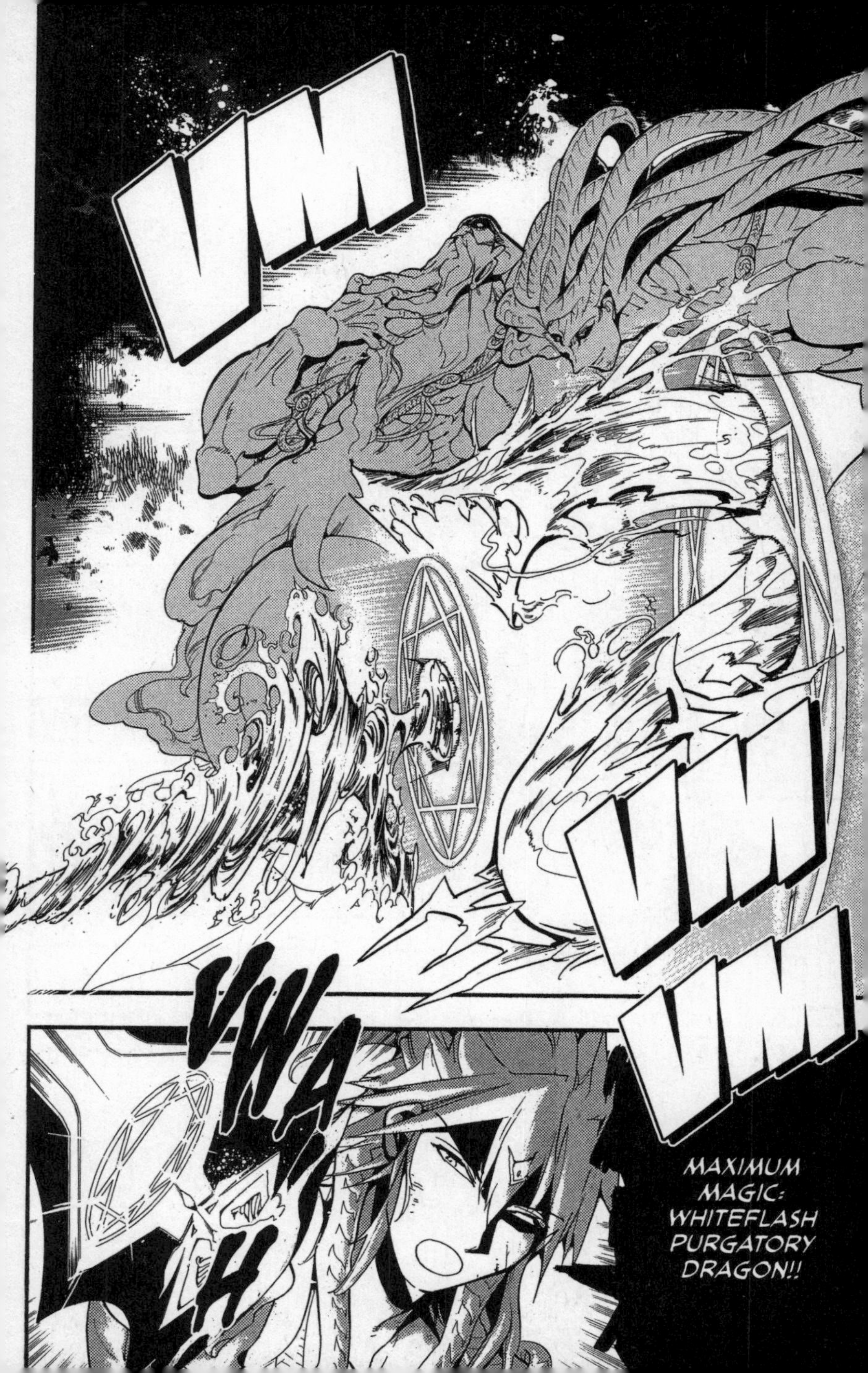
VM
VM
VM
MAXIMUM MAGIC: WHITEFLASH PURGATORY DRAGON!!

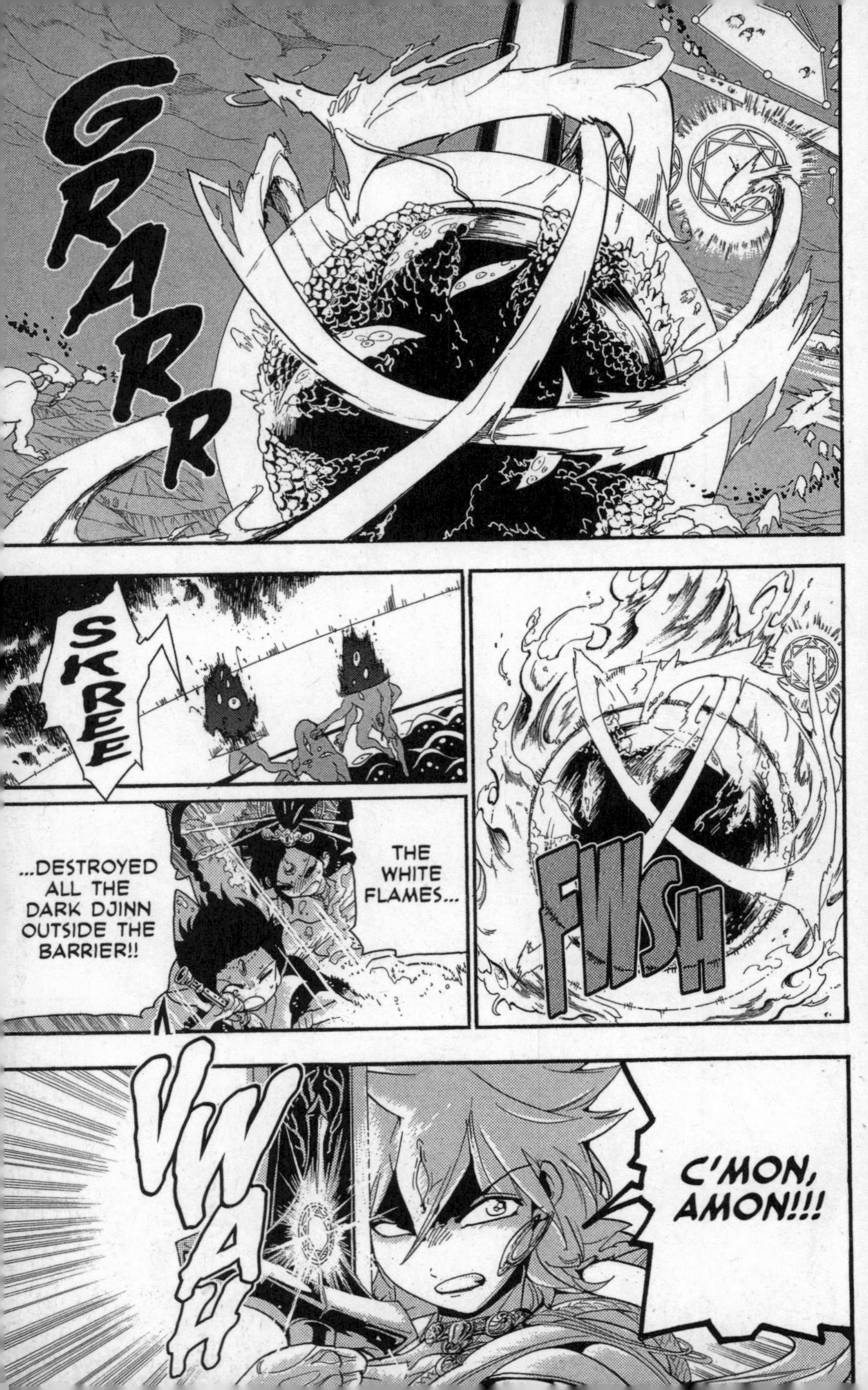
GRARR
FWSH
SKREE
THE WHITE FLAMES...
...DESTROYED ALL THE DARK DJINN OUTSIDE THE BARRIER!!
C'MON, AMON!!!
VWA

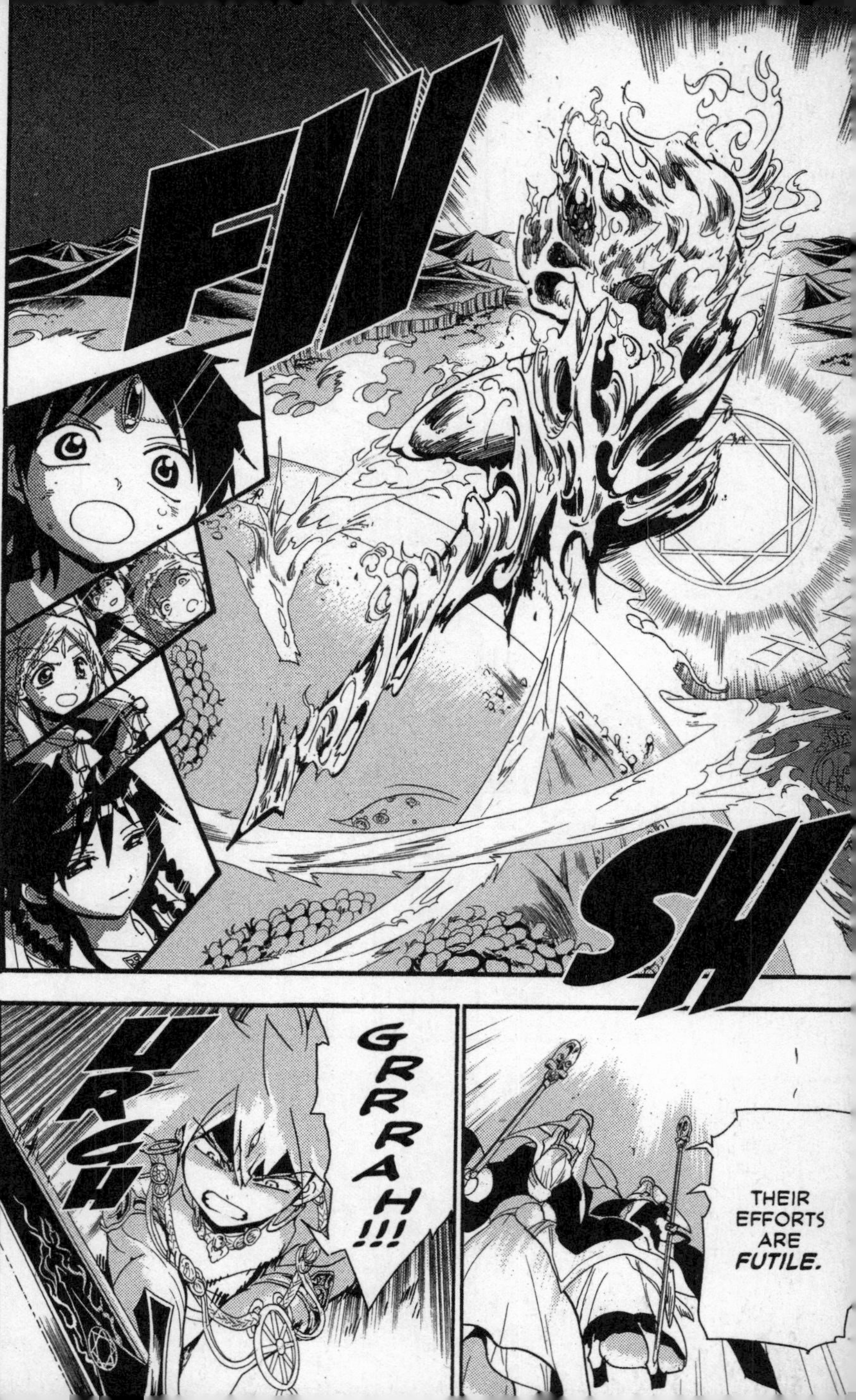
FW
SH
THEIR EFFORTS ARE FUTILE.
GRRRAH!!!
URGH

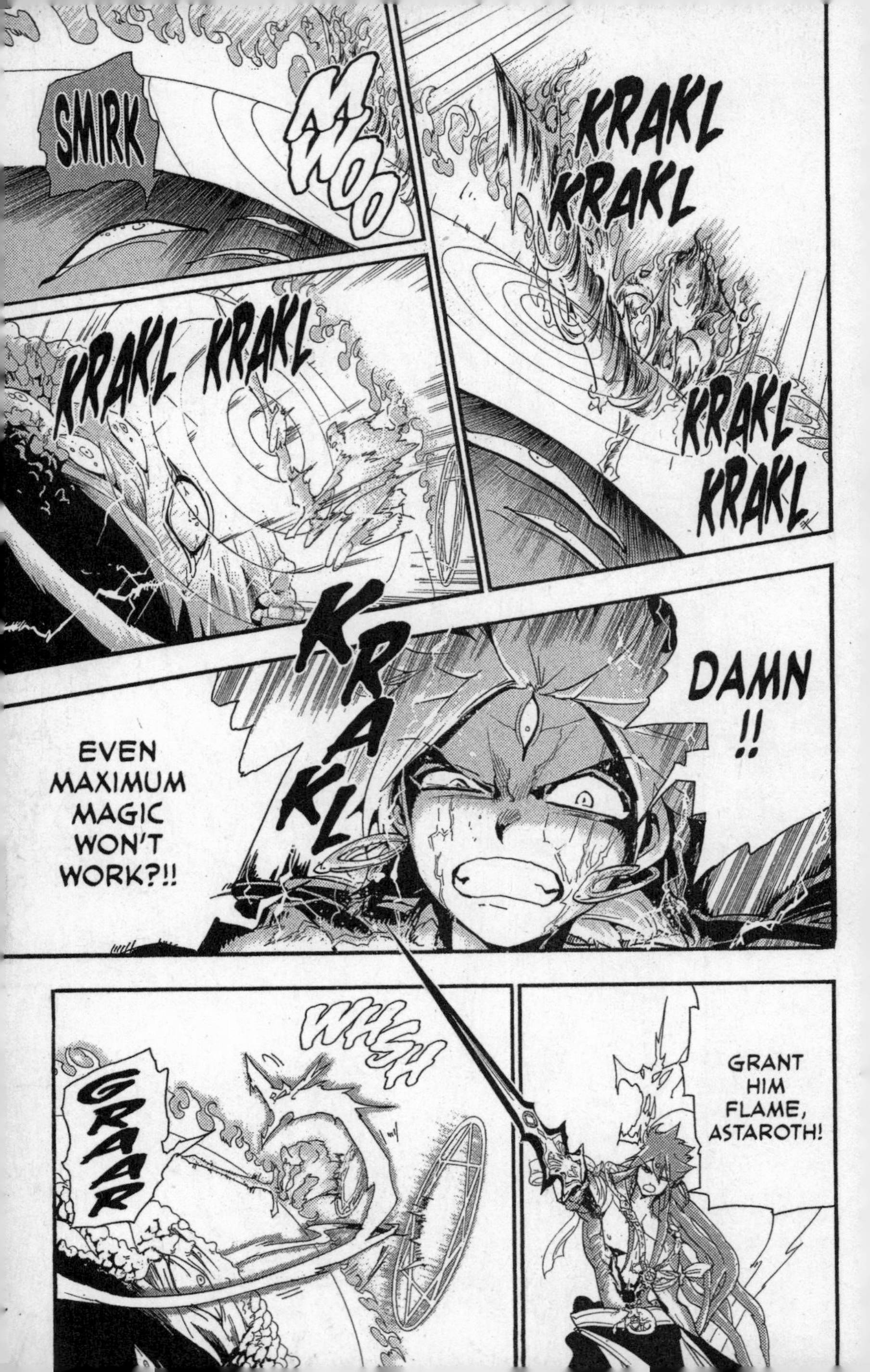
KRAKL
KRAKL
KRAKL
KRAKL
WOO
SMIRK
KRAKL KRAKL
DAMN!!
KRAKL
EVEN MAXIMUM MAGIC WON'T WORK?!!
GRANT HIM FLAME, ASTAROTH!
WHSH
GRAAR

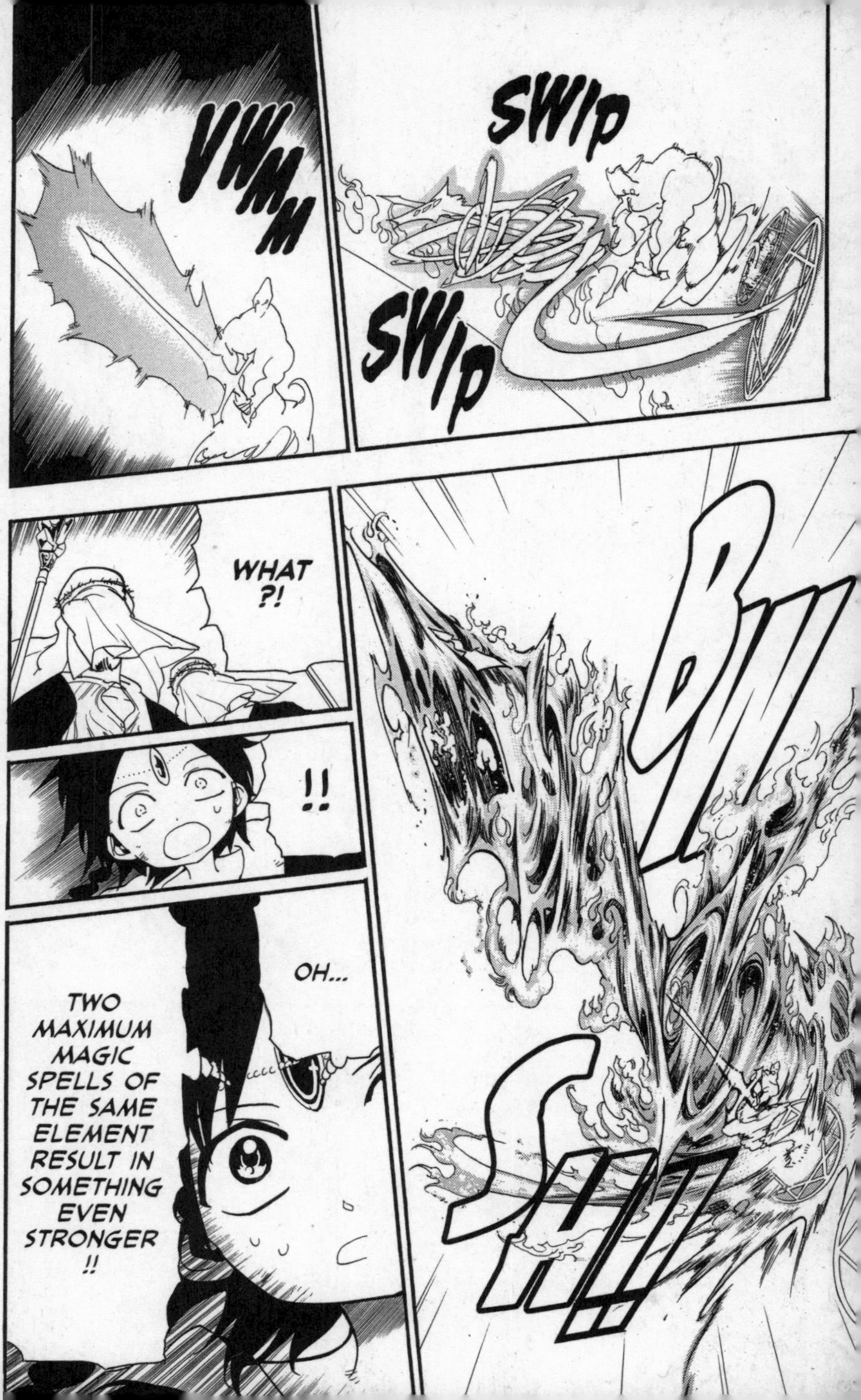
SWIP
SWIP
VWMMM
BWSH!!
WHAT?!
!!
OH...
TWO MAXIMUM MAGIC SPELLS OF THE SAME ELEMENT RESULT IN SOMETHING EVEN STRONGER!!

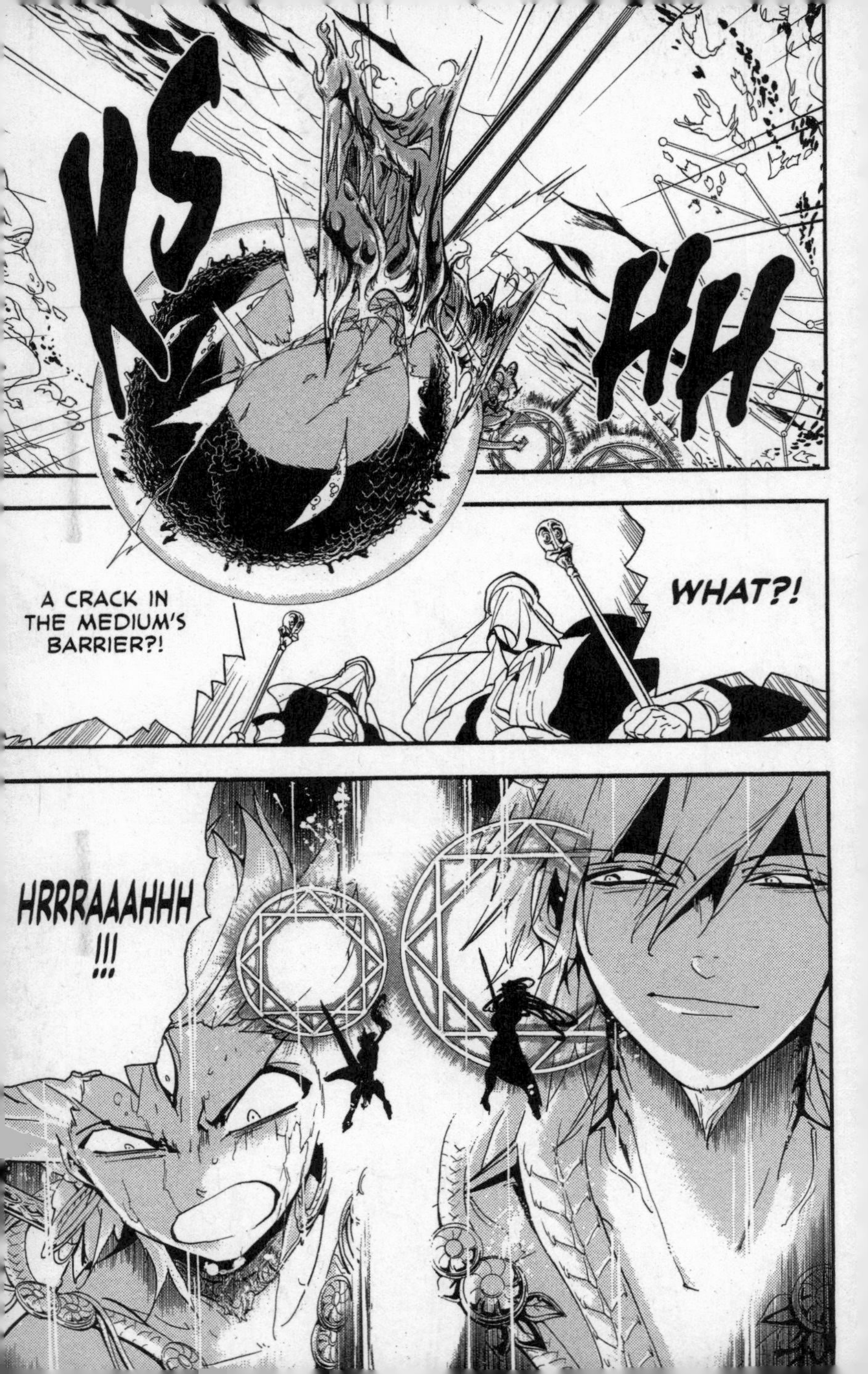
KSHH
WHAT?!
A CRACK IN THE MEDIUM'S BARRIER?!
HRRRAAAHHH!!!

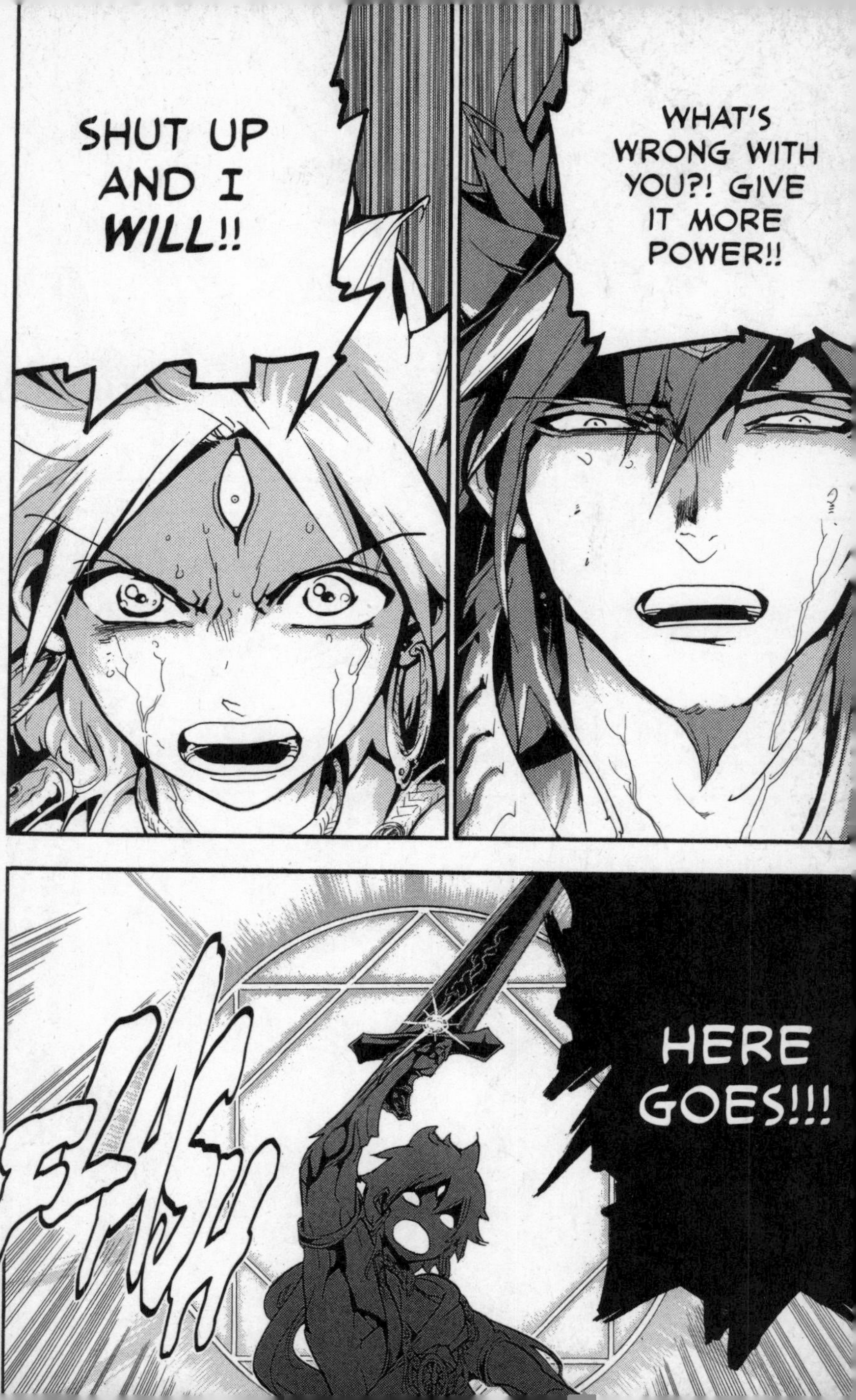
WHAT'S WRONG WITH YOU?! GIVE IT MORE POWER!!
SHUT UP AND I WILL!!
HERE GOES!!!

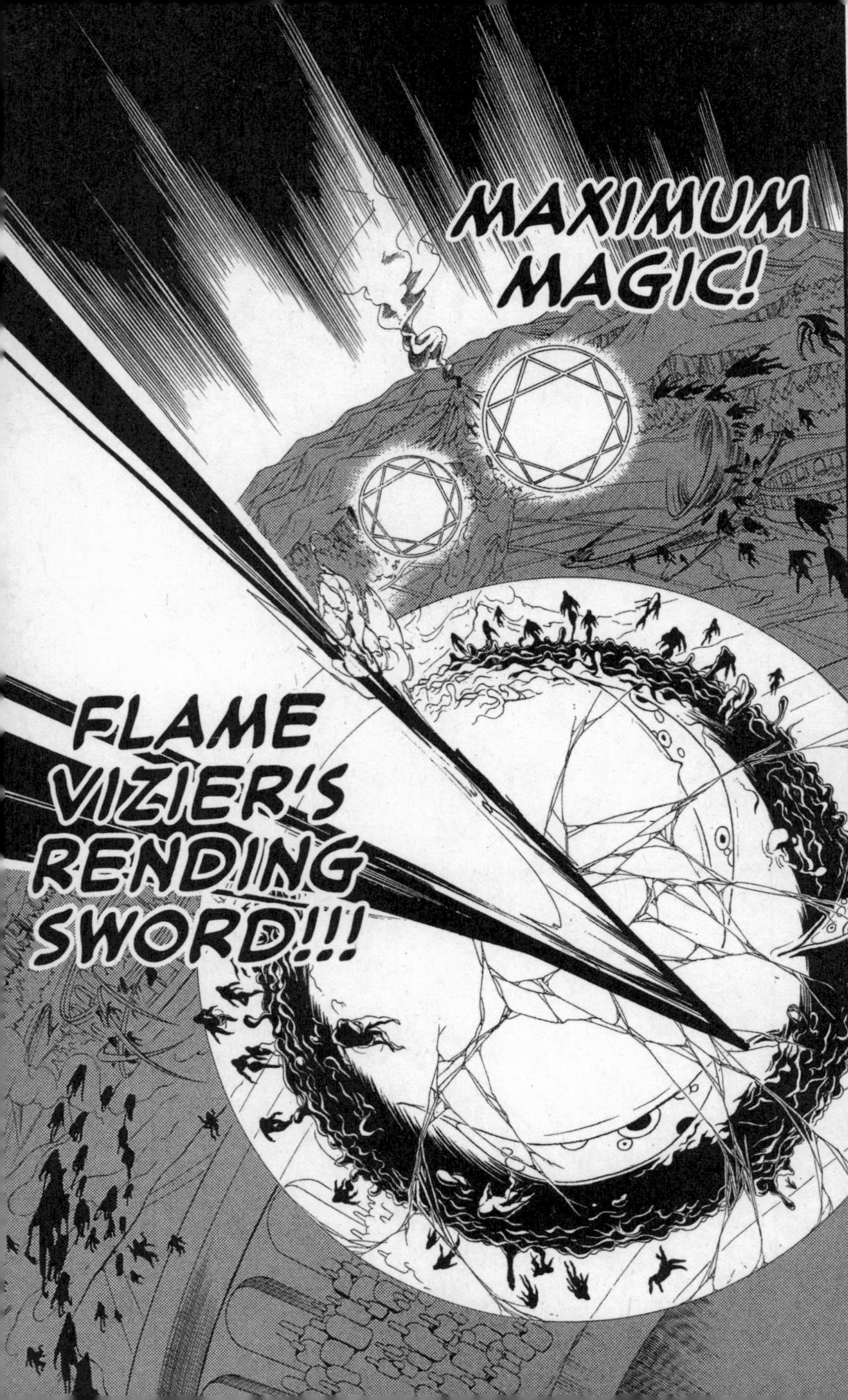
MAXIMUM MAGIC!
FLAME VIZIER'S RENDING SWORD!!!

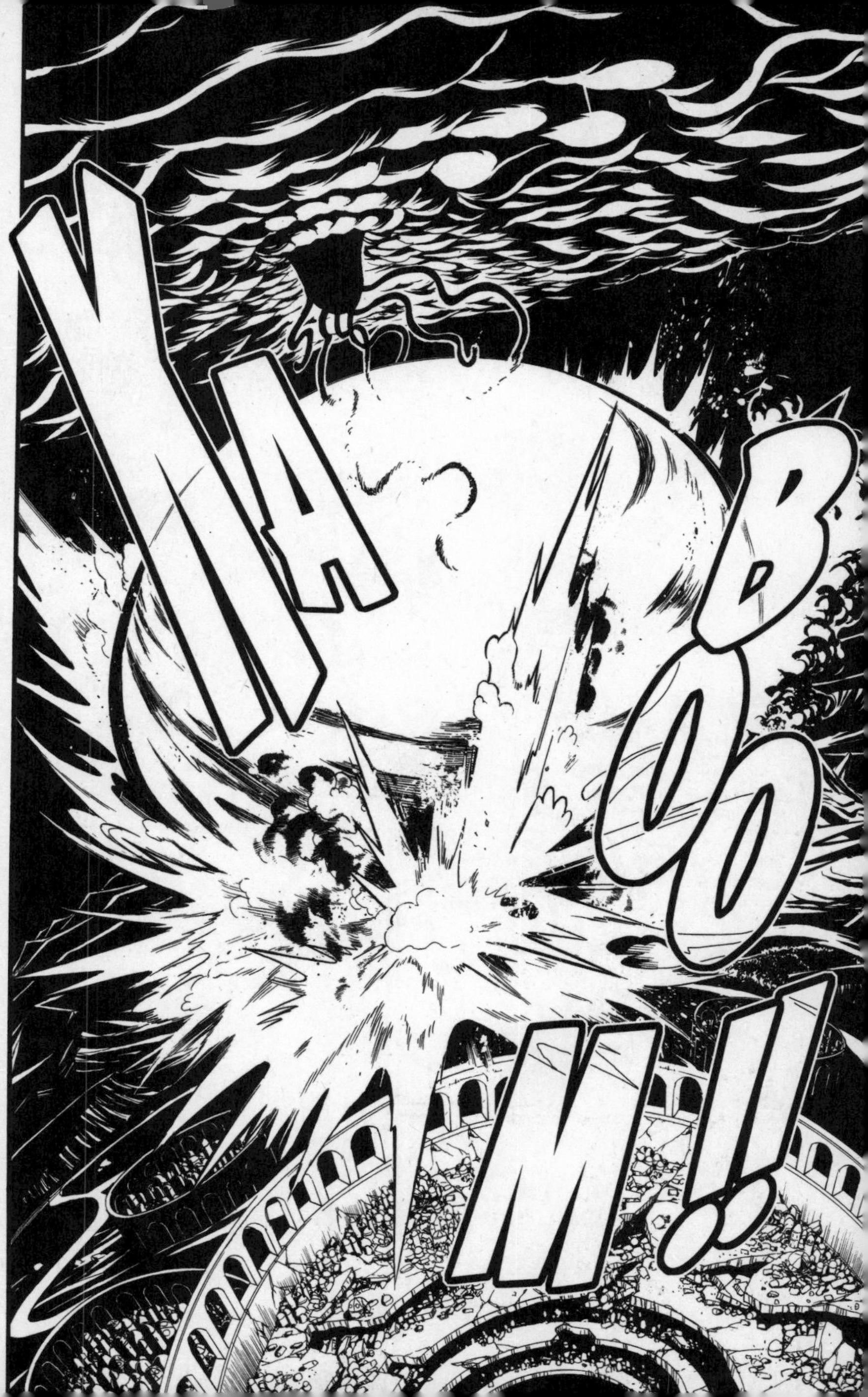
KABOOM!!

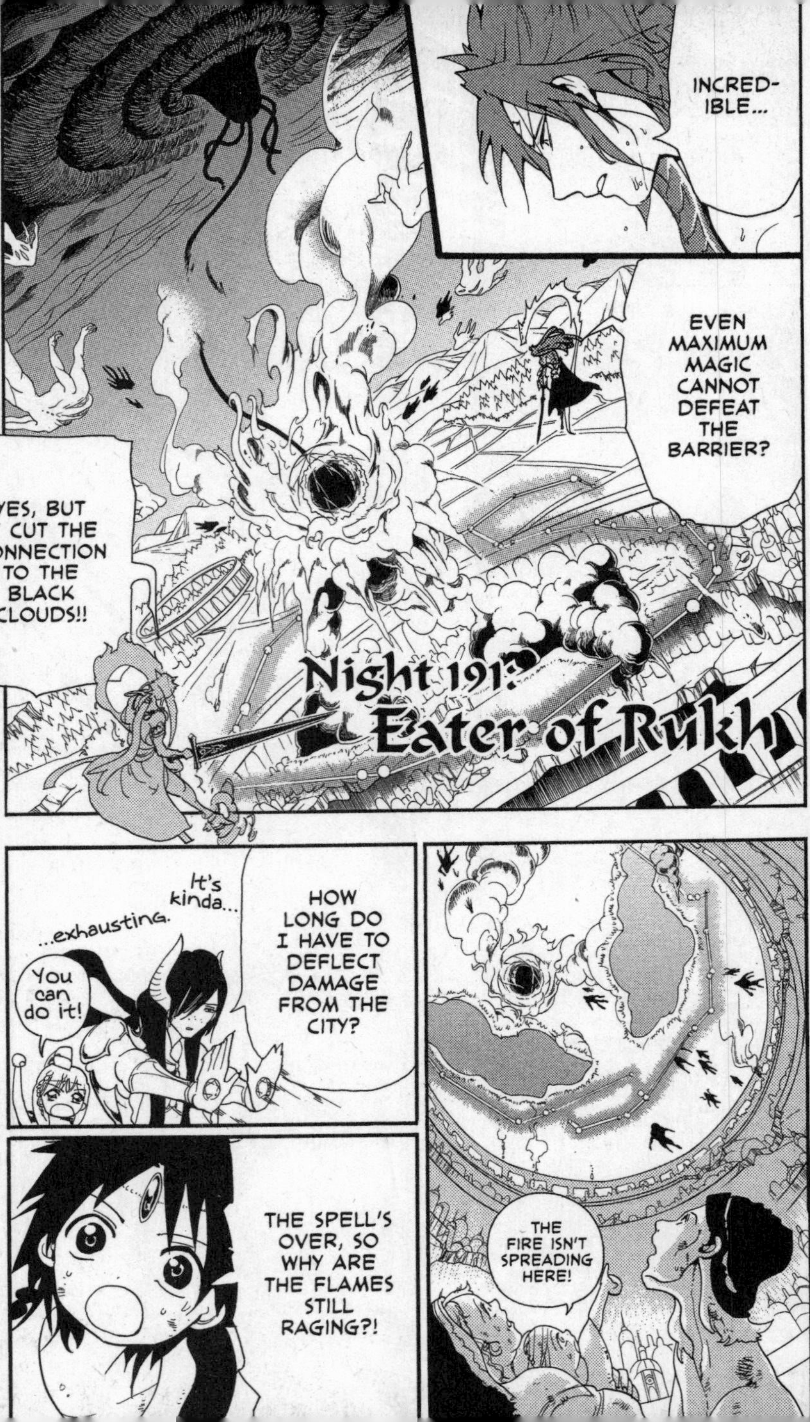
INCRED-IBLE...
EVEN MAXIMUM MAGIC CANNOT DEFEAT THE BARRIER?
YES, BUT IT CUT THE CONNECTION TO THE BLACK CLOUDS!!
Night 191: Eater of Rukh
THE FIRE ISN'T SPREADING HERE!
HOW LONG DO I HAVE TO DEFLECT DAMAGE FROM THE CITY?
It's kinda...
...exhausting.
You can do it!
THE SPELL'S OVER, SO WHY ARE THE FLAMES STILL RAGING?!

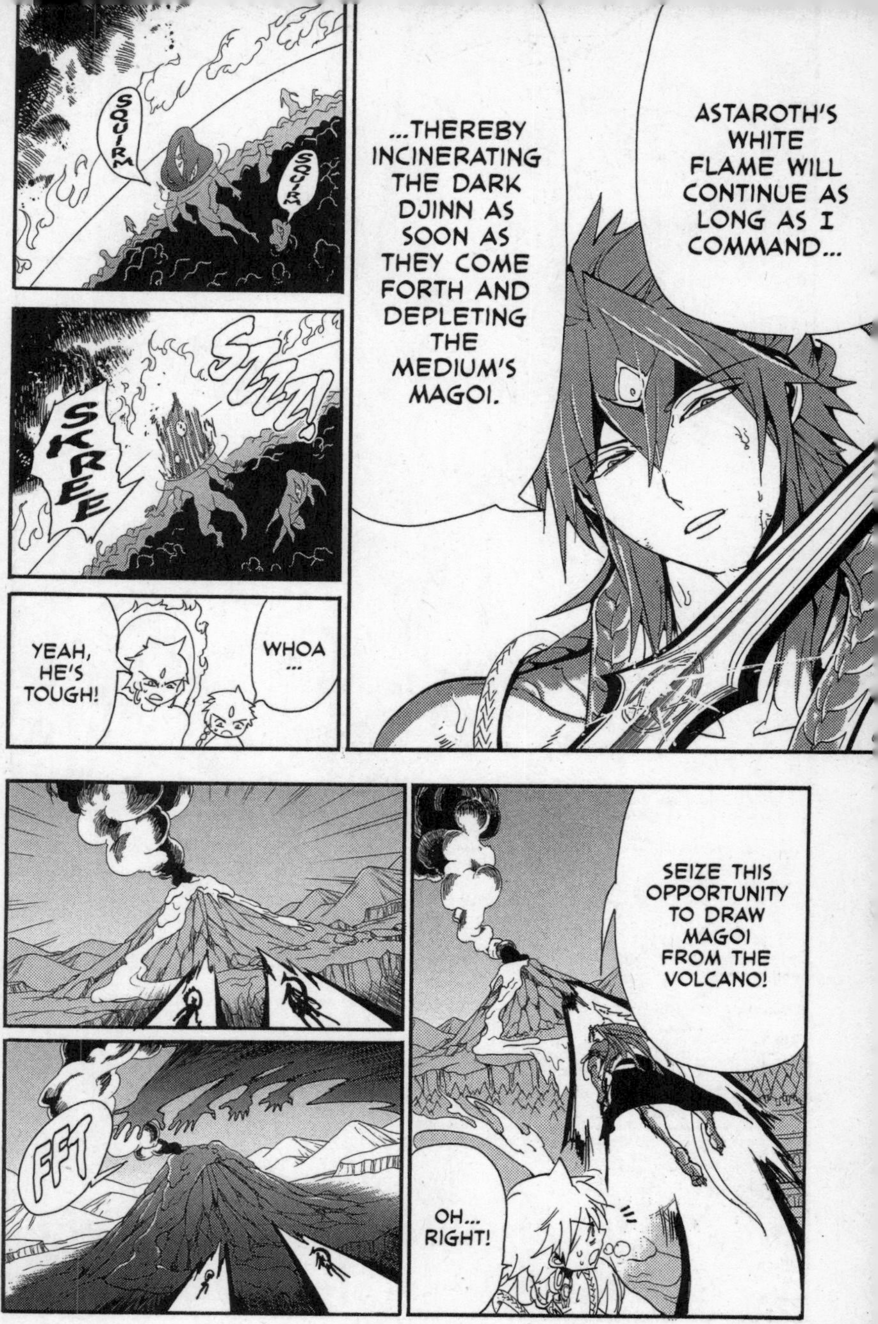
ASTAROTH'S WHITE FLAME WILL CONTINUE AS LONG AS I COMMAND...
...THEREBY INCINERATING THE DARK DJINN AS SOON AS THEY COME FORTH AND DEPLETING THE MEDIUM'S MAGOI.
SQUIRM
SQUIRM
SKREE
WHOA ...
YEAH, HE'S TOUGH!
SEIZE THIS OPPORTUNITY TO DRAW MAGOI FROM THE VOLCANO!
OH... RIGHT!
FFT

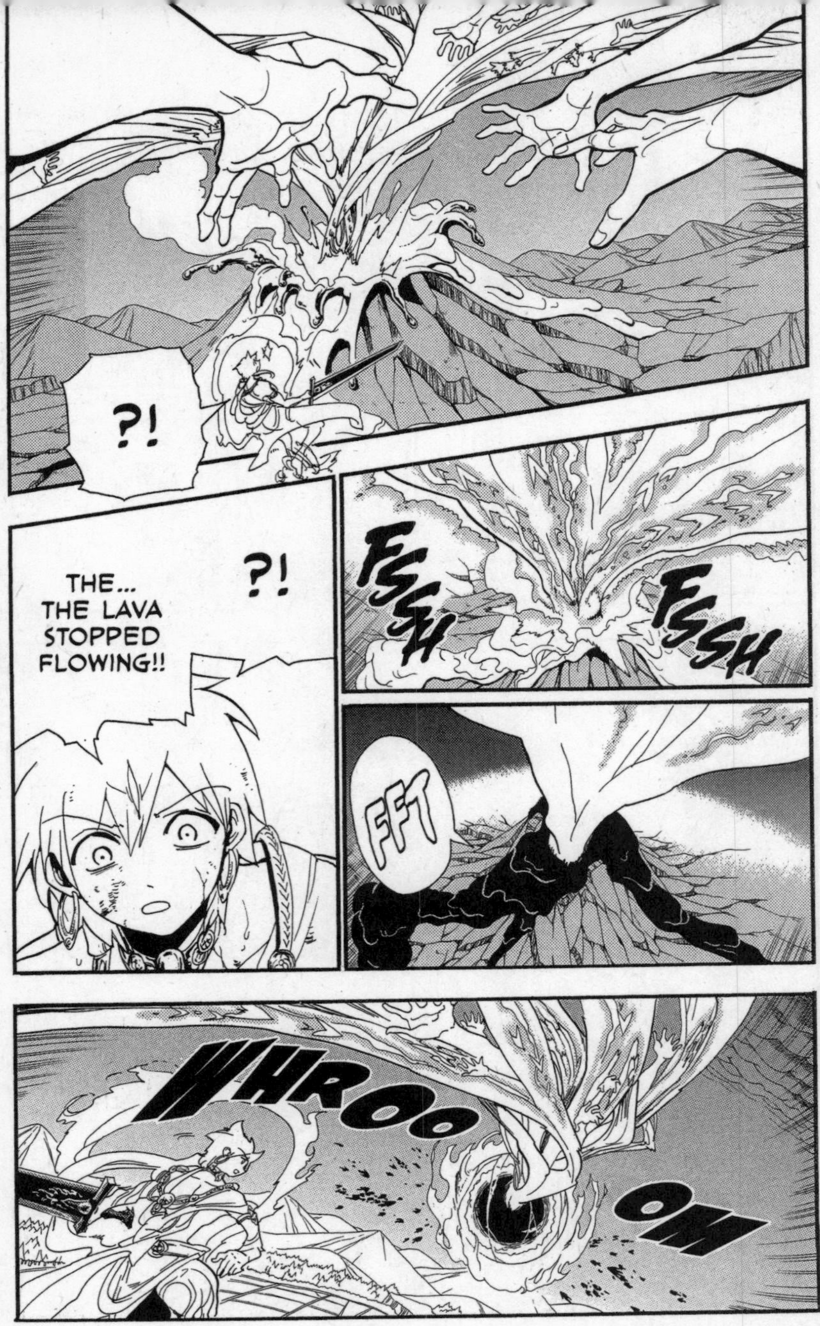
?!
FSSH
FSSH
FFT
?!
THE... THE LAVA STOPPED FLOWING!!
WHROOOOM

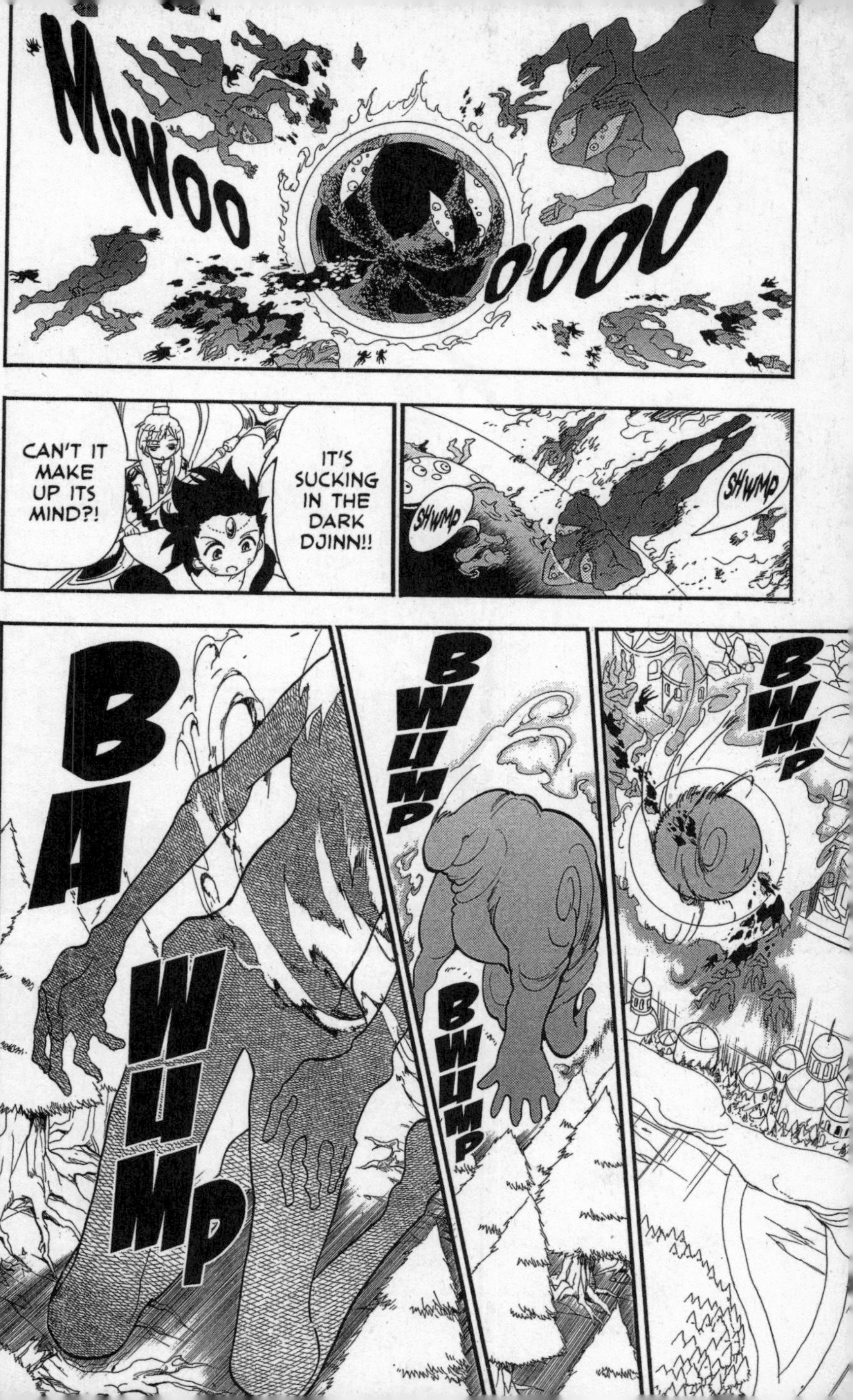
MWOOOOOOO
SHWMP
SHWMP
IT'S SUCKING IN THE DARK DJINN!!
CAN'T IT MAKE UP ITS MIND?!
BWUMP
BWUMP
BWUMP
BA
WUMP

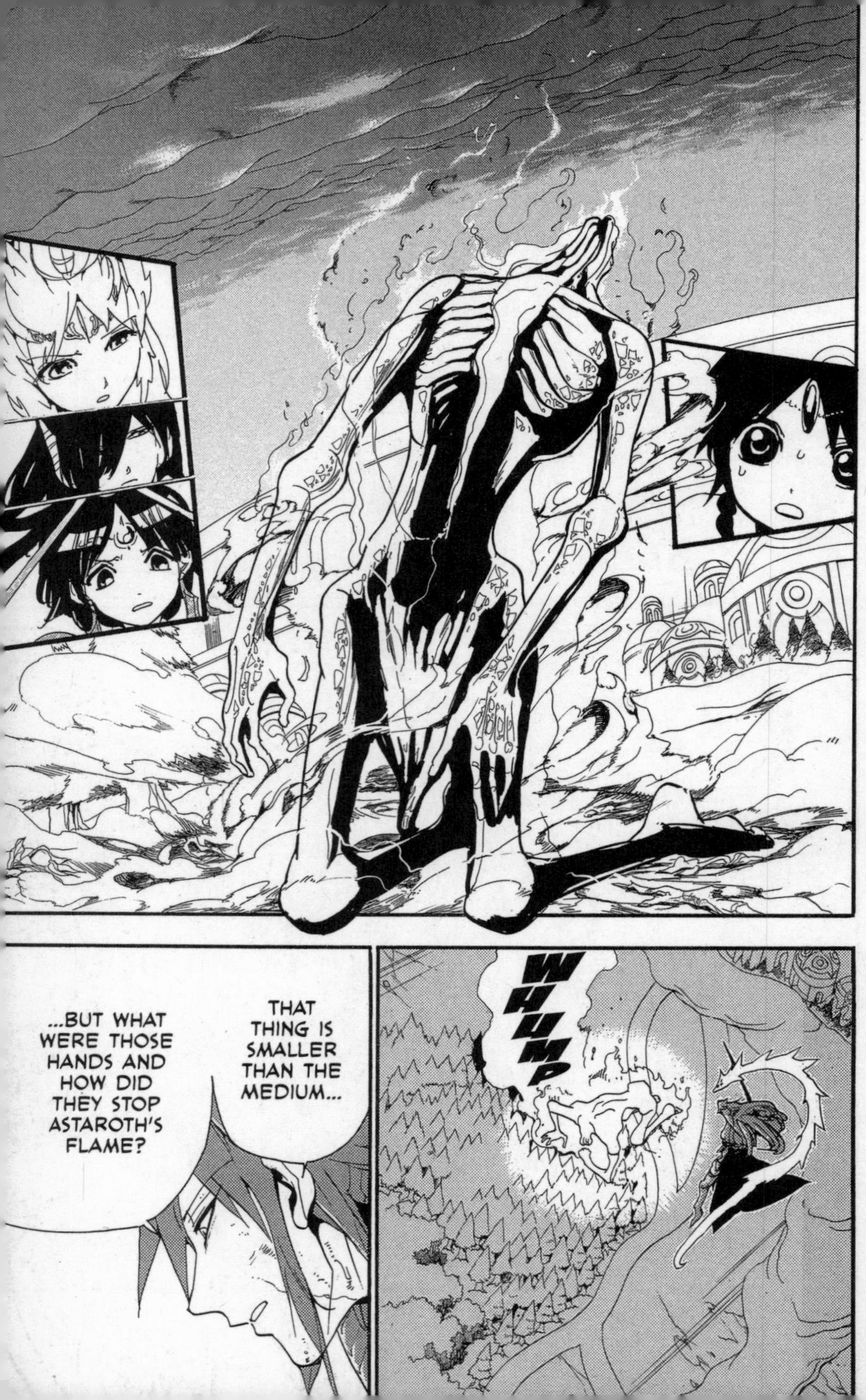
WHUMP
THAT THING IS SMALLER THAN THE MEDIUM...
...BUT WHAT WERE THOSE HANDS AND HOW DID THEY STOP ASTAROTH'S FLAME?

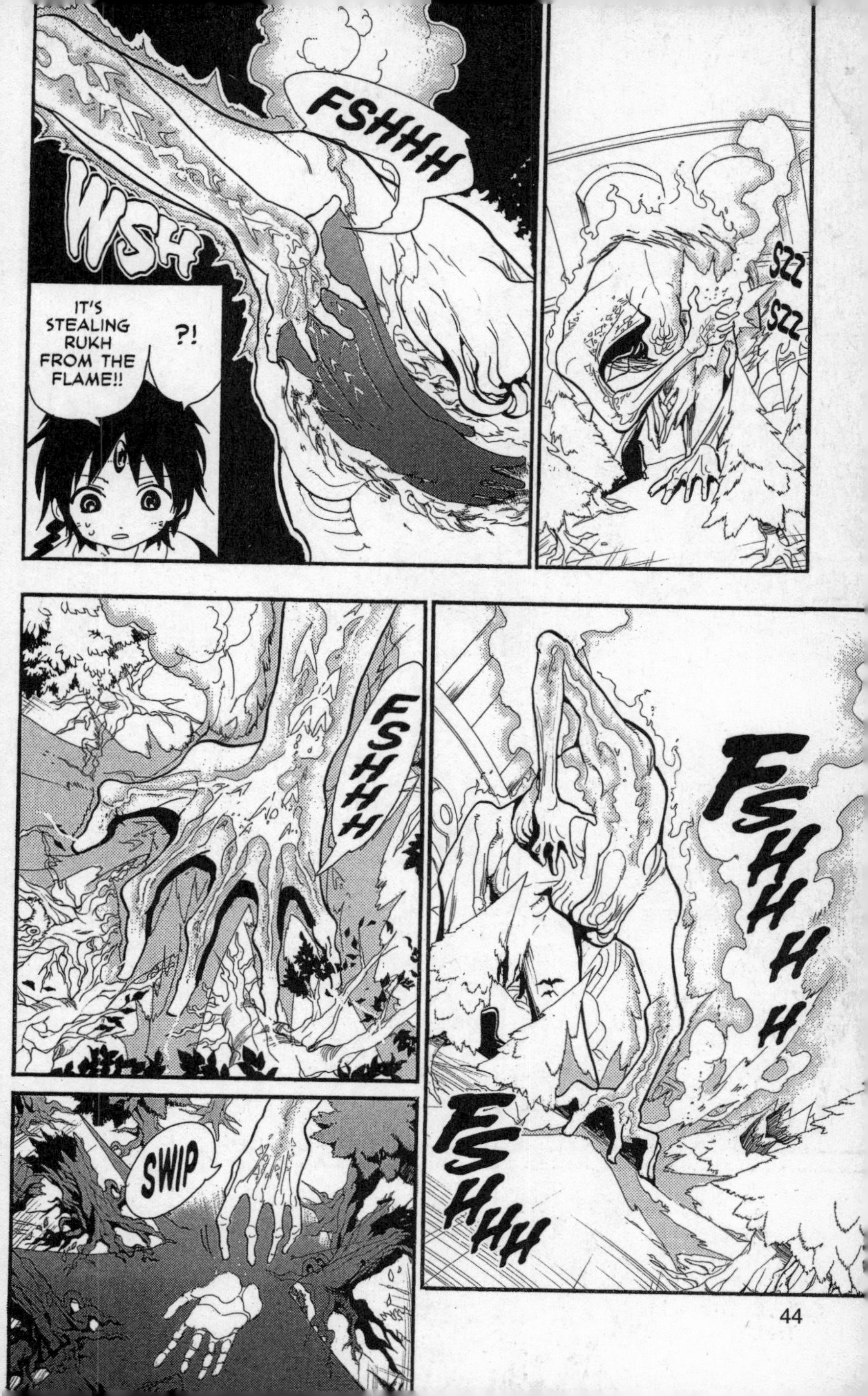
SZZ
SZZ
FSHHHH
WSH
?!
IT'S STEALING RUKH FROM THE FLAME!!
FSHHHHH
FSHHHH
FSHHHH
SWIP

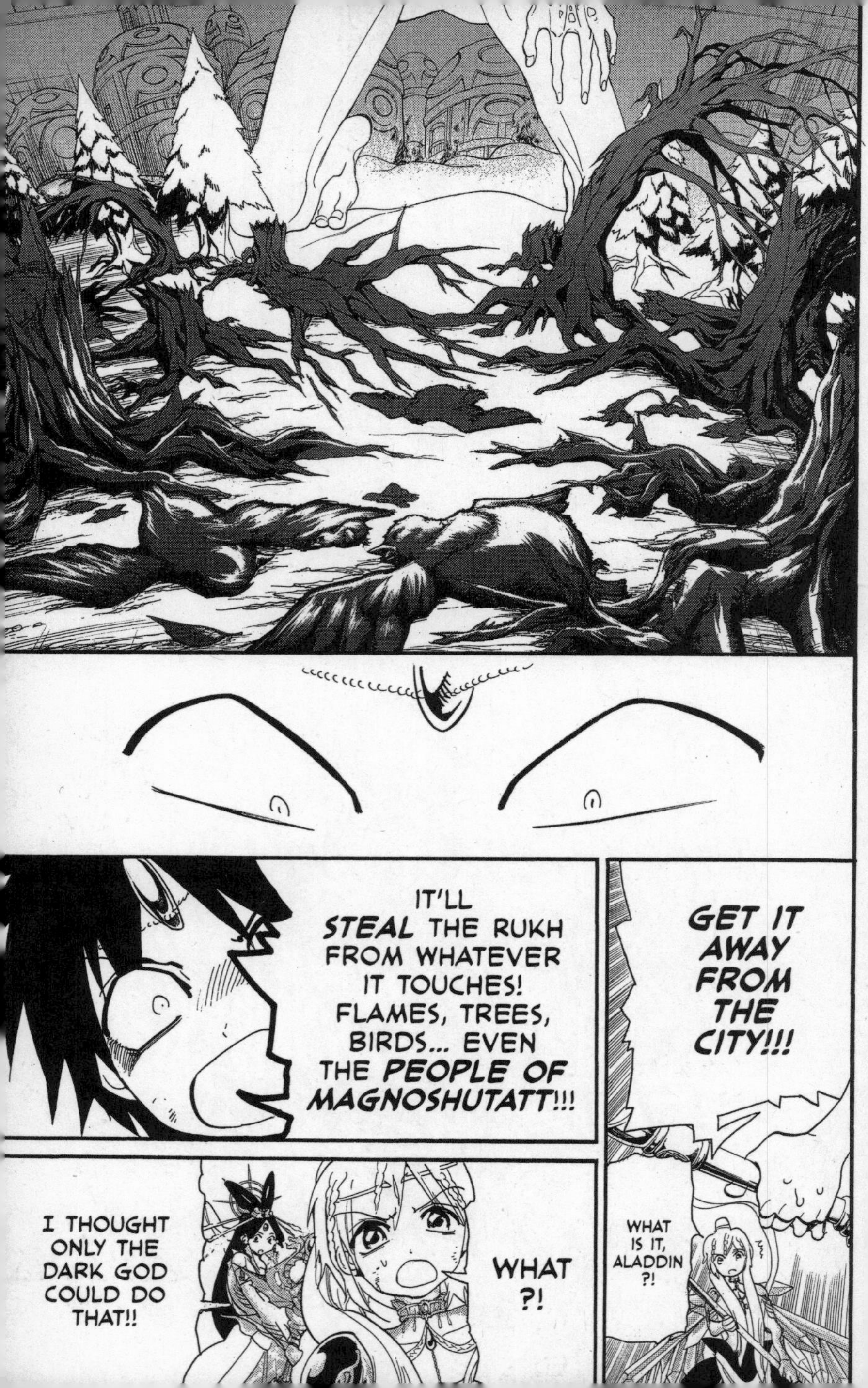
GET IT AWAY FROM THE CITY!!!
WHAT IS IT, ALADDIN?!
IT'LL STEAL THE RUKH FROM WHATEVER IT TOUCHES! FLAMES, TREES, BIRDS... EVEN THE PEOPLE OF MAGNOSHUTATT!!!
WHAT?!
I THOUGHT ONLY THE DARK GOD COULD DO THAT!!

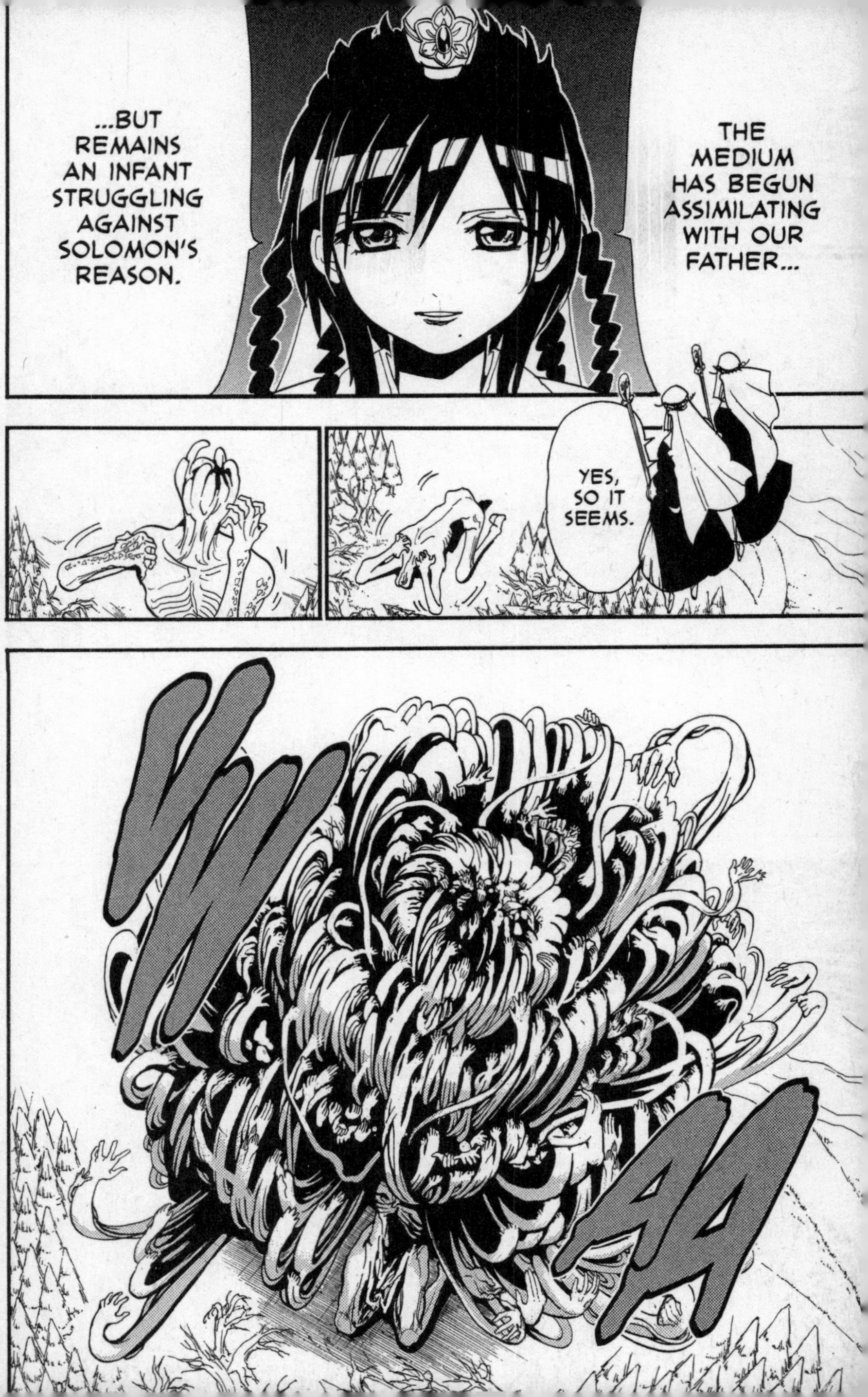
THE MEDIUM HAS BEGUN ASSIMILATING WITH OUR FATHER...
...BUT REMAINS AN INFANT STRUGGLING AGAINST SOLOMON'S REASON.
YES, SO IT SEEMS.

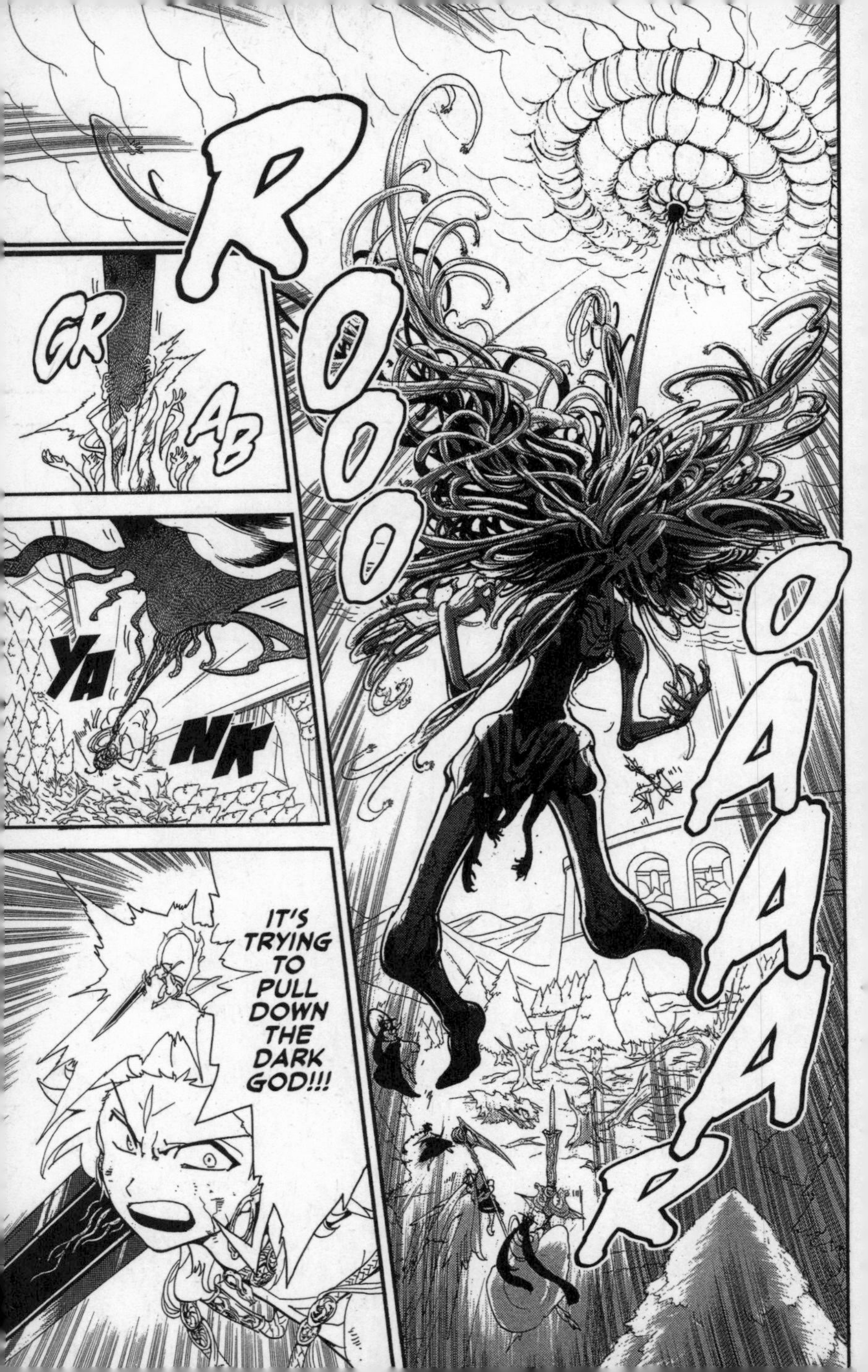
ROOOOAAAR
GRAB
YANK
IT'S TRYING TO PULL DOWN THE DARK GOD!!!

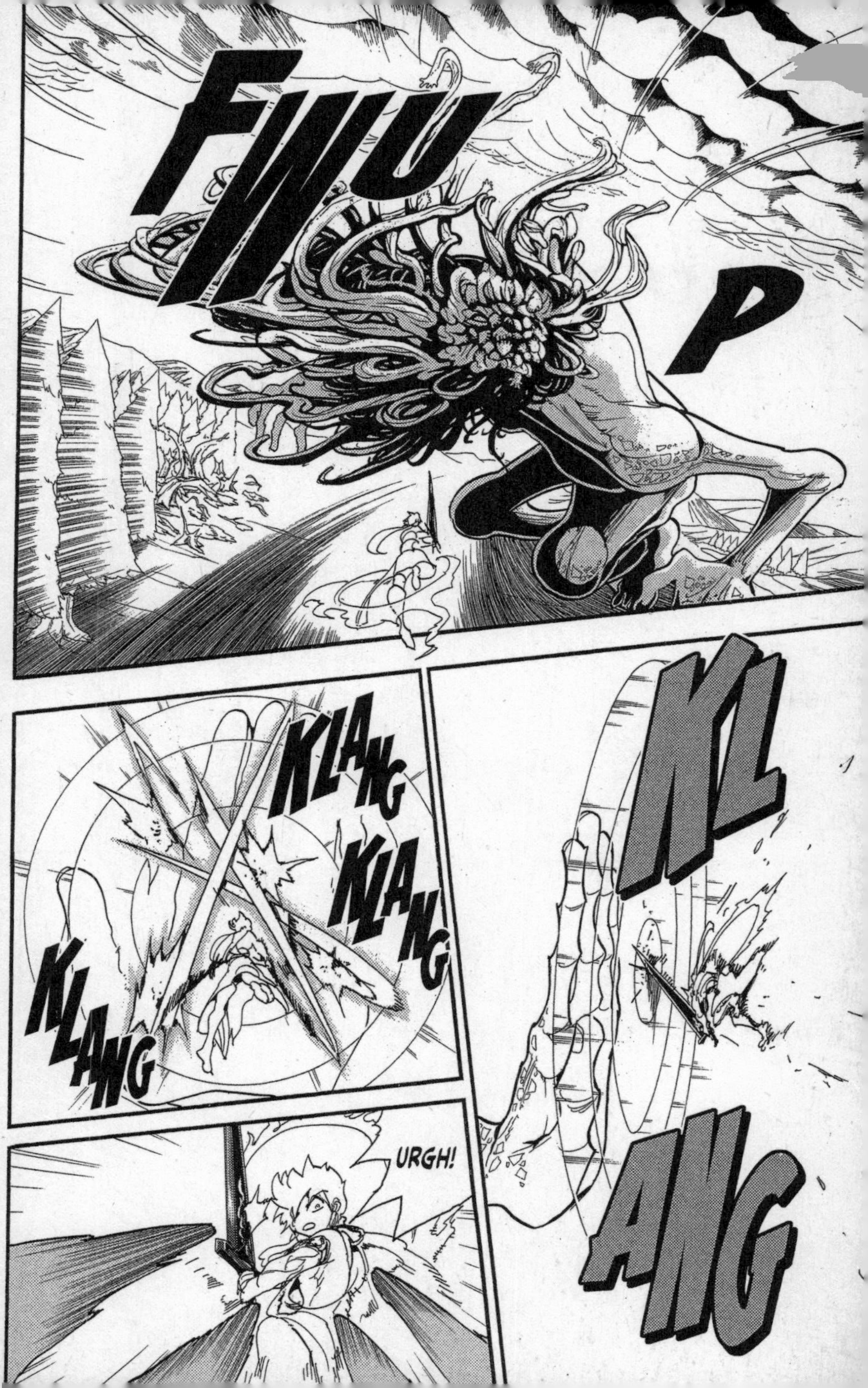
FWUP
KLANG
KLANG
KLANG
KLANG
URGH!

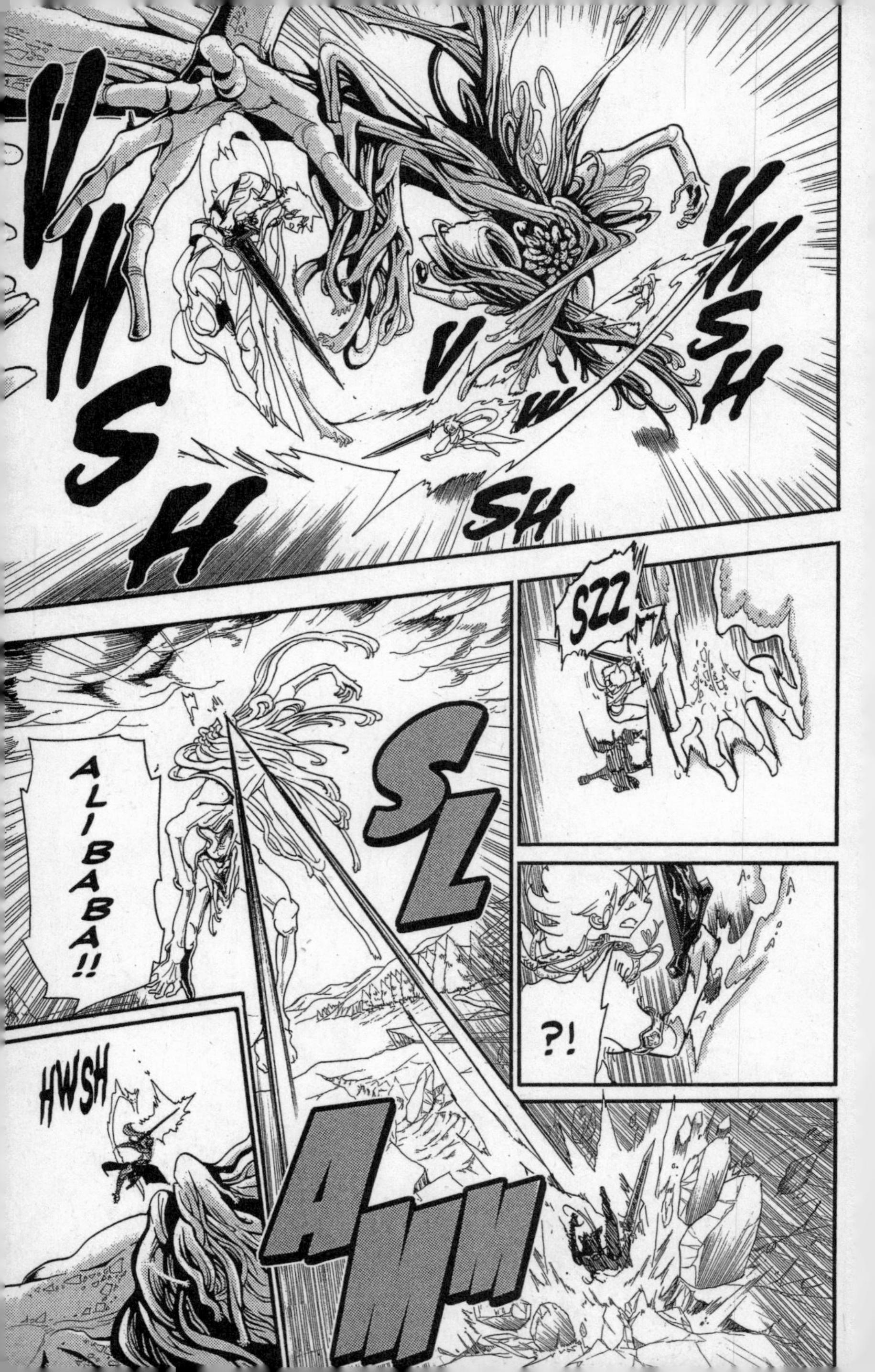
VWSH
VW
SH
VWSH
SZZ
?!
SL
ALIBABA!!
AM
HWSH

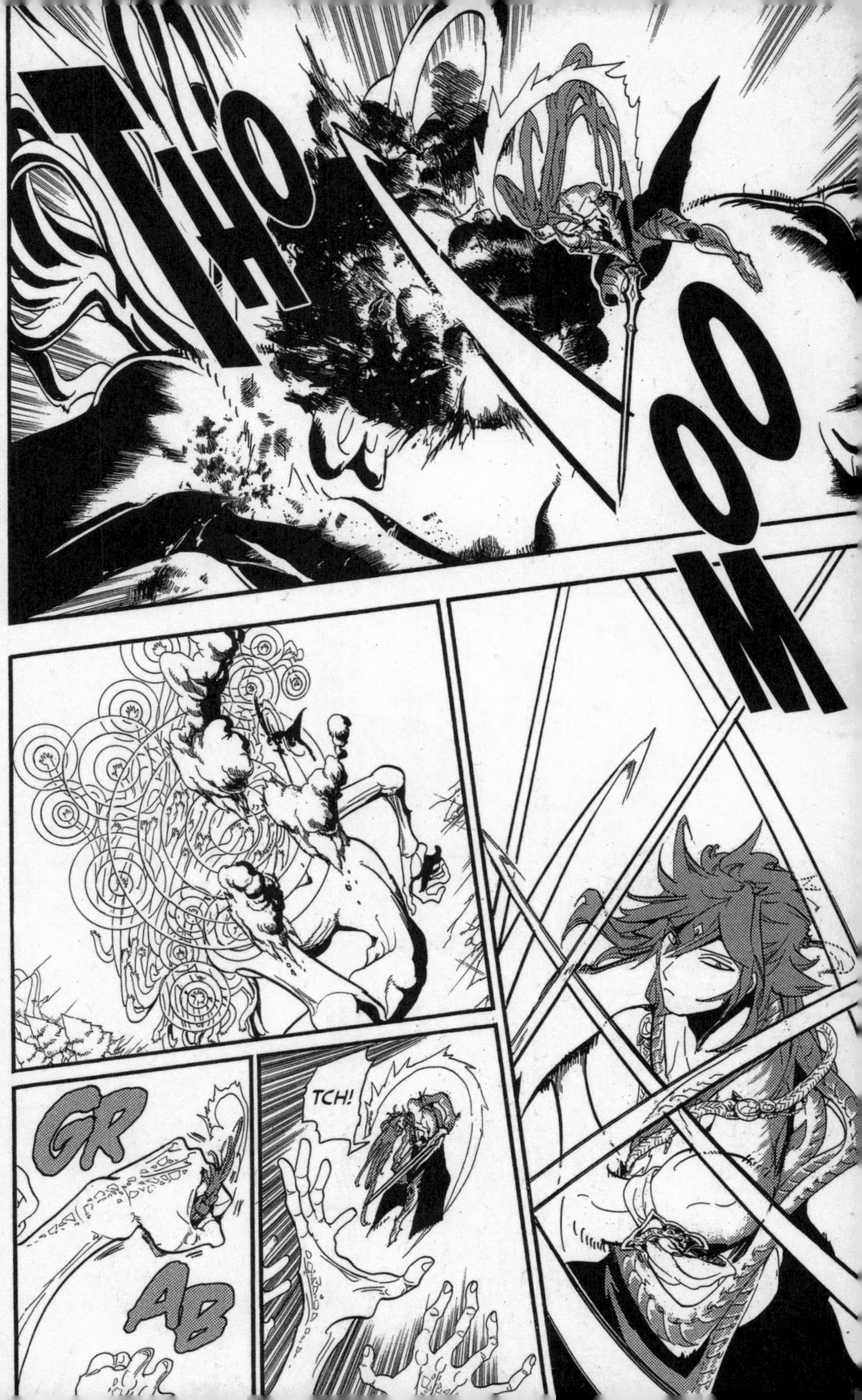
THOOOM
TCH!
GRAB

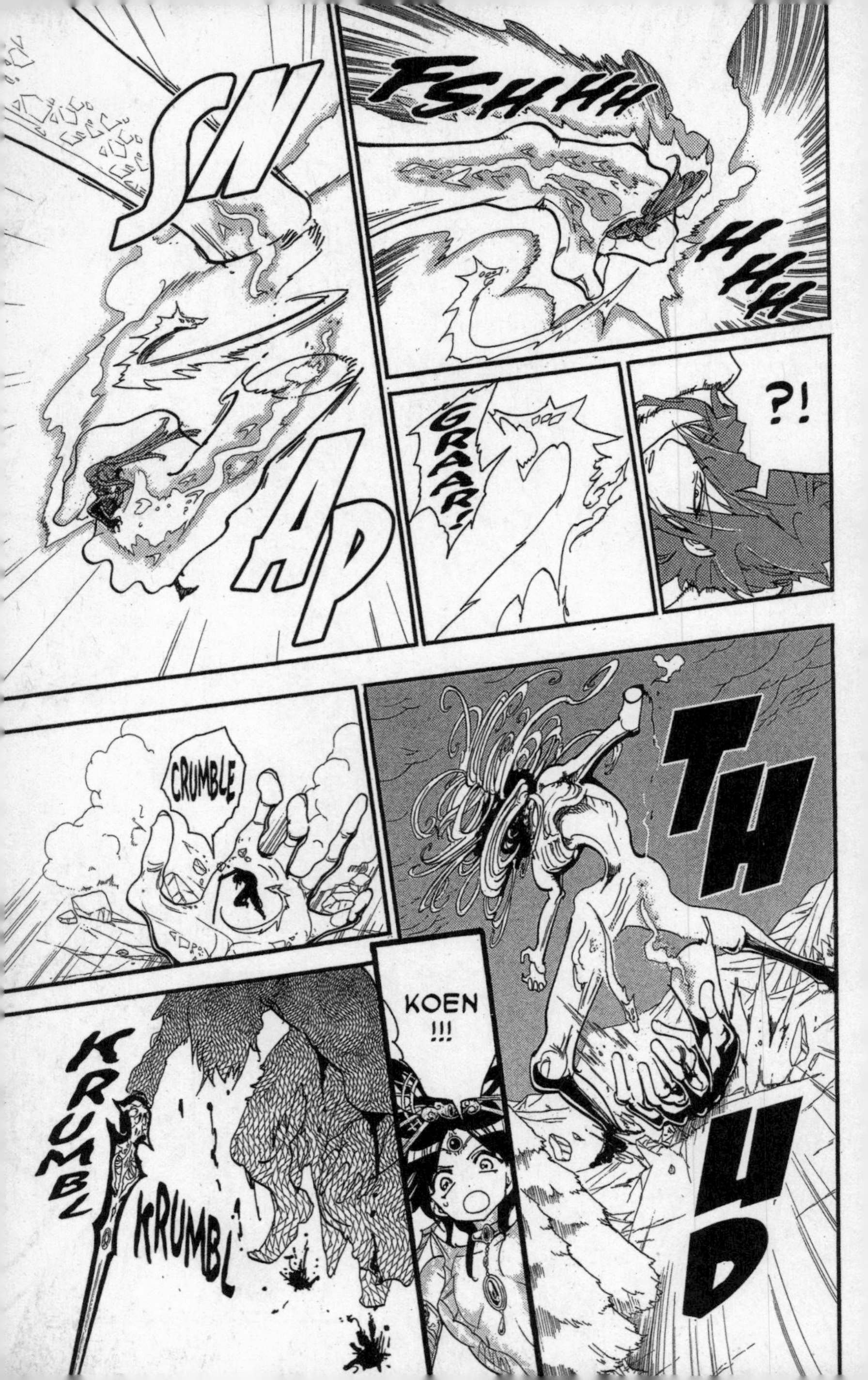
FSHHHH
HHH
?!
GRAAR!
SNAP
THUD
CRUMBLE
KOEN !!!
KRUMBL
KRUMBL

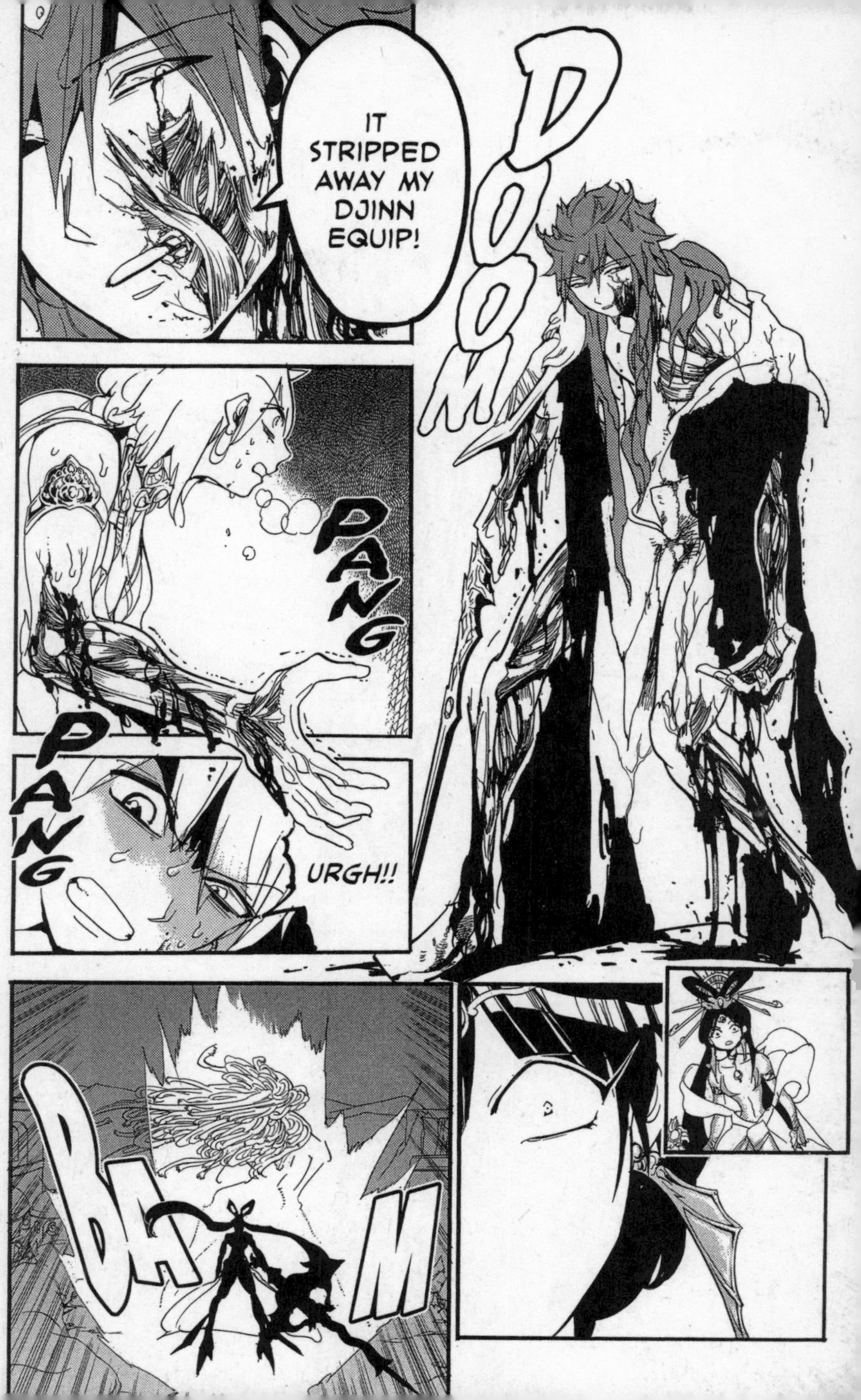
DOOOM
IT STRIPPED AWAY MY DJINN EQUIP!
PANG
PANG
URGH!!
BAM

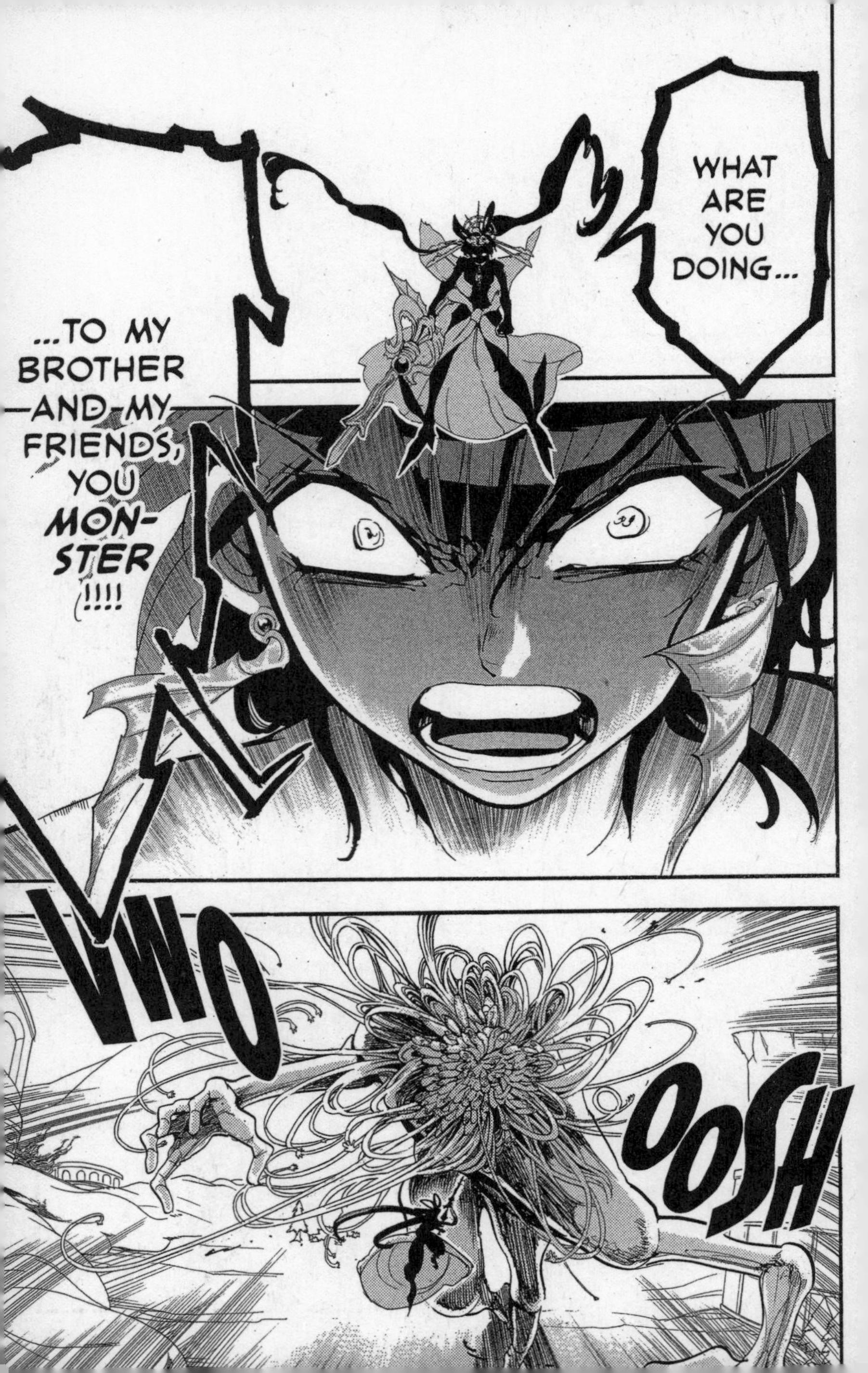
WHAT ARE YOU DOING...
...TO MY BROTHER AND MY FRIENDS, YOU MONSTER!!!!
VWOOOSH

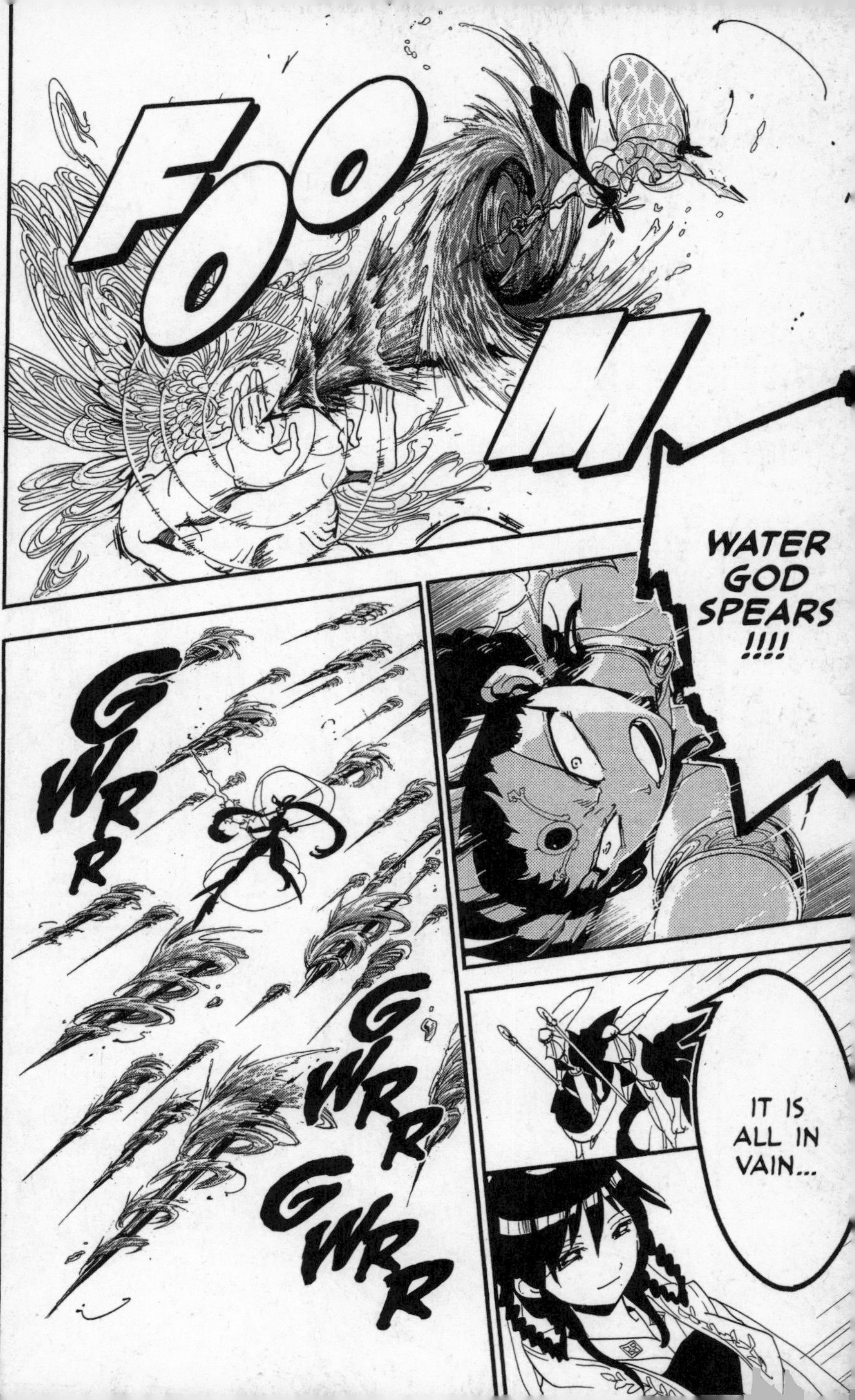
FOOM
WATER GOD SPEARS!!!!
IT IS ALL IN VAIN...
GWRR
GWRR
GWRR

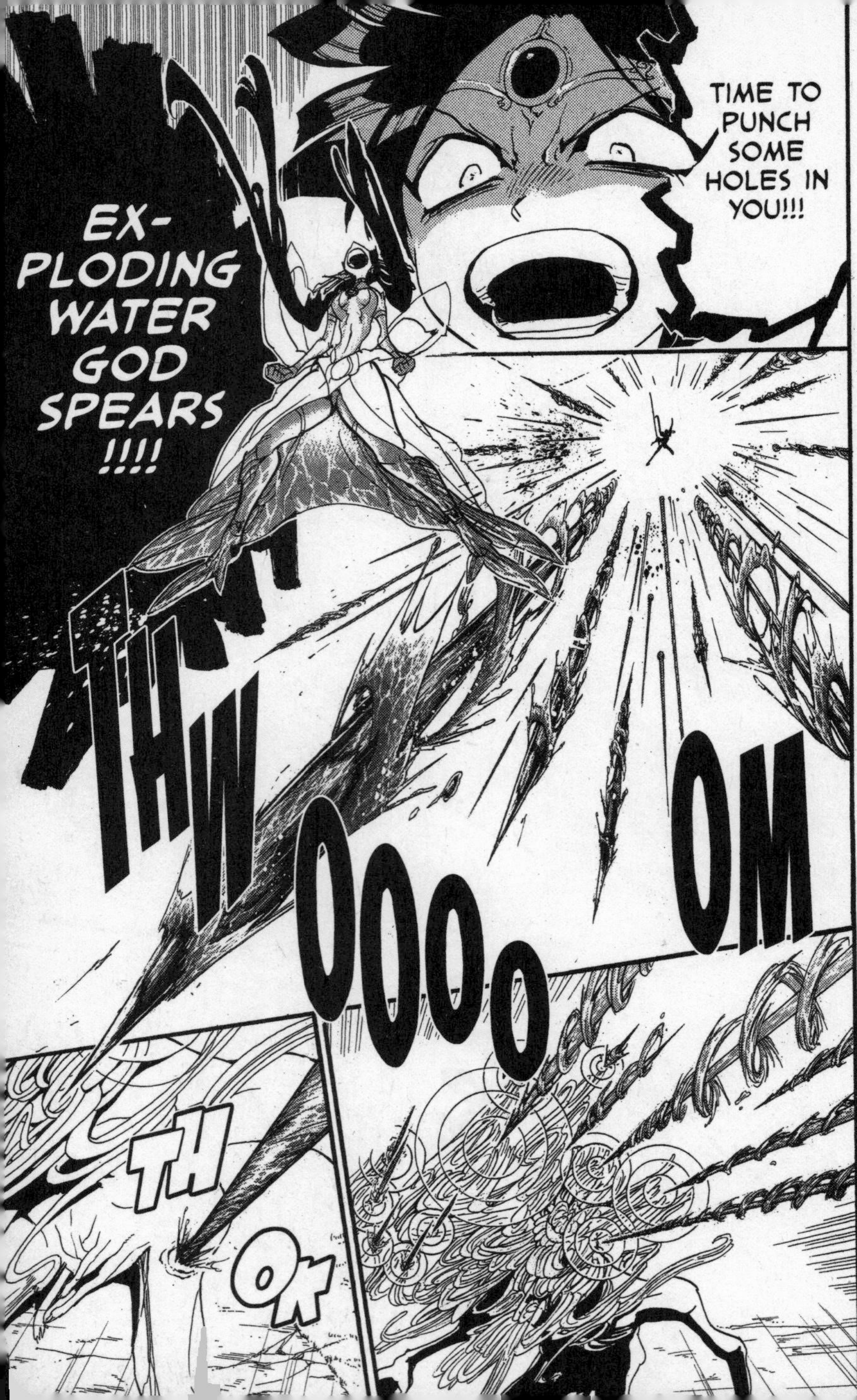
TIME TO PUNCH SOME HOLES IN YOU!!!
EX-PLODING WATER GOD SPEARS !!!!
THWOOOOOM
THOK

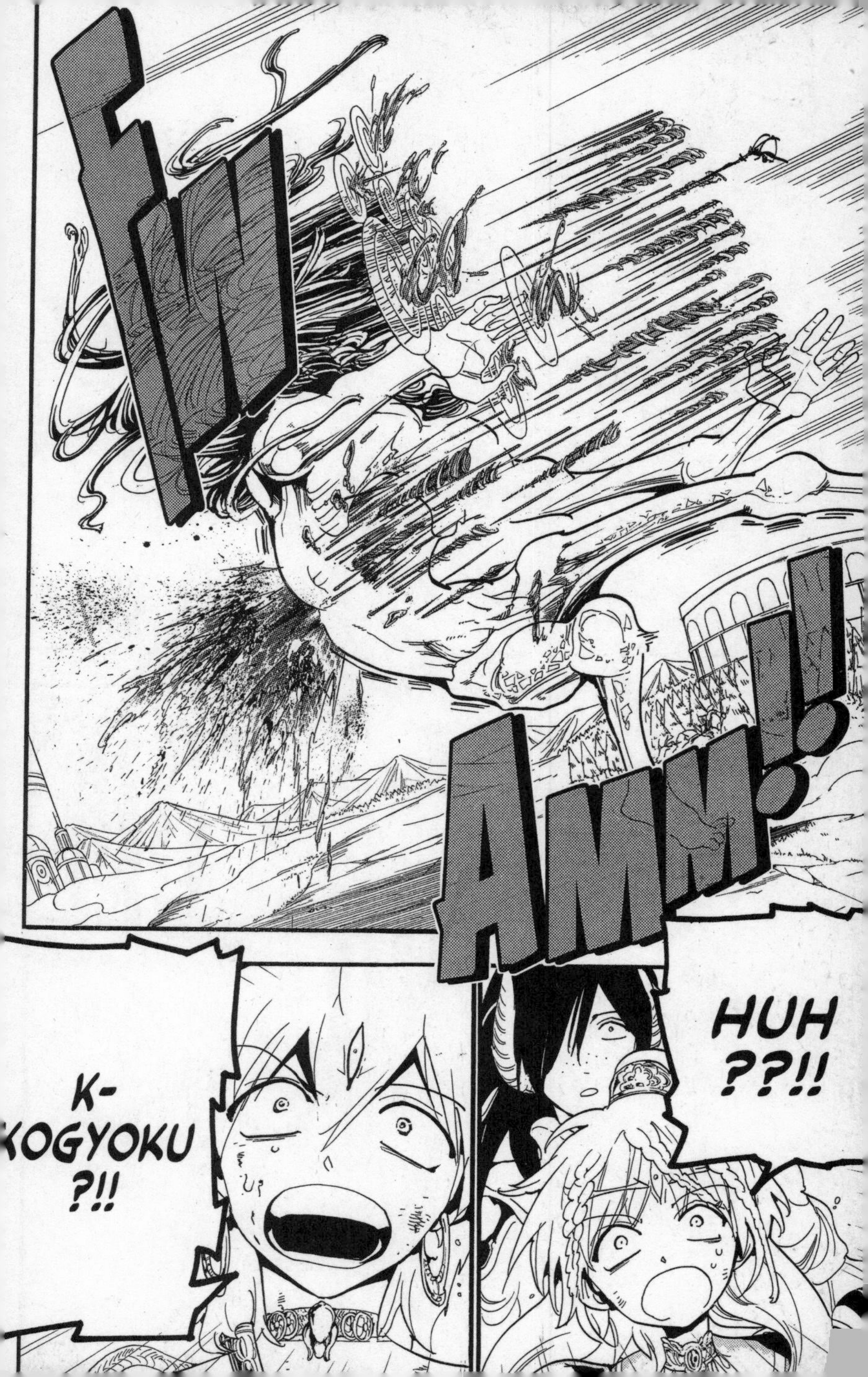
AMM!!
HUH ??!!
K-KOGYOKU ?!!

Night 192: Relentless Assault

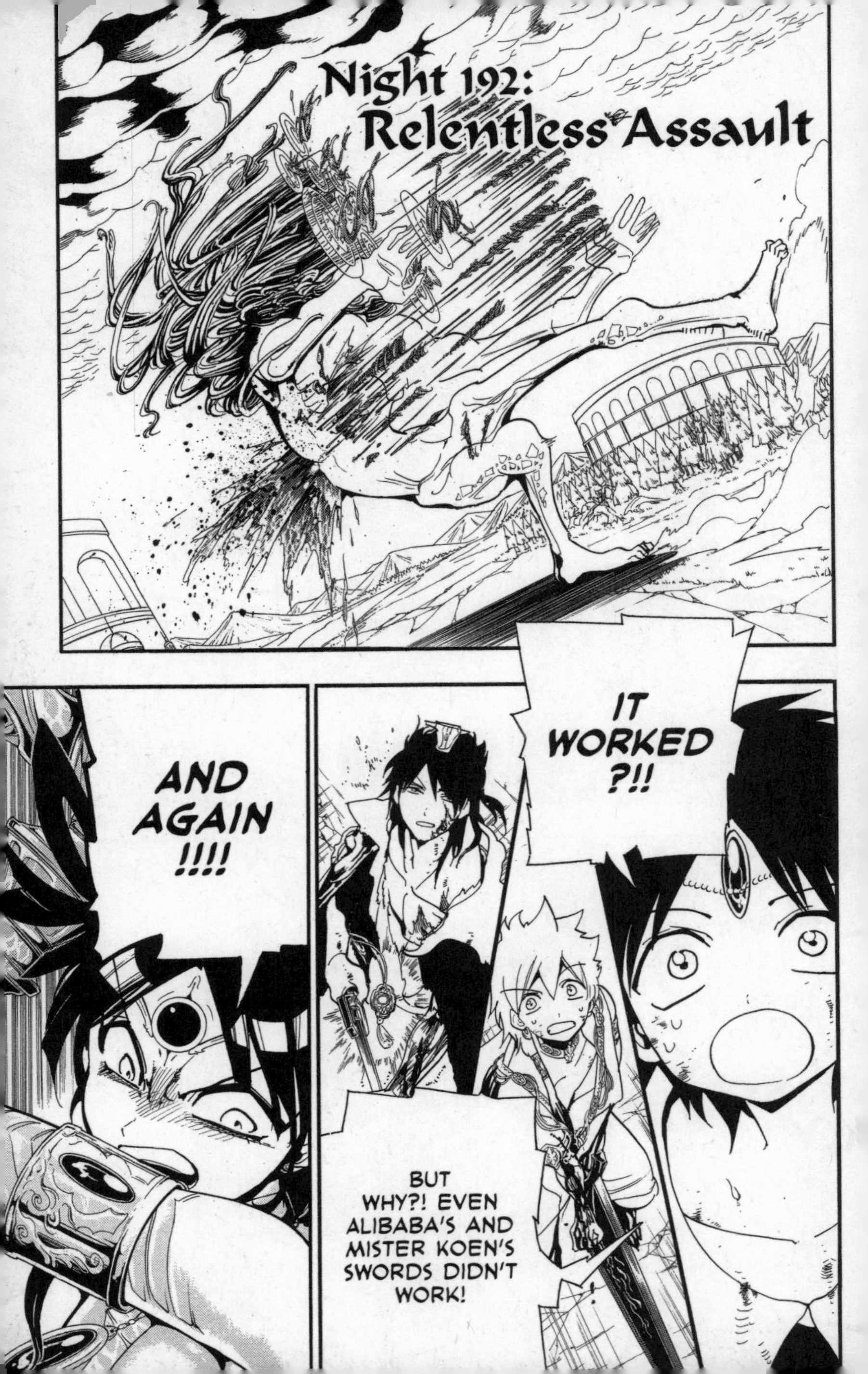
IT WORKED?!!
BUT WHY?! EVEN ALIBABA'S AND MISTER KOEN'S SWORDS DIDN'T WORK!
AND AGAIN!!!!

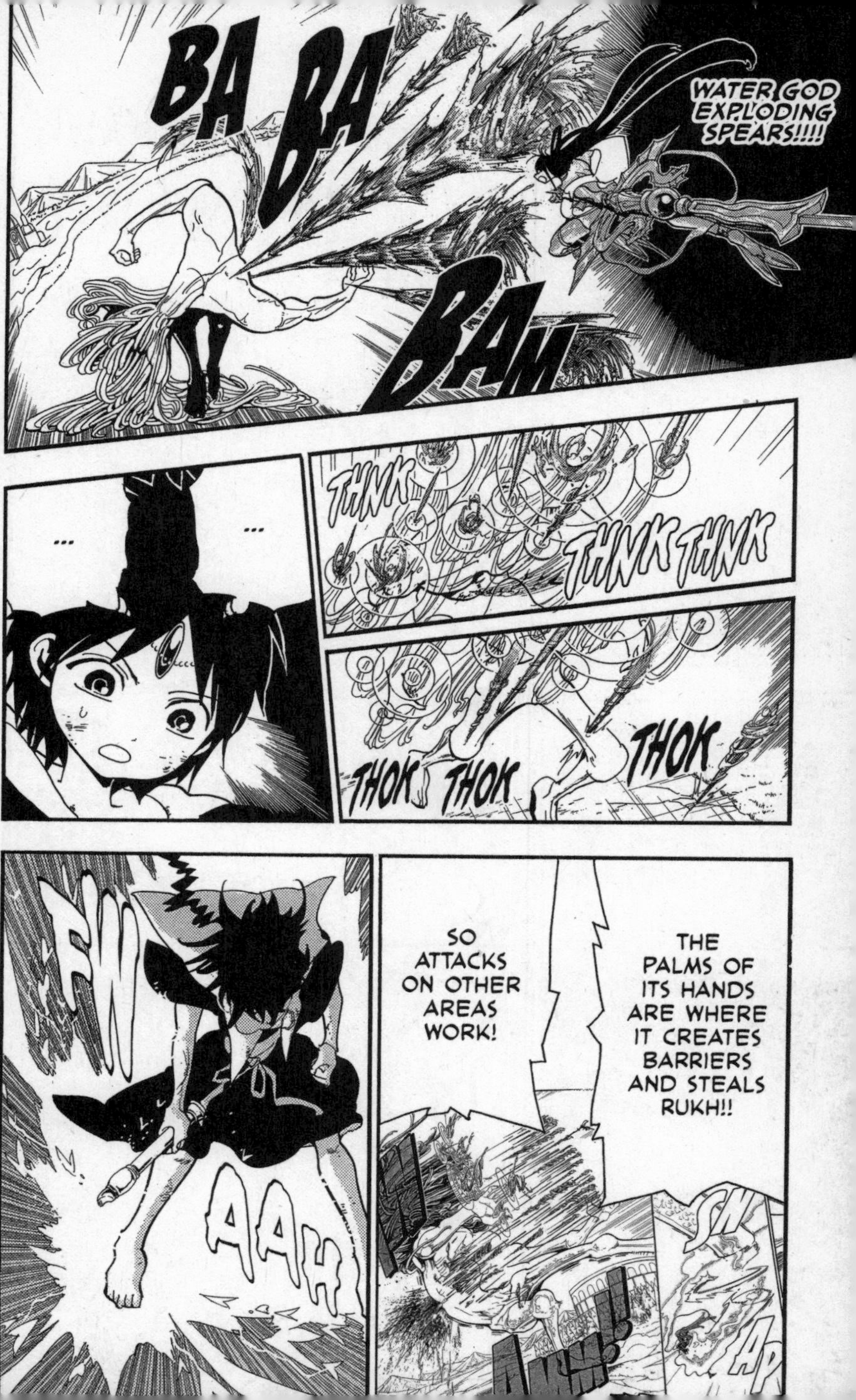
WATER GOD EXPLODING SPEARS!!!!
BA BA
BAM
THNK
THNK THNK
THOK
THOK
THOK
...
...
THE PALMS OF ITS HANDS ARE WHERE IT CREATES BARRIERS AND STEALS RUKH!!
SO ATTACKS ON OTHER AREAS WORK!
SNK
FW
AAH

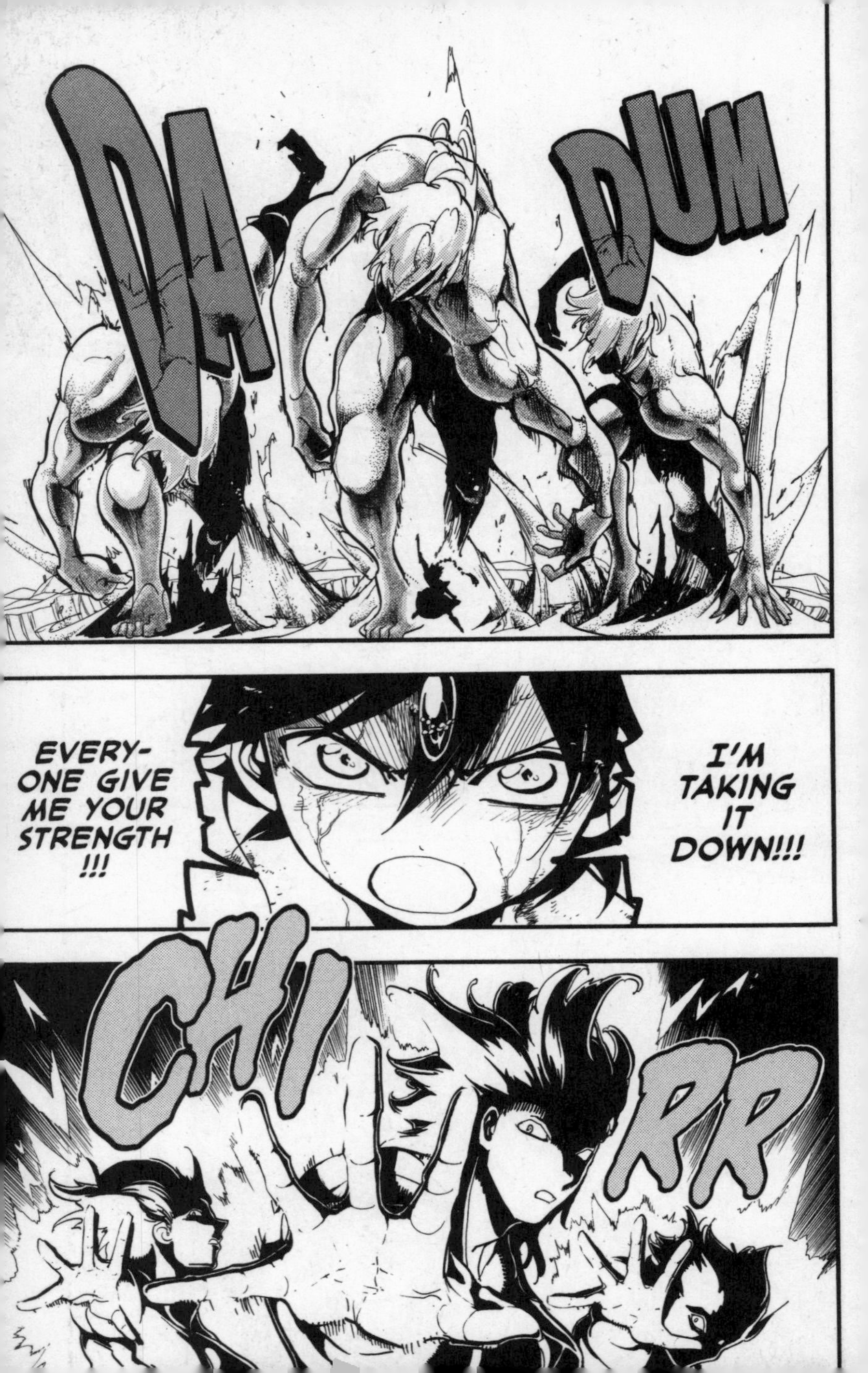
DA DUM
I'M TAKING IT DOWN!!!
EVERY-ONE GIVE ME YOUR STRENGTH!!!
CHI RR

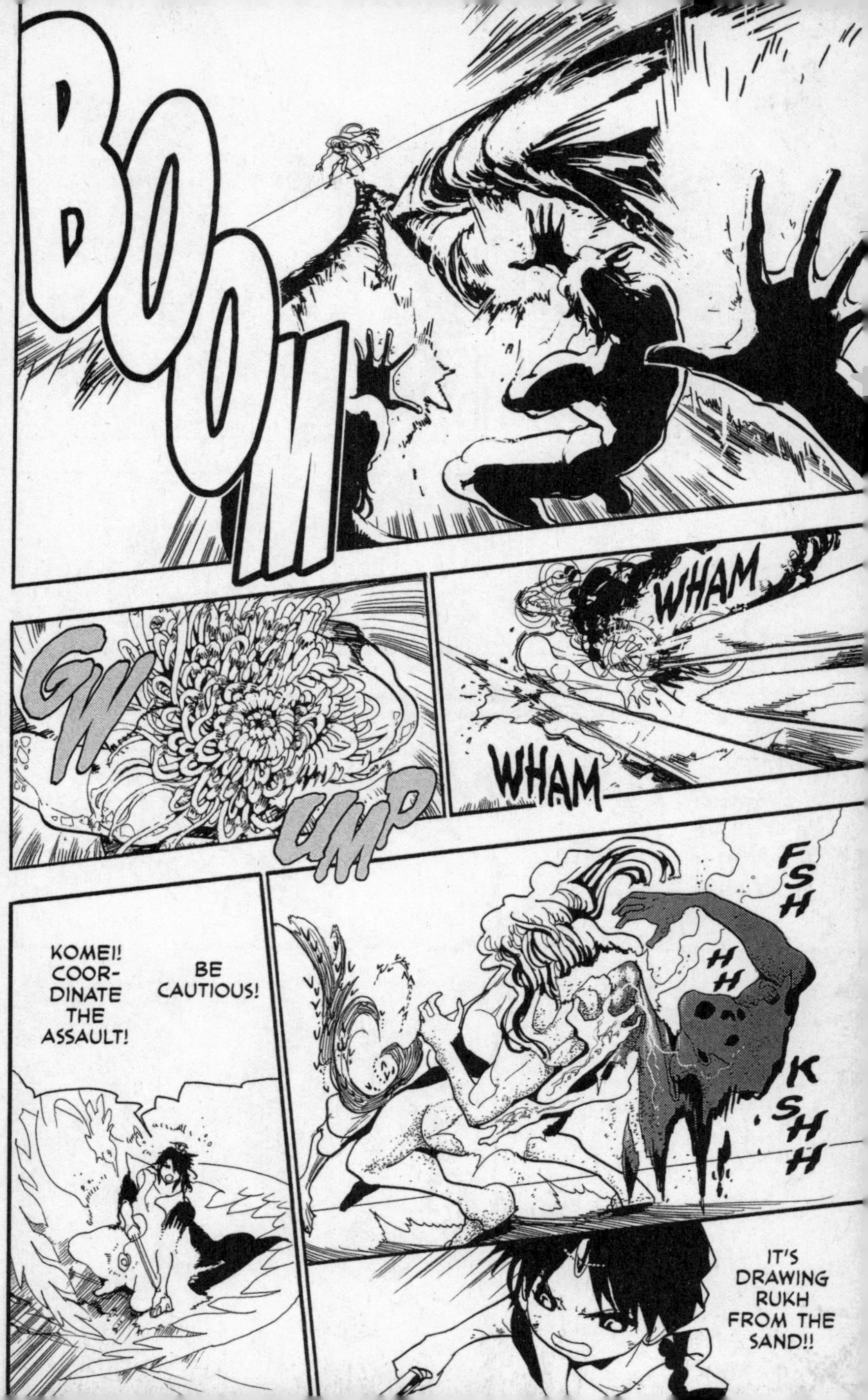
BOOM
WHAM
WHAM
GWUMP
FSH
HH
KSHH
IT'S DRAWING RUKH FROM THE SAND!!
BE CAUTIOUS!
KOMEI! COOR-DINATE THE ASSAULT!

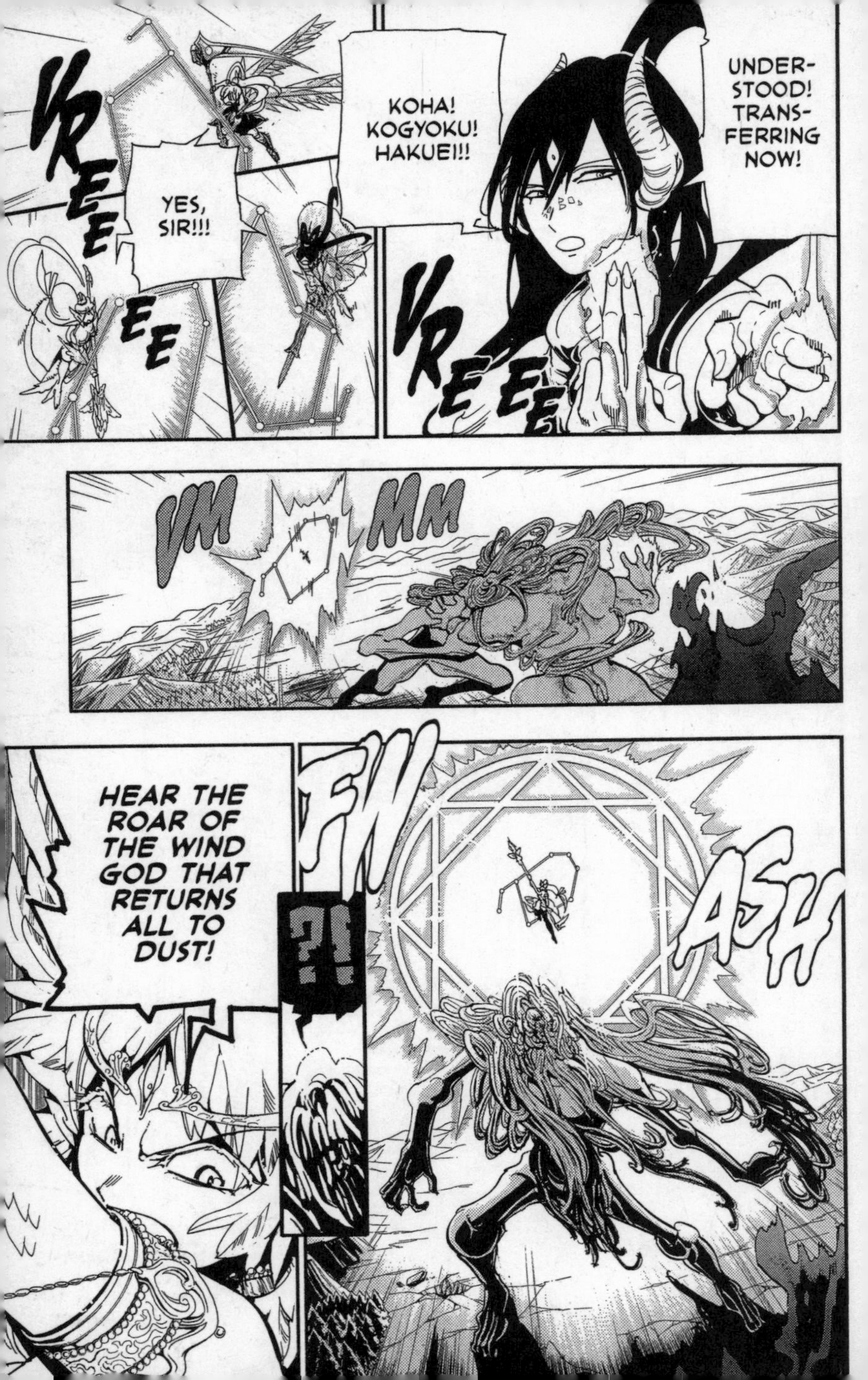
UNDER-
STOOD!
TRANS-
FERRING
NOW!
KOHA!
KOGYOKU!
HAKUEI!!!
VREEEE
VREEEE
YES,
SIR!!!
VMMMM
FWASH
?!
HEAR THE
ROAR OF
THE WIND
GOD THAT
RETURNS
ALL TO
DUST!

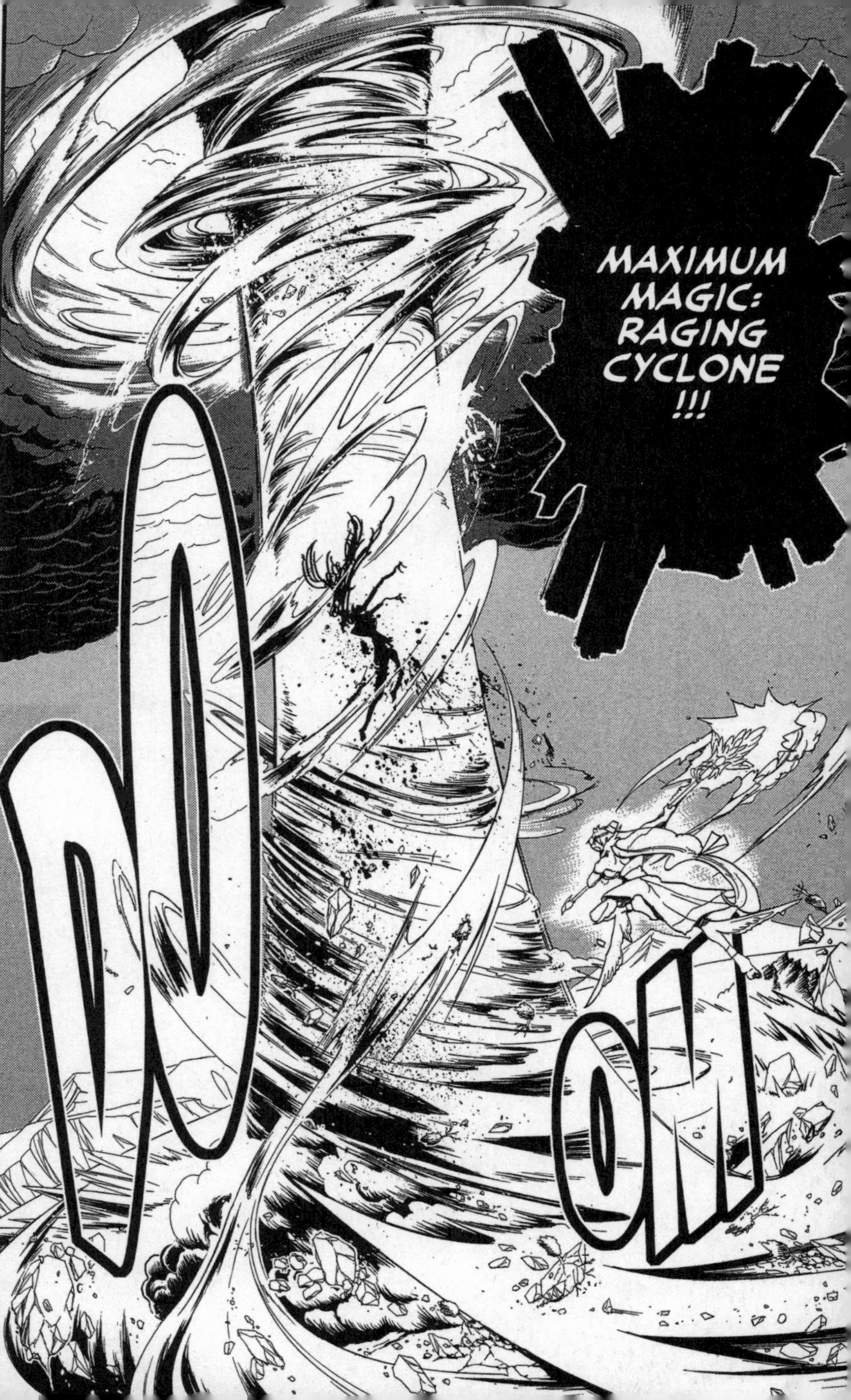
MAXIMUM MAGIC: RAGING CYCLONE !!!

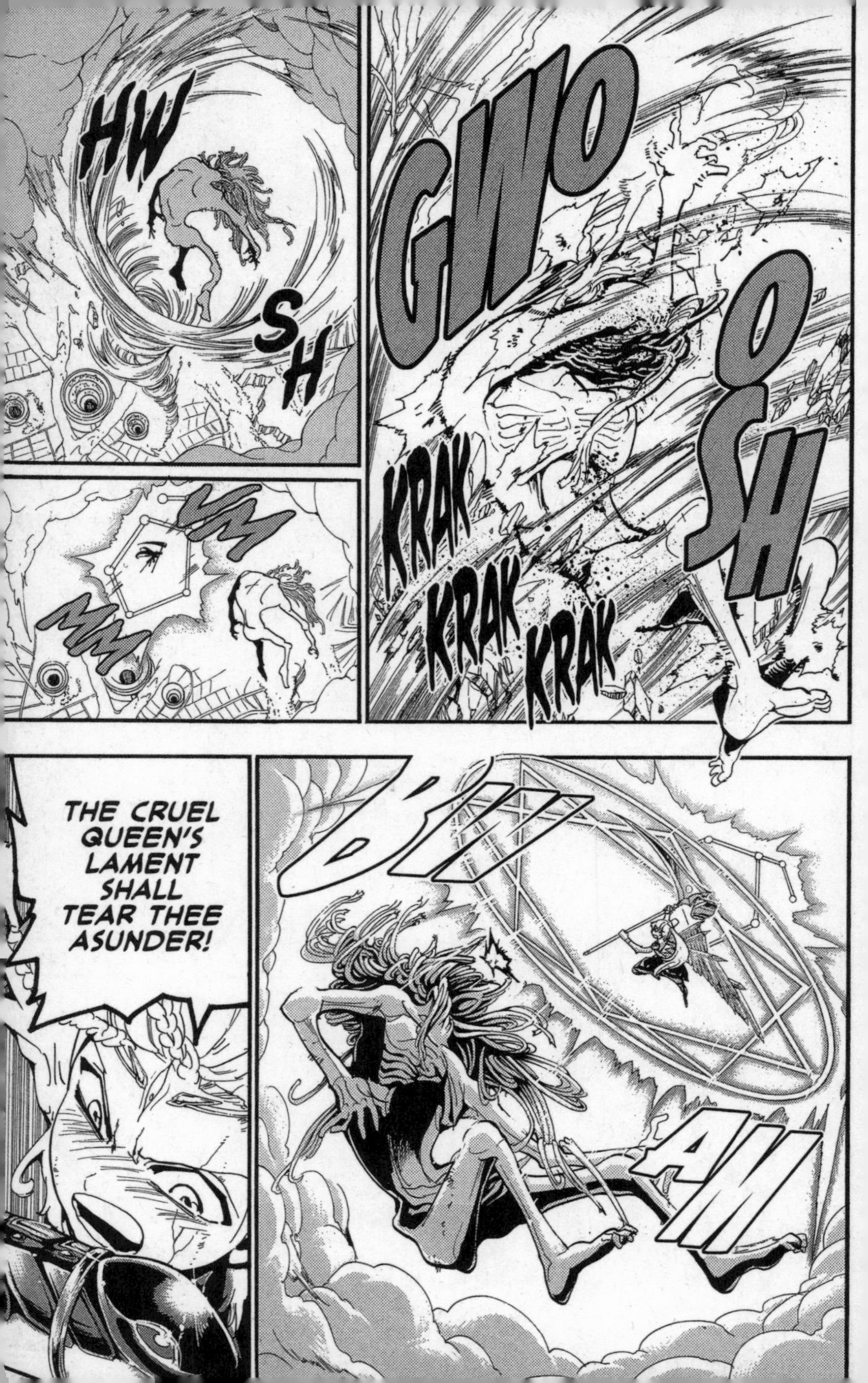
KRAK
KRAK
KRAK
HWSH
VMMM
THE CRUEL QUEEN'S LAMENT SHALL TEAR THEE ASUNDER!

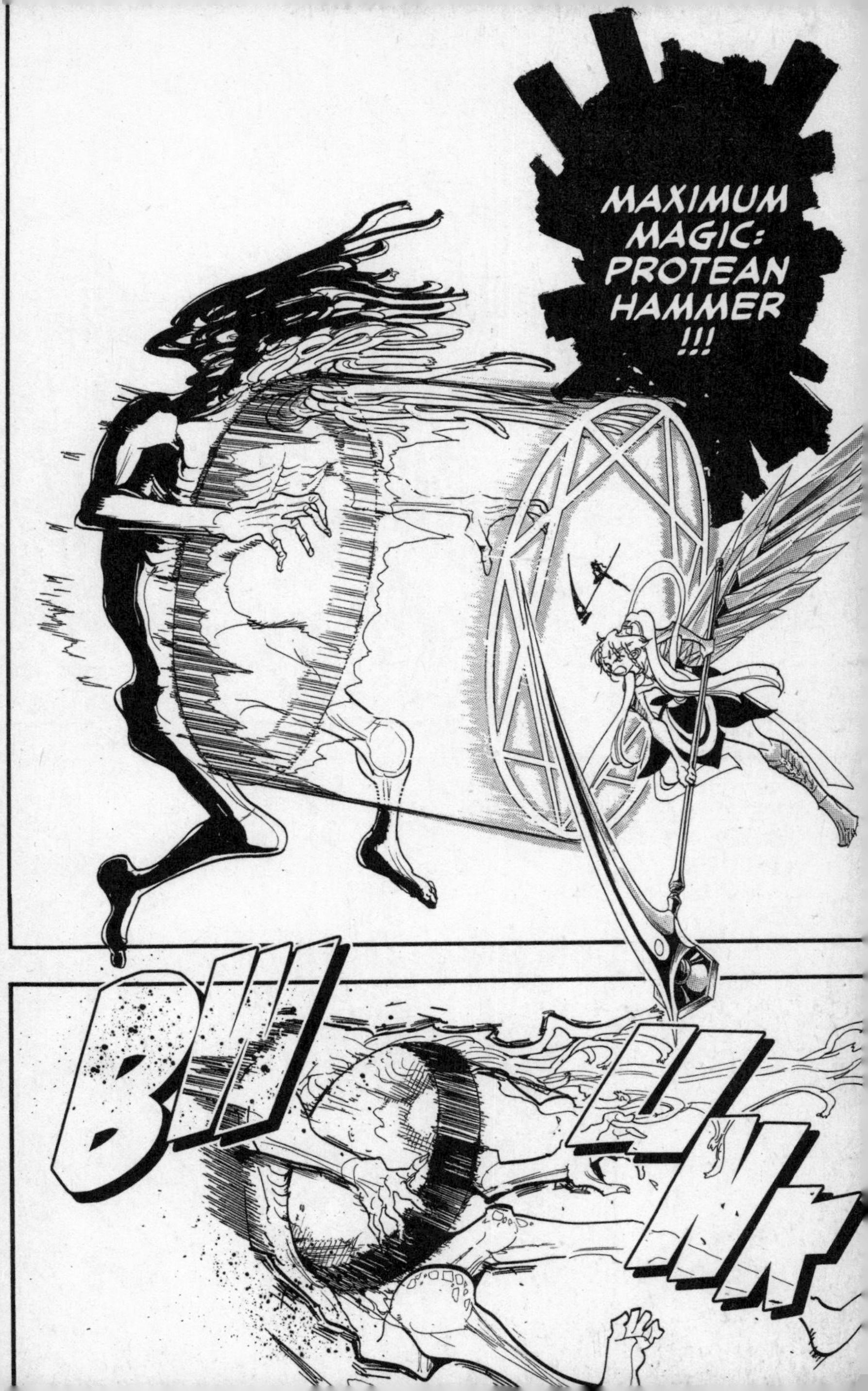
MAXIMUM MAGIC: PROTEAN HAMMER !!!
BWUNK!

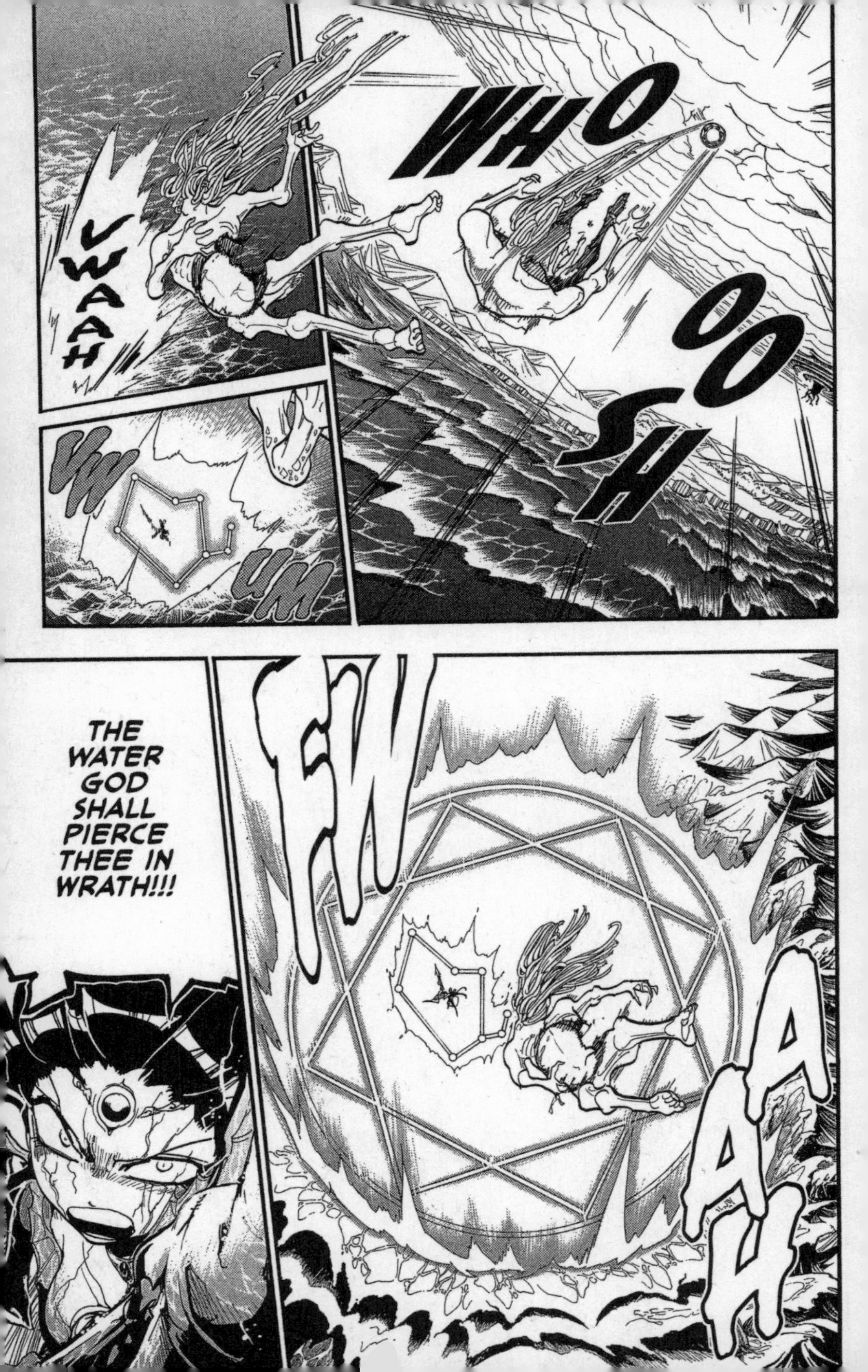
WHOOOSH
UWAAH
VWUM
FWAAH
THE WATER GOD SHALL PIERCE THEE IN WRATH!!!

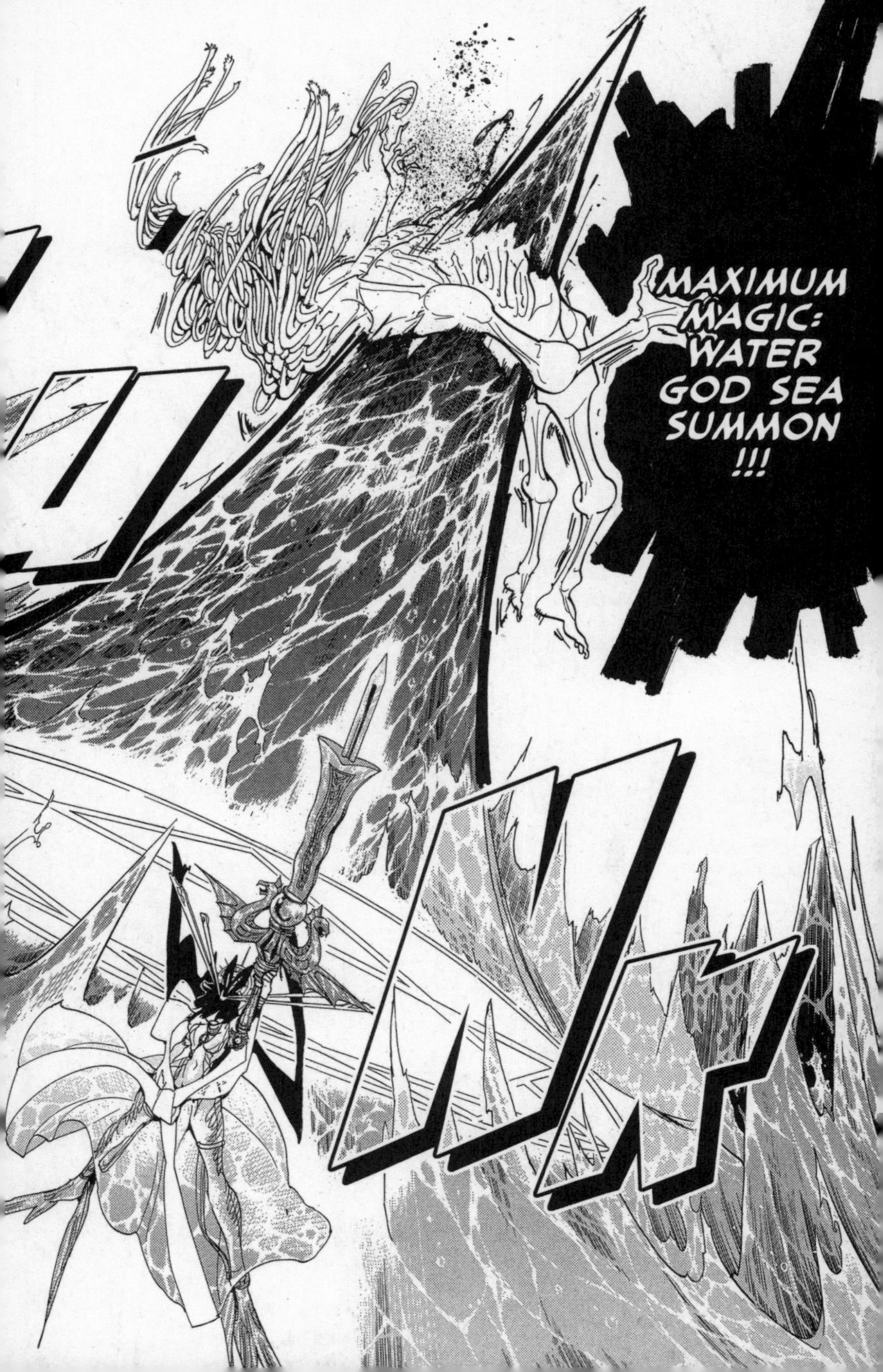
MAXIMUM MAGIC: WATER GOD SEA SUMMON !!!

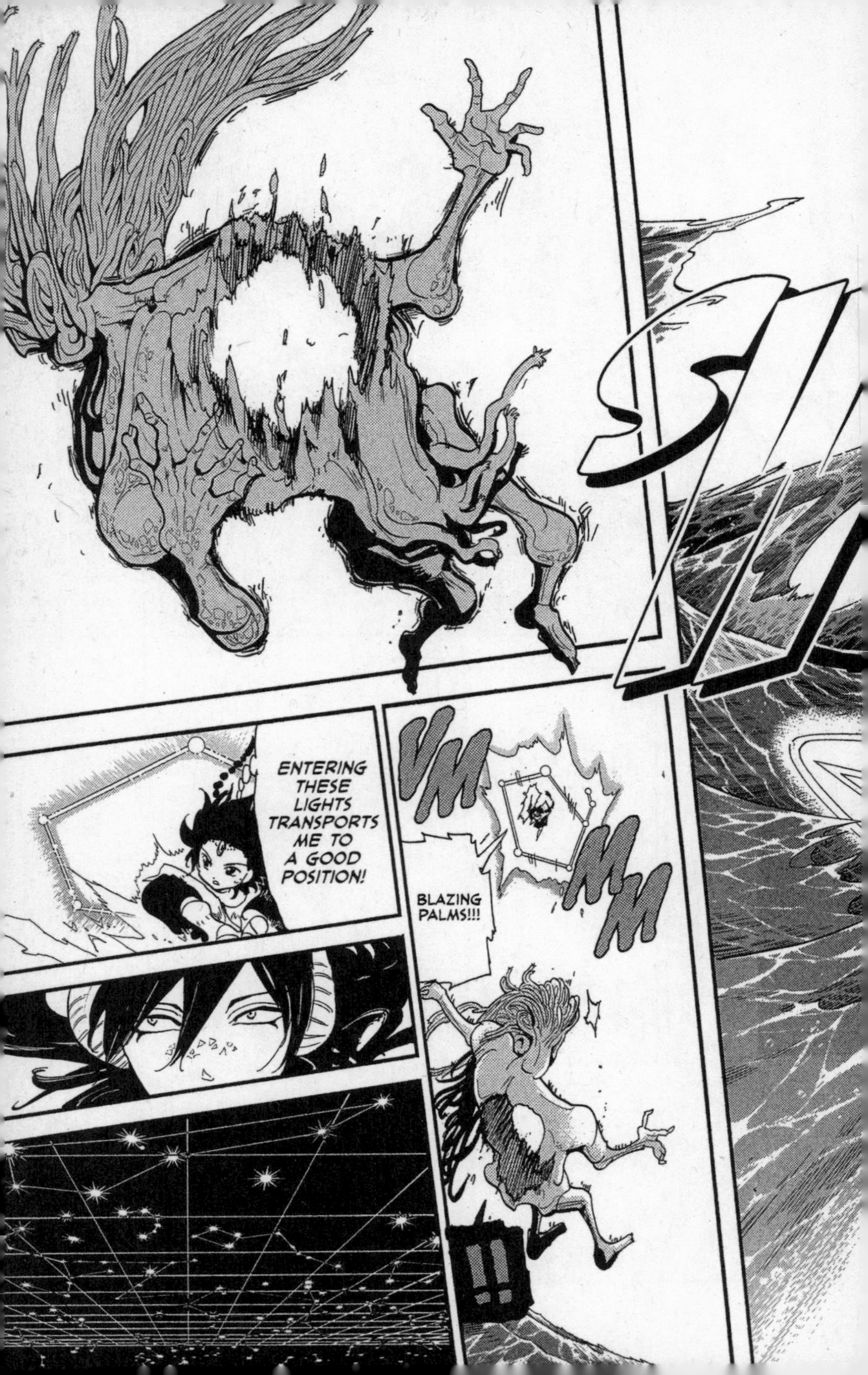
VMMMM
BLAZING PALMS!!!
ENTERING THESE LIGHTS TRANSPORTS ME TO A GOOD POSITION!

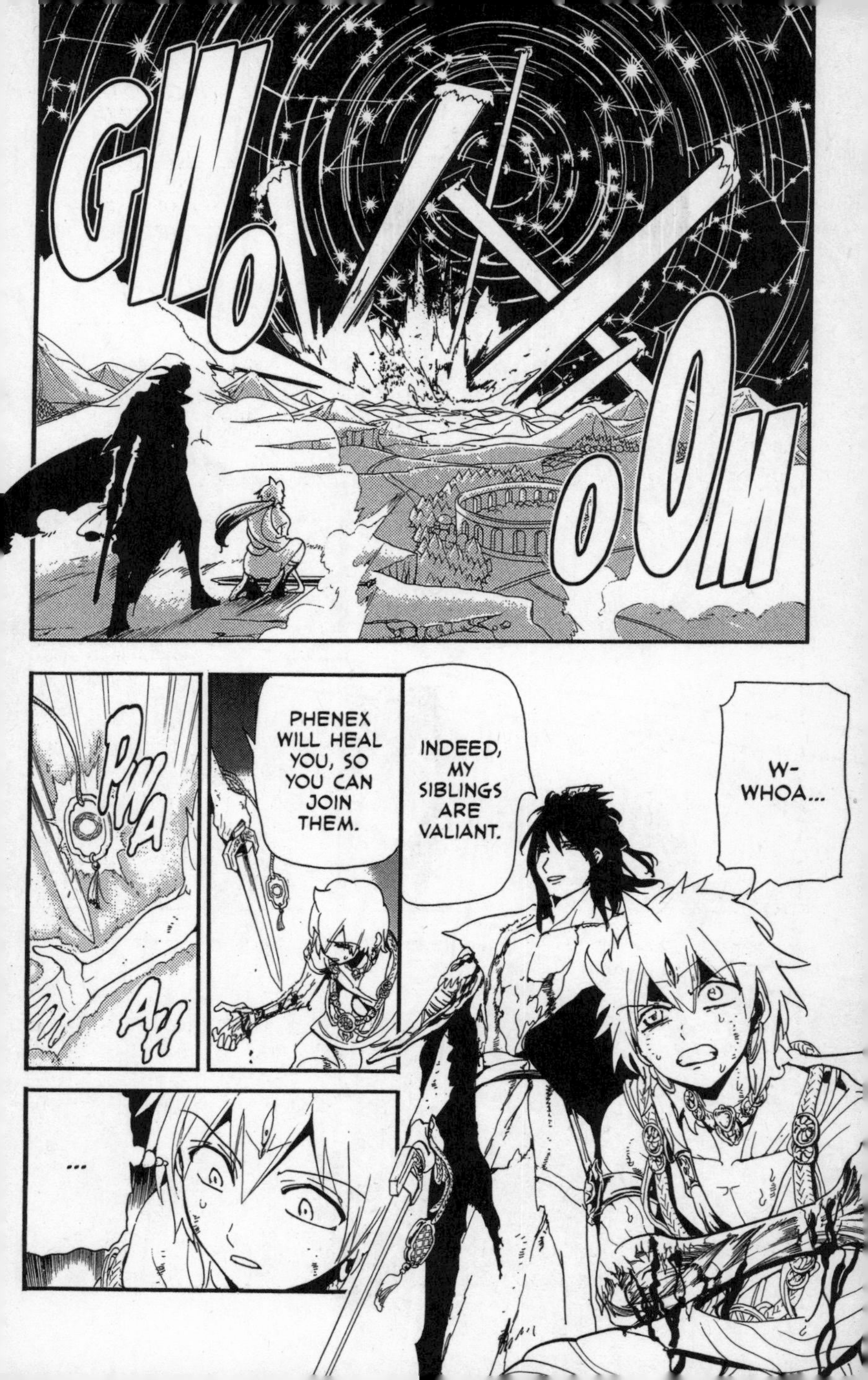
GWOOOOM
W-WHOA...
INDEED, MY SIBLINGS ARE VALIANT.
PHENEX WILL HEAL YOU, SO YOU CAN JOIN THEM.
PWA
AH
...

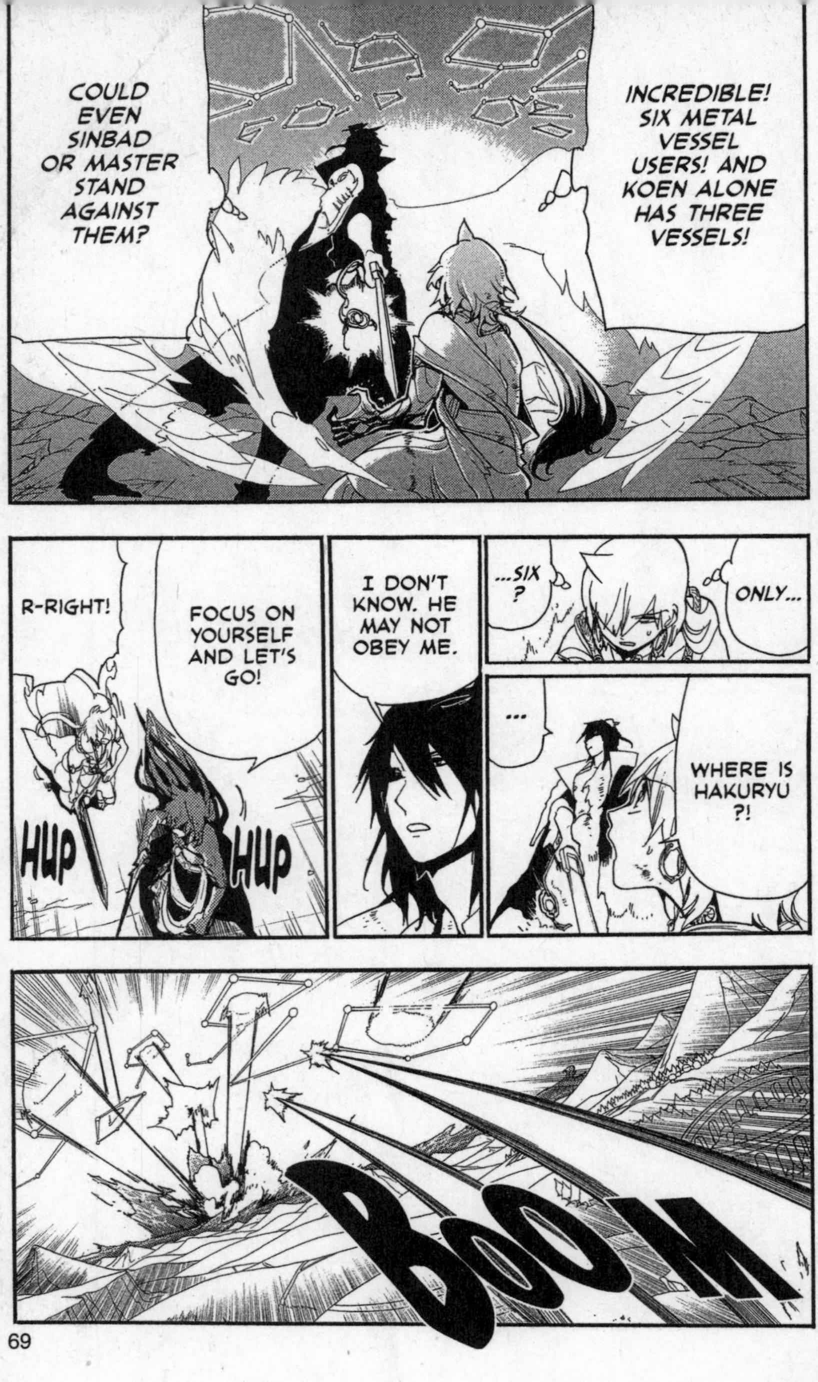
INCREDIBLE! SIX METAL VESSEL USERS! AND KOEN ALONE HAS THREE VESSELS!
COULD EVEN SINBAD OR MASTER STAND AGAINST THEM?
ONLY...
...SIX ?
WHERE IS HAKURYU ?!
...
I DON'T KNOW. HE MAY NOT OBEY ME.
FOCUS ON YOURSELF AND LET'S GO!
R-RIGHT!
HUP
HUP
BOOM

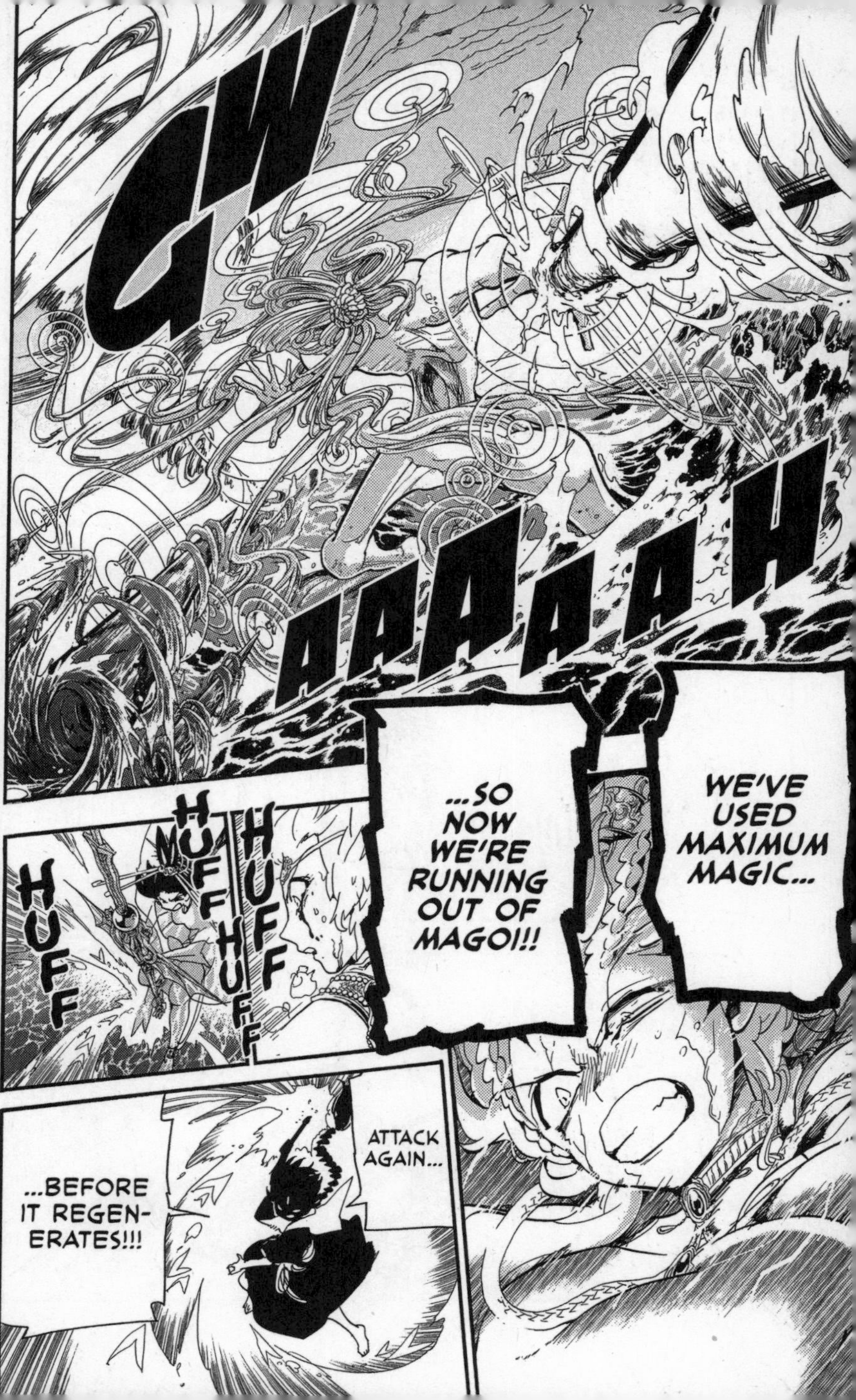
GWAAAAAH
WE'VE USED MAXIMUM MAGIC...
...SO NOW WE'RE RUNNING OUT OF MAGOI!!
HUFF
HUFF
HUFF
HUFF
ATTACK AGAIN...
...BEFORE IT REGENERATES!!!

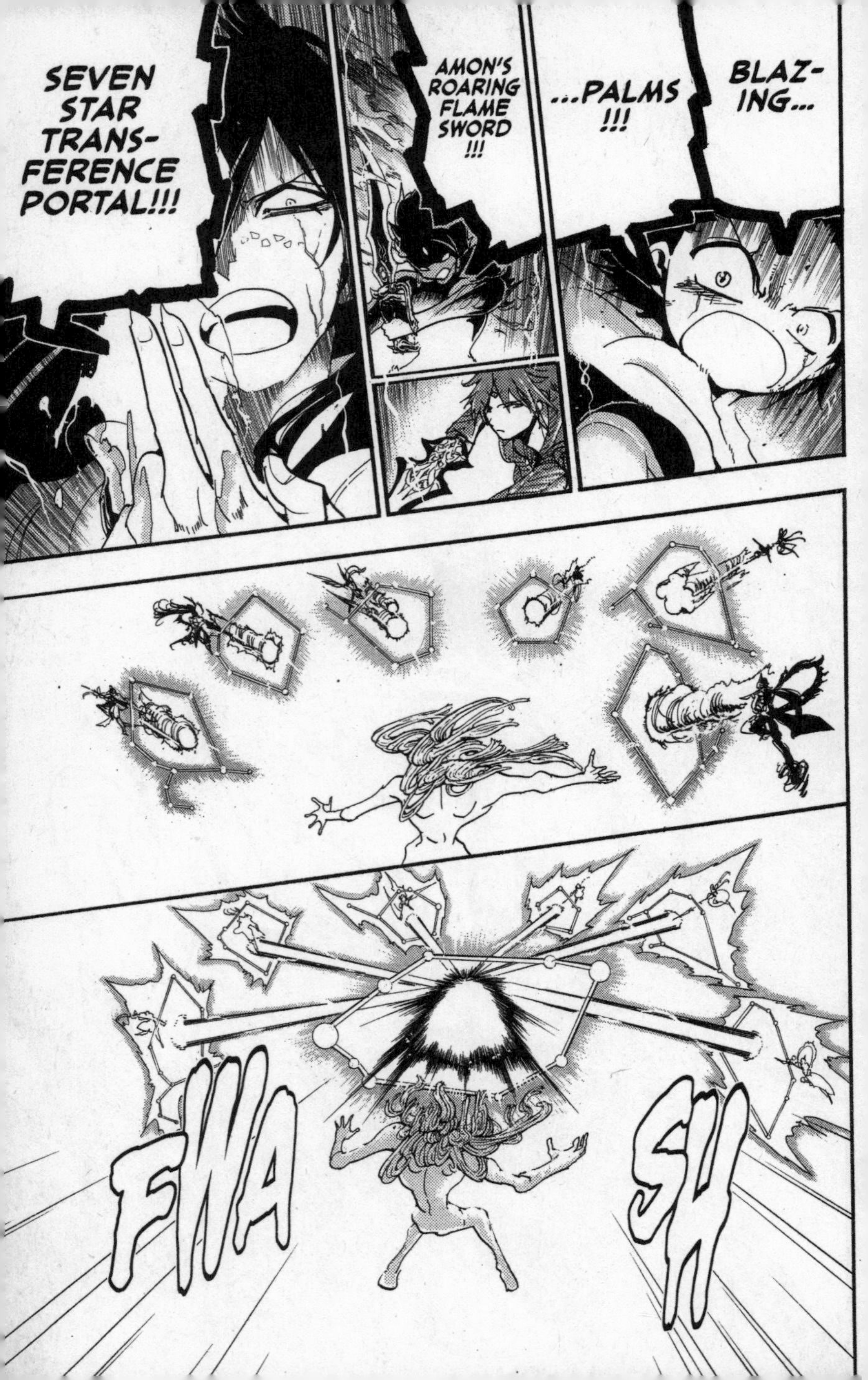

BLAZ-ING...
...PALMS !!!
AMON'S ROARING FLAME SWORD !!!
SEVEN STAR TRANS-FERENCE PORTAL!!!
FWASH

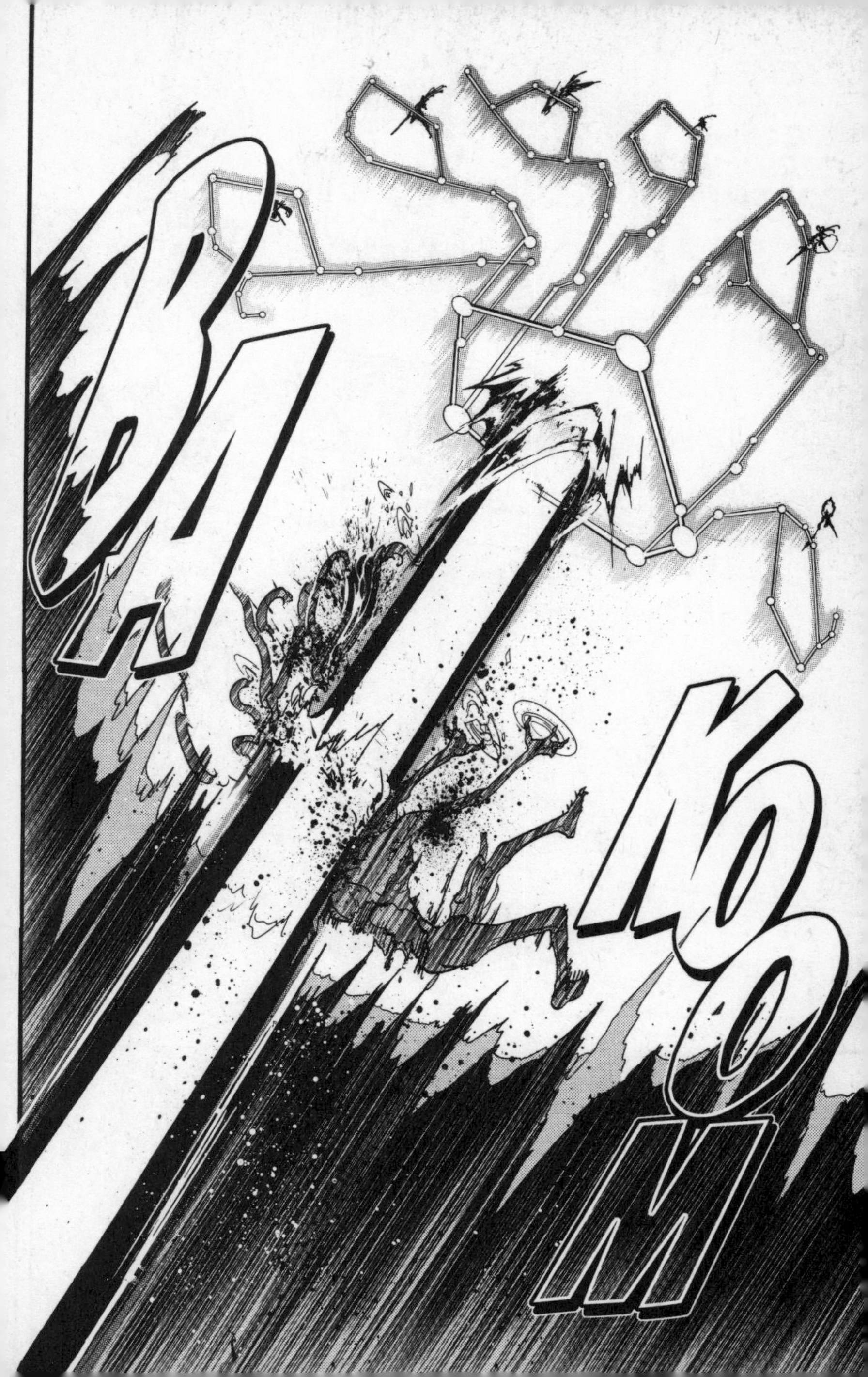
GAKOOH

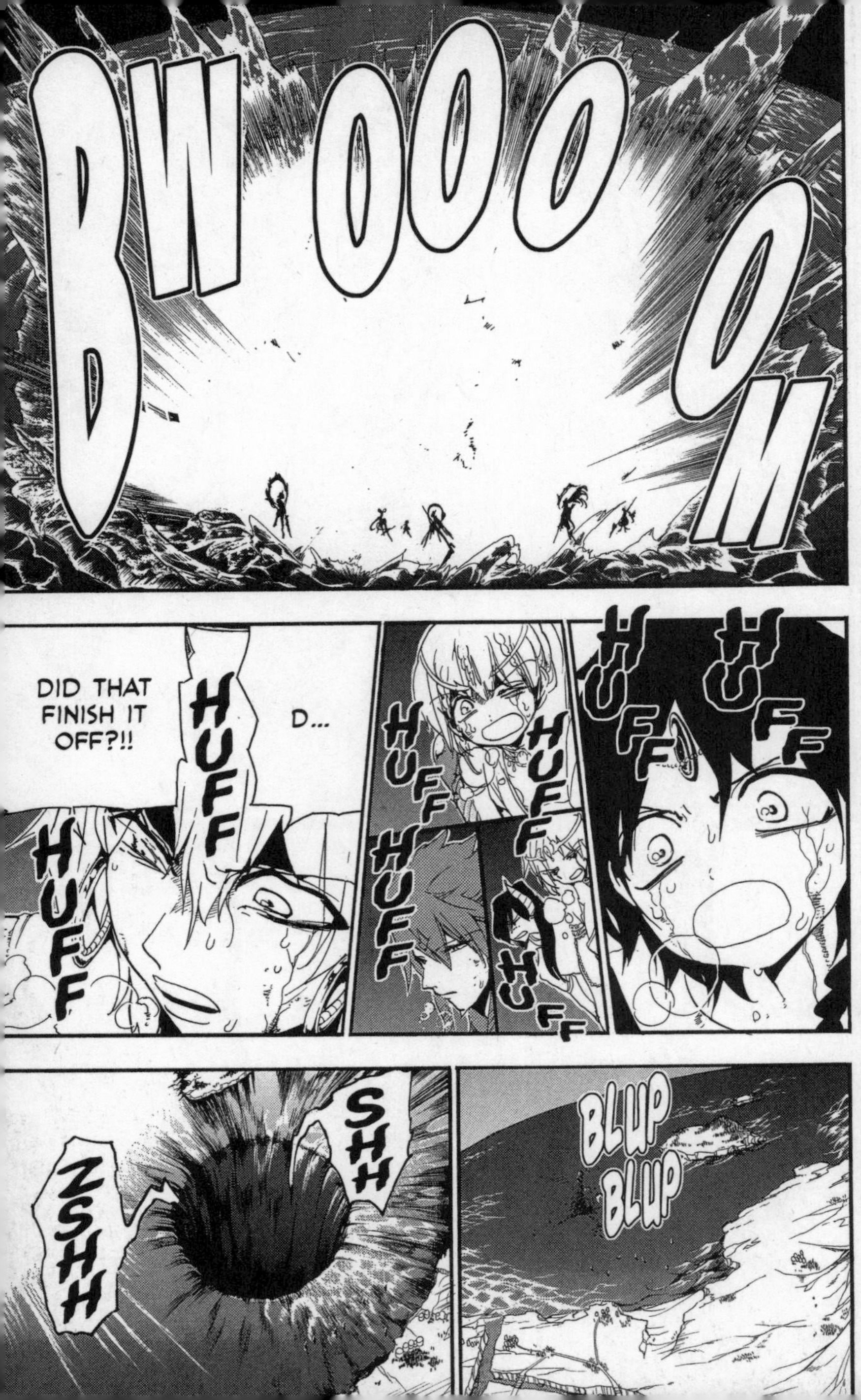
BWOOOOOM
HUFF
HUFF
HUFF
HUFF
HUFF
HUFF
HUFF
D...
HUFF
DID THAT FINISH IT OFF?!!
HUFF
BLUP BLUP
SHH
ZSHH

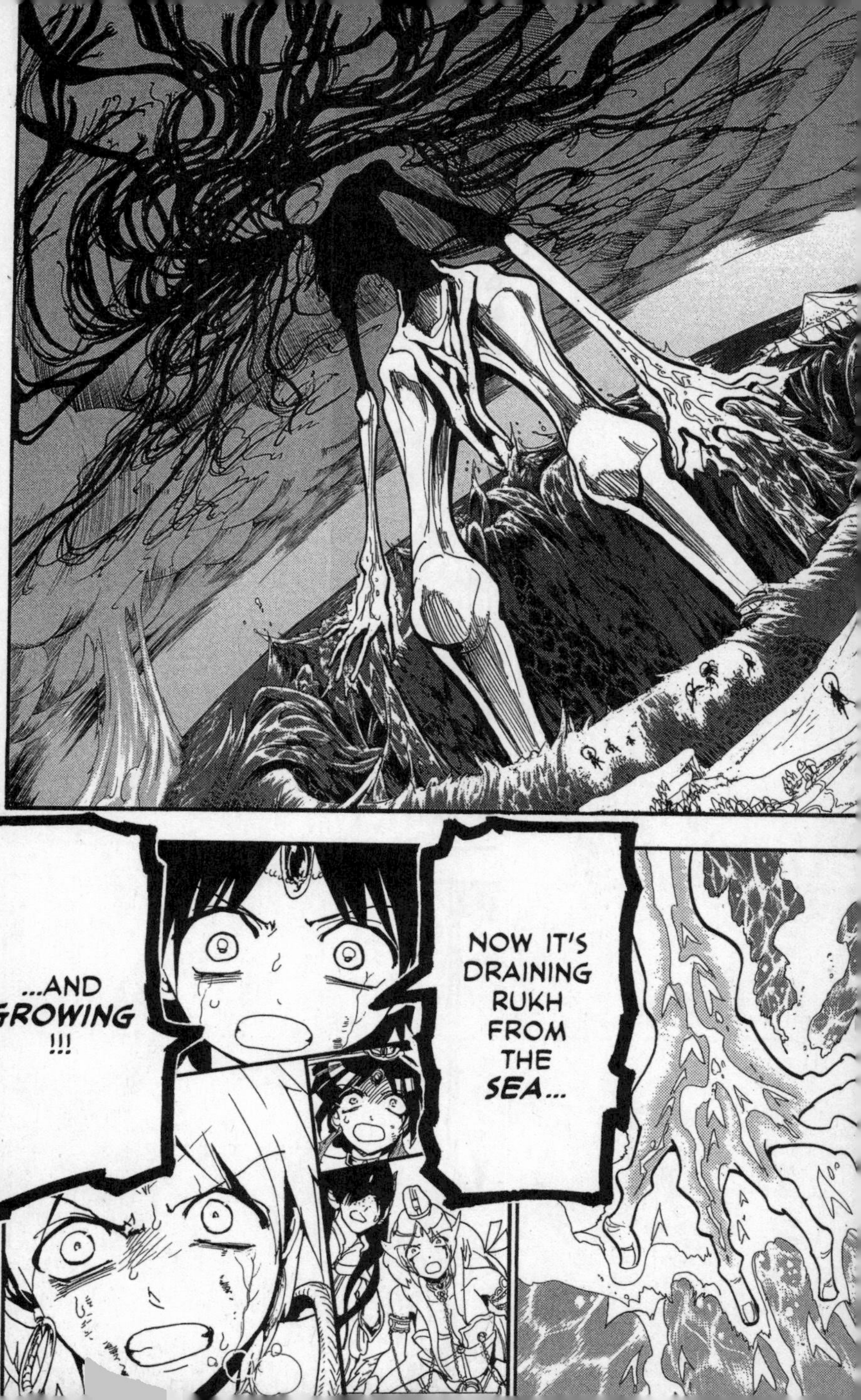
NOW IT'S DRAINING RUKH FROM THE SEA...
...AND GROWING!!!

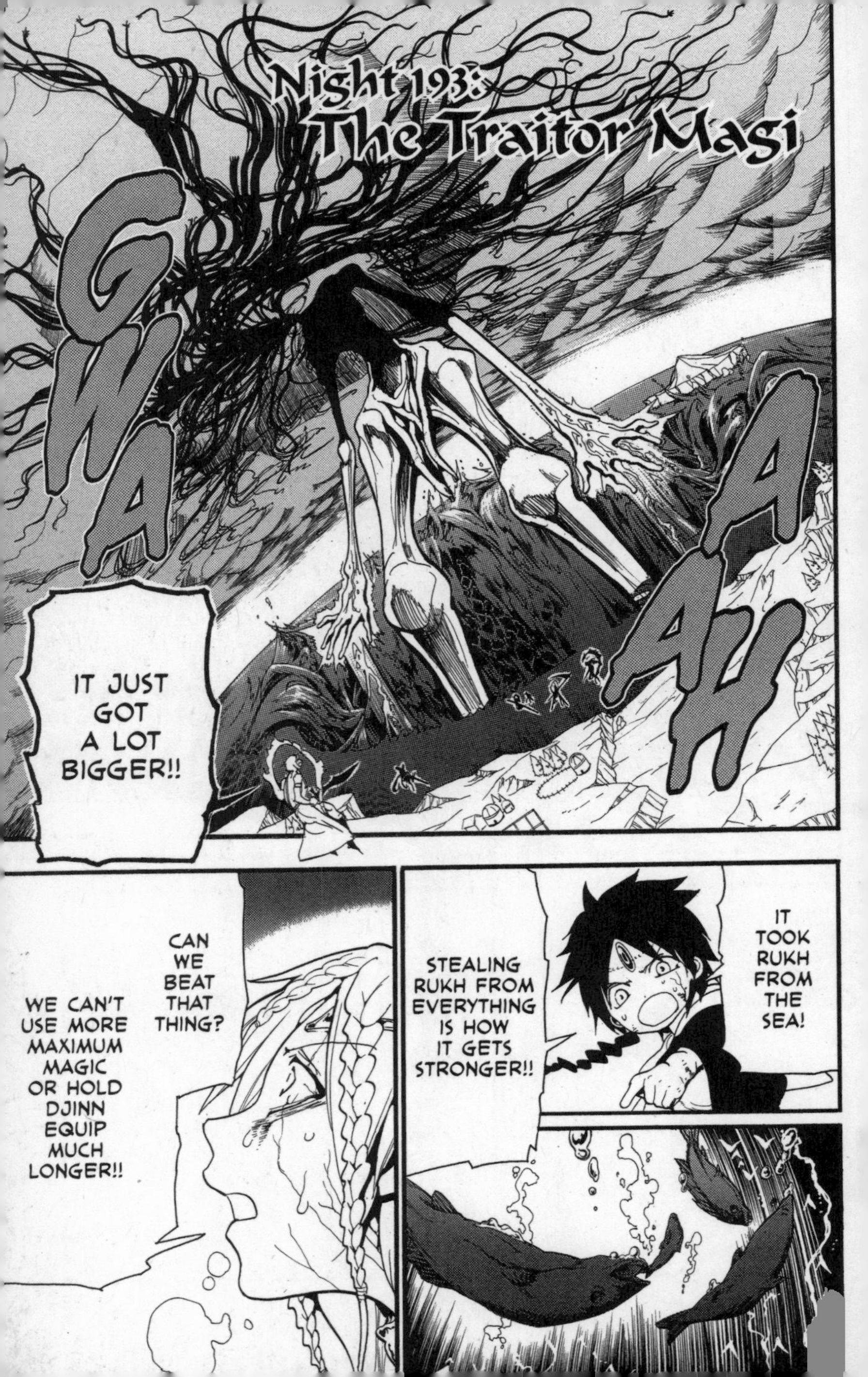
Night 193:
The Traitor Magi
GWAAAH
IT JUST GOT A LOT BIGGER!!
IT TOOK RUKH FROM THE SEA!
STEALING RUKH FROM EVERYTHING IS HOW IT GETS STRONGER!!
CAN WE BEAT THAT THING?
WE CAN'T USE MORE MAXIMUM MAGIC OR HOLD DJINN EQUIP MUCH LONGER!!

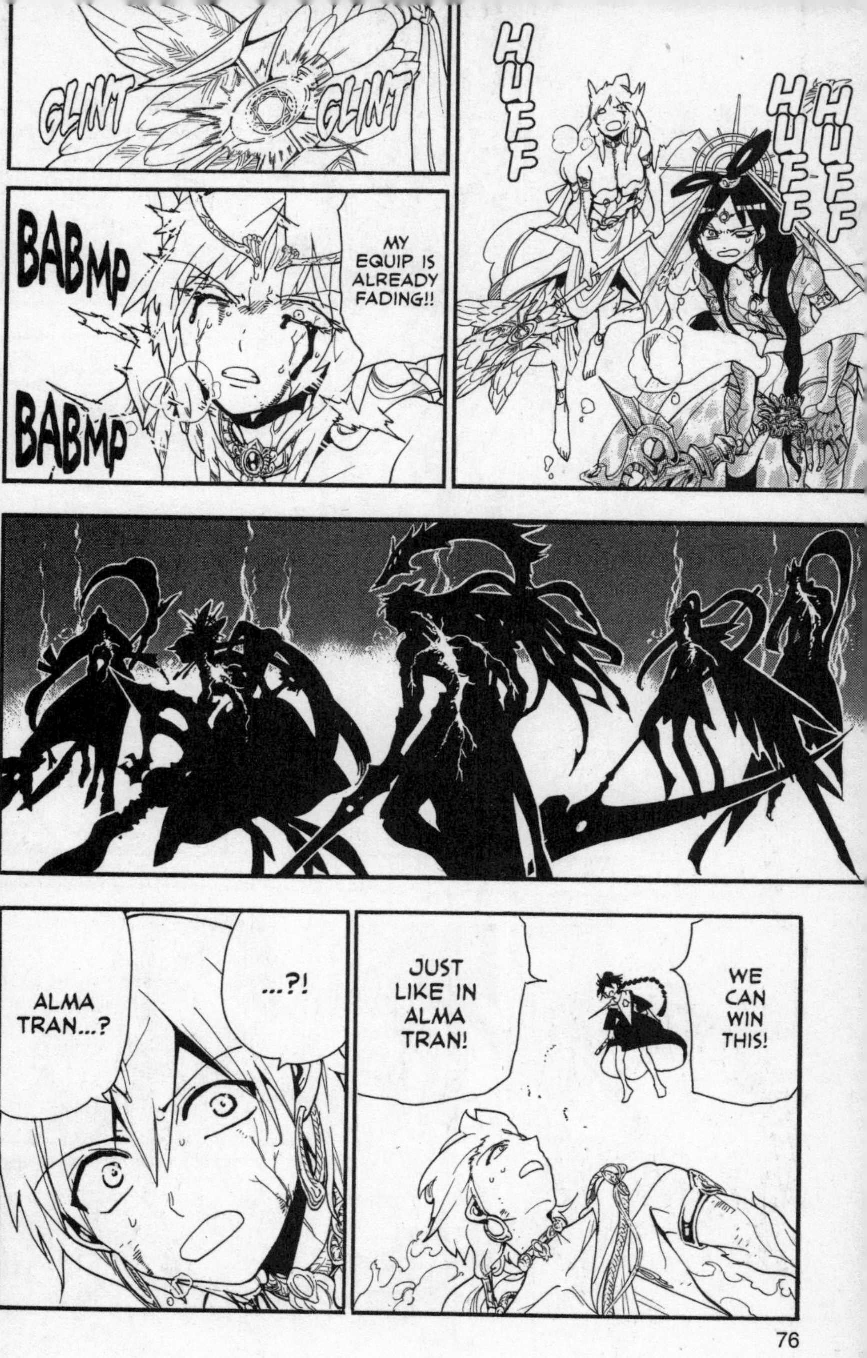
HUFF
HUFF
HUFF
GLINT
GLINT
MY EQUIP IS ALREADY FADING!!
BABMP
BABMP
WE CAN WIN THIS!
JUST LIKE IN ALMA TRAN!
...?!
ALMA TRAN...?

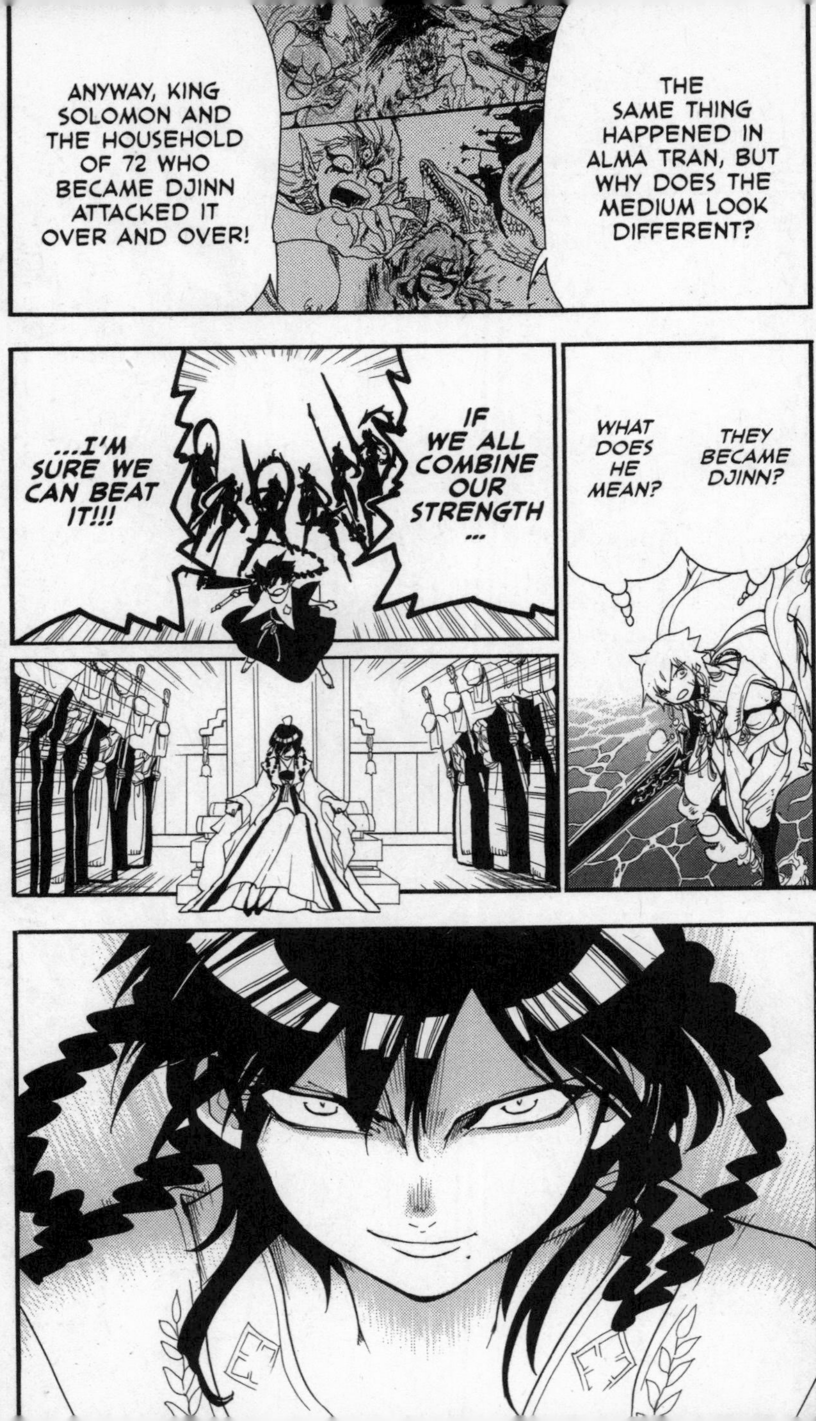
THE SAME THING HAPPENED IN ALMA TRAN, BUT WHY DOES THE MEDIUM LOOK DIFFERENT?
ANYWAY, KING SOLOMON AND THE HOUSEHOLD OF 72 WHO BECAME DJINN ATTACKED IT OVER AND OVER!
THEY BECAME DJINN?
WHAT DOES HE MEAN?
IF WE ALL COMBINE OUR STRENGTH ...
...I'M SURE WE CAN BEAT IT!!!

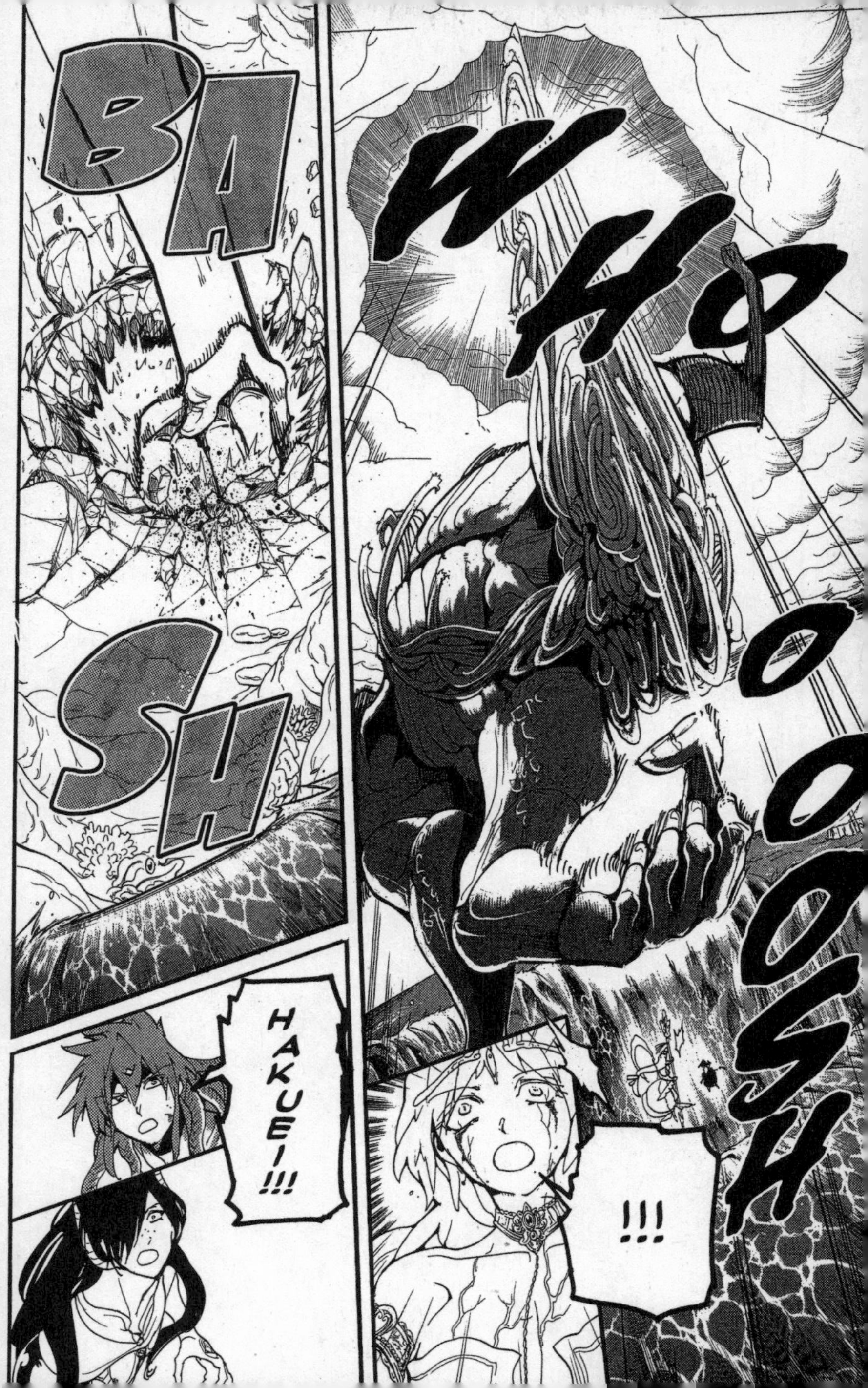
WHOOOOSH
BASH
!!!
HAKUEI!!!

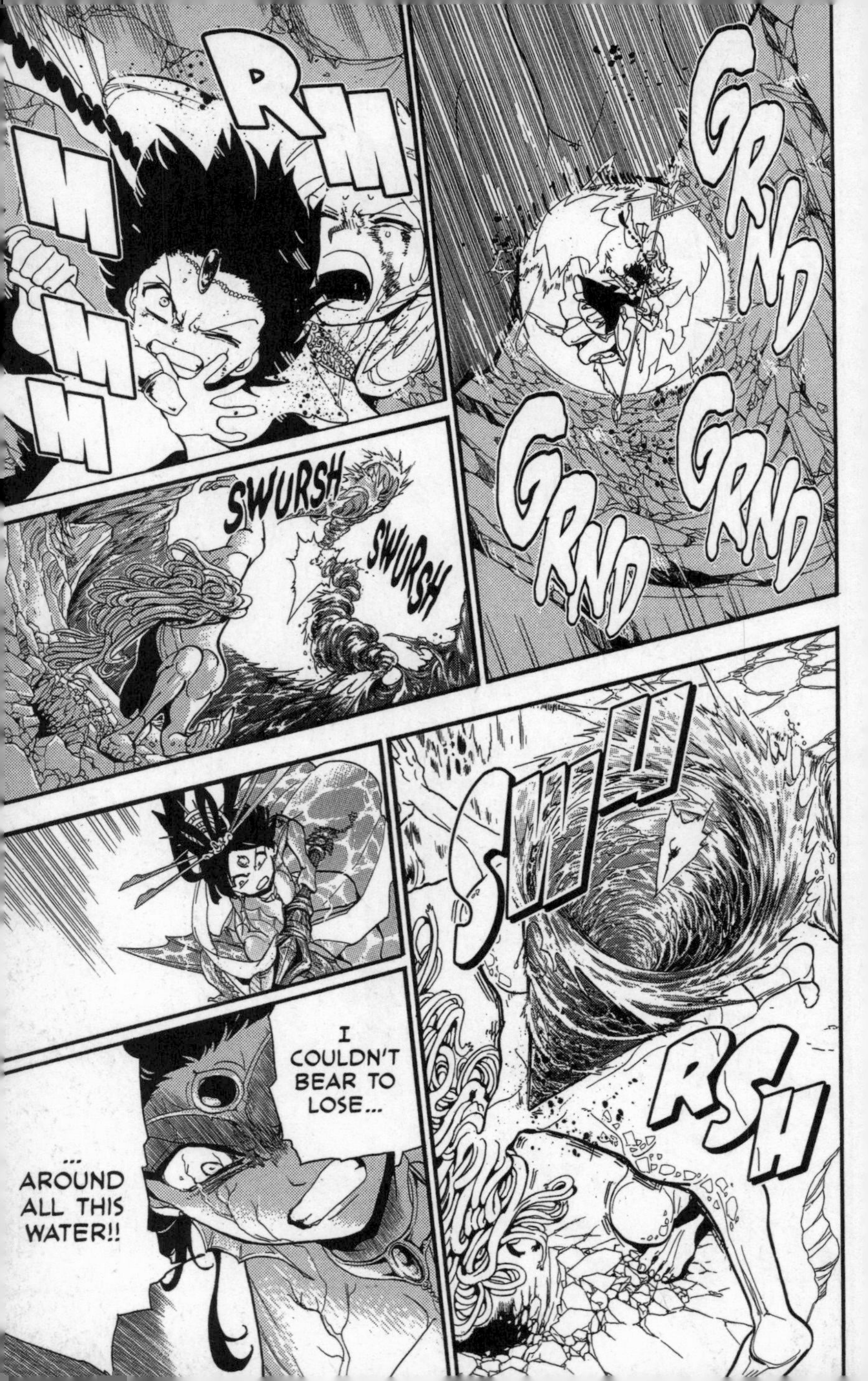
GRND
GRND
GRND
RM
MMMM
SWURSH
SWURSH
SHH!!
RSH
I COULDN'T BEAR TO LOSE...
...AROUND ALL THIS WATER!!

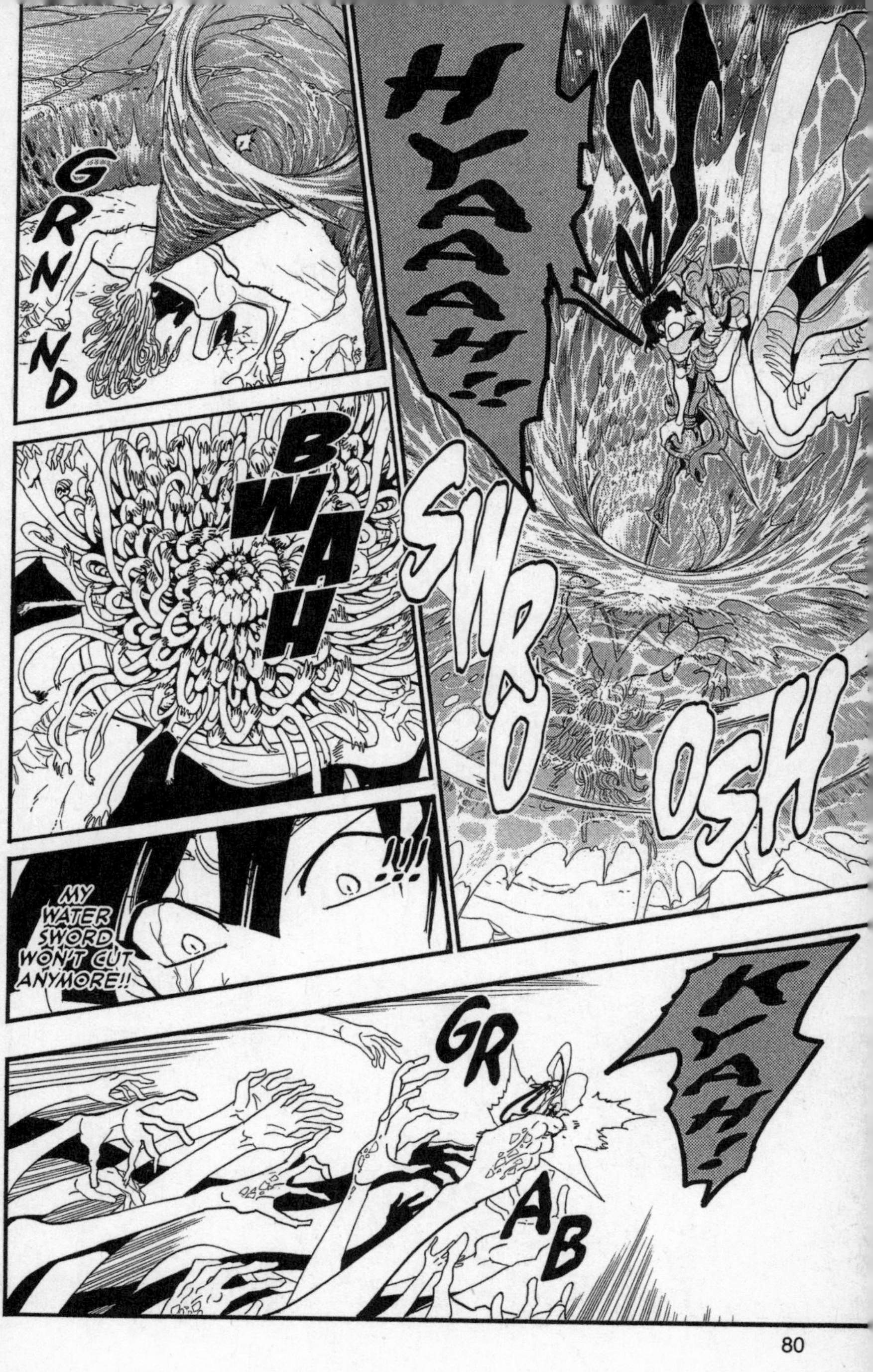
HYAAAH!!
SWROOSH
GRNND
BWAAH
!!!!
MY WATER SWORD WON'T CUT ANYMORE!!
KYAH!
GRAB

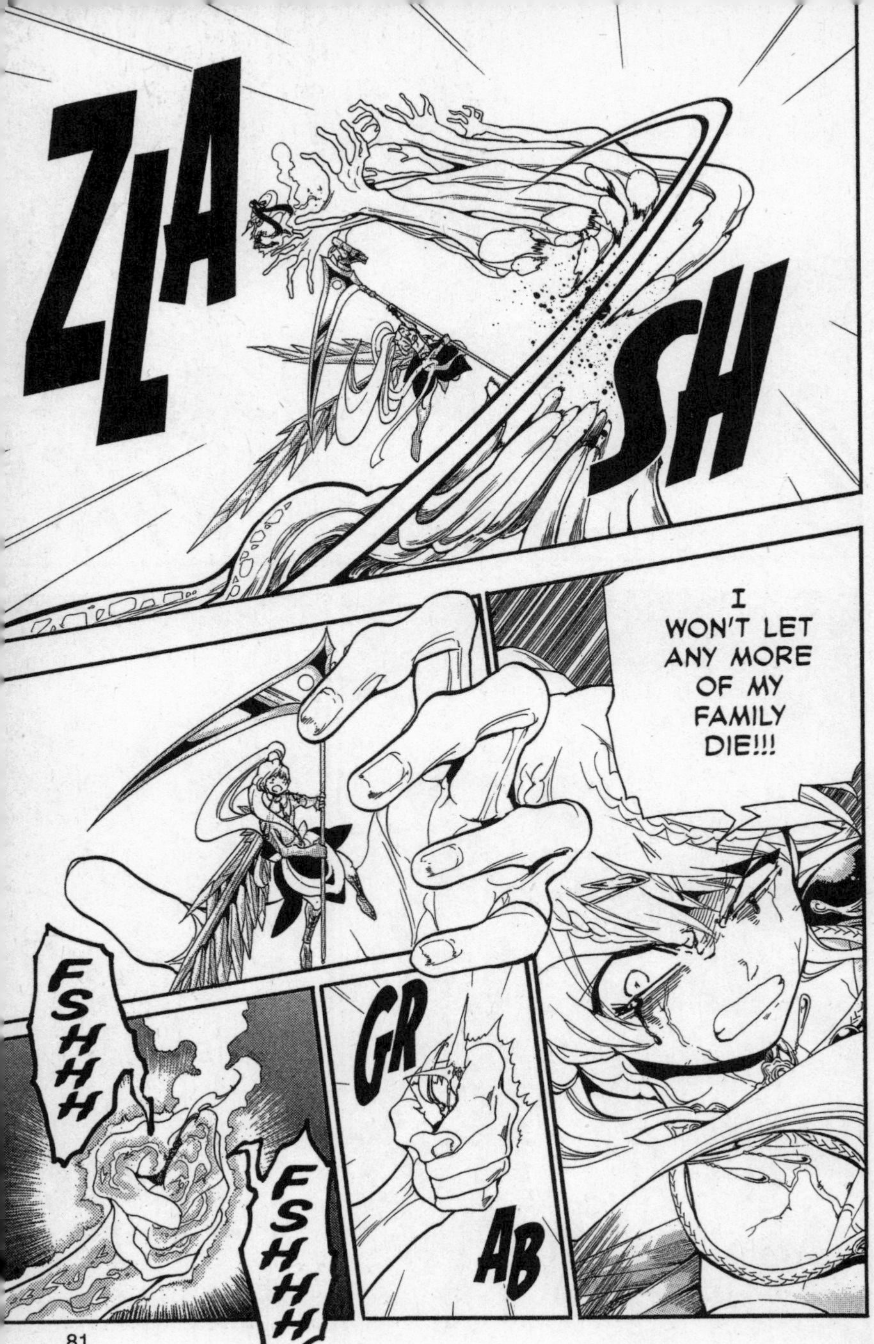
ZLASH
I WON'T LET ANY MORE OF MY FAMILY DIE!!!
GRAB
FSHHH
FSHHH

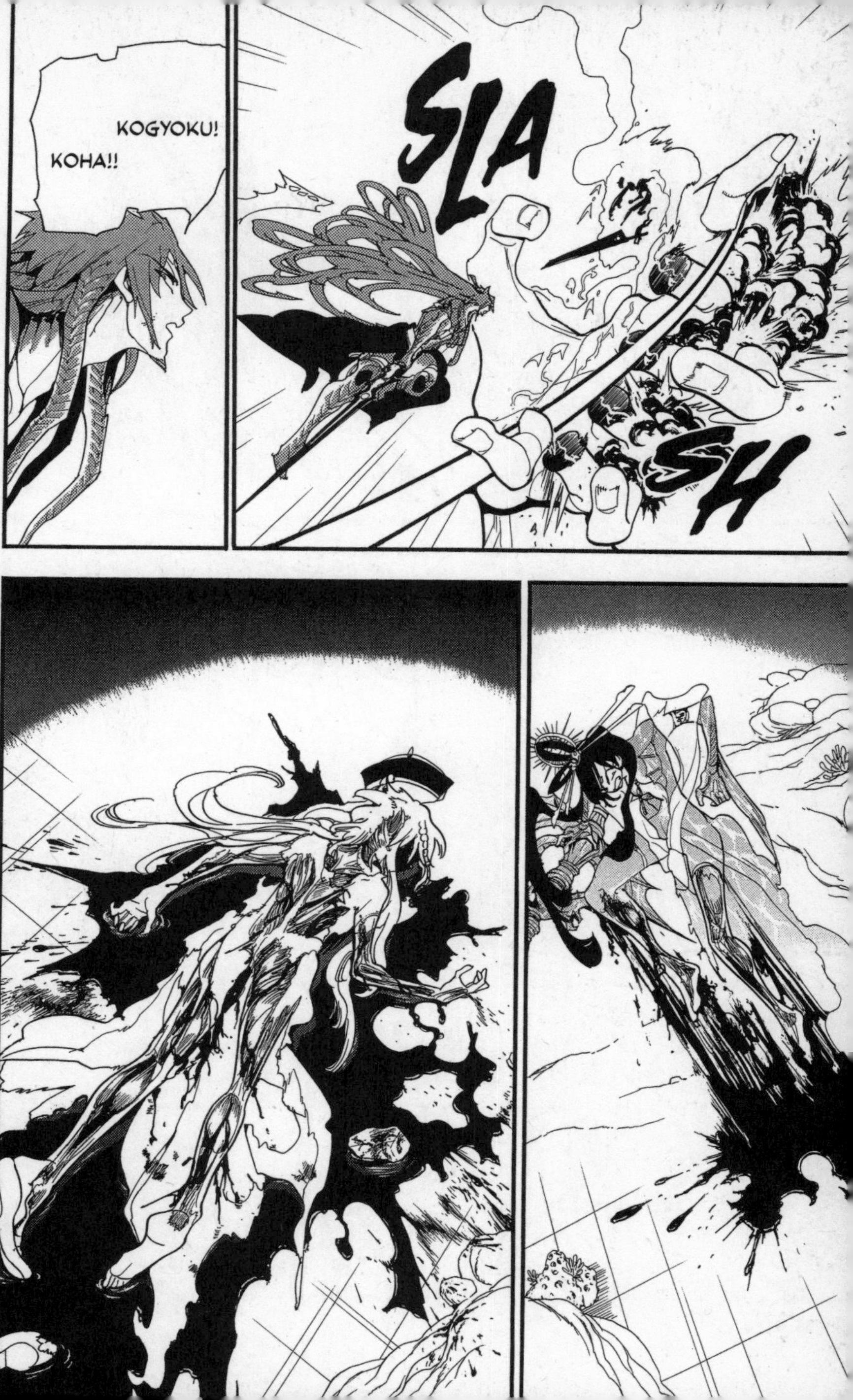
SLA
SH
KOGYOKU!
KOHA!!

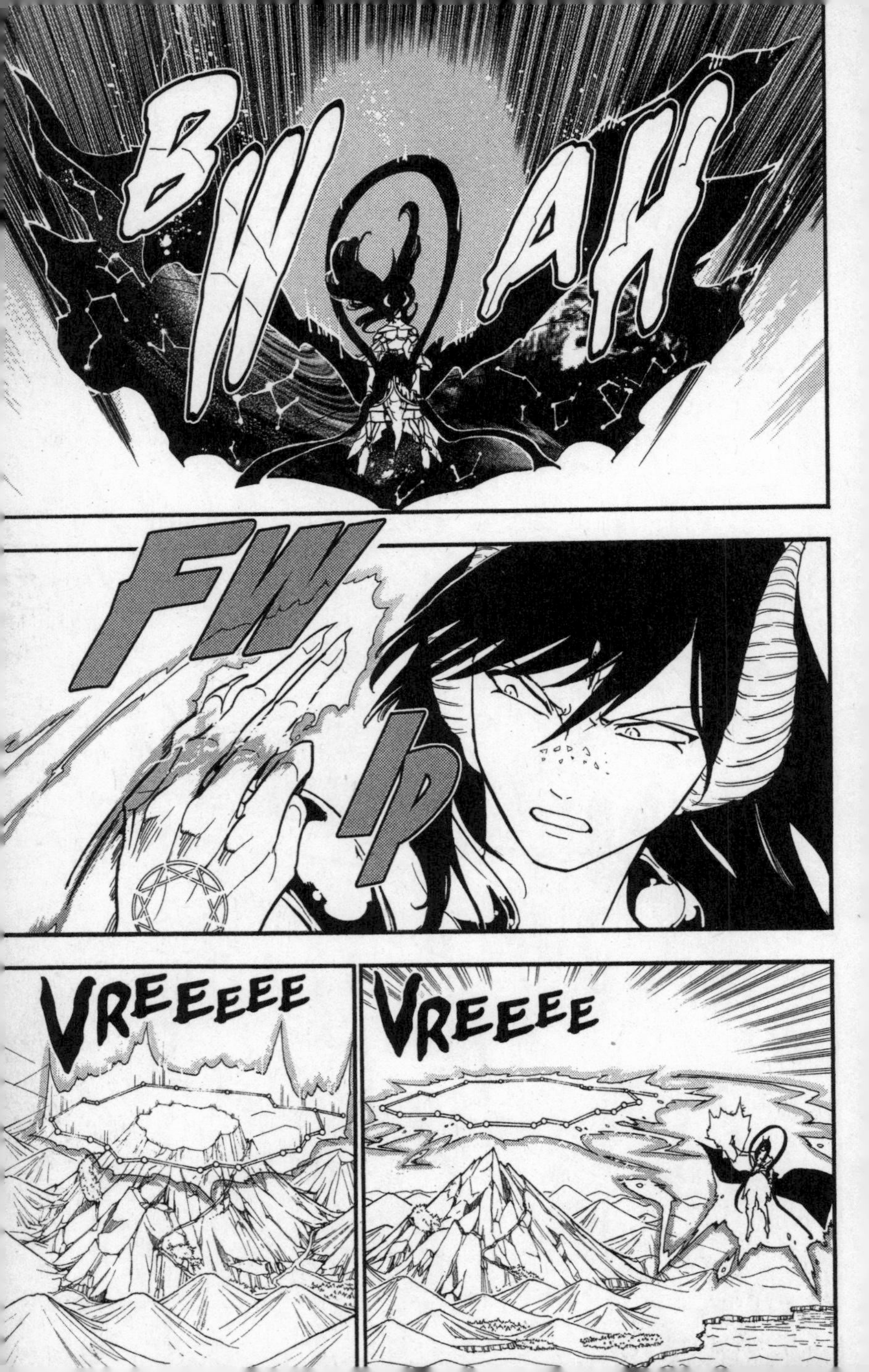
BWAH
FWIP
VREEEE
VREEEEE

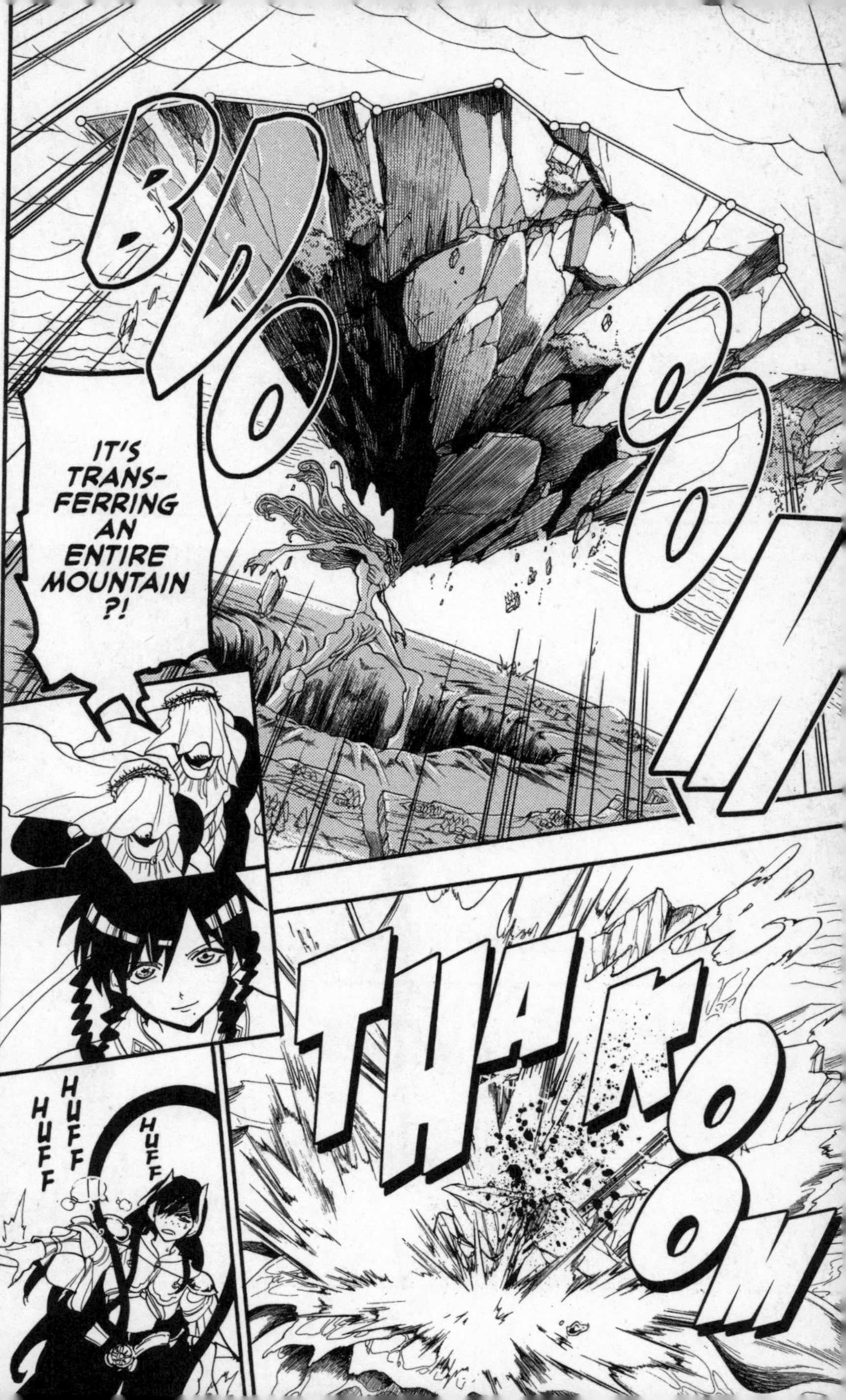
BOOOOM
IT'S TRANS-FERRING AN ENTIRE MOUNTAIN?!
THA-KOOOM
HUFF HUFF
HUFF HUFF

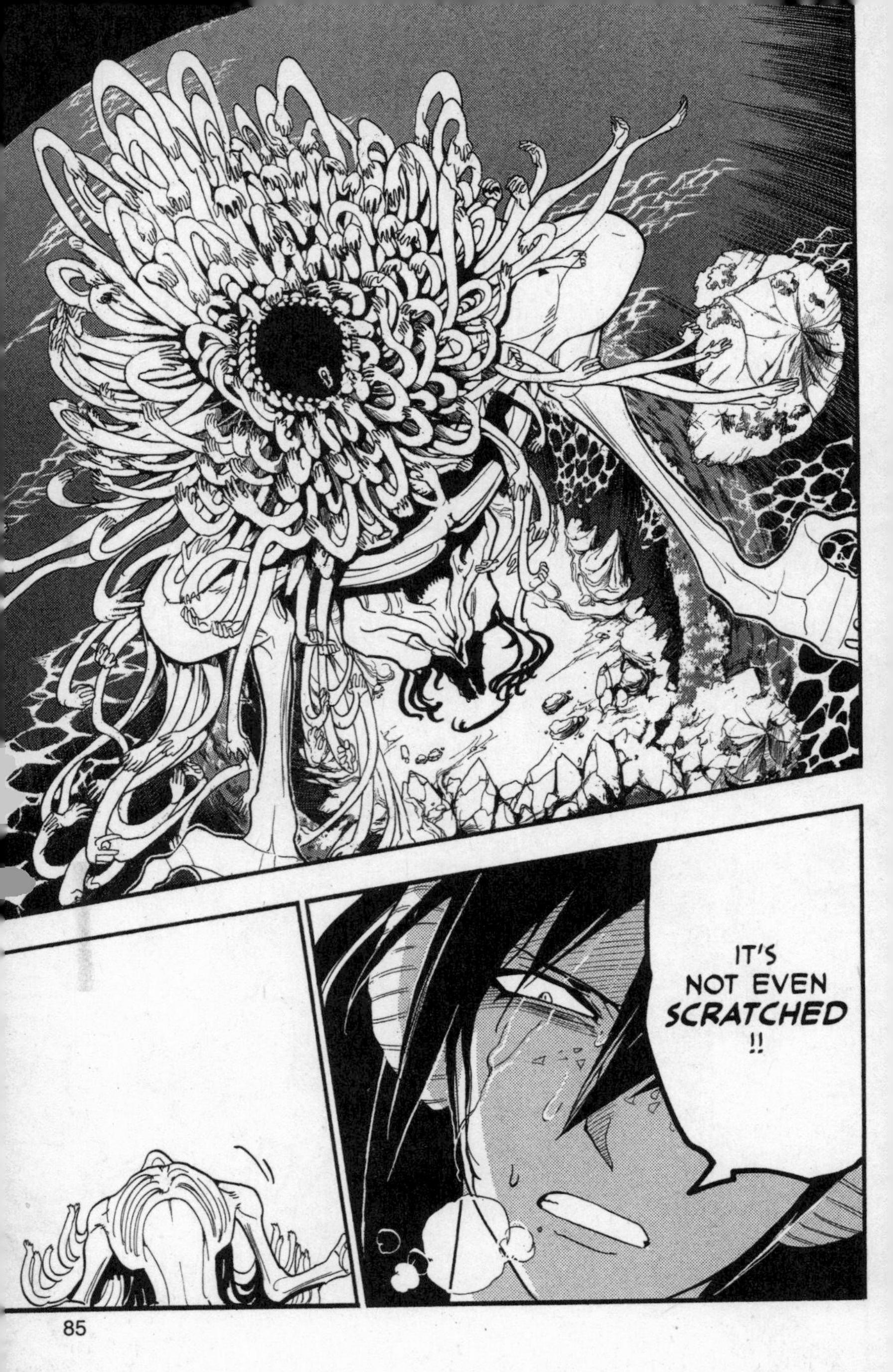
IT'S NOT EVEN SCRATCHED !!

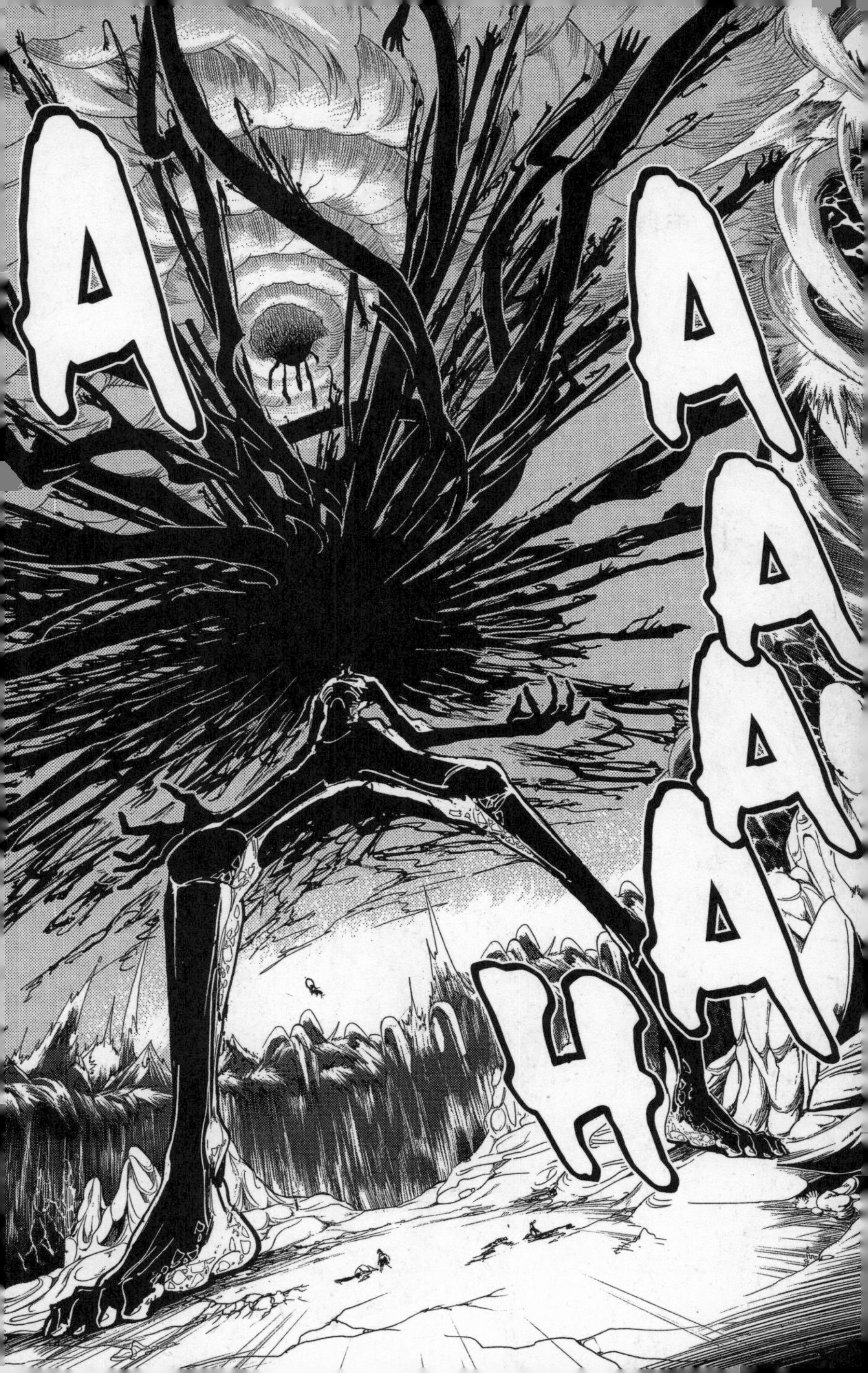
AAAAAH

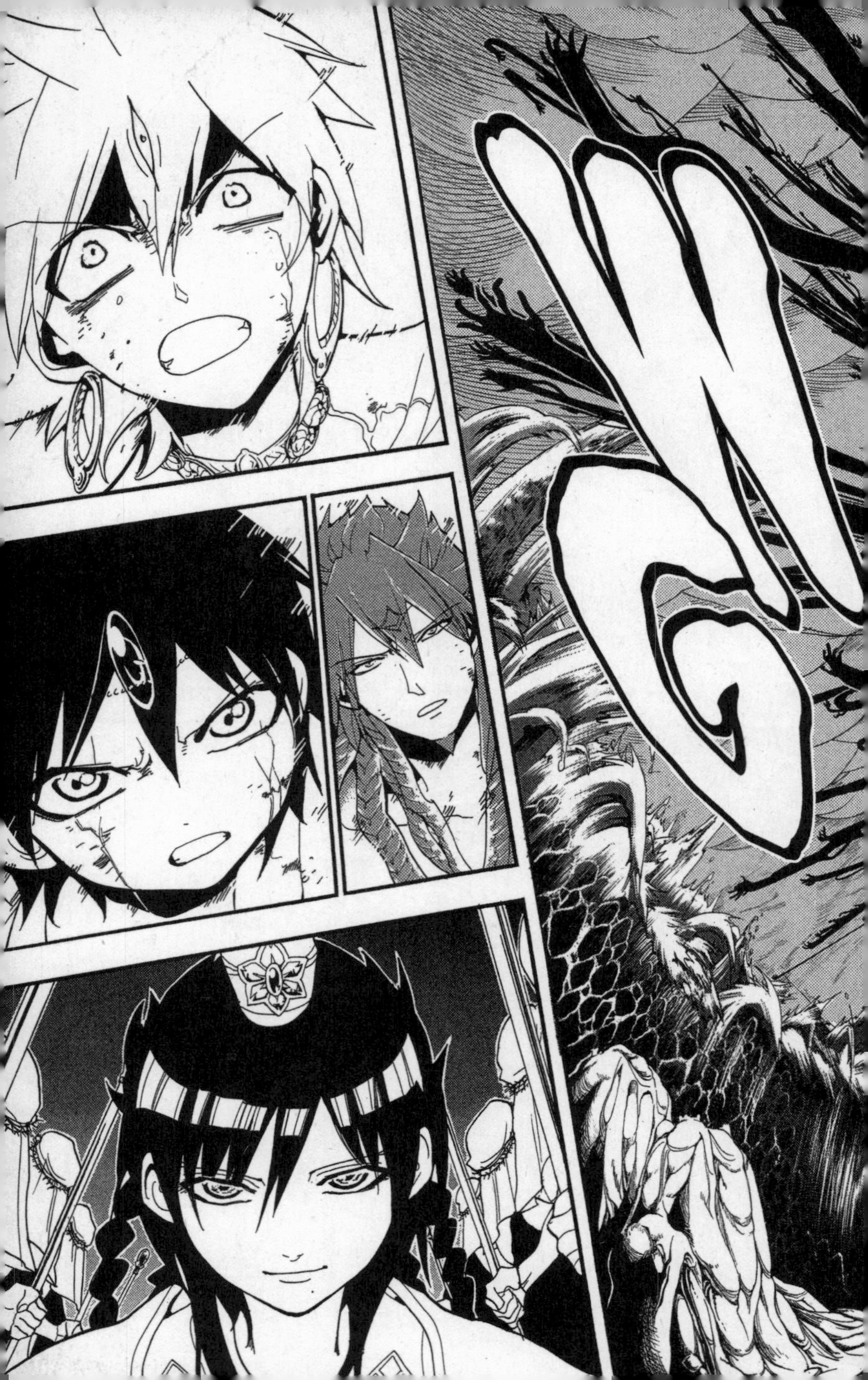

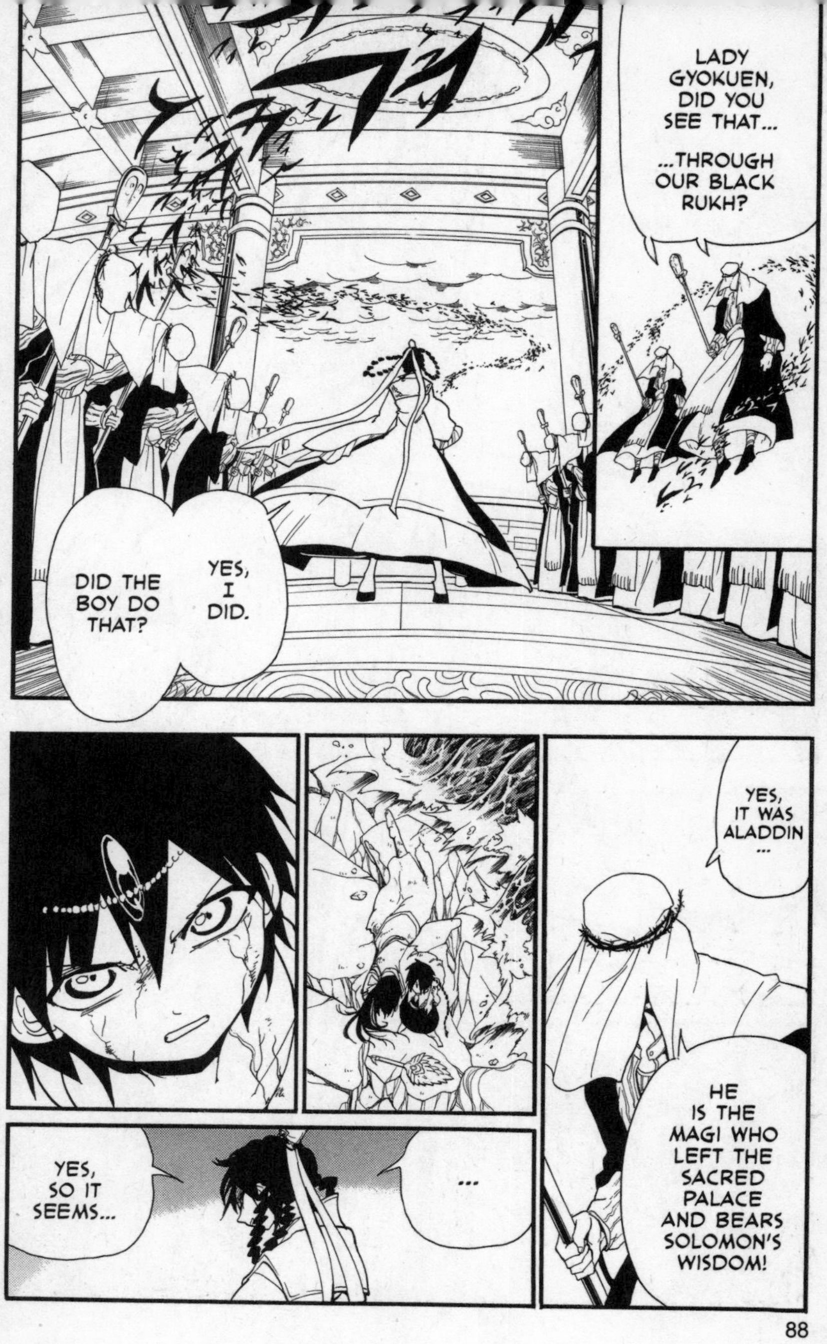
LADY GYOKUEN, DID YOU SEE THAT...
...THROUGH OUR BLACK RUKH?
YES, I DID.
DID THE BOY DO THAT?
YES, IT WAS ALADDIN ...
HE IS THE MAGI WHO LEFT THE SACRED PALACE AND BEARS SOLOMON'S WISDOM!
...
YES, SO IT SEEMS...

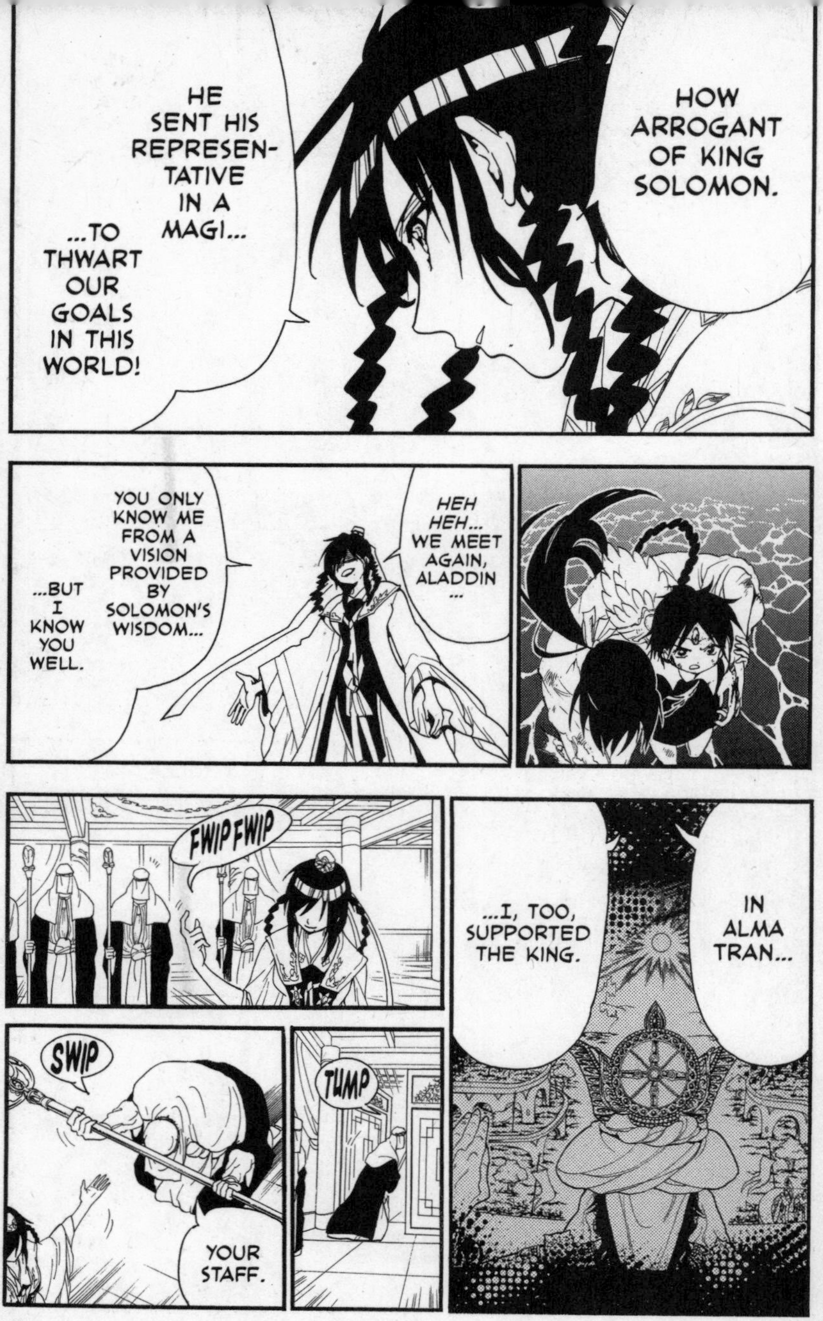
HOW ARROGANT OF KING SOLOMON.
HE SENT HIS REPRESEN-TATIVE IN A MAGI...
...TO THWART OUR GOALS IN THIS WORLD!
HEH HEH... WE MEET AGAIN, ALADDIN...
YOU ONLY KNOW ME FROM A VISION PROVIDED BY SOLOMON'S WISDOM...
...BUT I KNOW YOU WELL.
IN ALMA TRAN...
...I, TOO, SUPPORTED THE KING.
FWIPFWIP
TUMP
SWIP
YOUR STAFF.

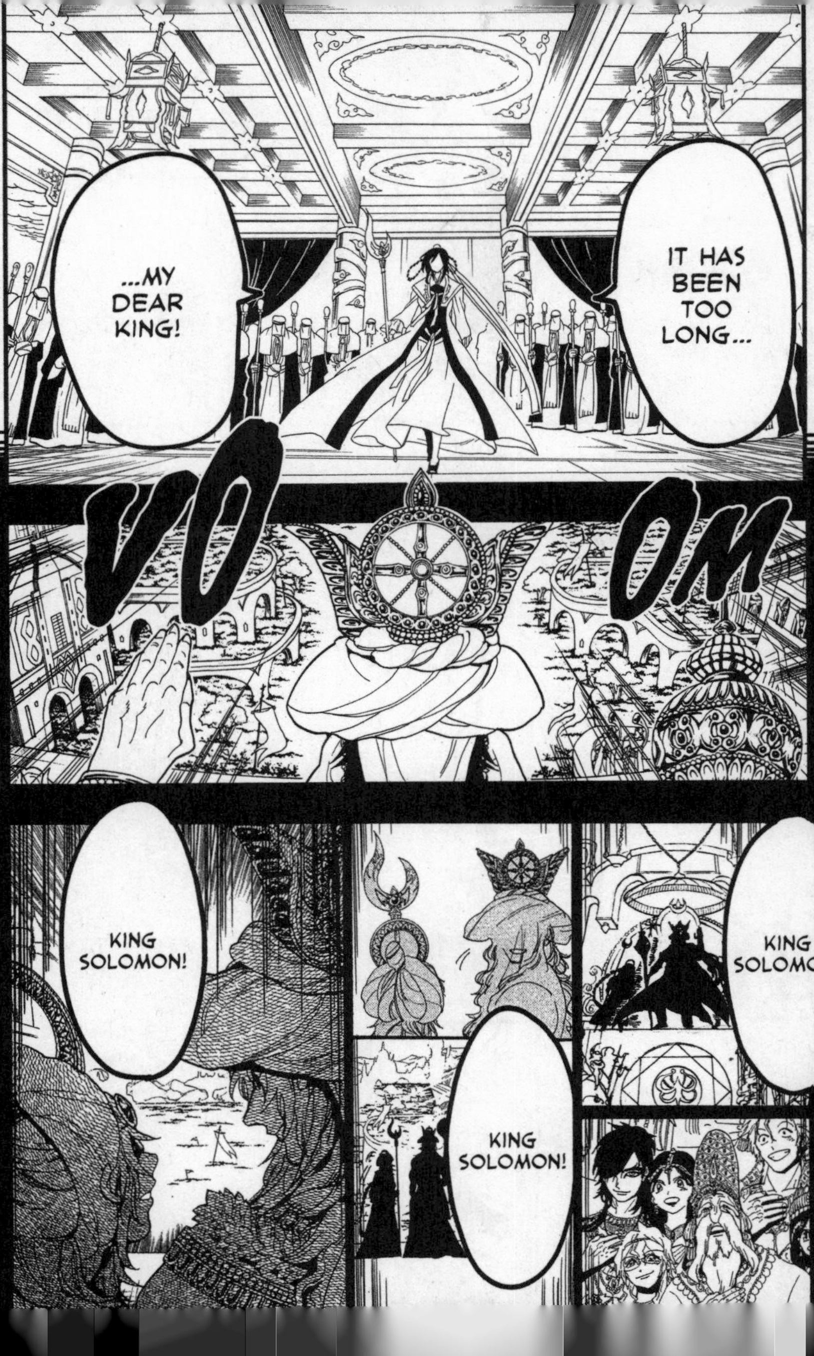
IT HAS BEEN TOO LONG...
...MY DEAR KING!
VOOM
KING SOLOMON!
KING SOLOMON!
KING SOLOMON!

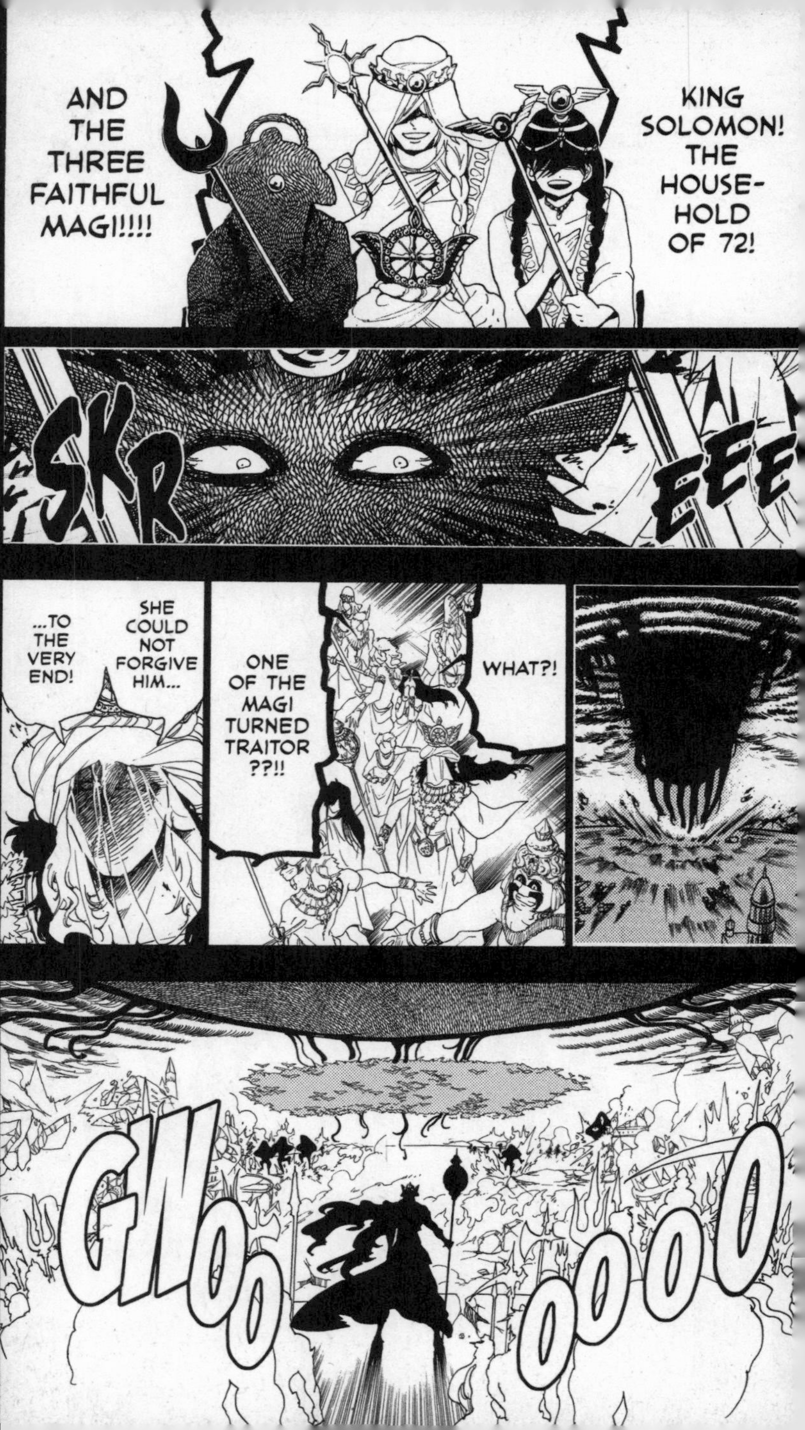
KING SOLOMON! THE HOUSEHOLD OF 72!
AND THE THREE FAITHFUL MAGI!!!!
SKREEE
WHAT?!
ONE OF THE MAGI TURNED TRAITOR??!!
SHE COULD NOT FORGIVE HIM...
...TO THE VERY END!
GNOOOOOOO

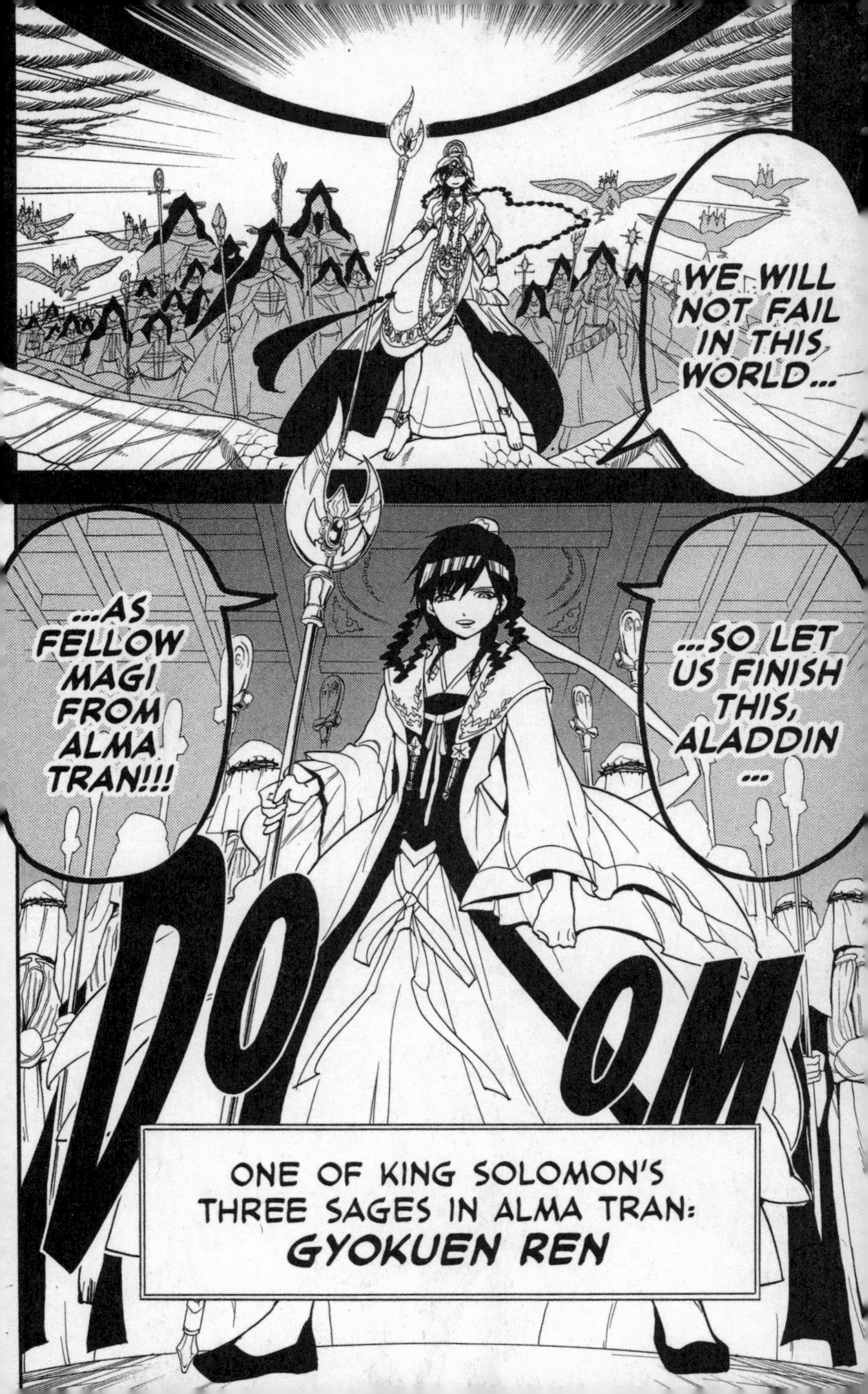
WE WILL NOT FAIL IN THIS WORLD...
...SO LET US FINISH THIS, ALADDIN ...
...AS FELLOW MAGI FROM ALMA TRAN!!!
DOOOM
ONE OF KING SOLOMON'S THREE SAGES IN ALMA TRAN: GYOKUEN REN

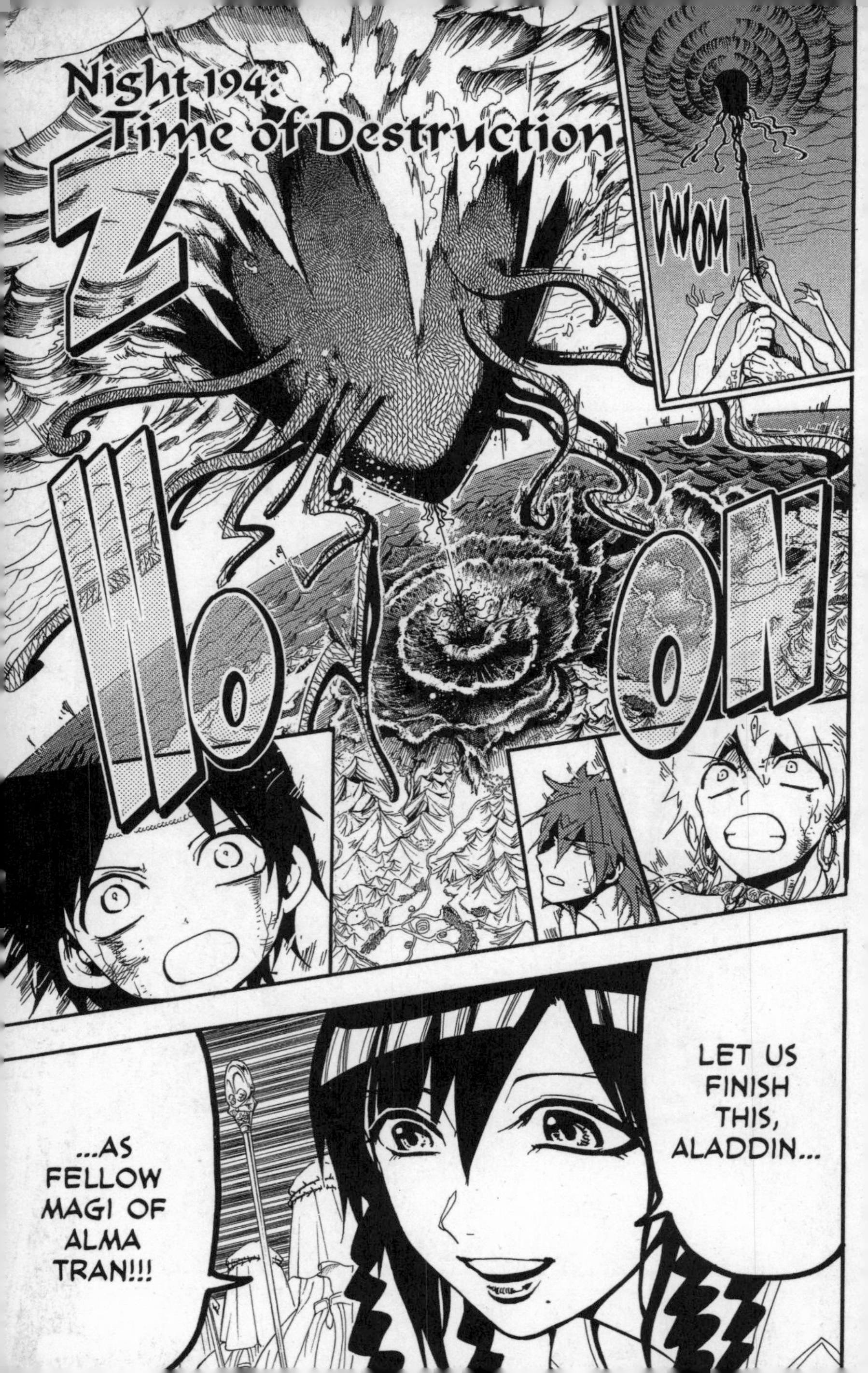
VWOM
Night 194: Time of Destruction
LET US FINISH THIS, ALADDIN...
...AS FELLOW MAGI OF ALMA TRAN!!!

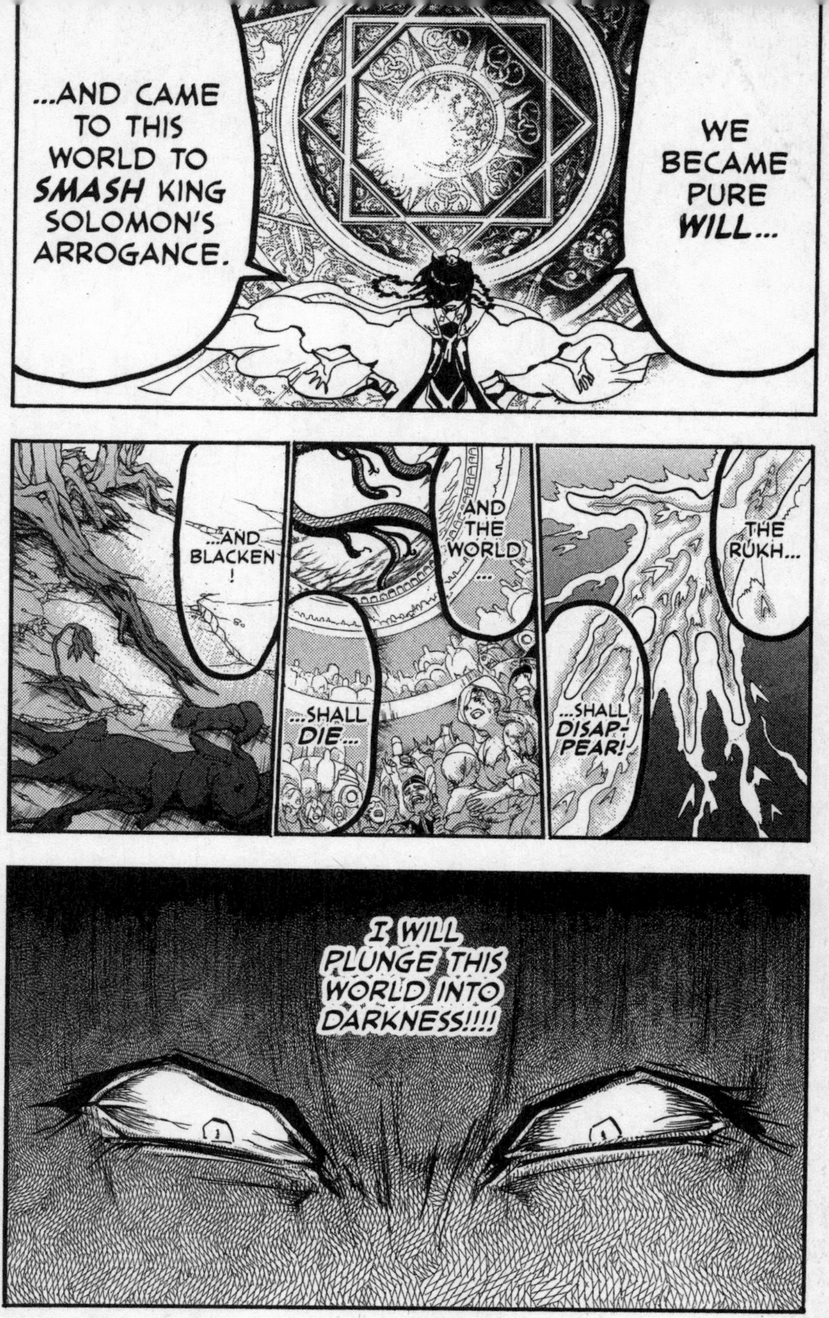
WE BECAME PURE WILL...
...AND CAME TO THIS WORLD TO SMASH KING SOLOMON'S ARROGANCE.
THE RUKH...
...SHALL DISAPPEAR!
AND THE WORLD...
...SHALL DIE...
...AND BLACKEN!
I WILL PLUNGE THIS WORLD INTO DARKNESS!!!!

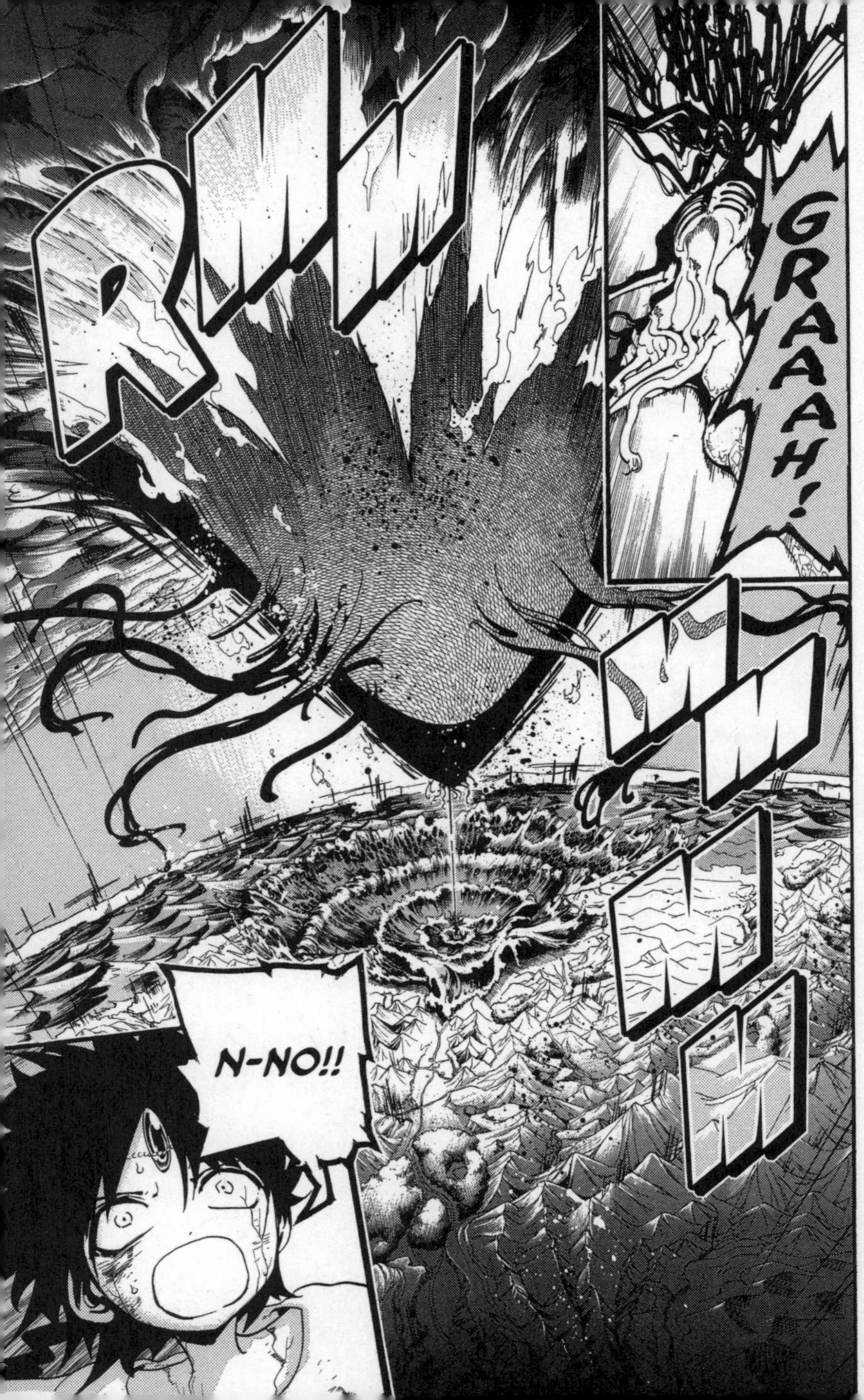
GRAAAH!
N-NO!!

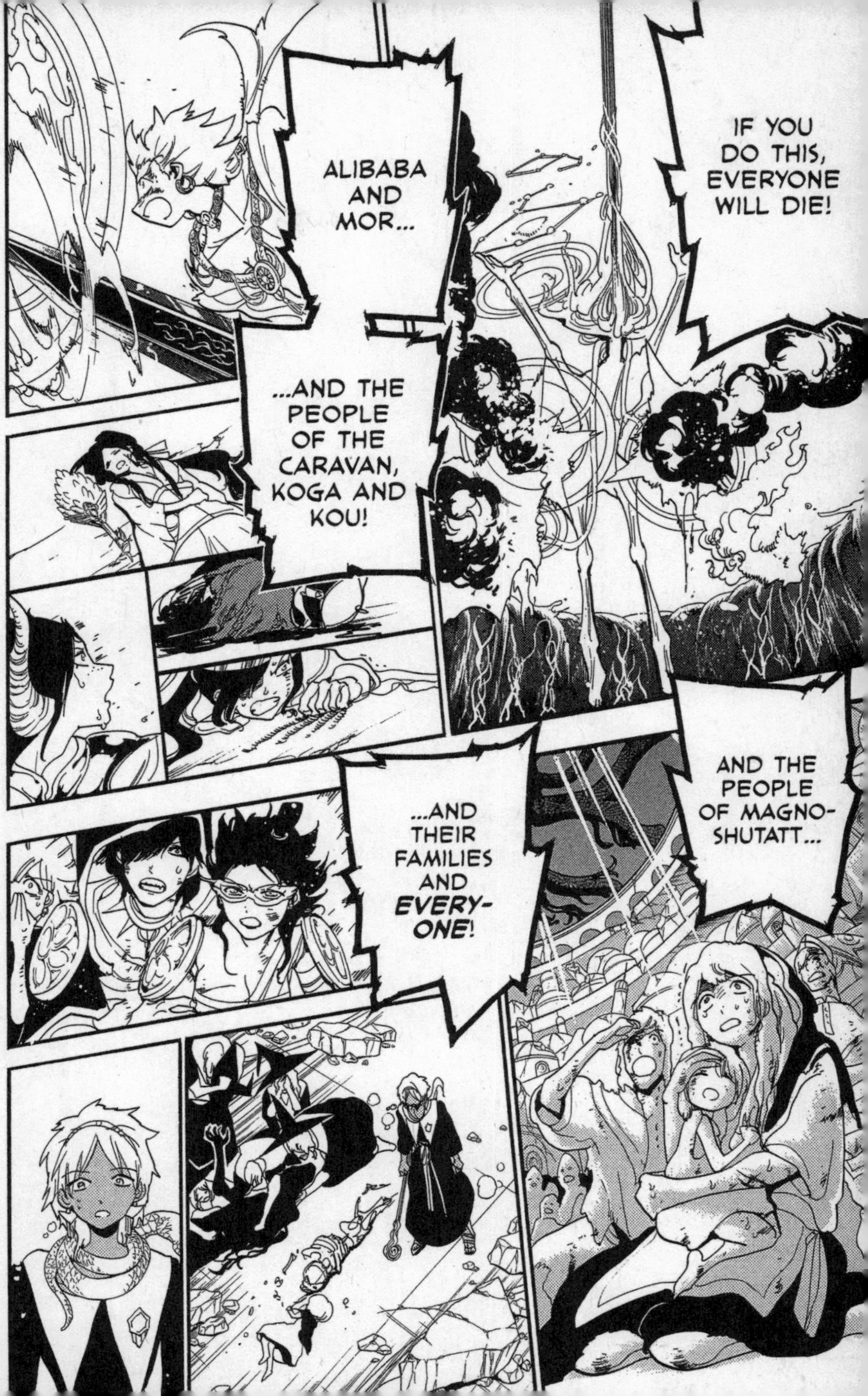
IF YOU DO THIS, EVERYONE WILL DIE!
ALIBABA AND MOR...
...AND THE PEOPLE OF THE CARAVAN, KOGA AND KOU!
AND THE PEOPLE OF MAGNO-SHUTATT...
...AND THEIR FAMILIES AND *EVERYONE*!

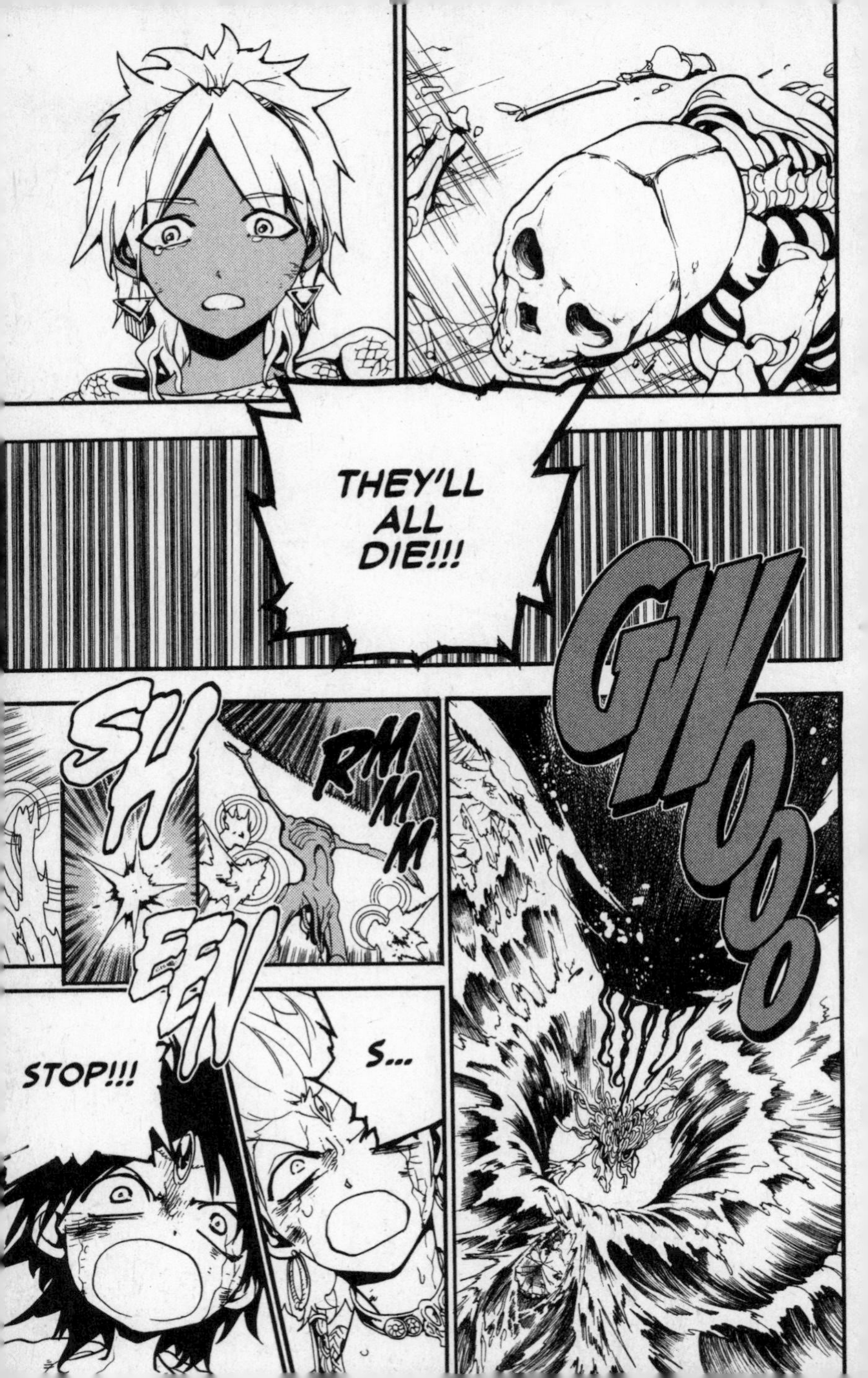
THEY'LL ALL DIE!!!
GWOOOO
RMMM
SHEEN
S...
STOP!!!

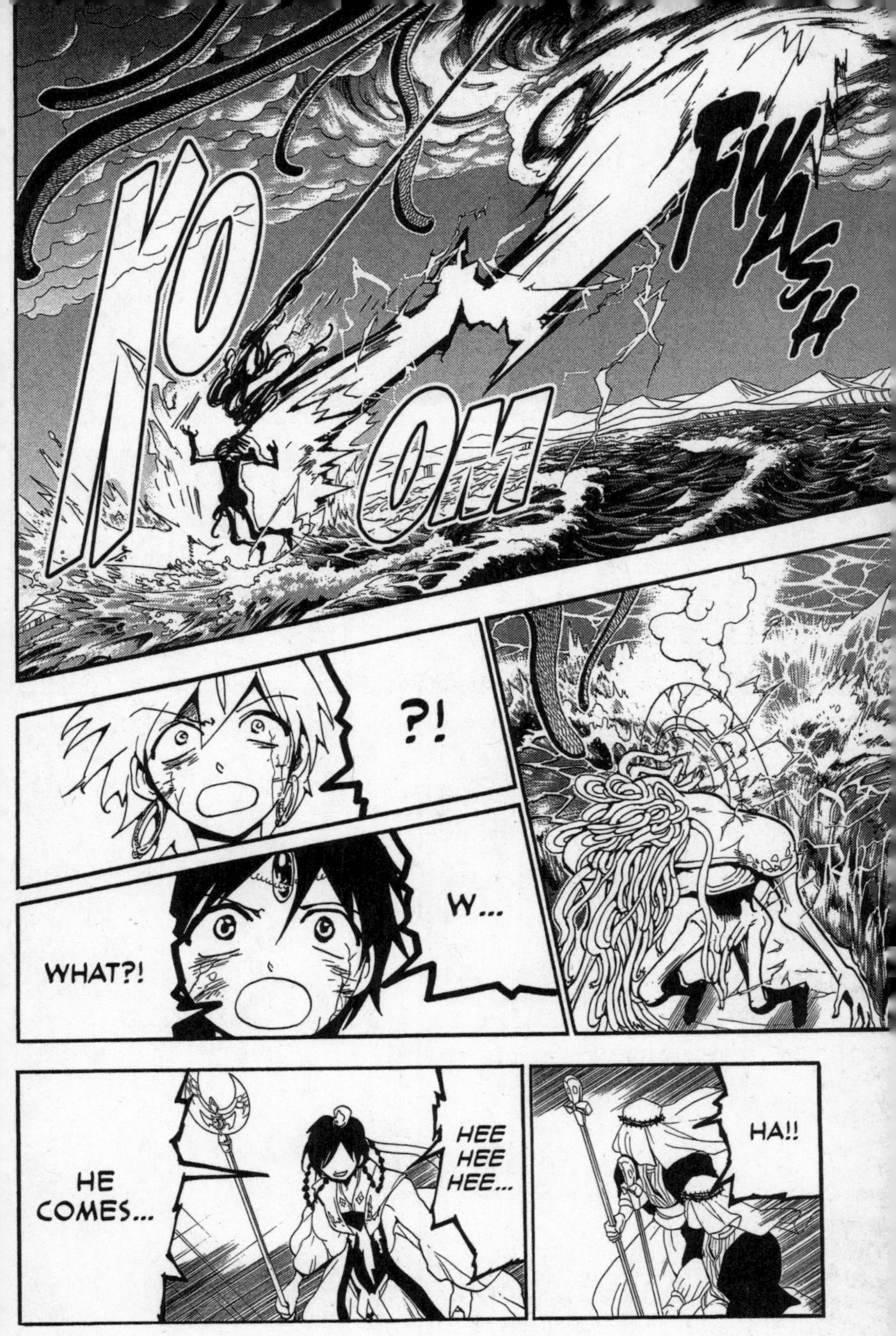
FWASH
KOOM
?!
W...
WHAT?!
HA!!
HEE HEE HEE...
HE COMES...

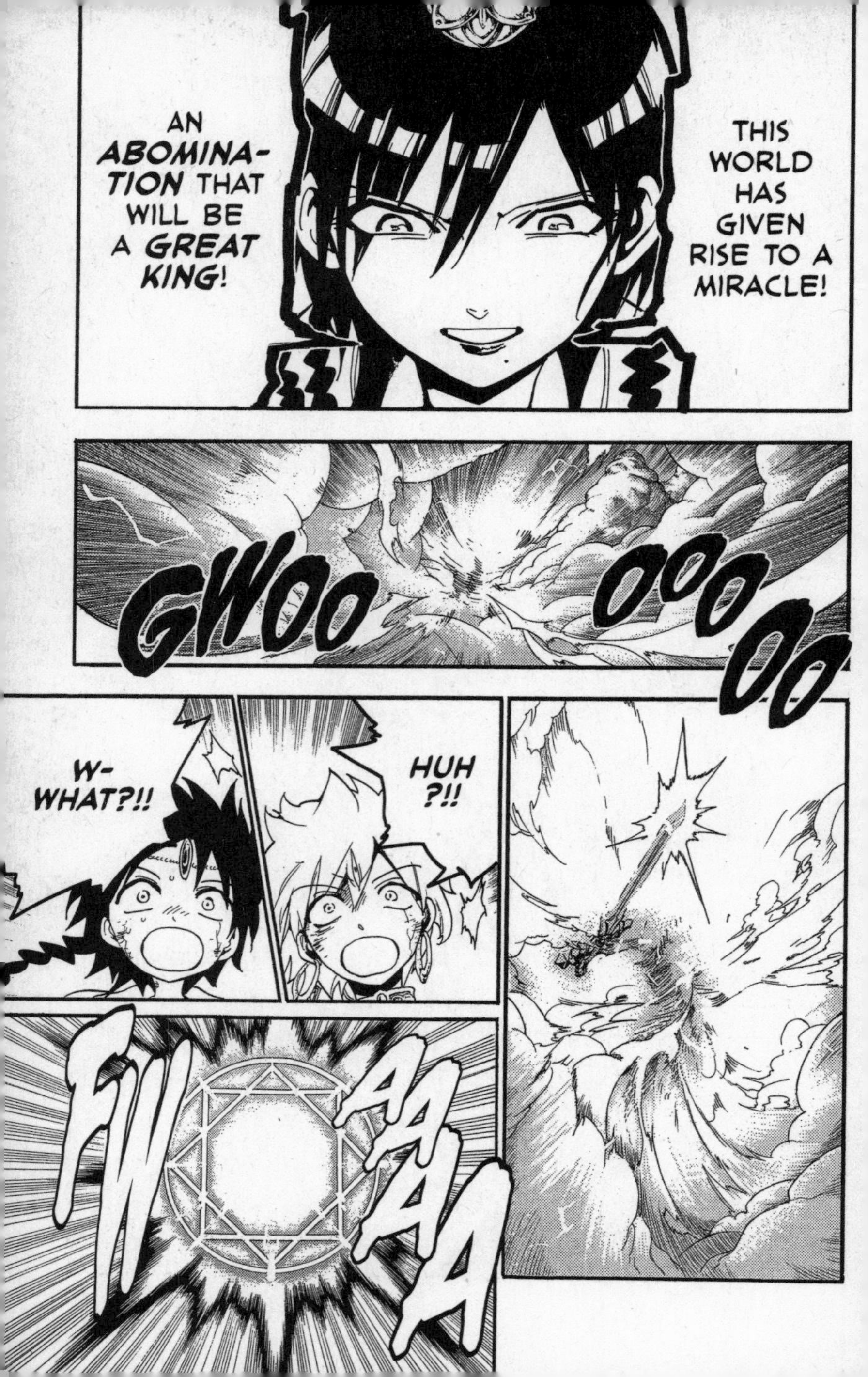
THIS WORLD HAS GIVEN RISE TO A MIRACLE!
AN ABOMINATION THAT WILL BE A GREAT KING!
GWOOOOOOO
HUH?!!
W-WHAT?!!
FWAAAAA

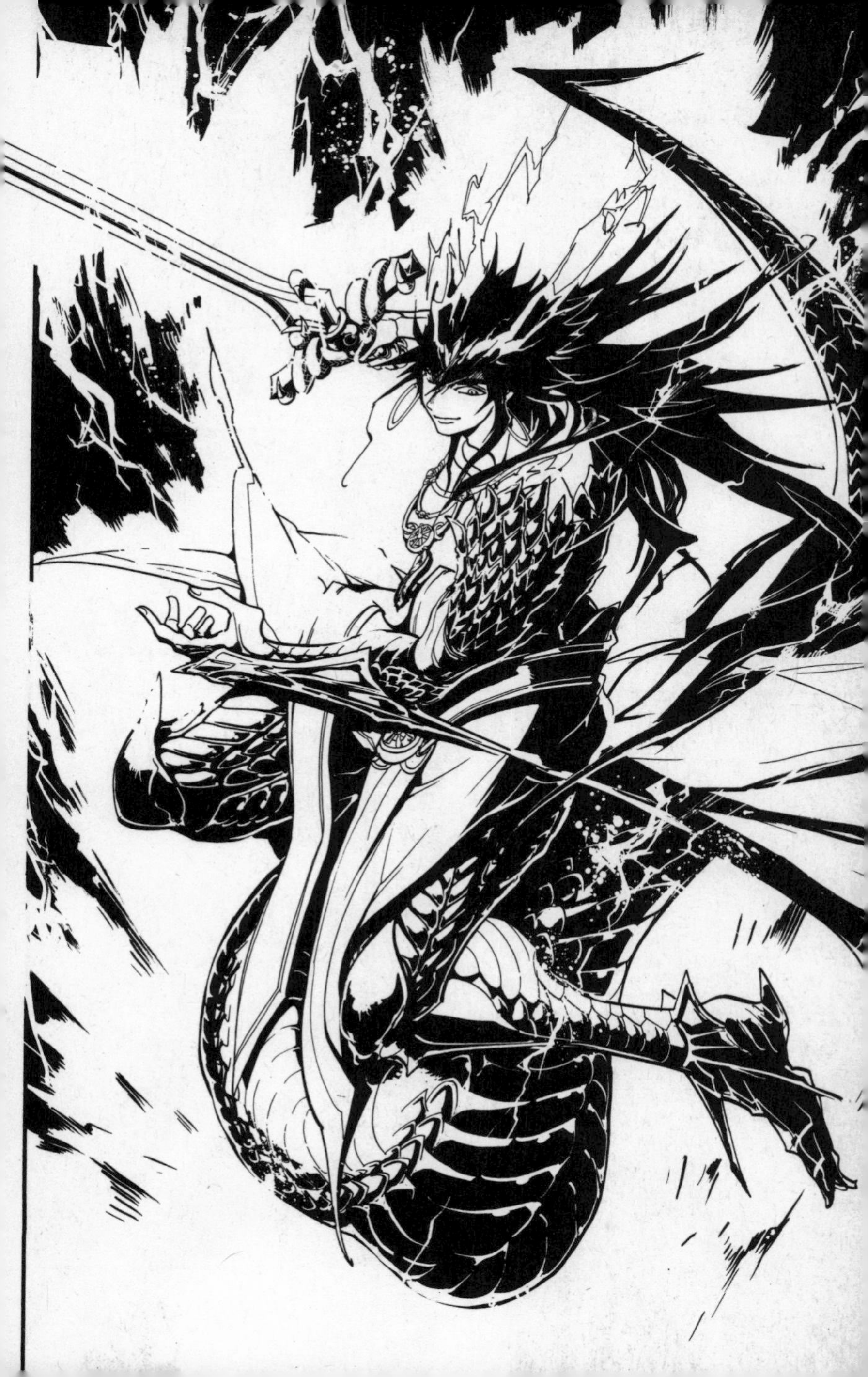

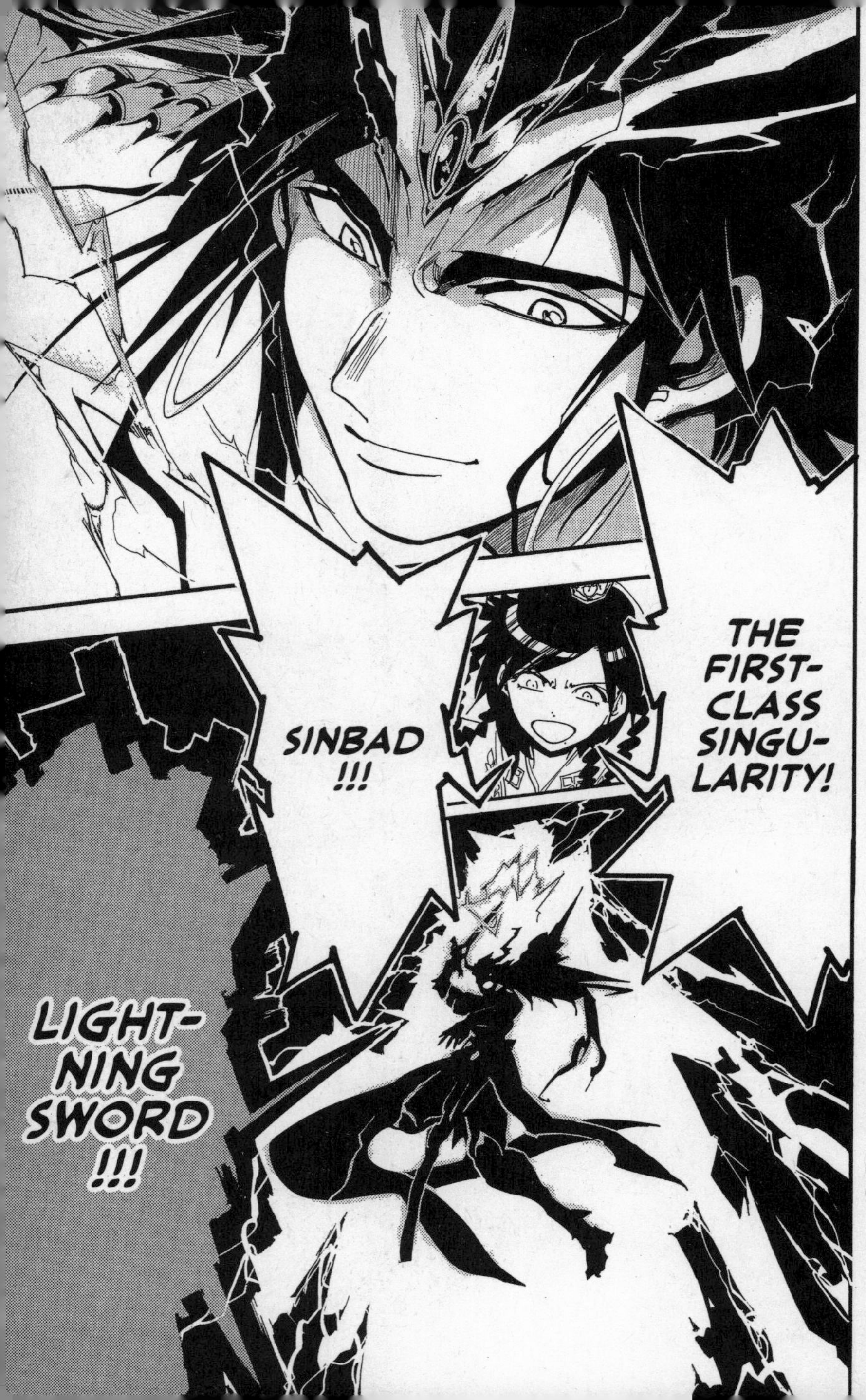
THE FIRST-CLASS SINGULARITY!
SINBAD!!!
LIGHTNING SWORD!!!

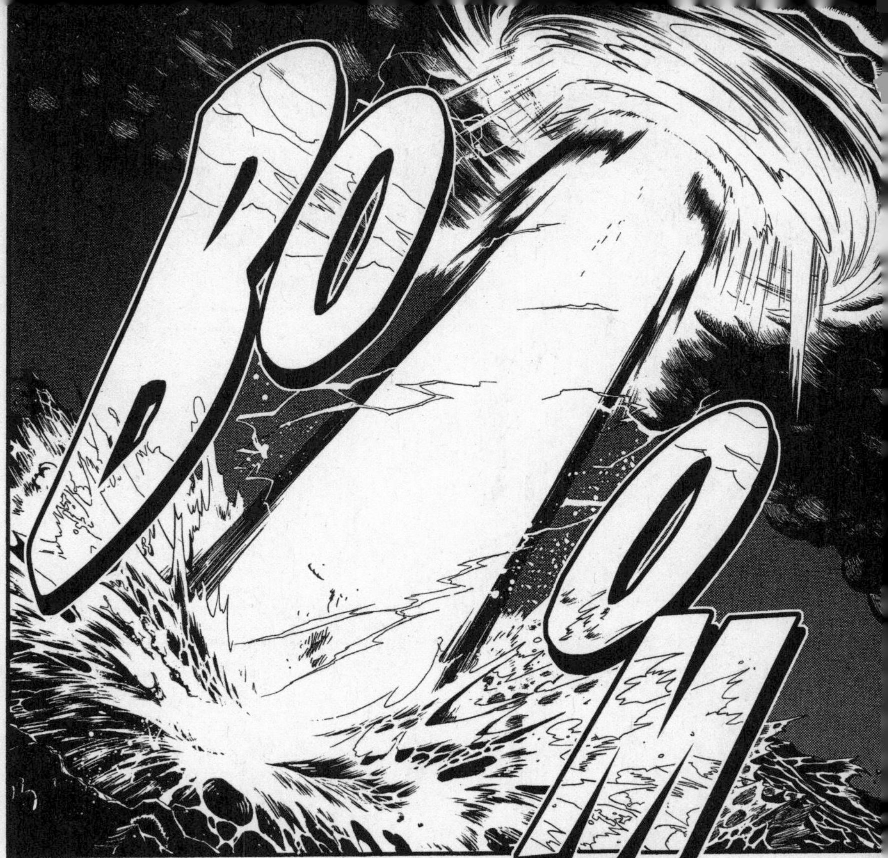
DOOM
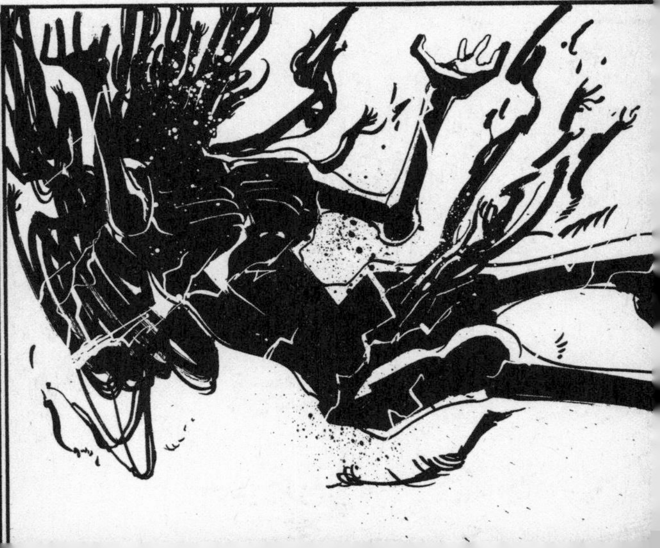
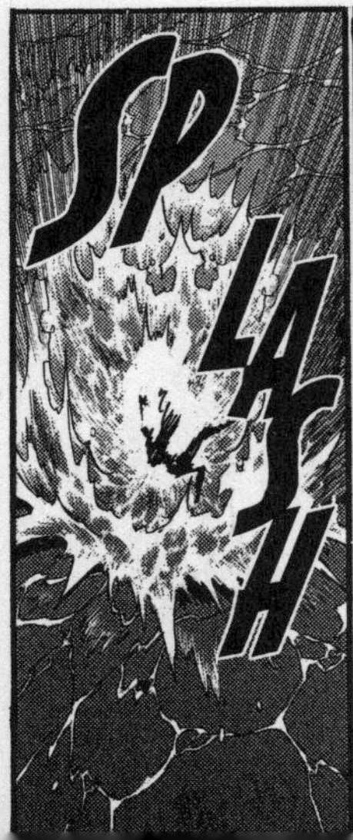

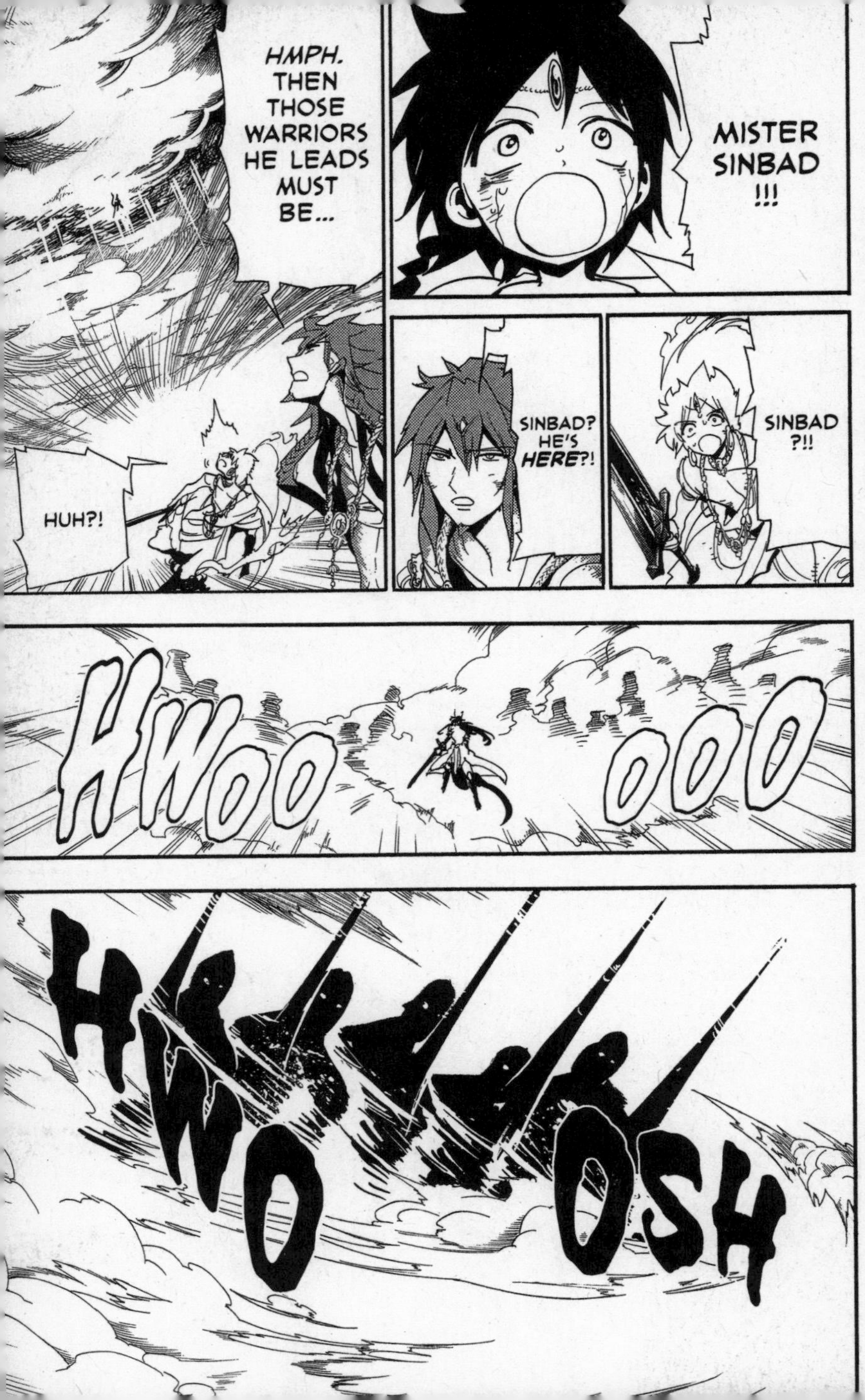
MISTER SINBAD !!!
SINBAD ?!!
SINBAD? HE'S *HERE*?!
HMPH. THEN THOSE WARRIORS HE LEADS MUST BE...
HUH?!
HWOOOOOO
HWOOSH

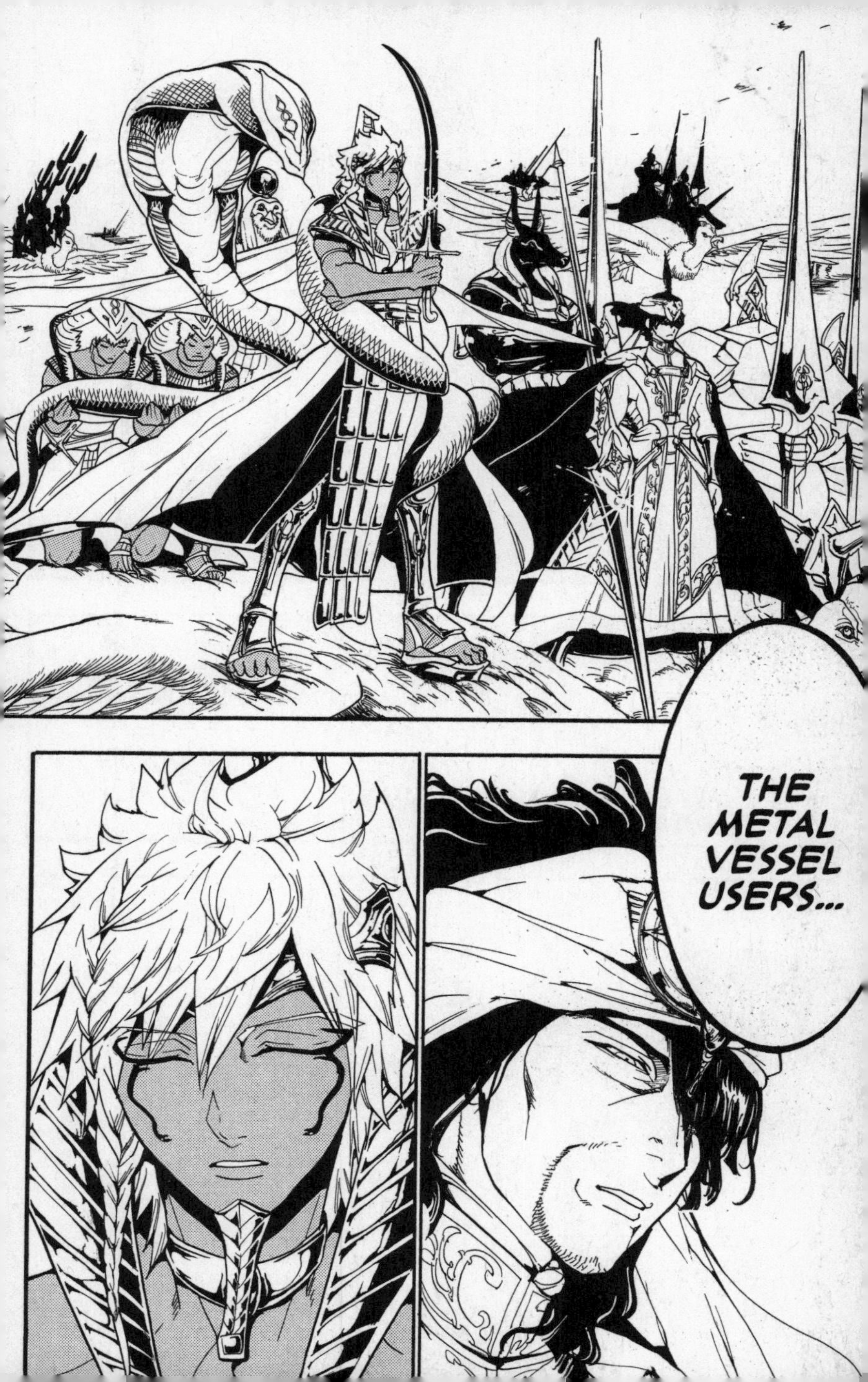
THE METAL VESSEL USERS...

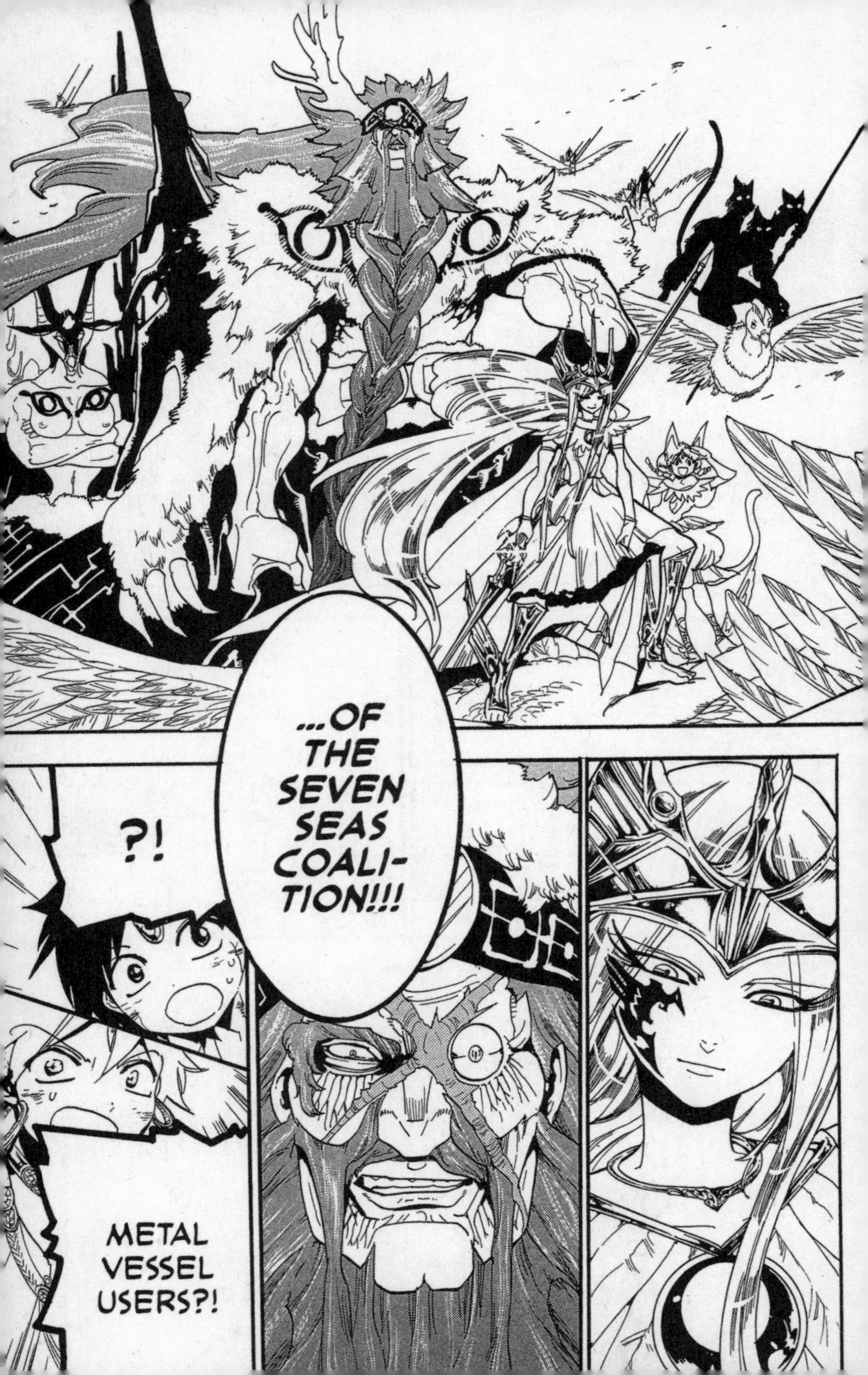
...OF THE SEVEN SEAS COALITION!!!
?!
METAL VESSEL USERS?!

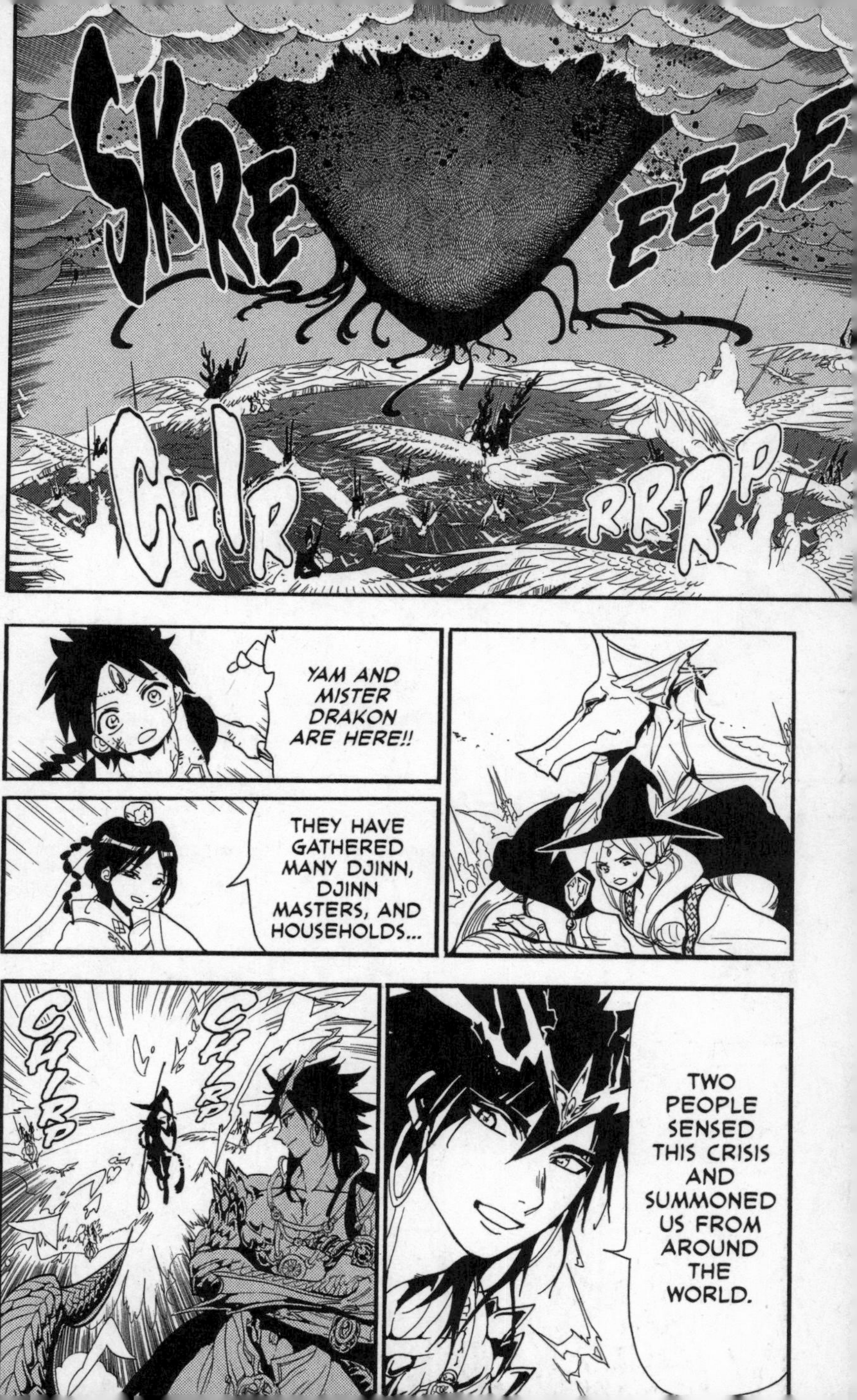
SKREEEEE
CHIRRRRP
YAM AND MISTER DRAKON ARE HERE!!
THEY HAVE GATHERED MANY DJINN, DJINN MASTERS, AND HOUSEHOLDS...
TWO PEOPLE SENSED THIS CRISIS AND SUMMONED US FROM AROUND THE WORLD.
CHIRP
CHIRP

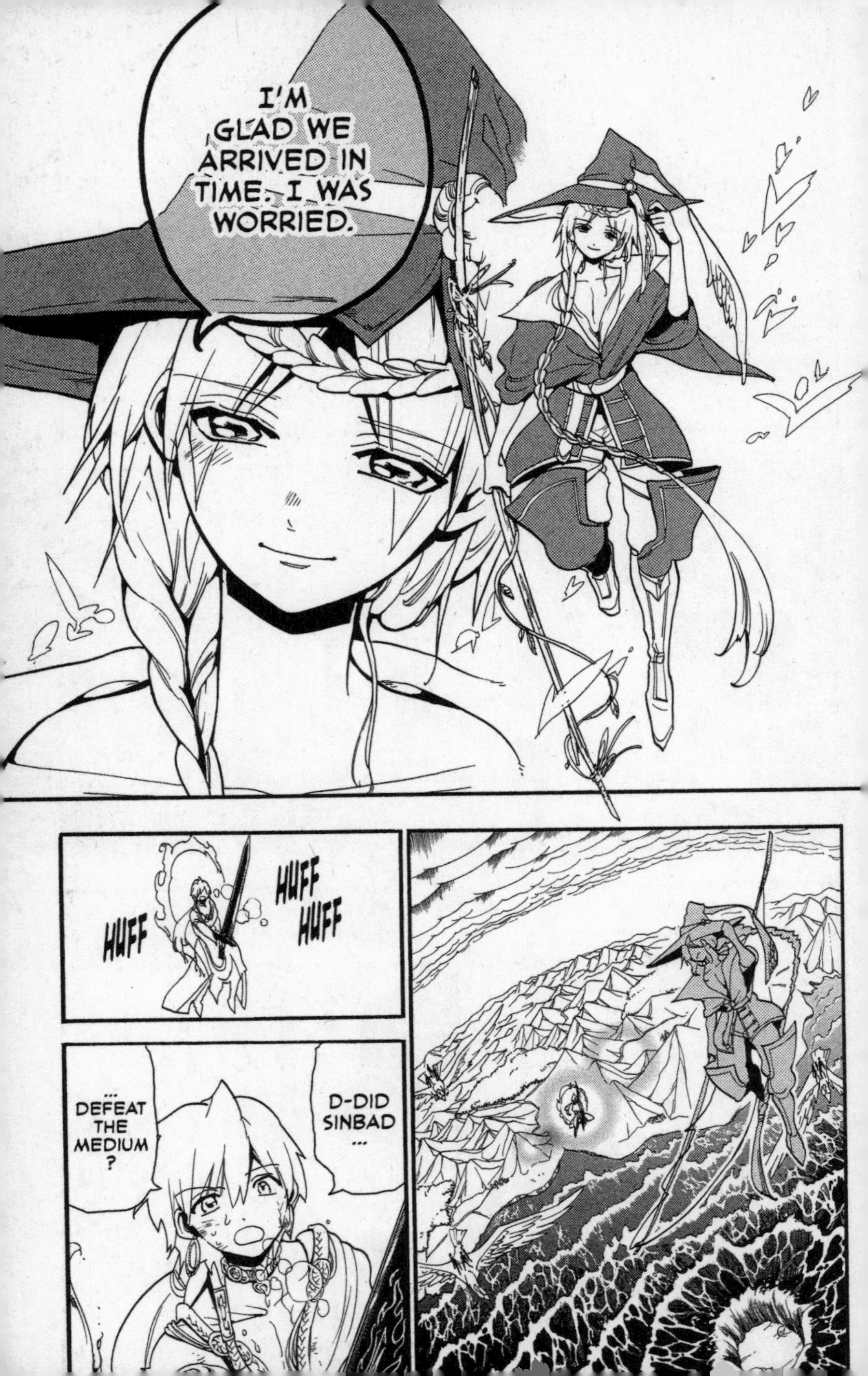
I'M GLAD WE ARRIVED IN TIME. I WAS WORRIED.
HUFF HUFF
HUFF
D-DID SINBAD...
...DEFEAT THE MEDIUM?

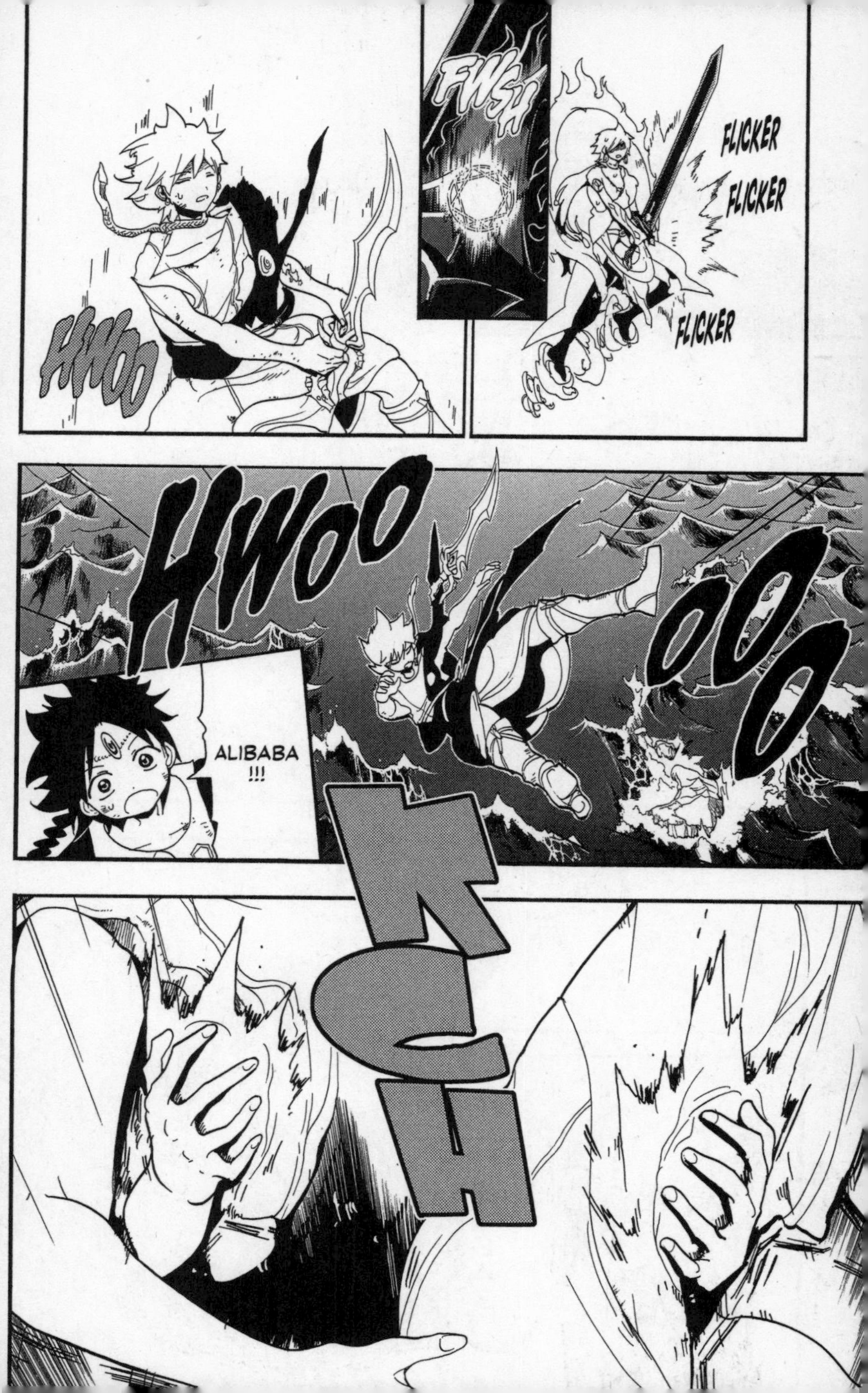
FWSH
FLICKER
FLICKER
FLICKER
HWOO
HWOO
OOO
ALIBABA
!!!
KCH

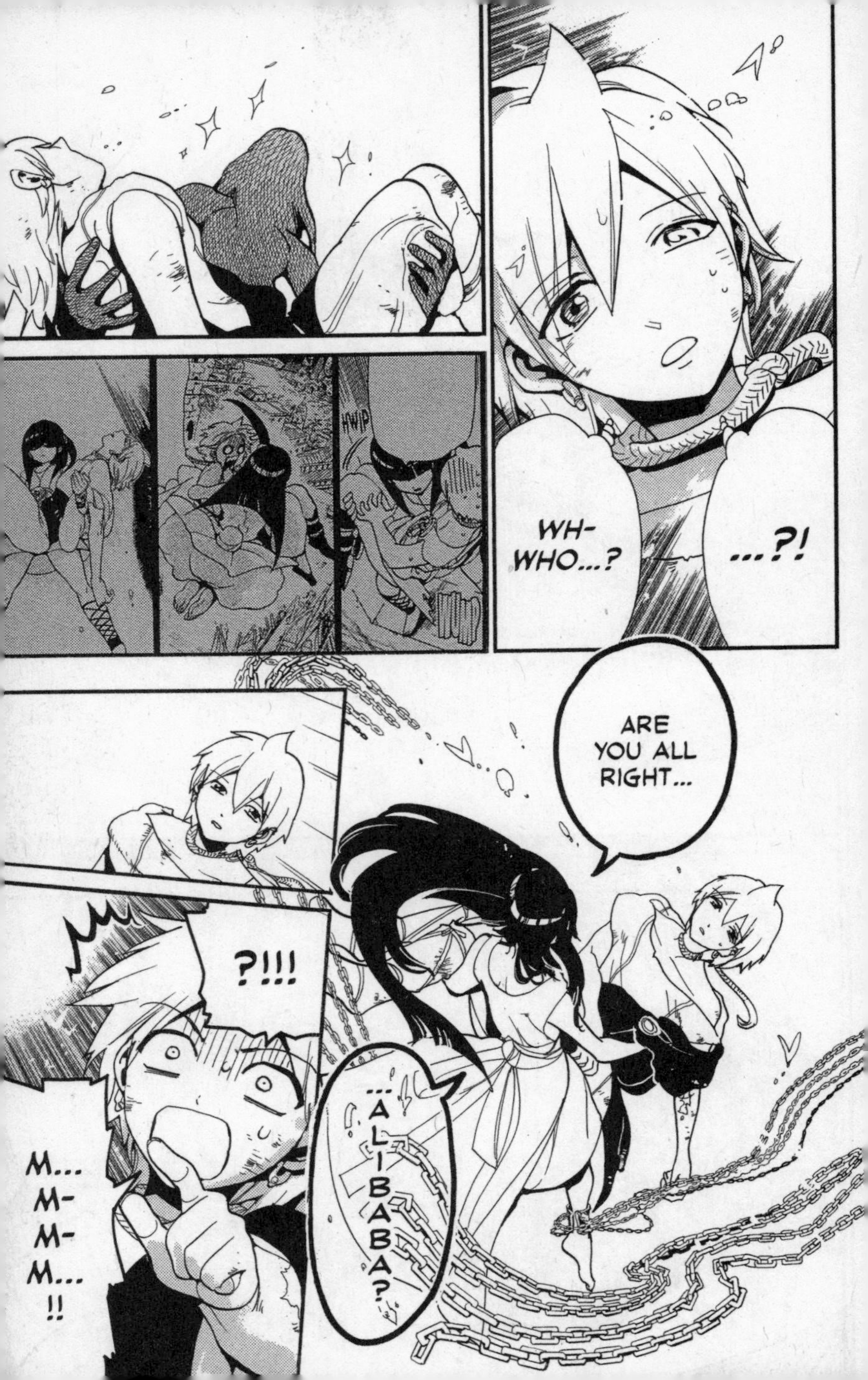
...?!
WH- WHO...?
HWIP
ARE YOU ALL RIGHT...
?!!!
...ALIBABA?
M... M- M- M...!!

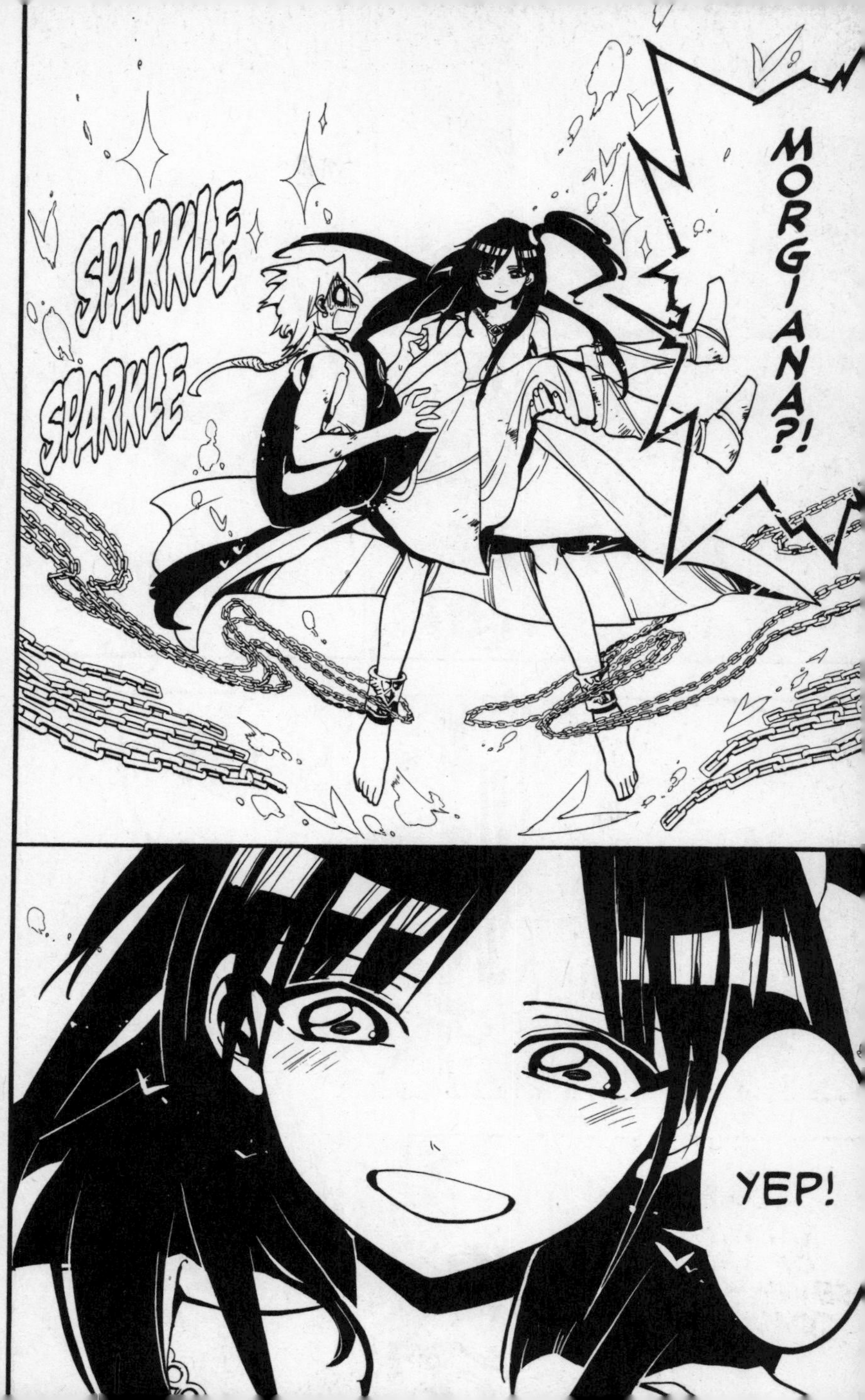
MORGIANA?!
SPARKLE
SPARKLE
YEP!

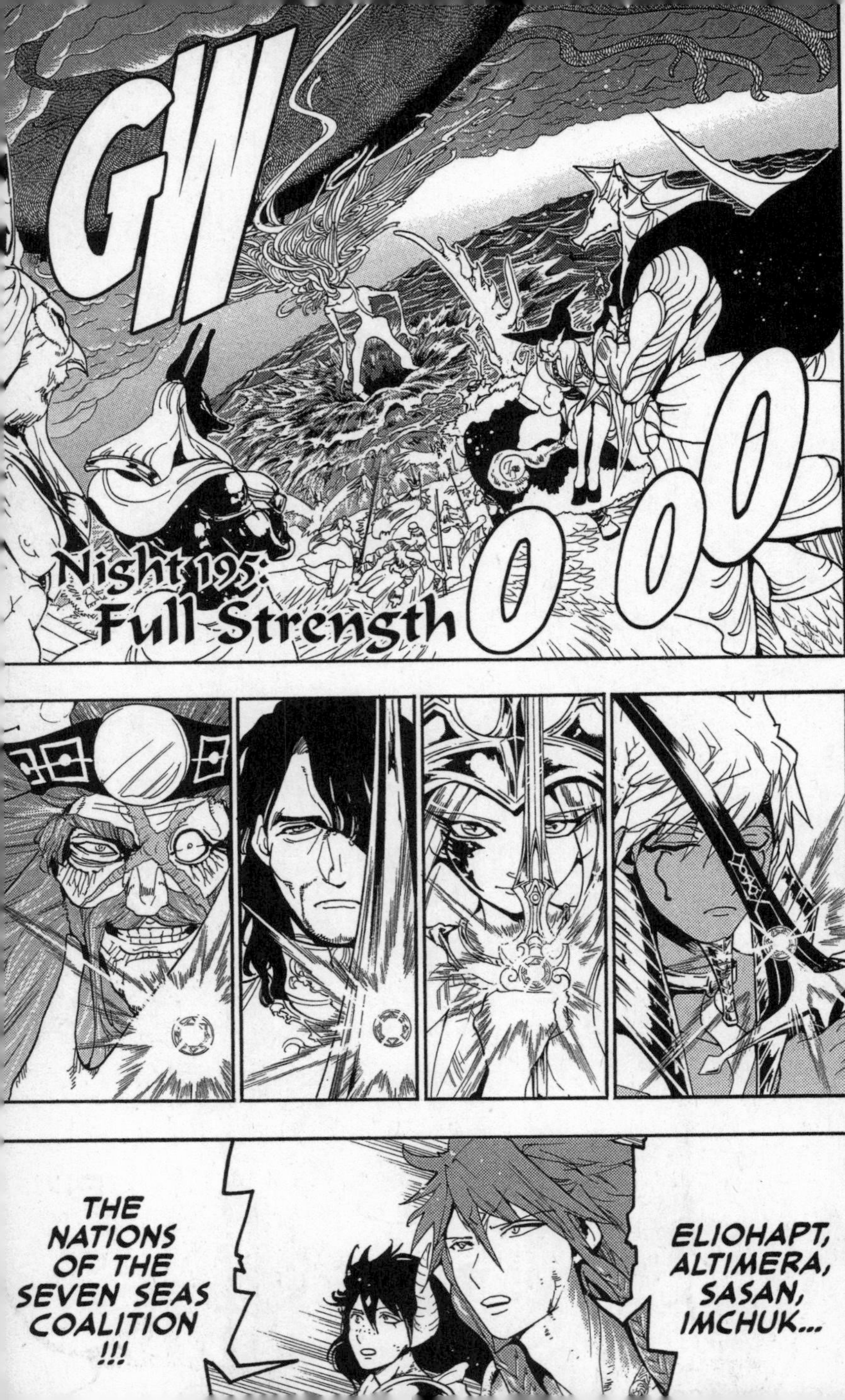
GWOOOO
Night 195: Full Strength
ELIOHAPT, ALTIMERA, SASAN, IMCHUK...
THE NATIONS OF THE SEVEN SEAS COALITION!!!

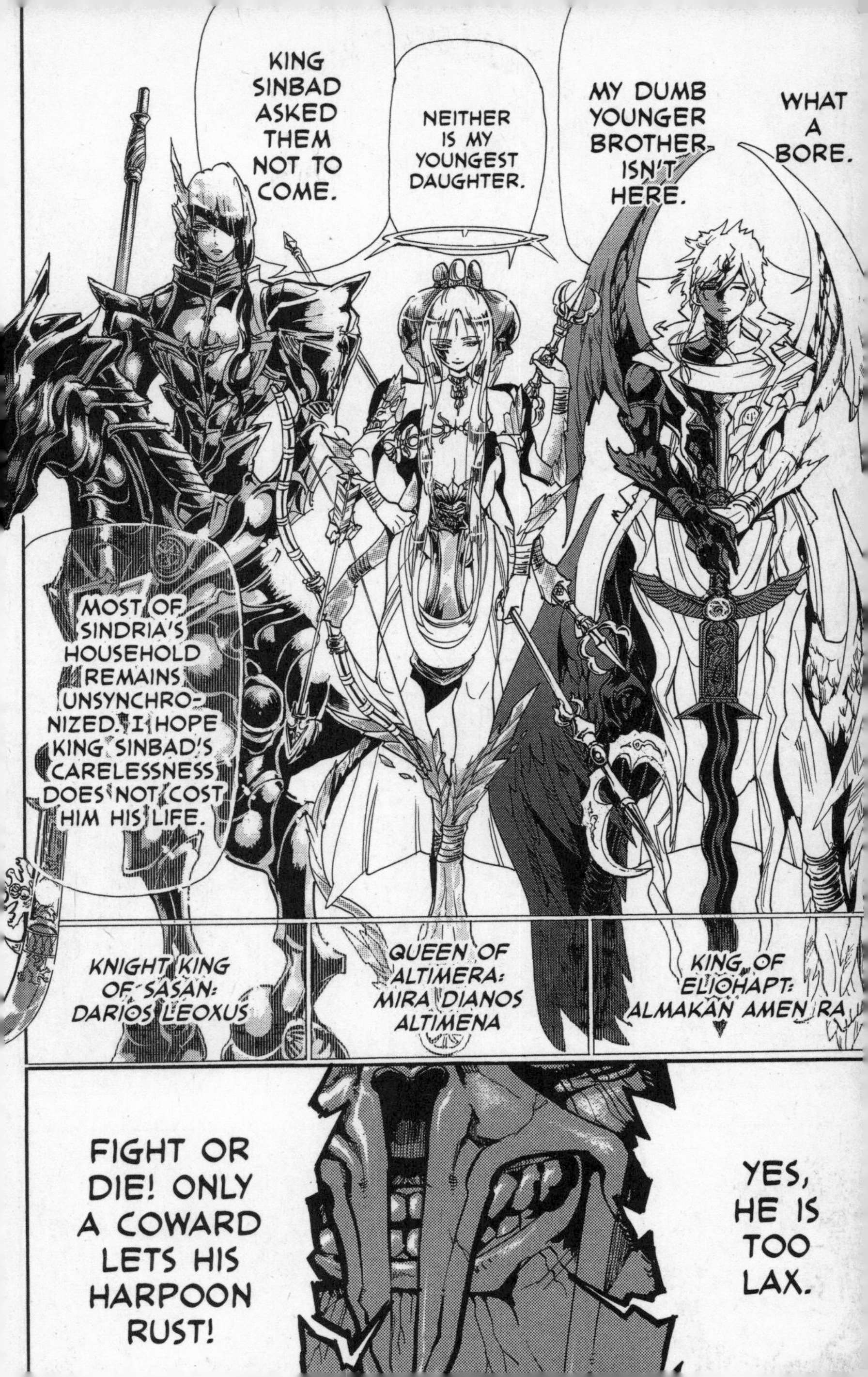
WHAT A BORE.
MY DUMB YOUNGER BROTHER ISN'T HERE.
NEITHER IS MY YOUNGEST DAUGHTER.
KING SINBAD ASKED THEM NOT TO COME.
MOST OF SINDRIA'S HOUSEHOLD REMAINS UNSYNCHRO-NIZED. I HOPE KING SINBAD'S CARELESSNESS DOES NOT COST HIM HIS LIFE.
KING OF ELIOHAPT: ALMAKAN AMEN RA
QUEEN OF ALTIMERA: MIRA DIANOS ALTIMENA
KNIGHT KING OF SASAN: DARIOS LEOXUS
YES, HE IS TOO LAX.
FIGHT OR DIE! ONLY A COWARD LETS HIS HARPOON RUST!

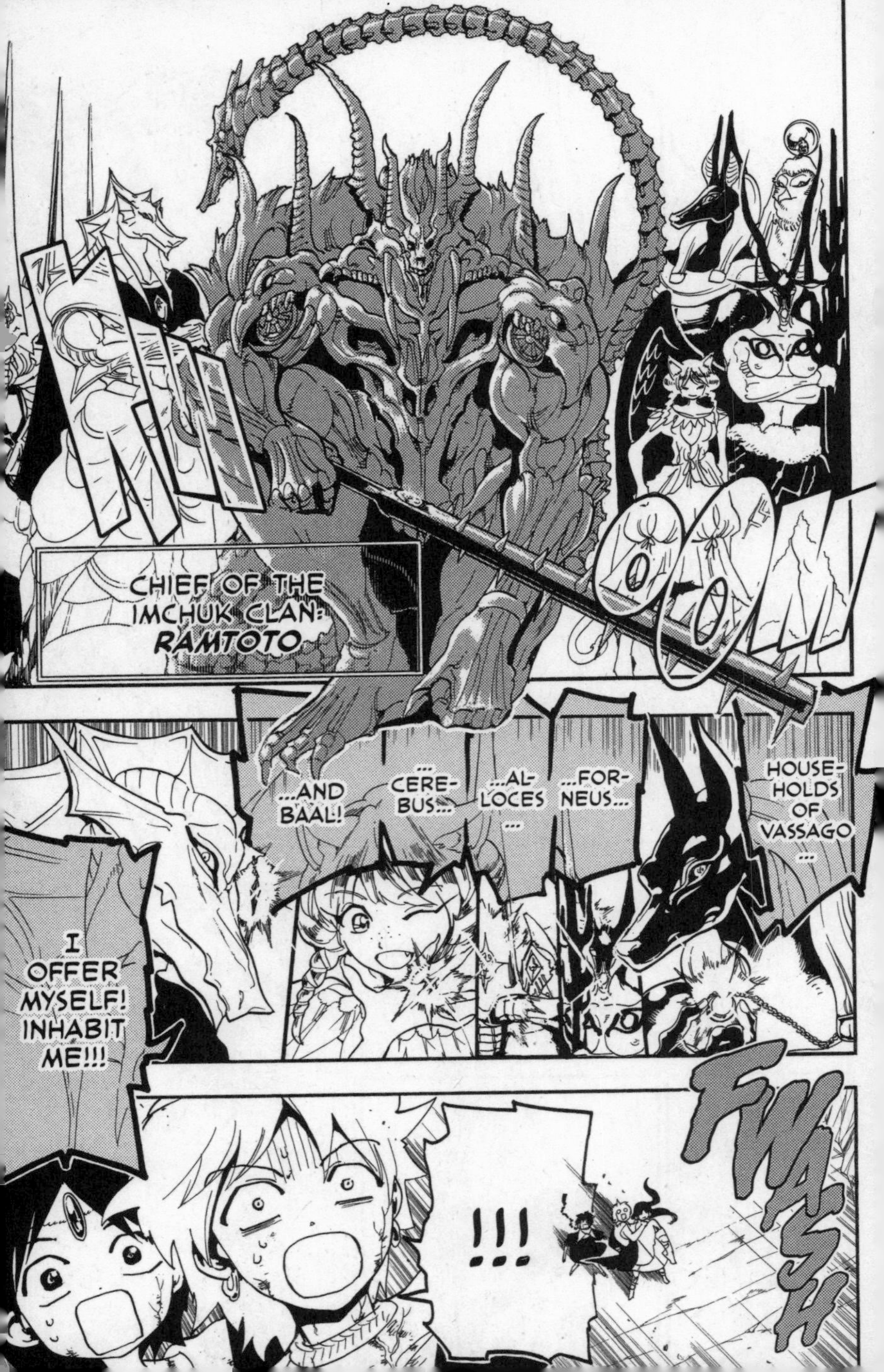
CHIEF OF THE IMCHUK CLAN: *RAMTOTO*
HOUSE-HOLDS OF VASSAGO...
...FOR-NEUS...
...AL-LOCES...
...CERE-BUS...
...AND BAAL!
I OFFER MYSELF! INHABIT ME!!!
FWASH
!!!

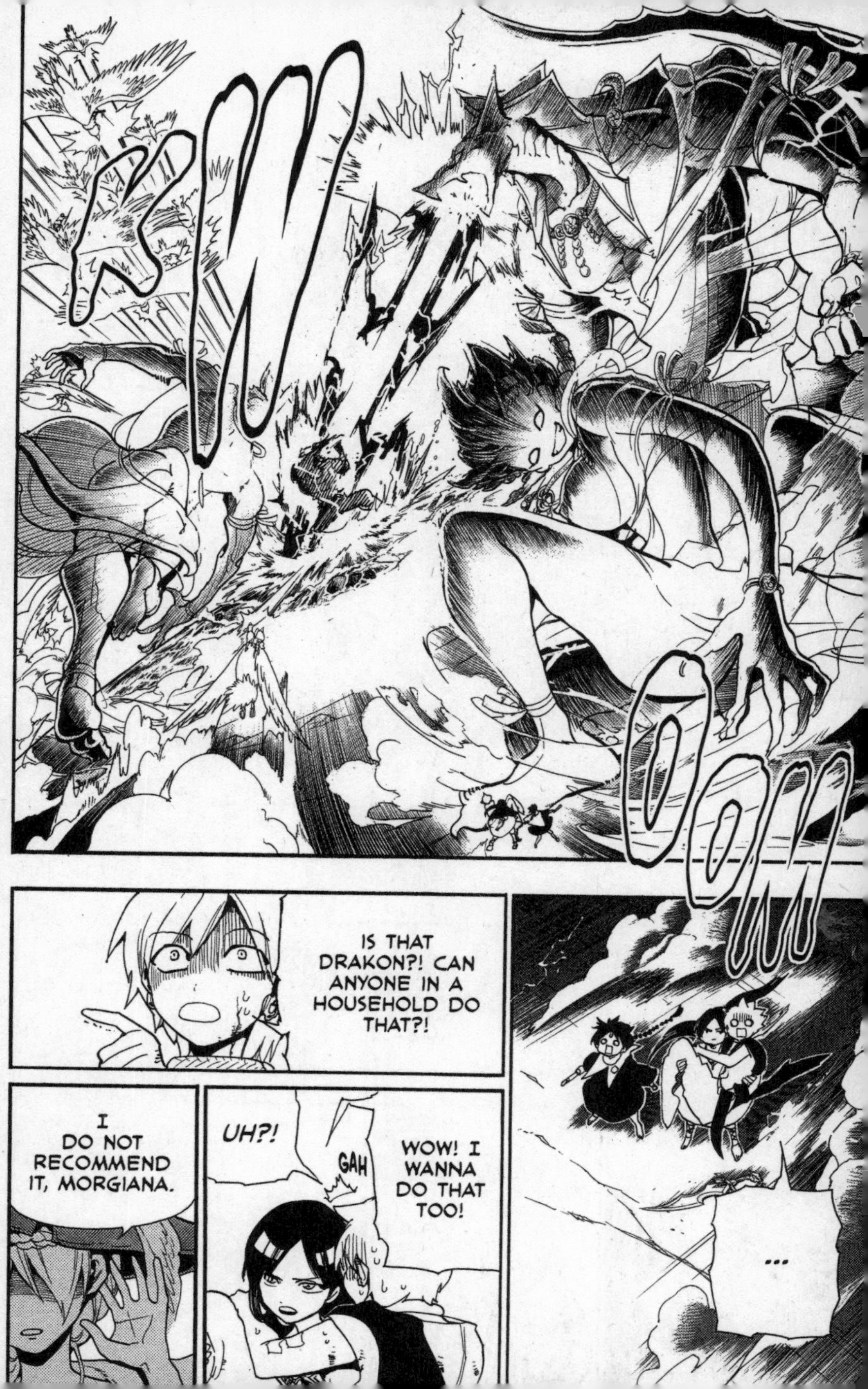

...
IS THAT DRAKON?! CAN ANYONE IN A HOUSEHOLD DO THAT?!
WOW! I WANNA DO THAT TOO!
GAH
UH?!
I DO NOT RECOMMEND IT, MORGIANA.

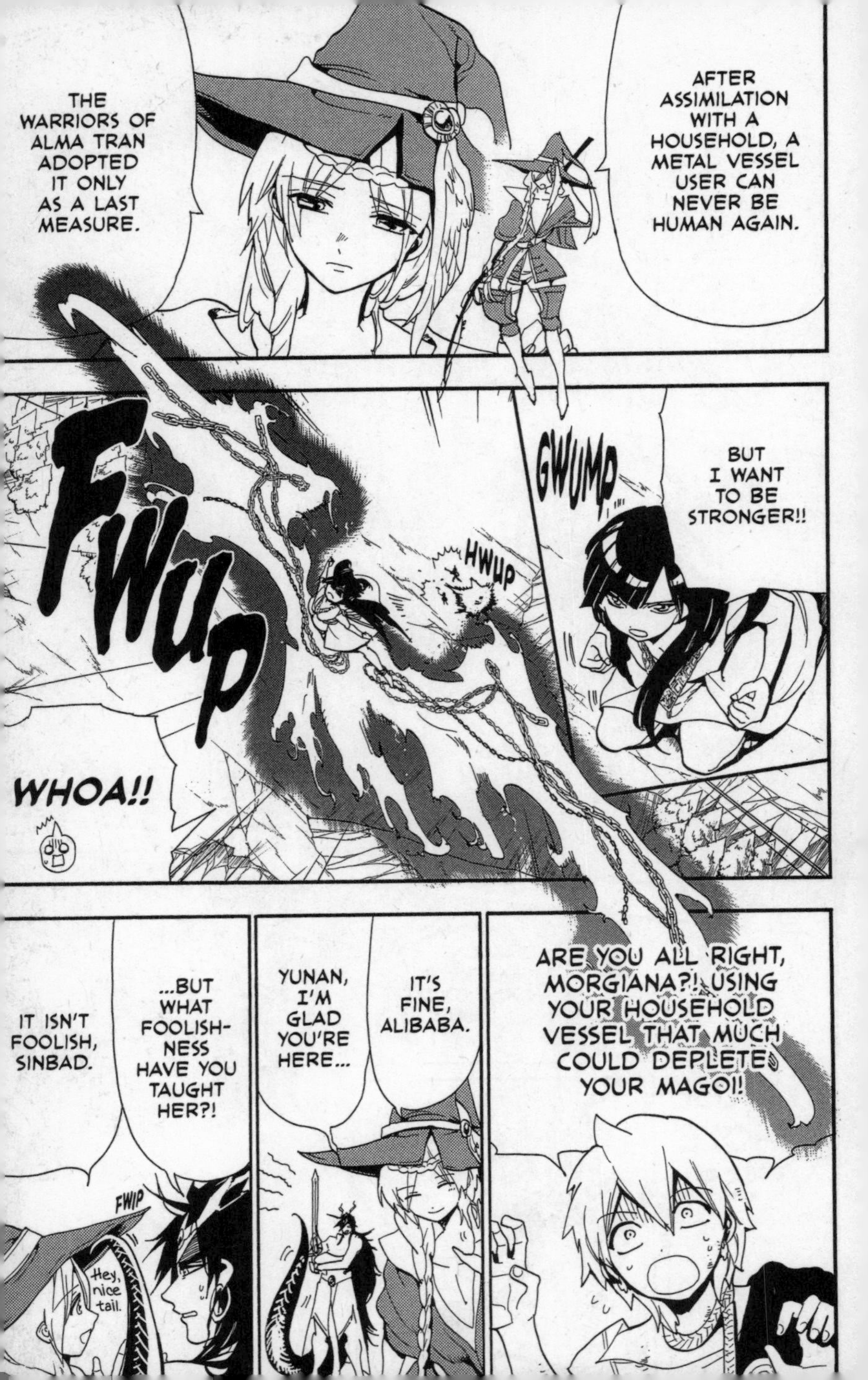
AFTER ASSIMILATION WITH A HOUSEHOLD, A METAL VESSEL USER CAN NEVER BE HUMAN AGAIN.
THE WARRIORS OF ALMA TRAN ADOPTED IT ONLY AS A LAST MEASURE.
GWUMP
BUT I WANT TO BE STRONGER!!
FWUP
HWUP
WHOA!!
ARE YOU ALL RIGHT, MORGIANA?! USING YOUR HOUSEHOLD VESSEL THAT MUCH COULD DEPLETE YOUR MAGOI!
IT'S FINE, ALIBABA.
YUNAN, I'M GLAD YOU'RE HERE...
...BUT WHAT FOOLISHNESS HAVE YOU TAUGHT HER?!
IT ISN'T FOOLISH, SINBAD.
FWIP
Hey, nice tail.

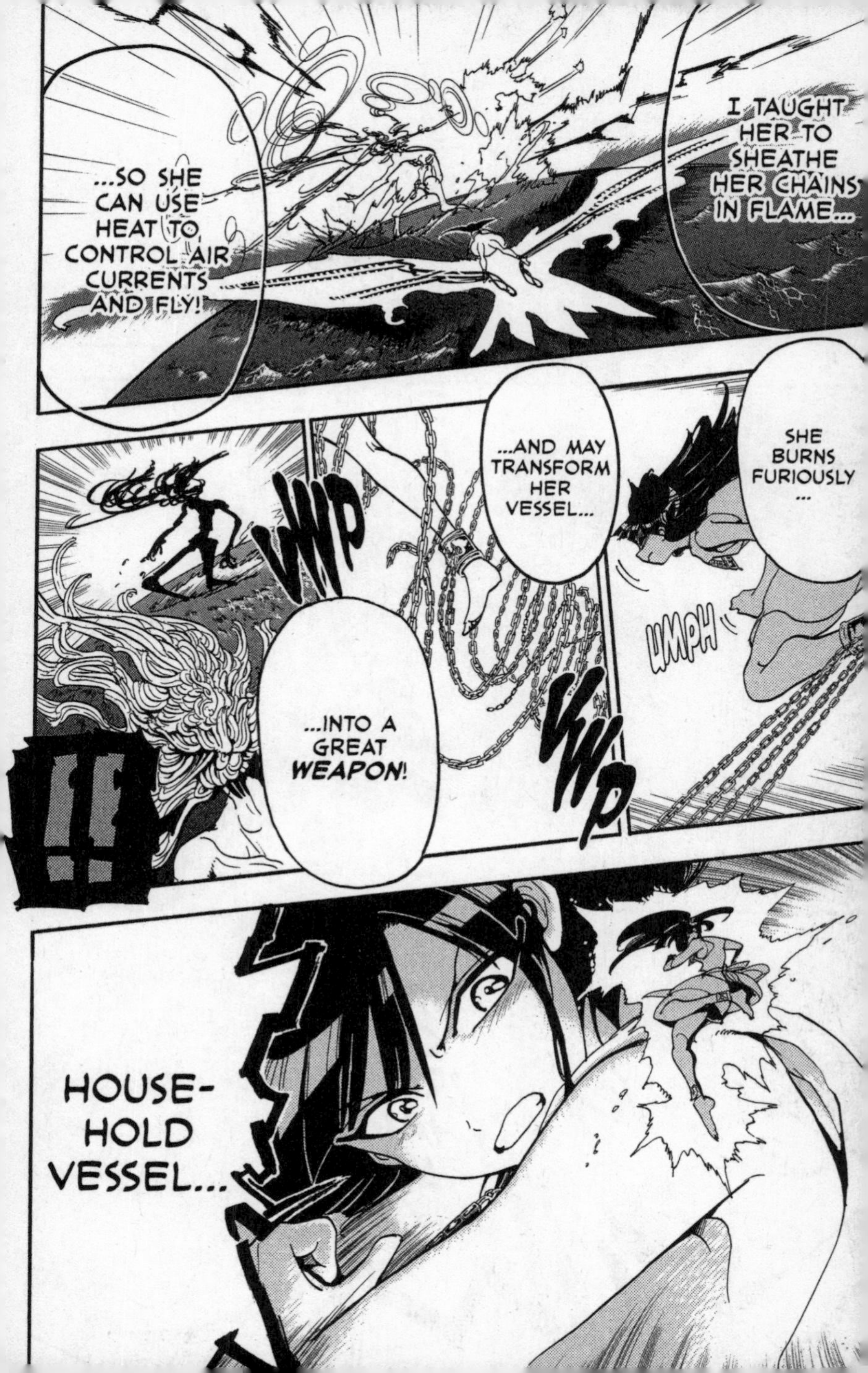
I TAUGHT HER TO SHEATHE HER CHAINS IN FLAME...
...SO SHE CAN USE HEAT TO CONTROL AIR CURRENTS AND FLY!
SHE BURNS FURIOUSLY ...
UMPH
...AND MAY TRANSFORM HER VESSEL...
WIP
WIP
...INTO A GREAT *WEAPON*!
!!
HOUSE-HOLD VESSEL...

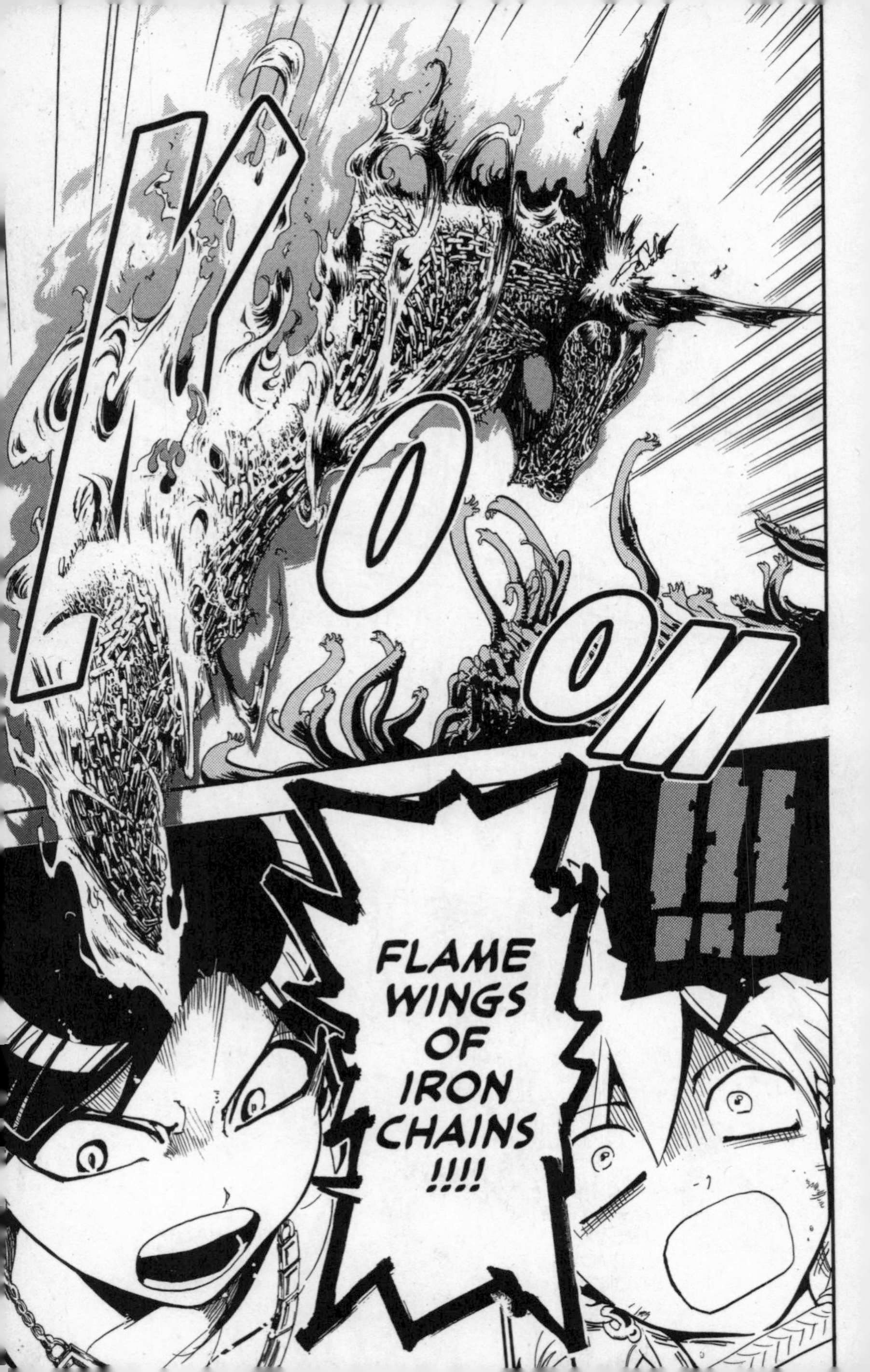
FLAME WINGS OF IRON CHAINS !!!!

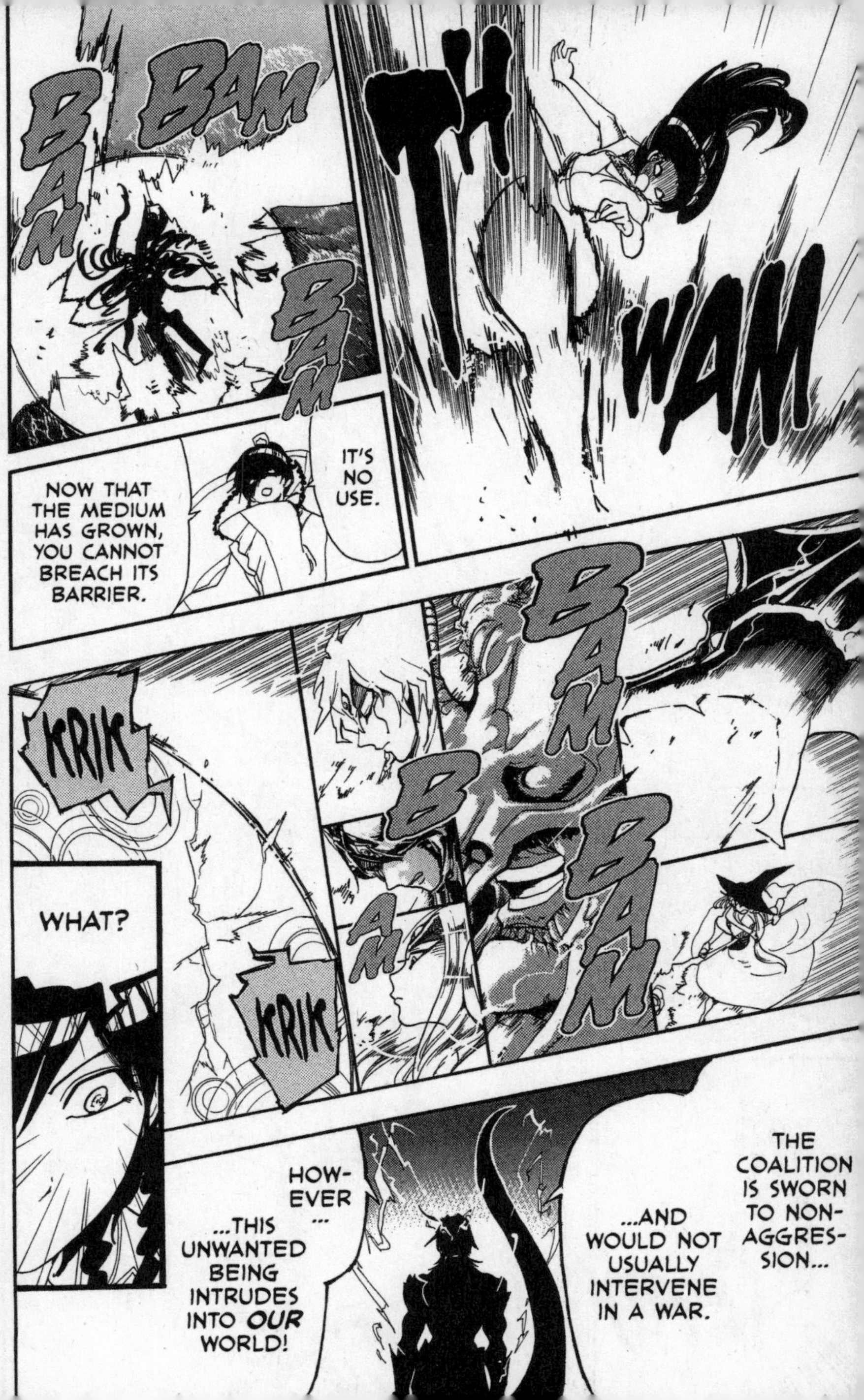

TH
WAM
BAM
BAM
BAM
IT'S NO USE.
NOW THAT THE MEDIUM HAS GROWN, YOU CANNOT BREACH ITS BARRIER.
BAM
BAM
BAM
KRIK
WHAT?
KRIK
THE COALITION IS SWORN TO NON-AGGRES-SION...
...AND WOULD NOT USUALLY INTERVENE IN A WAR.
HOW-EVER...
...THIS UNWANTED BEING INTRUDES INTO *OUR* WORLD!

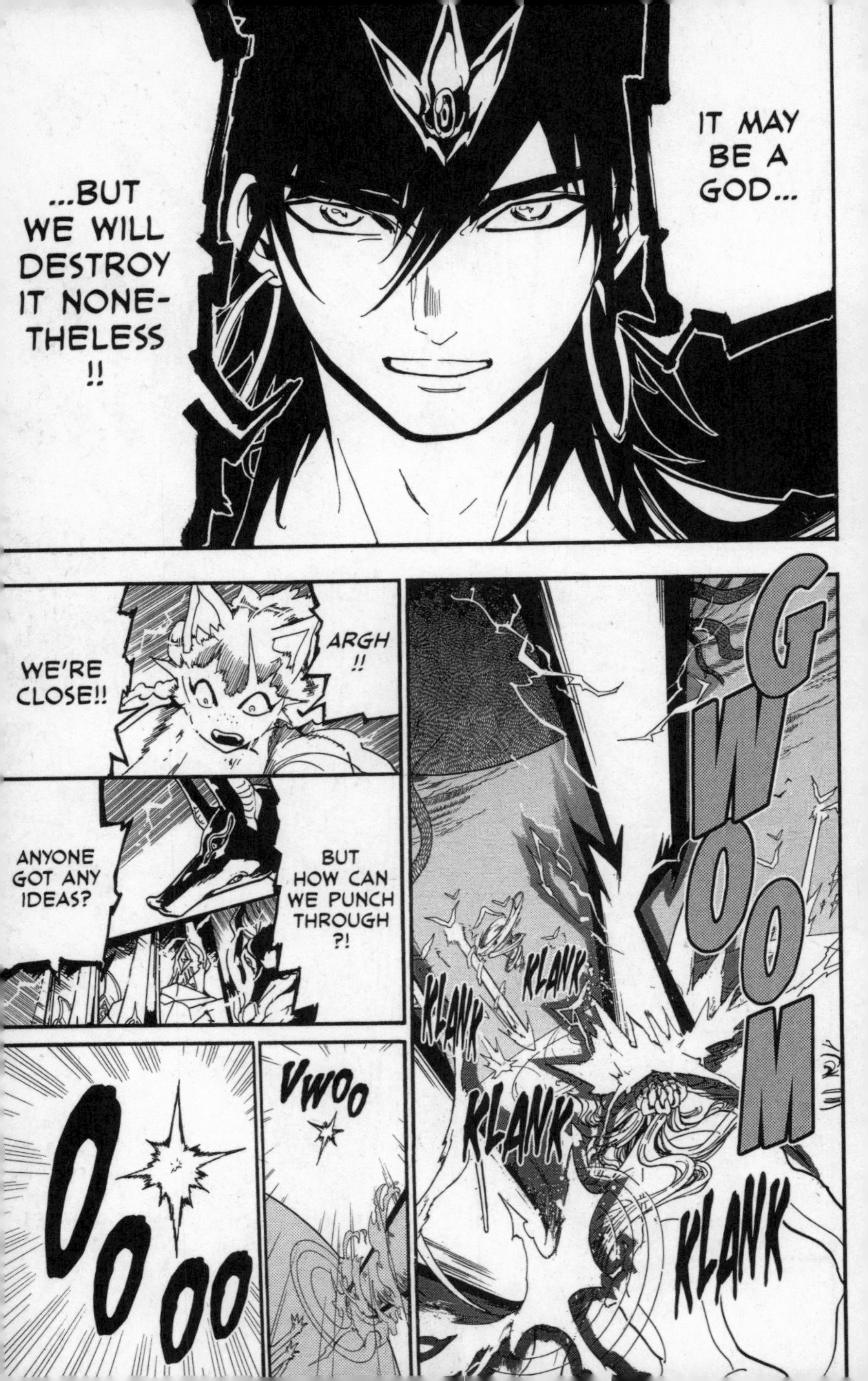
IT MAY BE A GOD...
...BUT WE WILL DESTROY IT NONE-THELESS!!
GWOOOM
KLANK
KLANK
KLANK
KLANK
KLANK
ARGH!!
WE'RE CLOSE!!
BUT HOW CAN WE PUNCH THROUGH?!
ANYONE GOT ANY IDEAS?
VWOO
OOOOO

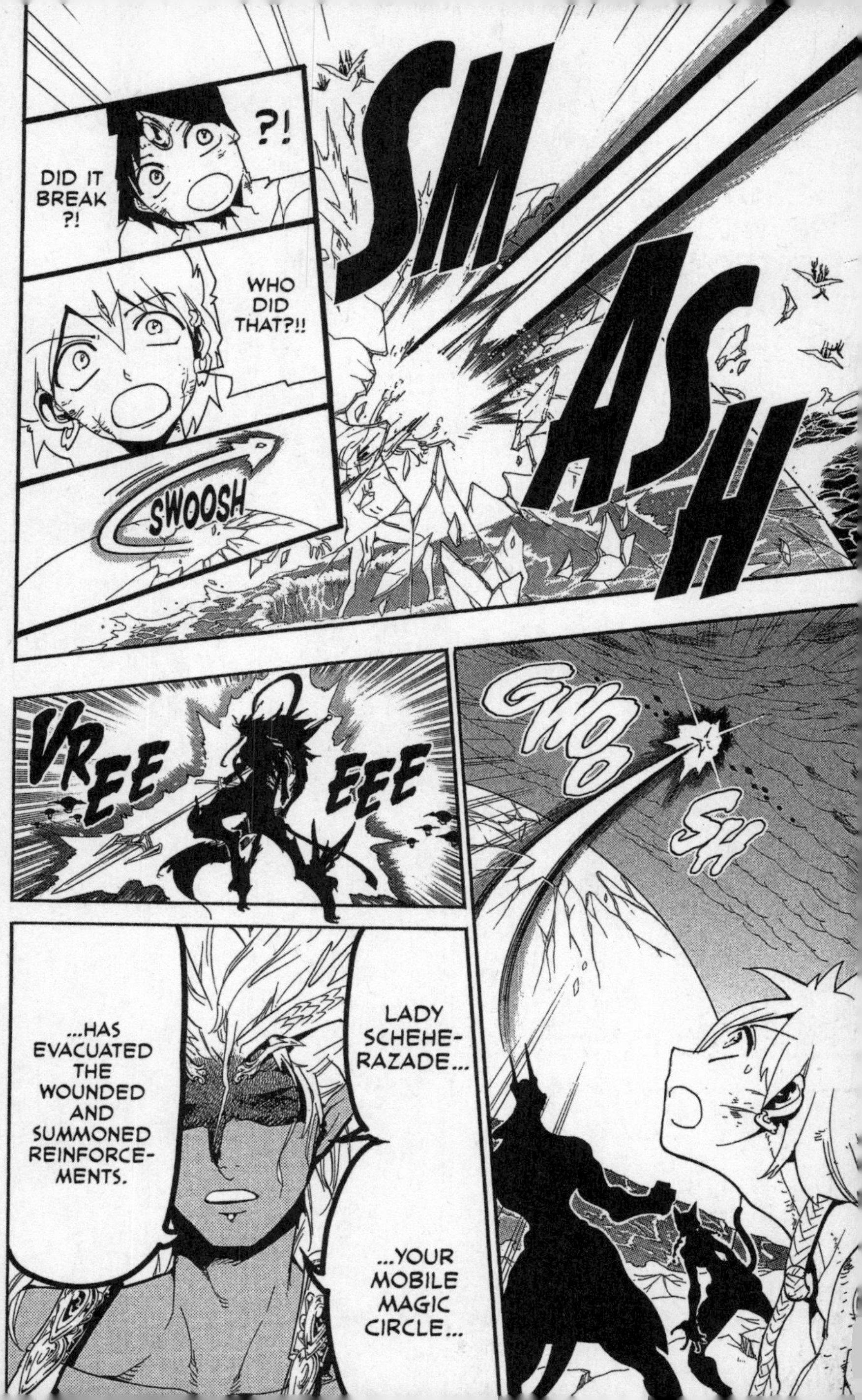
SHASH
?!
DID IT BREAK ?!
WHO DID THAT?!!
SWOOSH
GWOOSH
VREEEEEE
LADY SCHEHE-RAZADE...
...YOUR MOBILE MAGIC CIRCLE...
...HAS EVACUATED THE WOUNDED AND SUMMONED REINFORCE-MENTS.

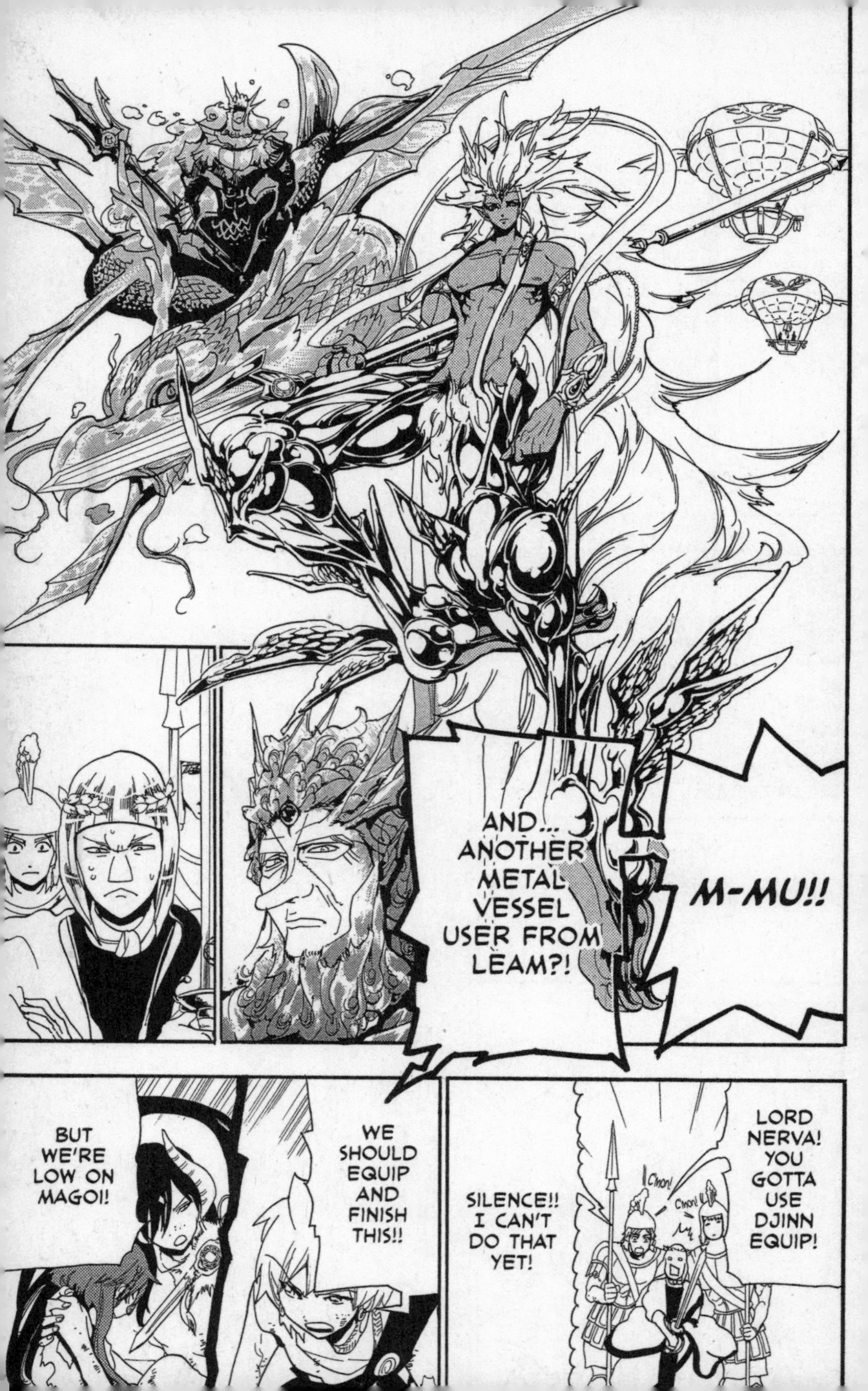
M-MU!!
AND... ANOTHER METAL VESSEL USER FROM LEAM?!
LORD NERVA! YOU GOTTA USE DJINN EQUIP!
C'mon!
C'mon!
SILENCE!! I CAN'T DO THAT YET!
WE SHOULD EQUIP AND FINISH THIS!!
BUT WE'RE LOW ON MAGOI!

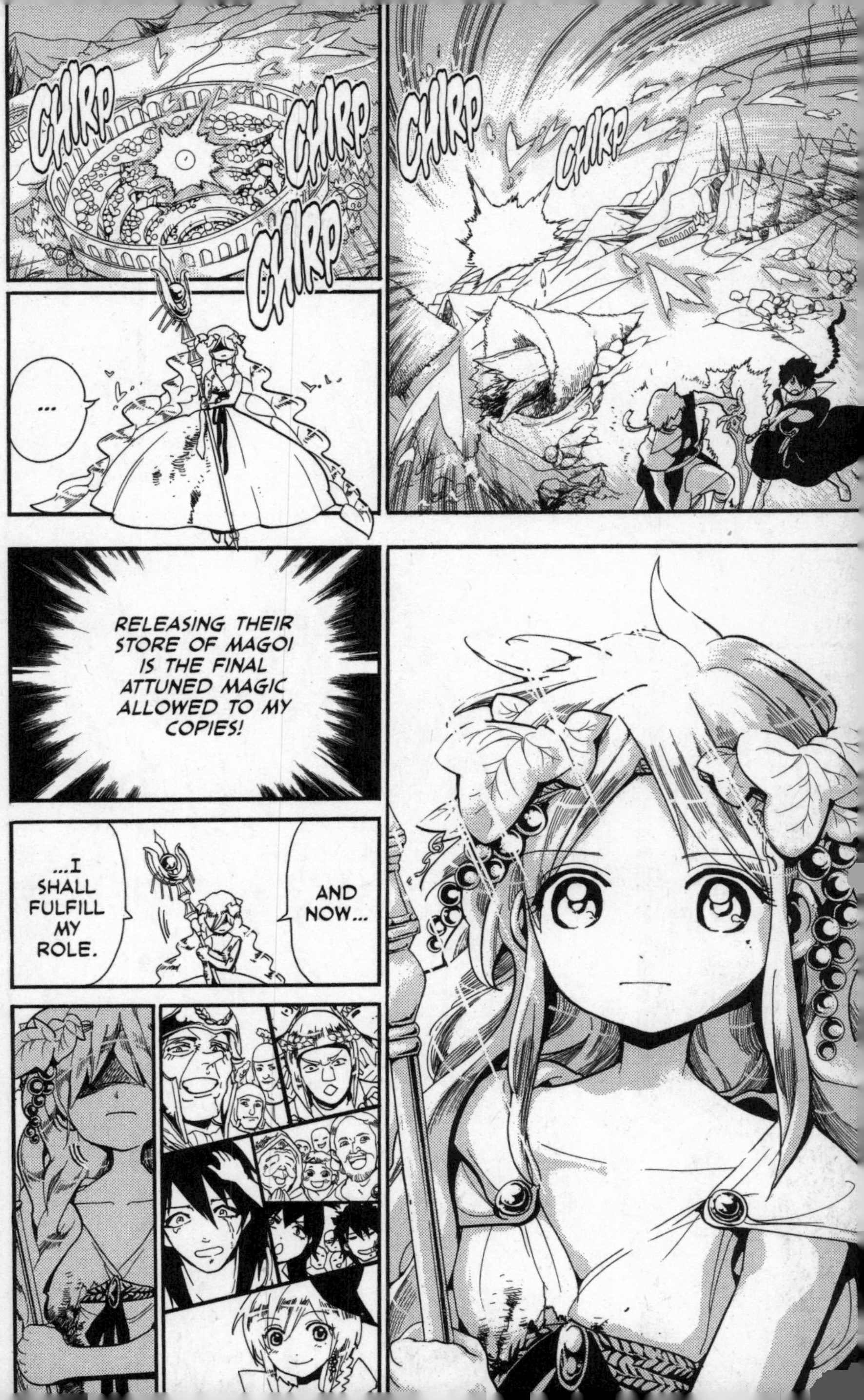

CHIRP
CHIRP
CHIRP
CHIRP
CHIRP
...
RELEASING THEIR STORE OF MAGOI IS THE FINAL ATTUNED MAGIC ALLOWED TO MY COPIES!
AND NOW...
...I SHALL FULFILL MY ROLE.

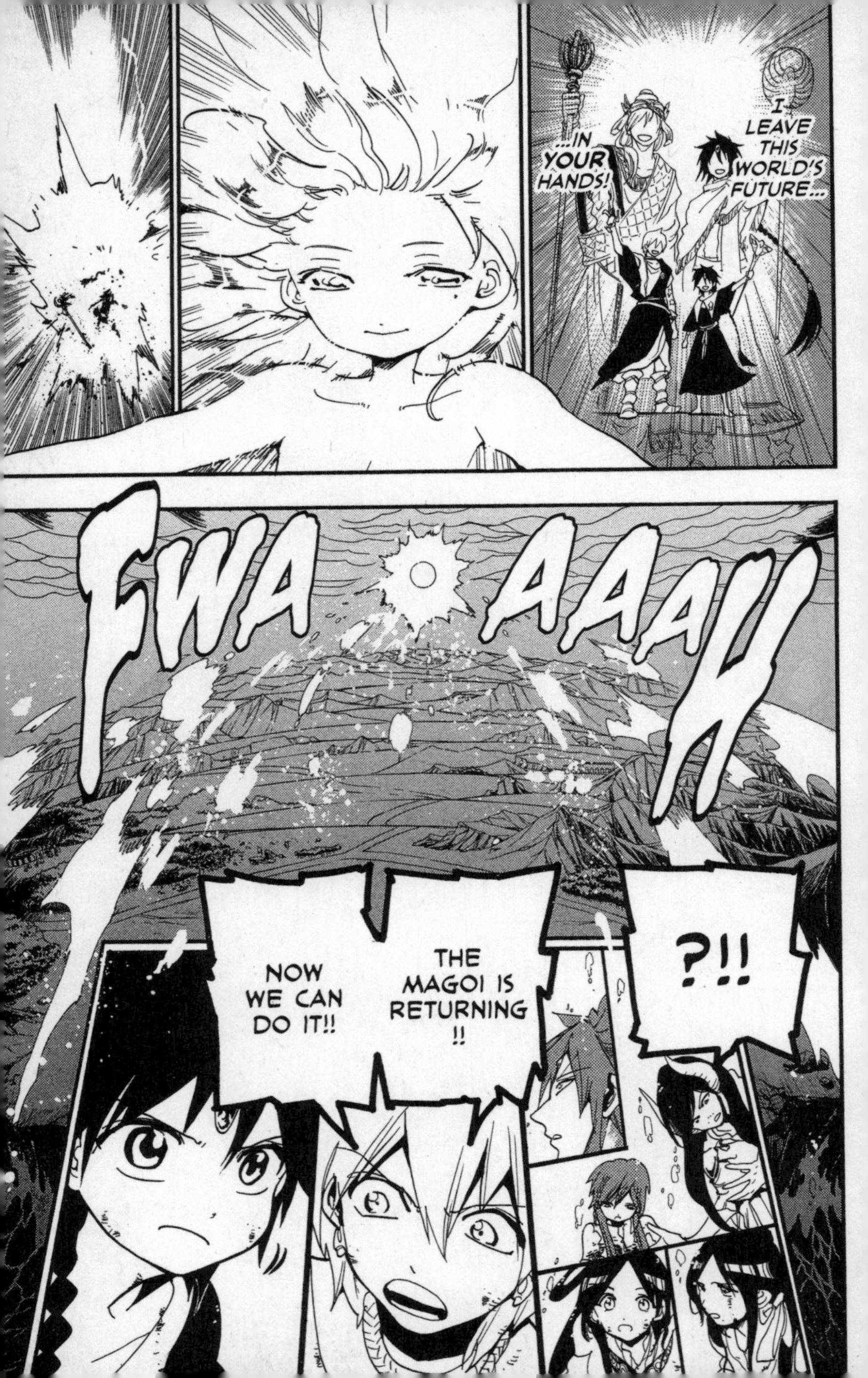
I LEAVE THIS WORLD'S FUTURE...
...IN YOUR HANDS!
FWAAAAH
?!!
THE MAGOI IS RETURNING !!
NOW WE CAN DO IT!!

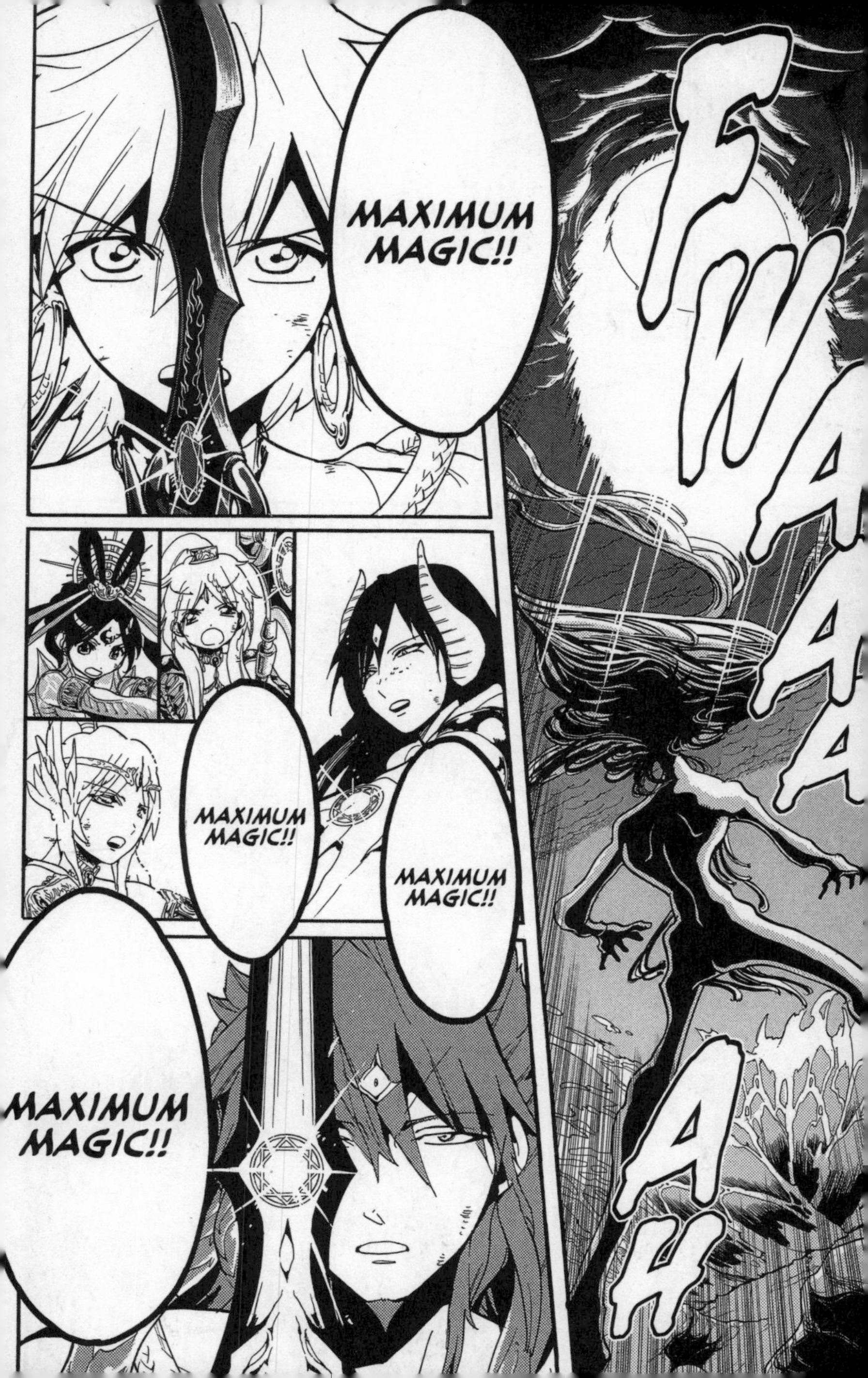
FWAAAAH
MAXIMUM MAGIC!!
MAXIMUM MAGIC!!
MAXIMUM MAGIC!!
MAXIMUM MAGIC!!

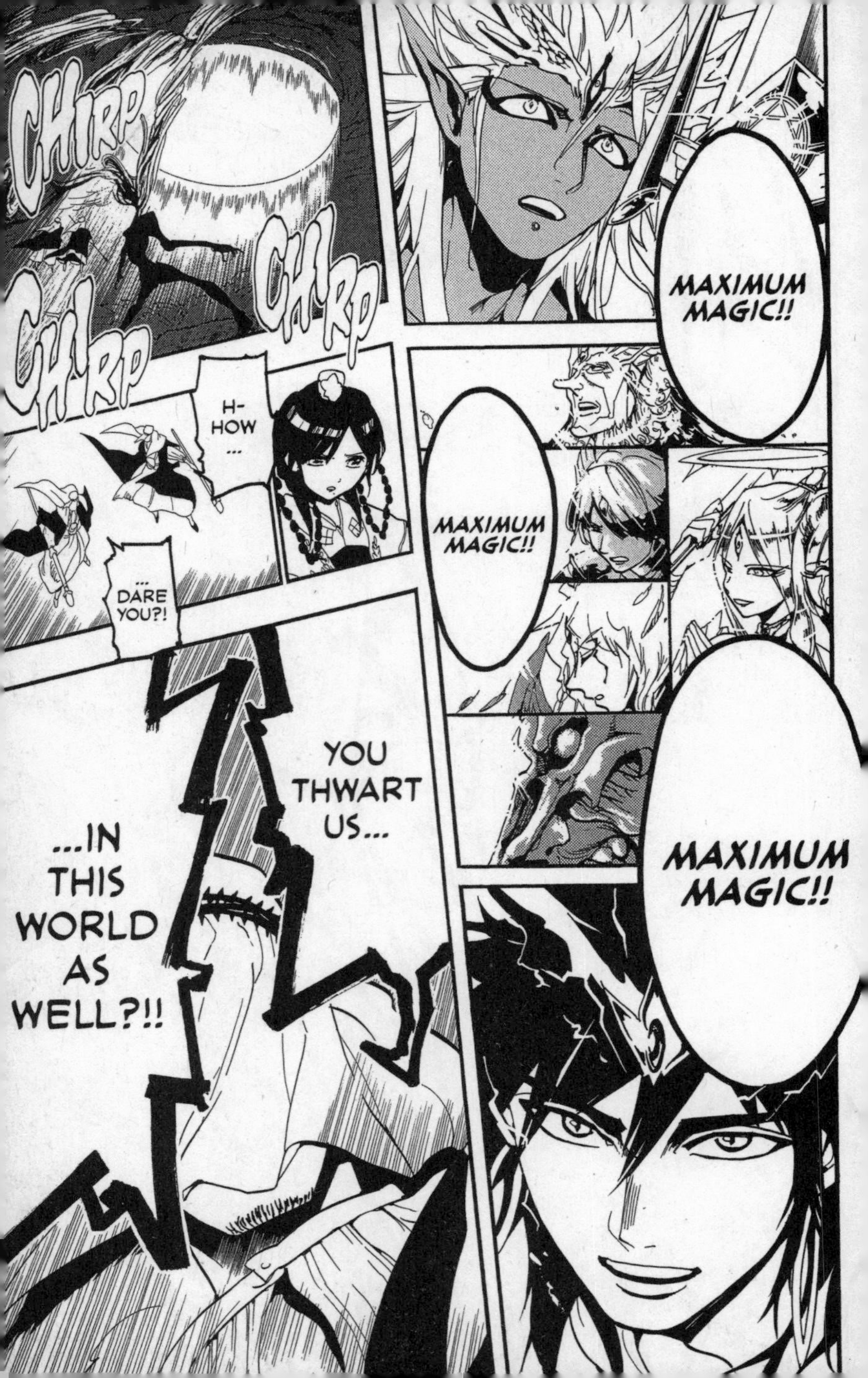
MAXIMUM MAGIC!!
CHIRP
CHIRP
CHIRP
MAXIMUM MAGIC!!
H- HOW ...
... DARE YOU?!
MAXIMUM MAGIC!!
YOU THWART US...
...IN THIS WORLD AS WELL?!!

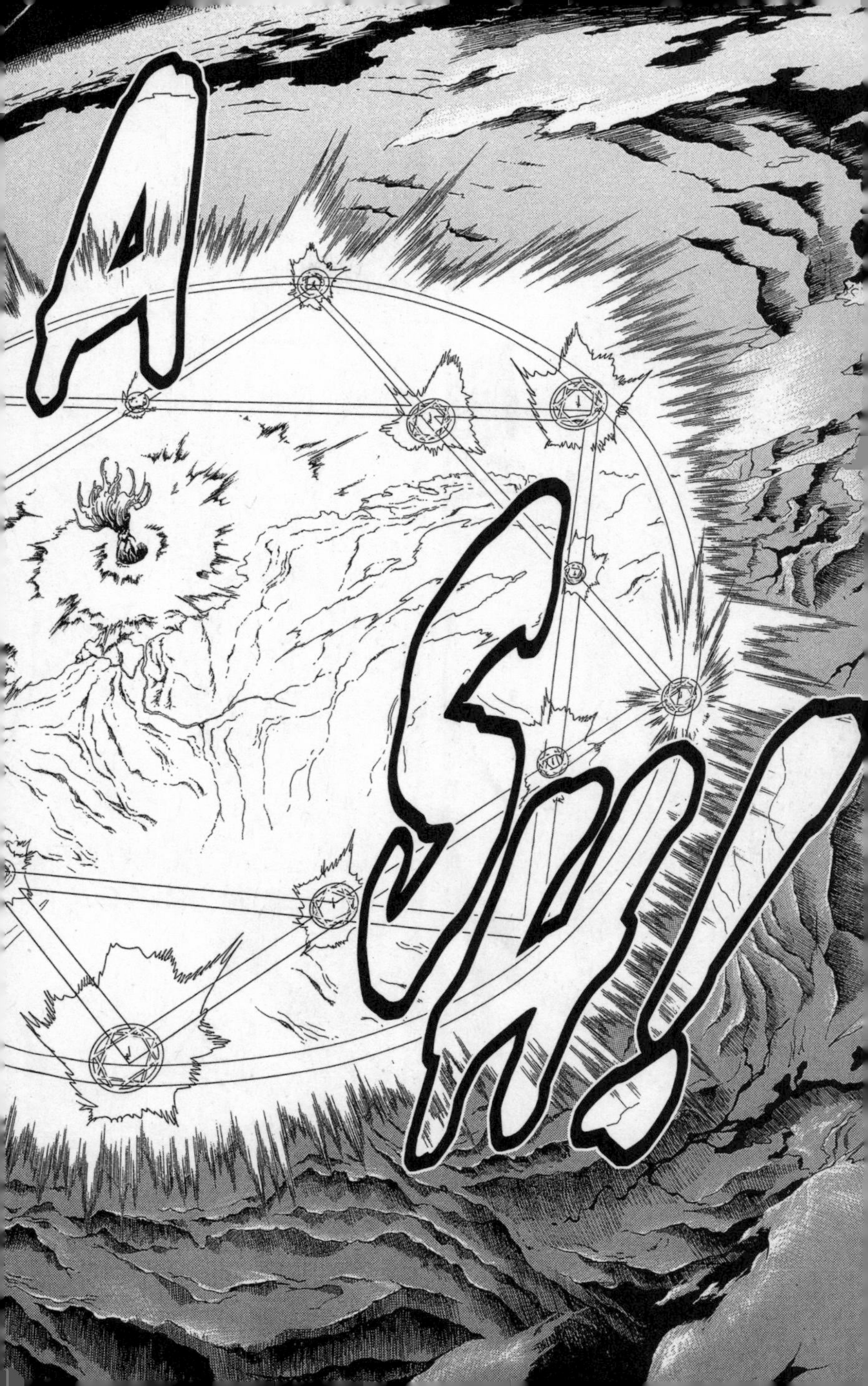

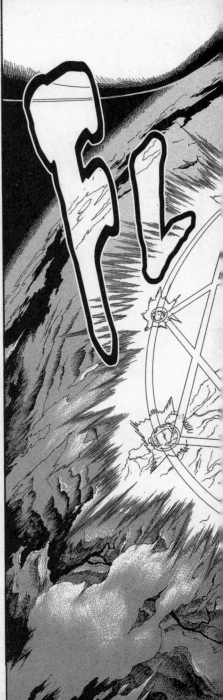

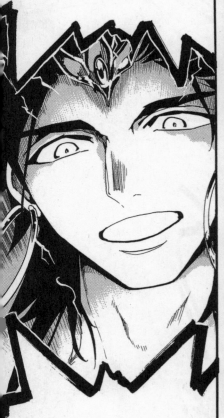

MAXIMUM MAGIC...

...LIGHTNING SWORD OF DESTRUCTION !!!

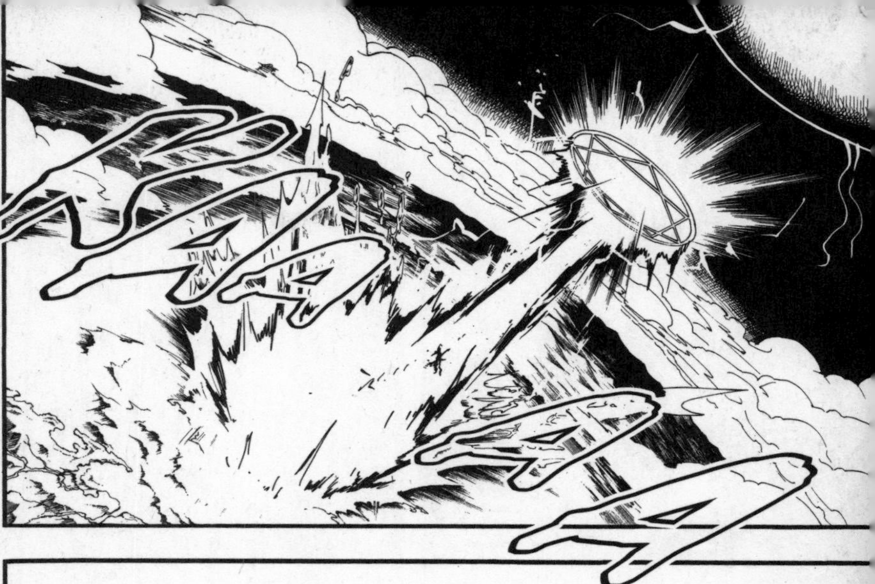

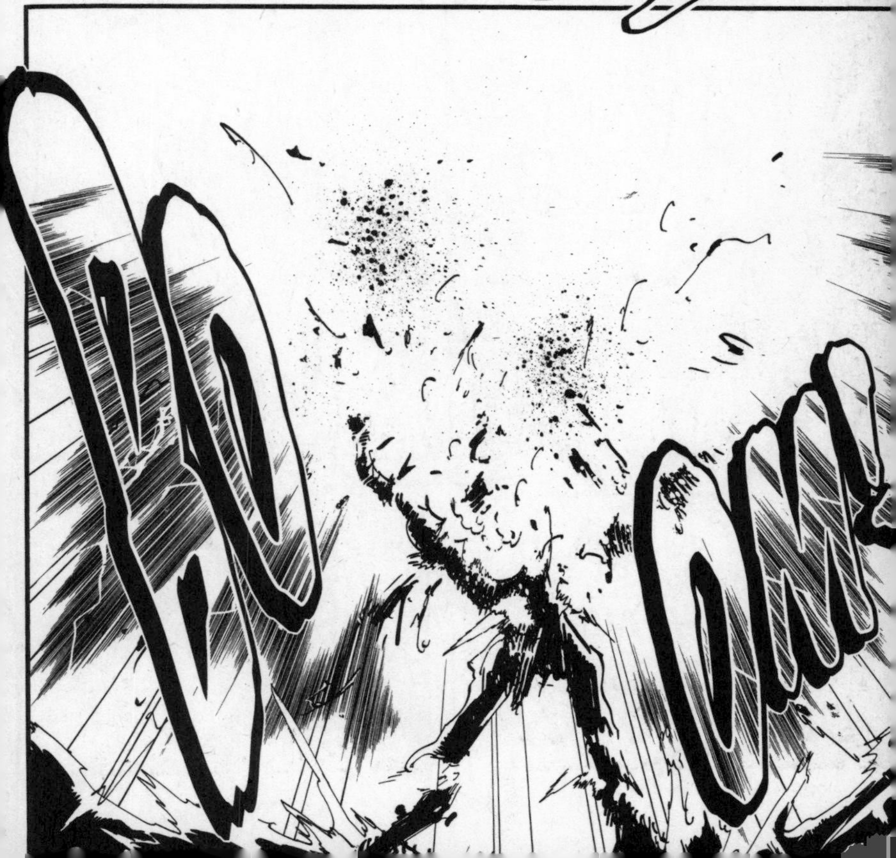
BOOM!

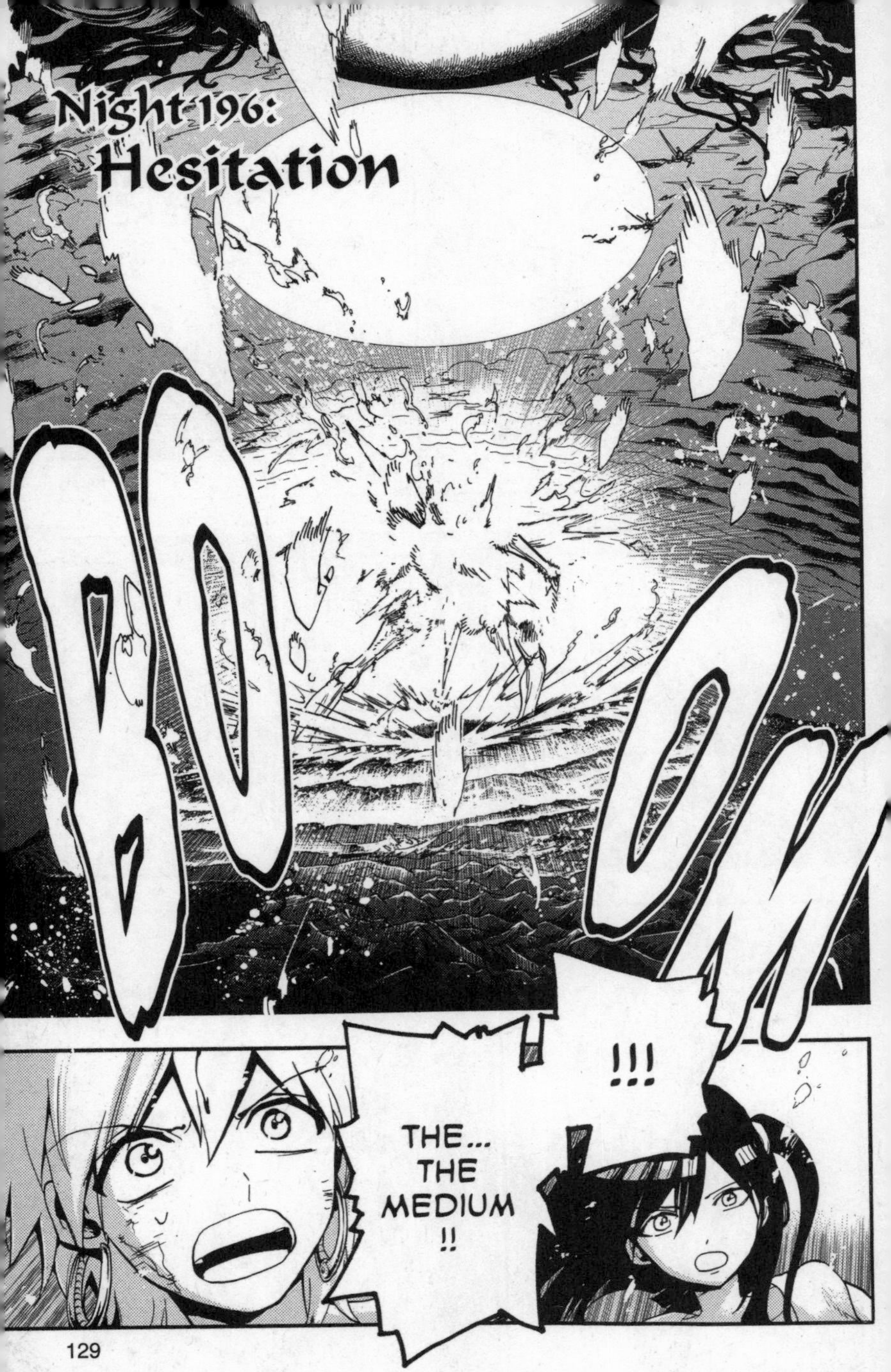
Night 196:
Hesitation
BOOM
!!!
THE... THE MEDIUM !!

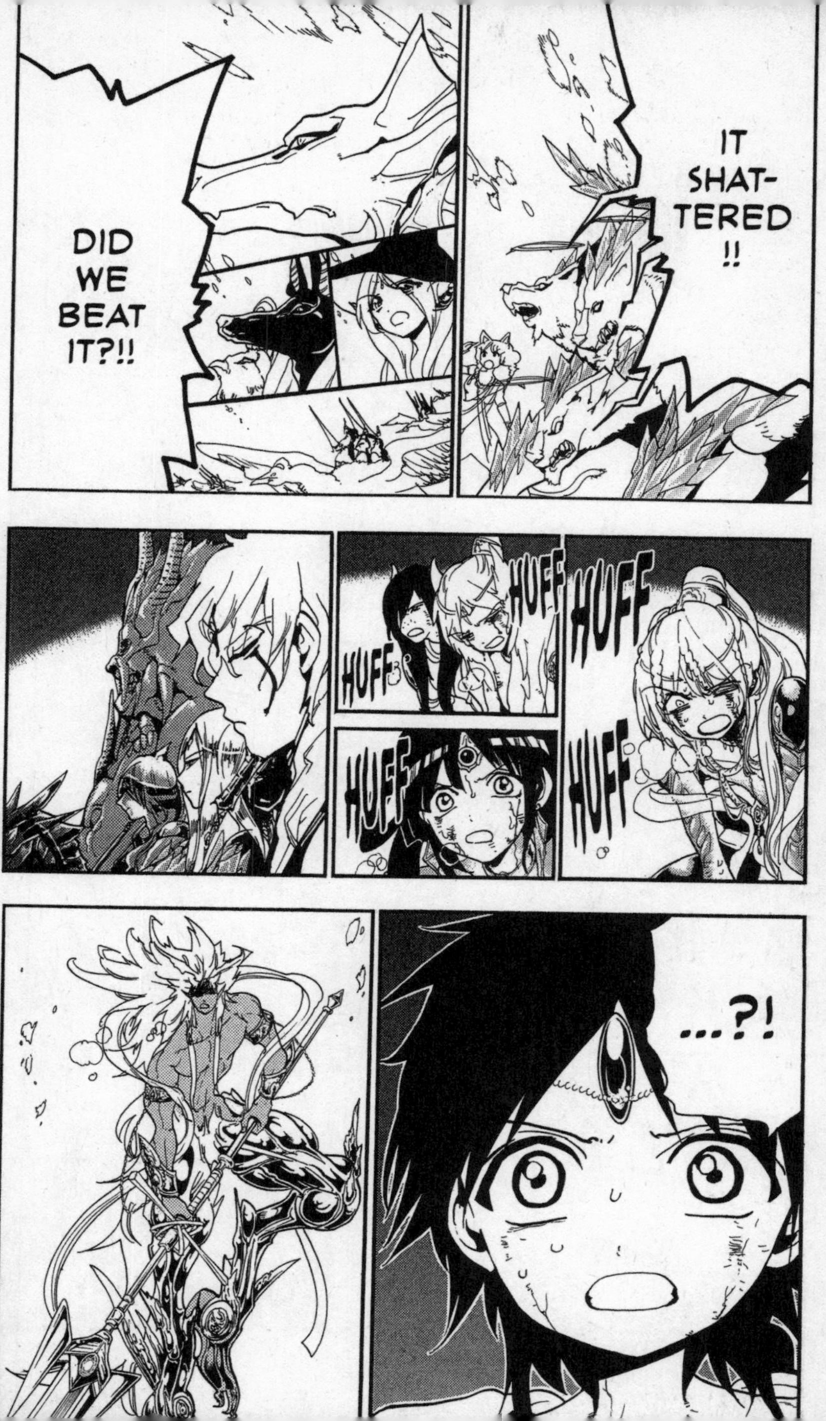
IT SHAT-TERED !!
DID WE BEAT IT?!!
HUFF
HUFF
HUFF
HUFF
HUFF
...?!

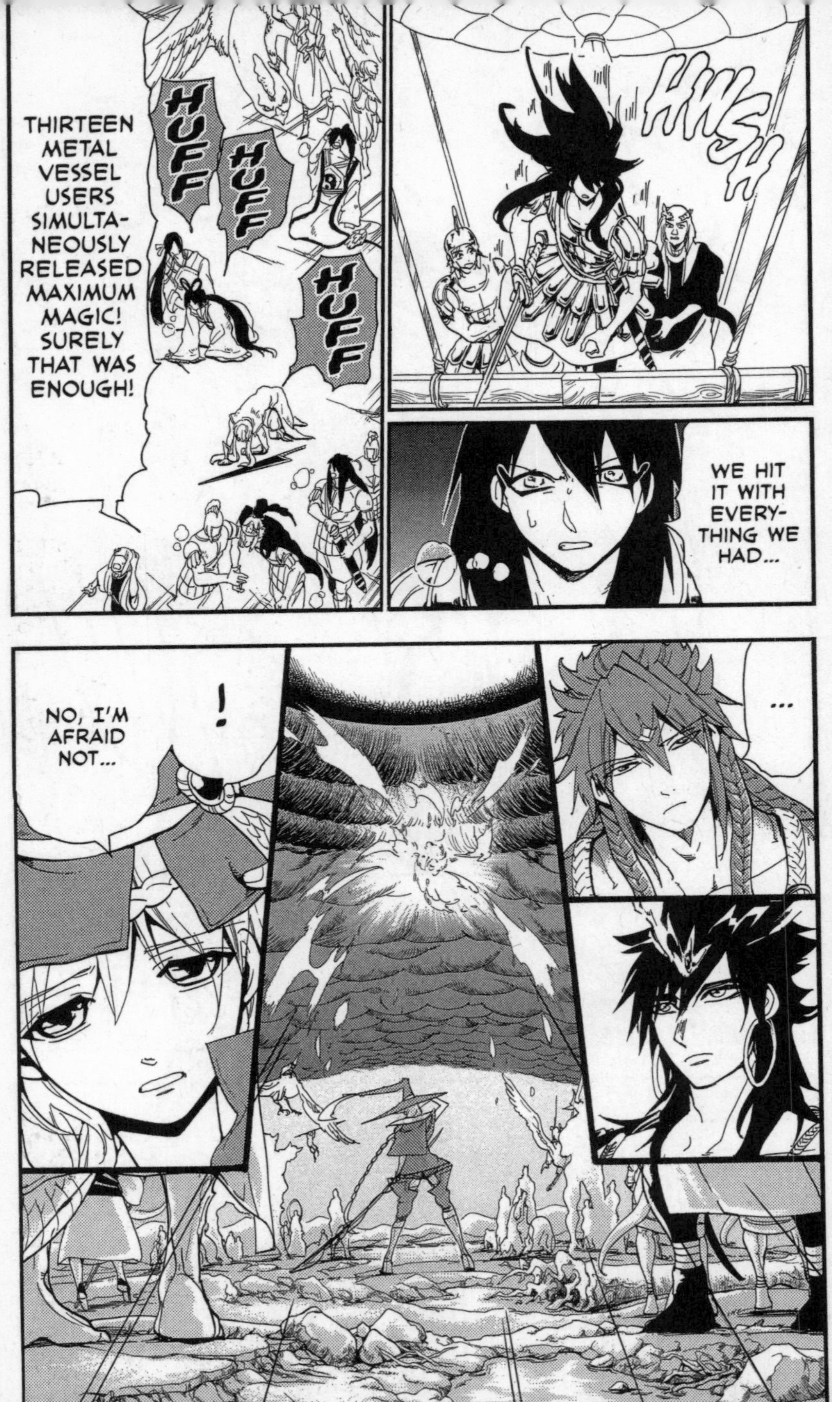
HWSH
WE HIT IT WITH EVERYTHING WE HAD...
HUFF
HUFF
HUFF
THIRTEEN METAL VESSEL USERS SIMULTANEOUSLY RELEASED MAXIMUM MAGIC! SURELY THAT WAS ENOUGH!
...
!
NO, I'M AFRAID NOT...

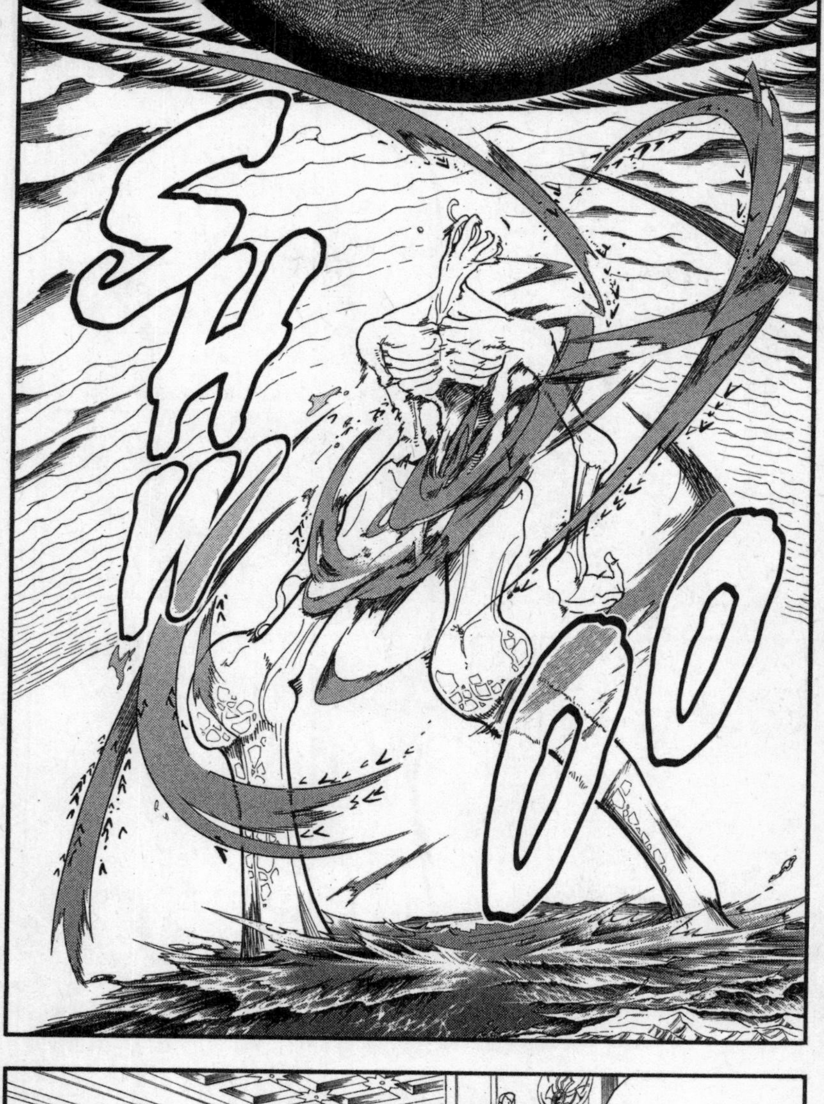
SHWOO

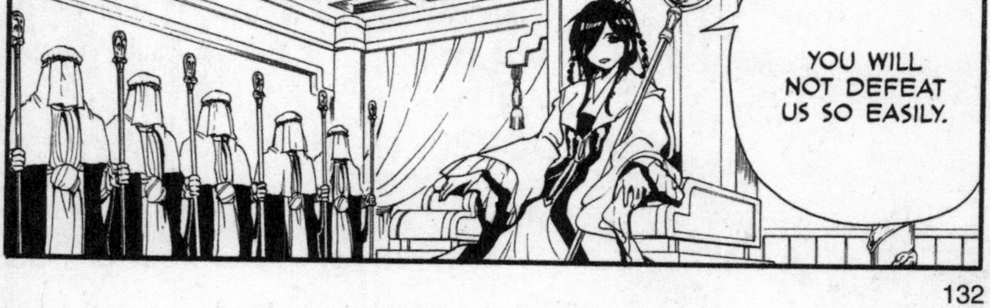
YOU WILL NOT DEFEAT US SO EASILY.

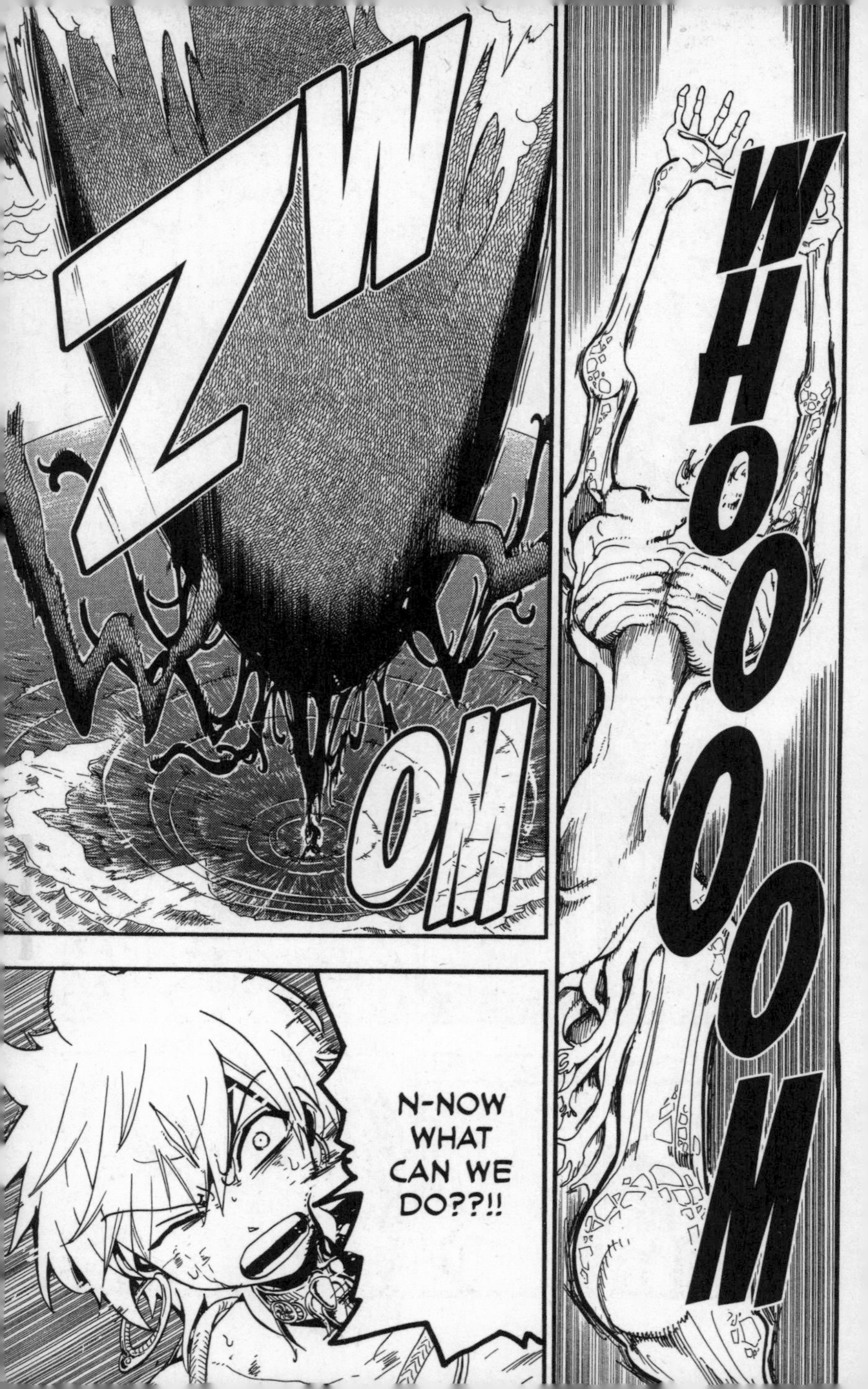
WHOOOOM
ZWOM
N-NOW WHAT CAN WE DO??!!

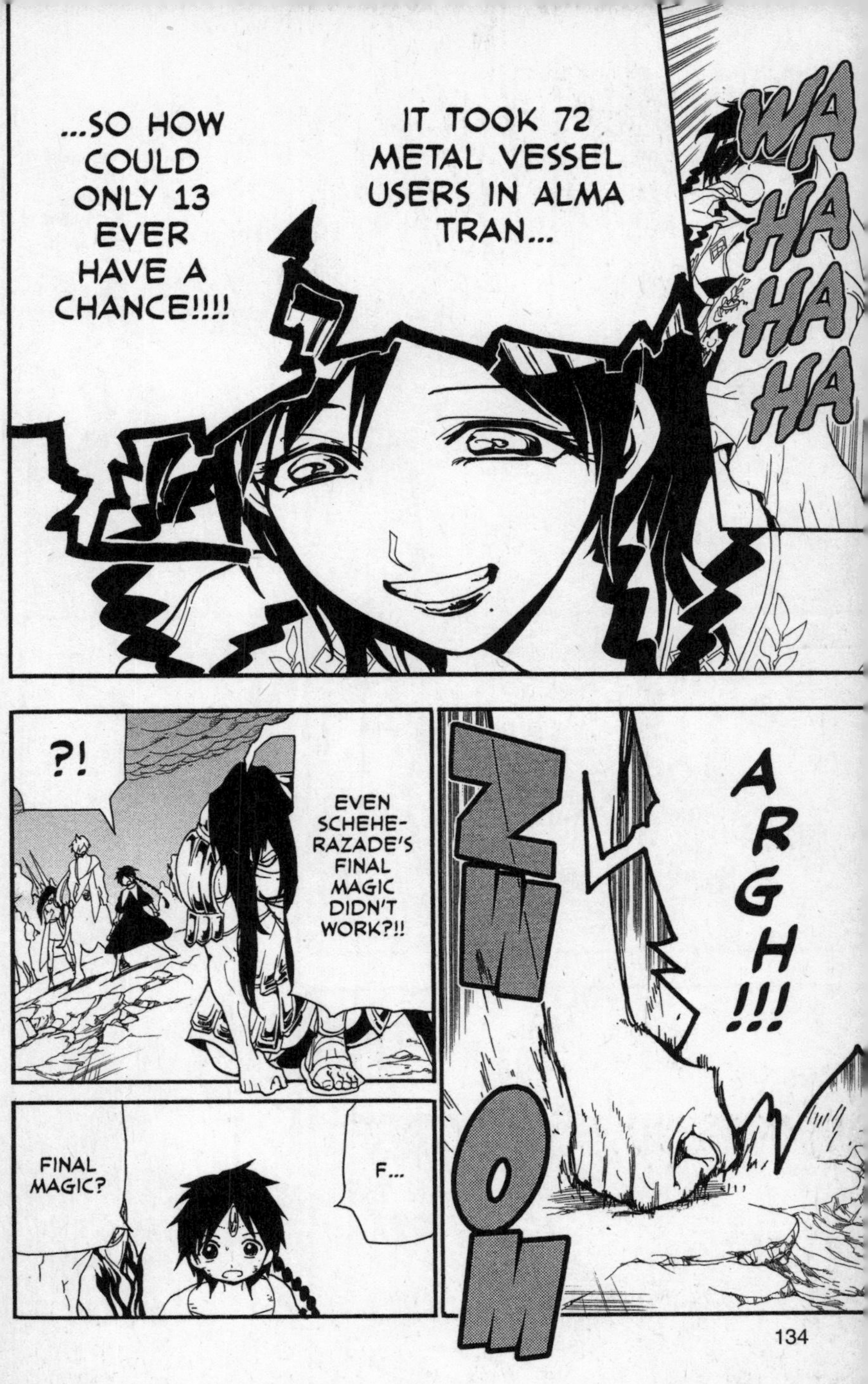
WAHAHAHAHA
IT TOOK 72 METAL VESSEL USERS IN ALMA TRAN...
...SO HOW COULD ONLY 13 EVER HAVE A CHANCE!!!!
ARGH!!!
EVEN SCHEHERAZADE'S FINAL MAGIC DIDN'T WORK?!!
?!
F...
FINAL MAGIC?

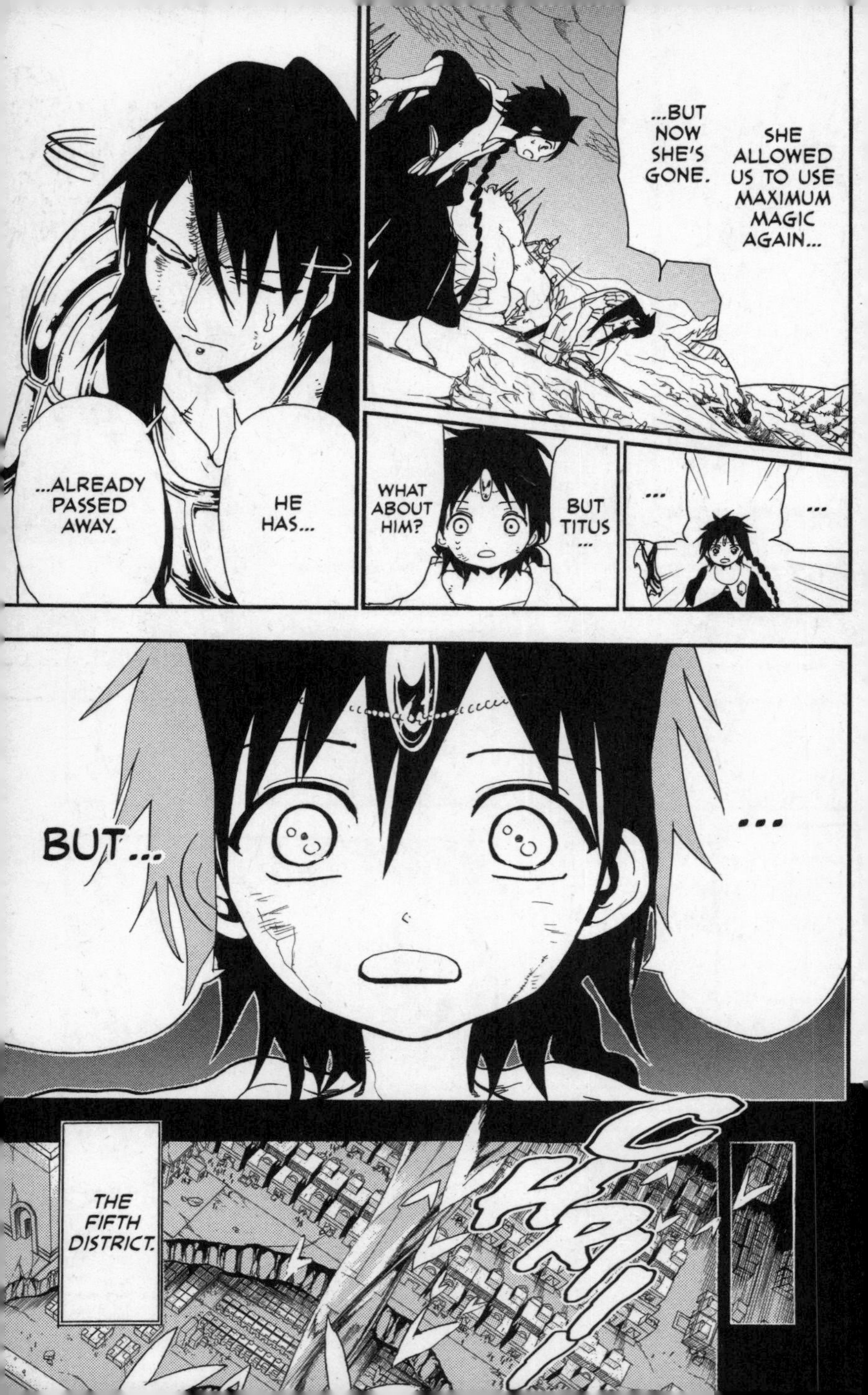
SHE ALLOWED US TO USE MAXIMUM MAGIC AGAIN...
...BUT NOW SHE'S GONE.
...
...
BUT TITUS ...
WHAT ABOUT HIM?
HE HAS...
...ALREADY PASSED AWAY.
...
BUT...
THE FIFTH DISTRICT.

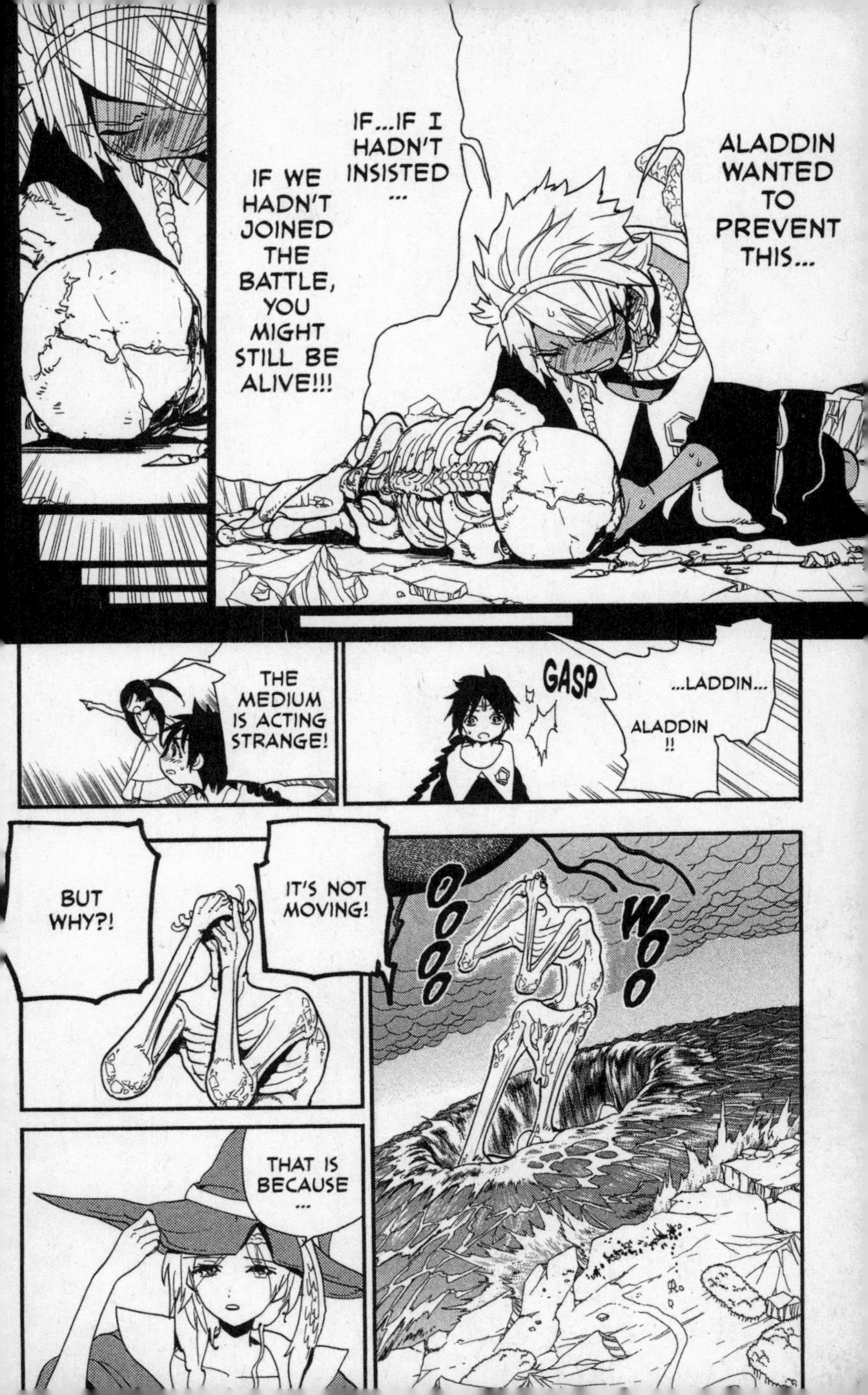
ALADDIN WANTED TO PREVENT THIS...
IF...IF I HADN'T INSISTED...
IF WE HADN'T JOINED THE BATTLE, YOU MIGHT STILL BE ALIVE!!!
...LADDIN...
GASP
ALADDIN !!
THE MEDIUM IS ACTING STRANGE!
WOOOOOOO
IT'S NOT MOVING!
BUT WHY?!
THAT IS BECAUSE...

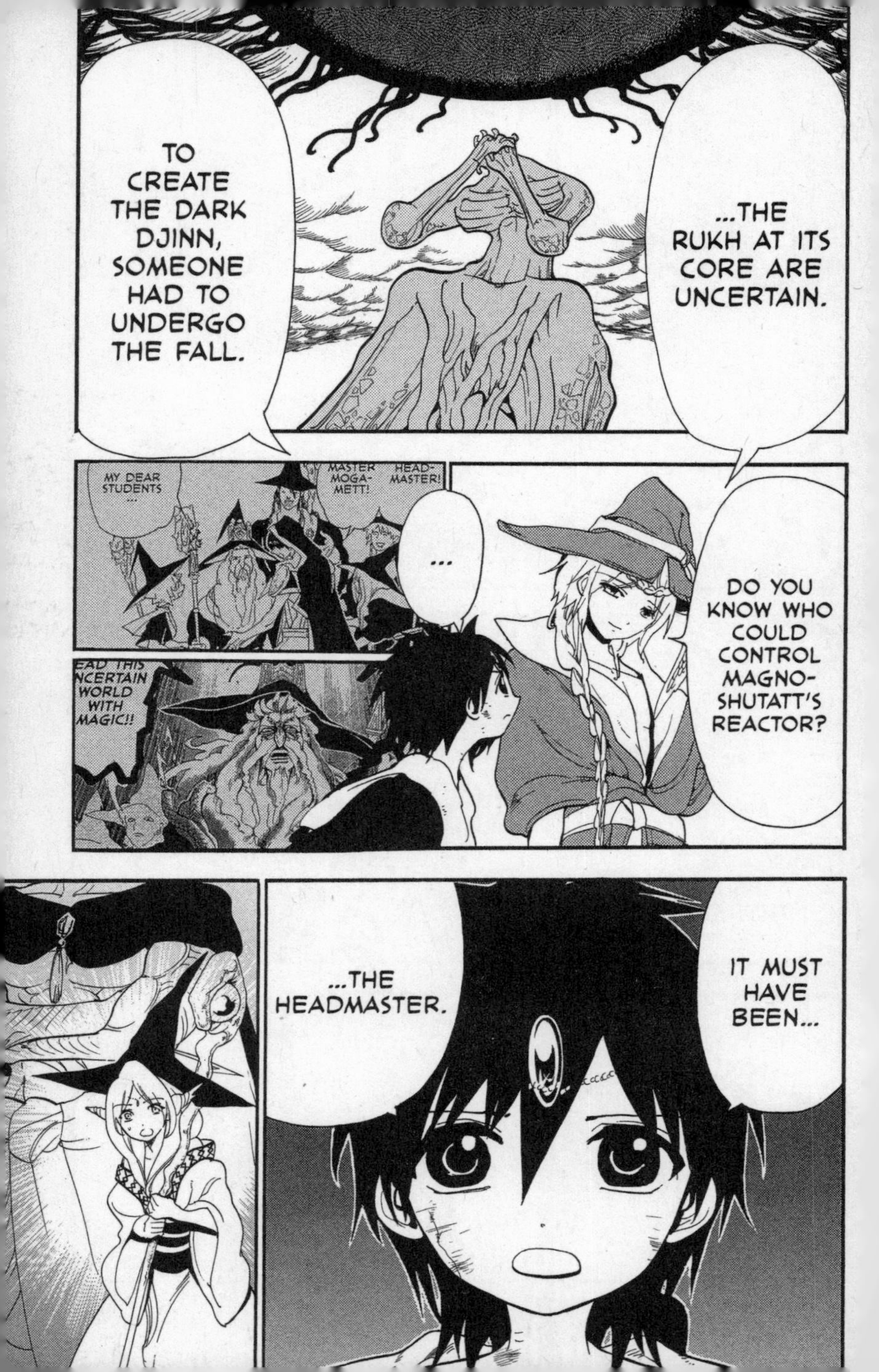
...THE RUKH AT ITS CORE ARE UNCERTAIN.
TO CREATE THE DARK DJINN, SOMEONE HAD TO UNDERGO THE FALL.
DO YOU KNOW WHO COULD CONTROL MAGNO-SHUTATT'S REACTOR?
...
HEAD-MASTER!
MASTER MOGA-METT!
MY DEAR STUDENTS ...
EAD THIS NCERTAIN WORLD WITH MAGIC!!
IT MUST HAVE BEEN...
...THE HEADMASTER.

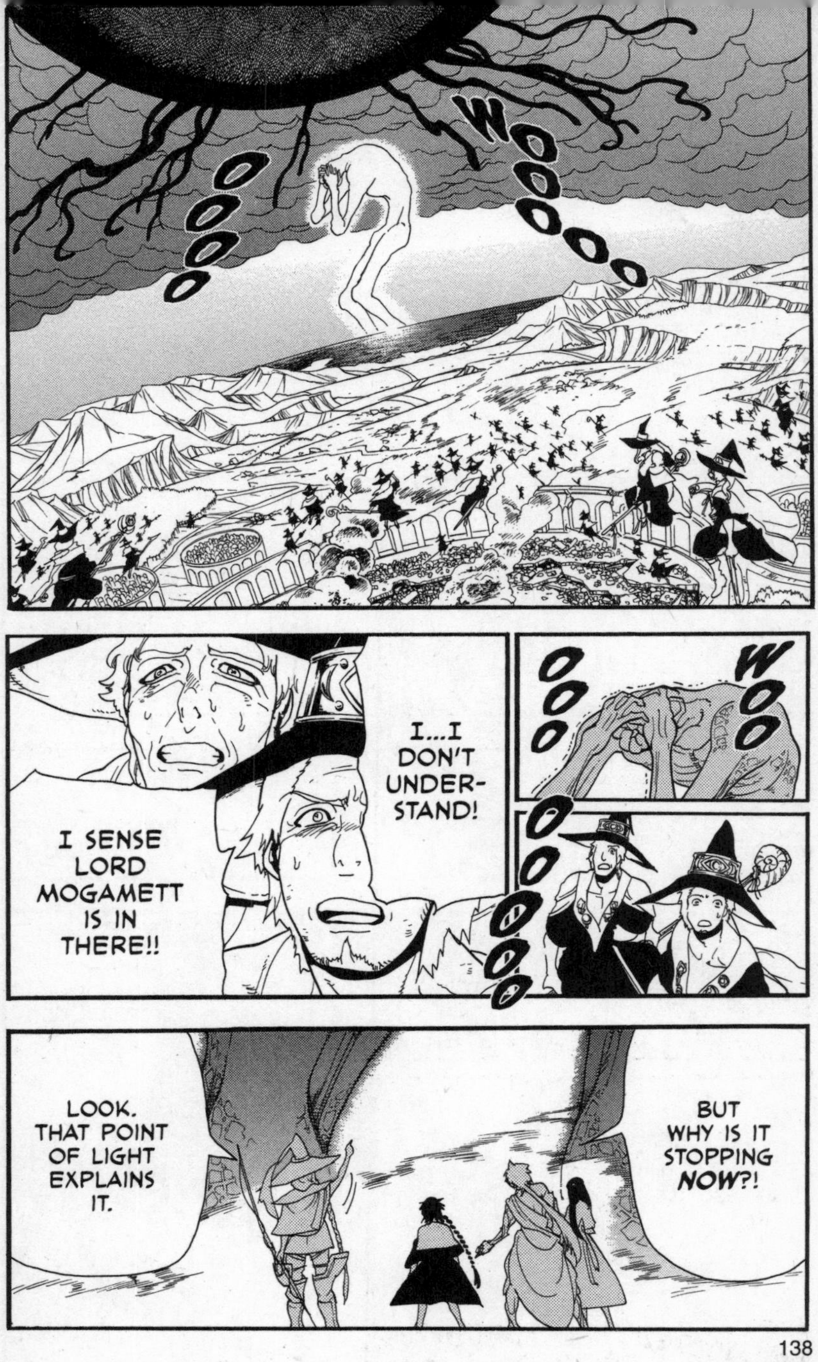
WOOOOOOOO
OOOOO
WOOOO
OOO
OOOOOO
I...I DON'T UNDER-STAND!
I SENSE LORD MOGAMETT IS IN THERE!!
BUT WHY IS IT STOPPING *NOW*?!
LOOK. THAT POINT OF LIGHT EXPLAINS IT.

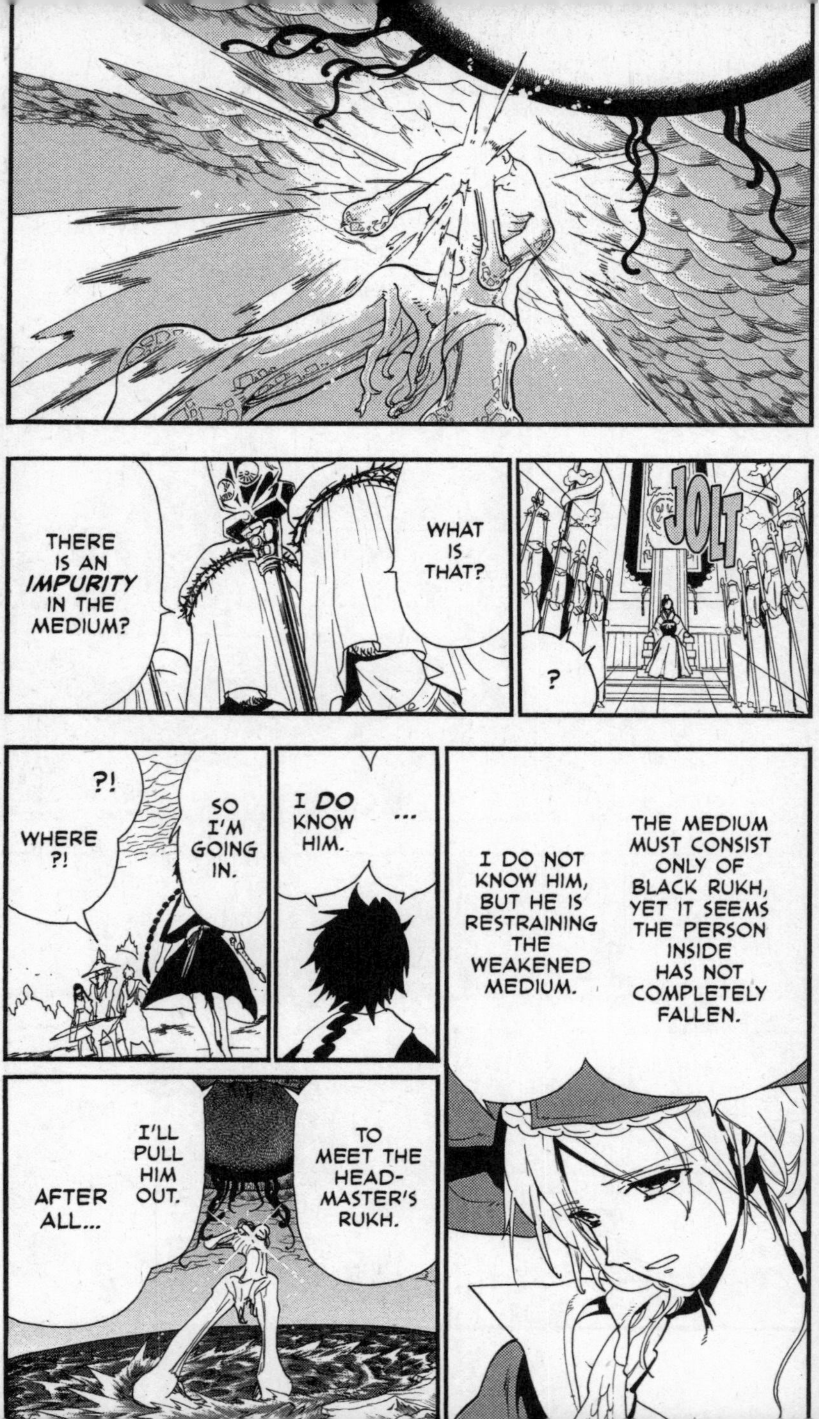
JOLT
?
WHAT IS THAT?
THERE IS AN *IMPURITY* IN THE MEDIUM?
THE MEDIUM MUST CONSIST ONLY OF BLACK RUKH, YET IT SEEMS THE PERSON INSIDE HAS NOT COMPLETELY FALLEN.
I DO NOT KNOW HIM, BUT HE IS RESTRAINING THE WEAKENED MEDIUM.
...
I *DO* KNOW HIM.
SO I'M GOING IN.
?!
WHERE ?!
TO MEET THE HEAD-MASTER'S RUKH.
I'LL PULL HIM OUT.
AFTER ALL...

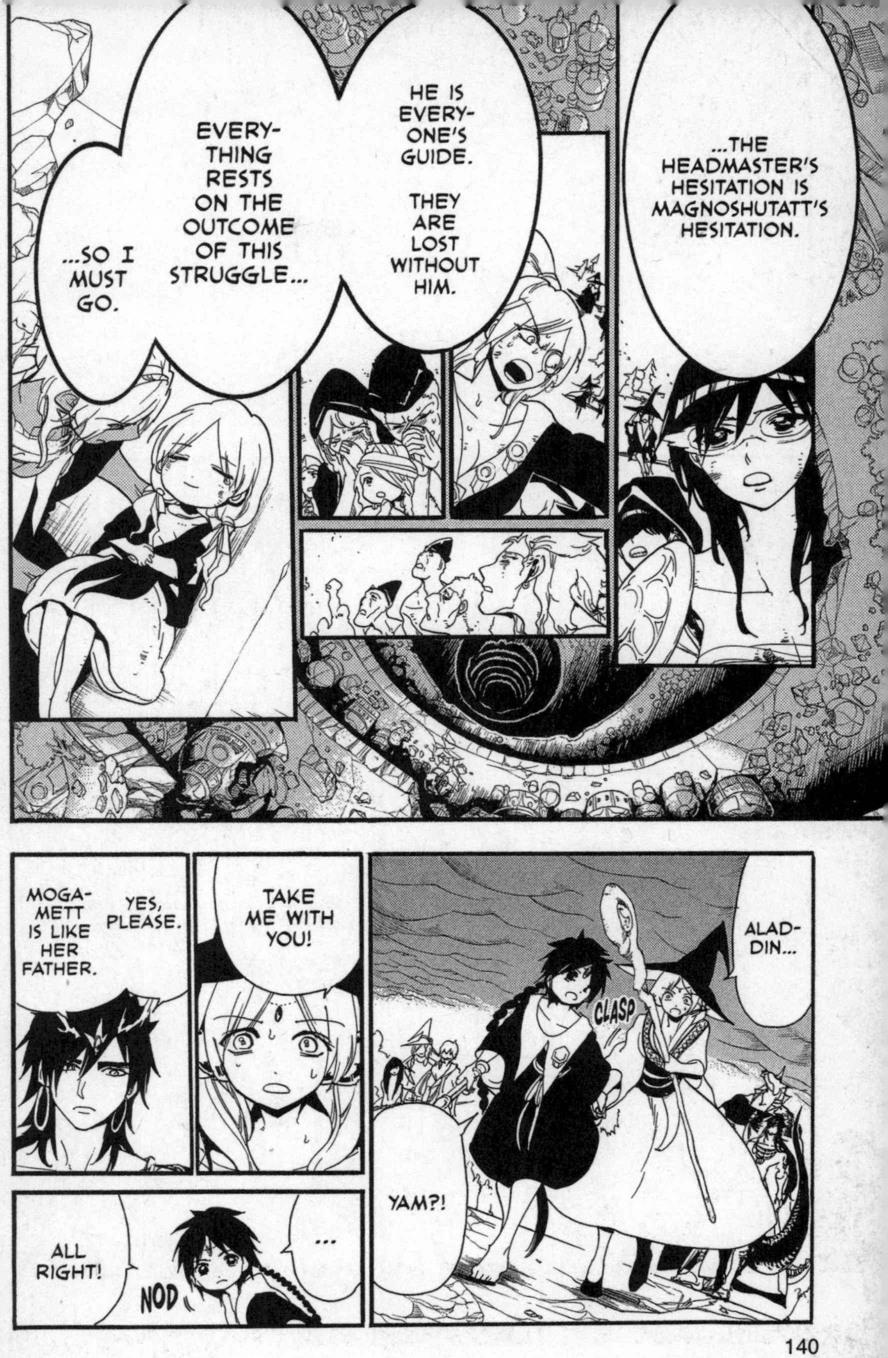
...THE HEADMASTER'S HESITATION IS MAGNOSHUTATT'S HESITATION.
HE IS EVERYONE'S GUIDE.
THEY ARE LOST WITHOUT HIM.
EVERYTHING RESTS ON THE OUTCOME OF THIS STRUGGLE...
...SO I MUST GO.
ALADDIN...
CLASP
YAM?!
TAKE ME WITH YOU!
YES, PLEASE.
MOGAMETT IS LIKE HER FATHER.
...
ALL RIGHT!
NOD

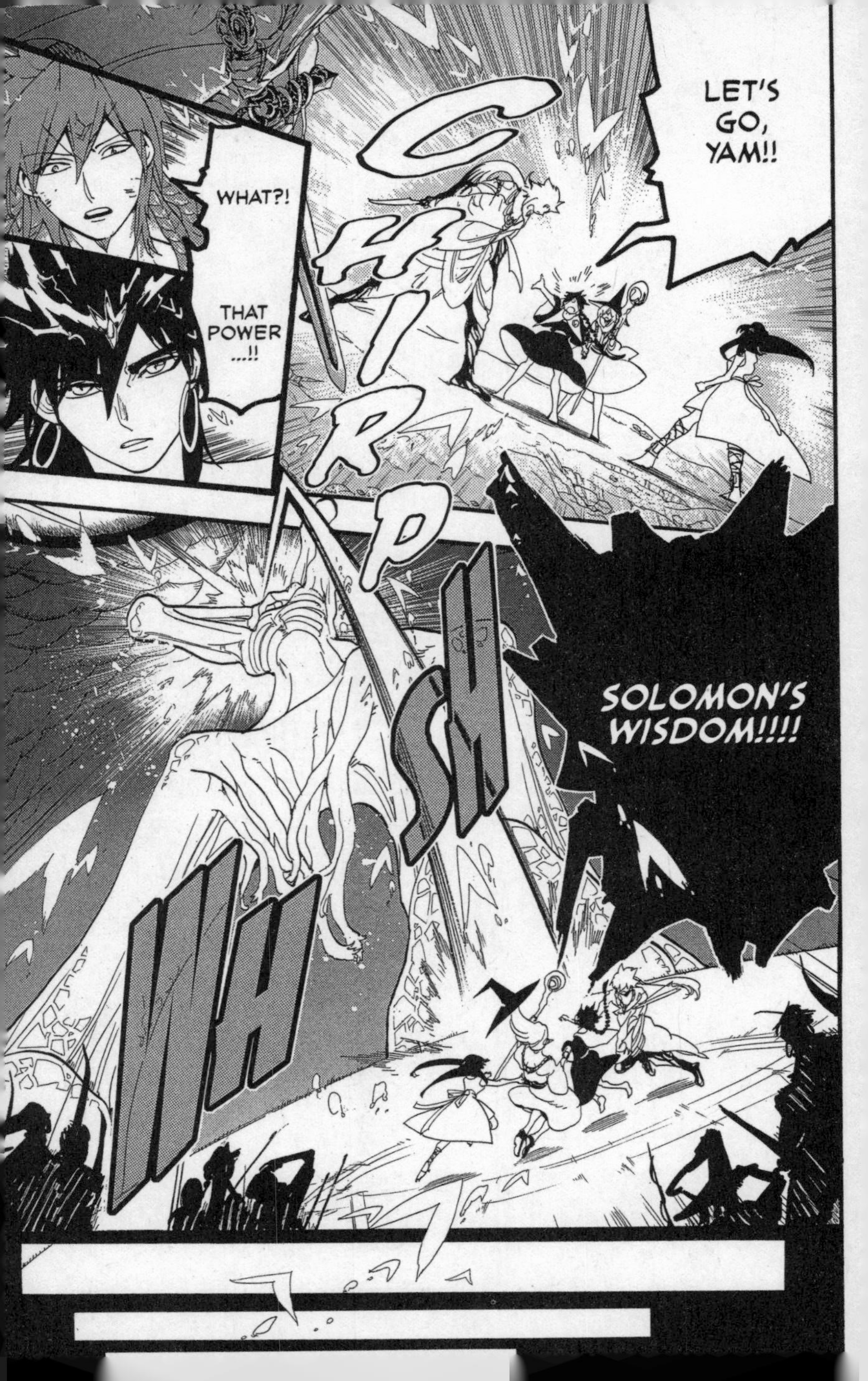
LET'S GO, YAM!!
CHIRPP
WHAT?!
THAT POWER ...!!
SOLOMON'S WISDOM!!!!

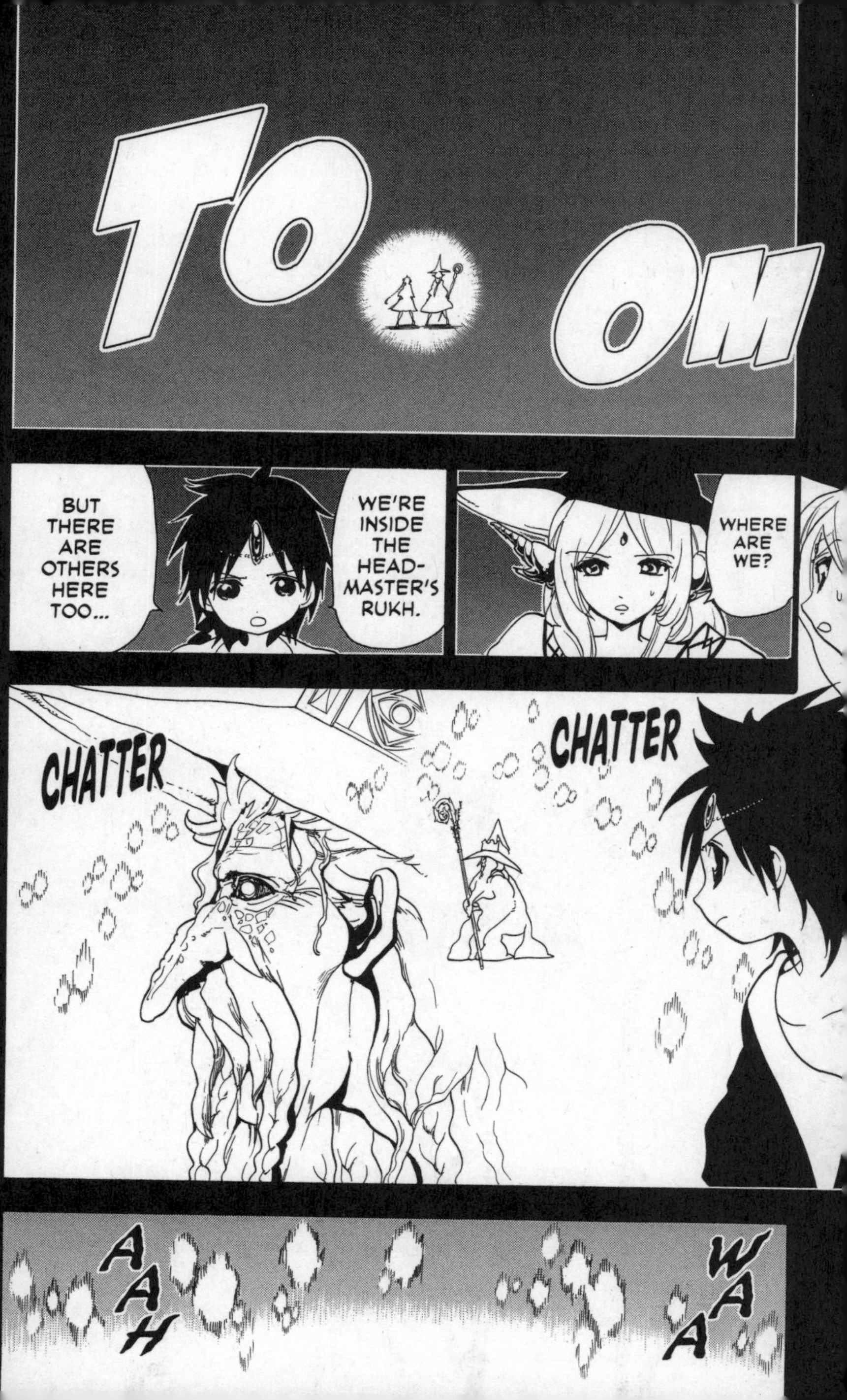
TO OM
WHERE ARE WE?
WE'RE INSIDE THE HEAD-MASTER'S RUKH.
BUT THERE ARE OTHERS HERE TOO...
CHATTER
CHATTER
WAA
AAH

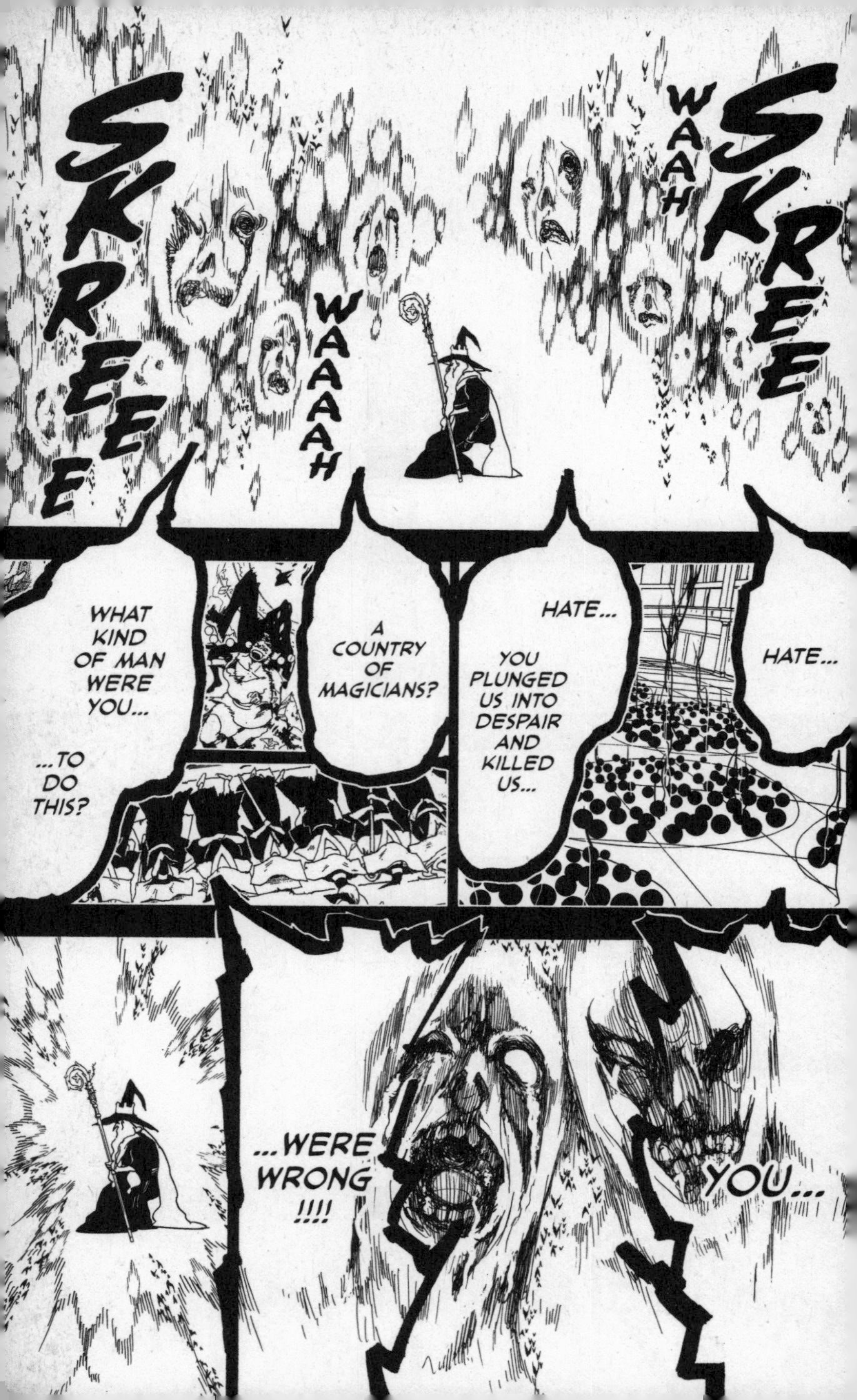

SKREE
WAAH
WAAAAH
SKREEE
HATE...
HATE...
YOU PLUNGED US INTO DESPAIR AND KILLED US...
A COUNTRY OF MAGICIANS?
WHAT KIND OF MAN WERE YOU...
...TO DO THIS?
YOU...
...WERE WRONG!!!!

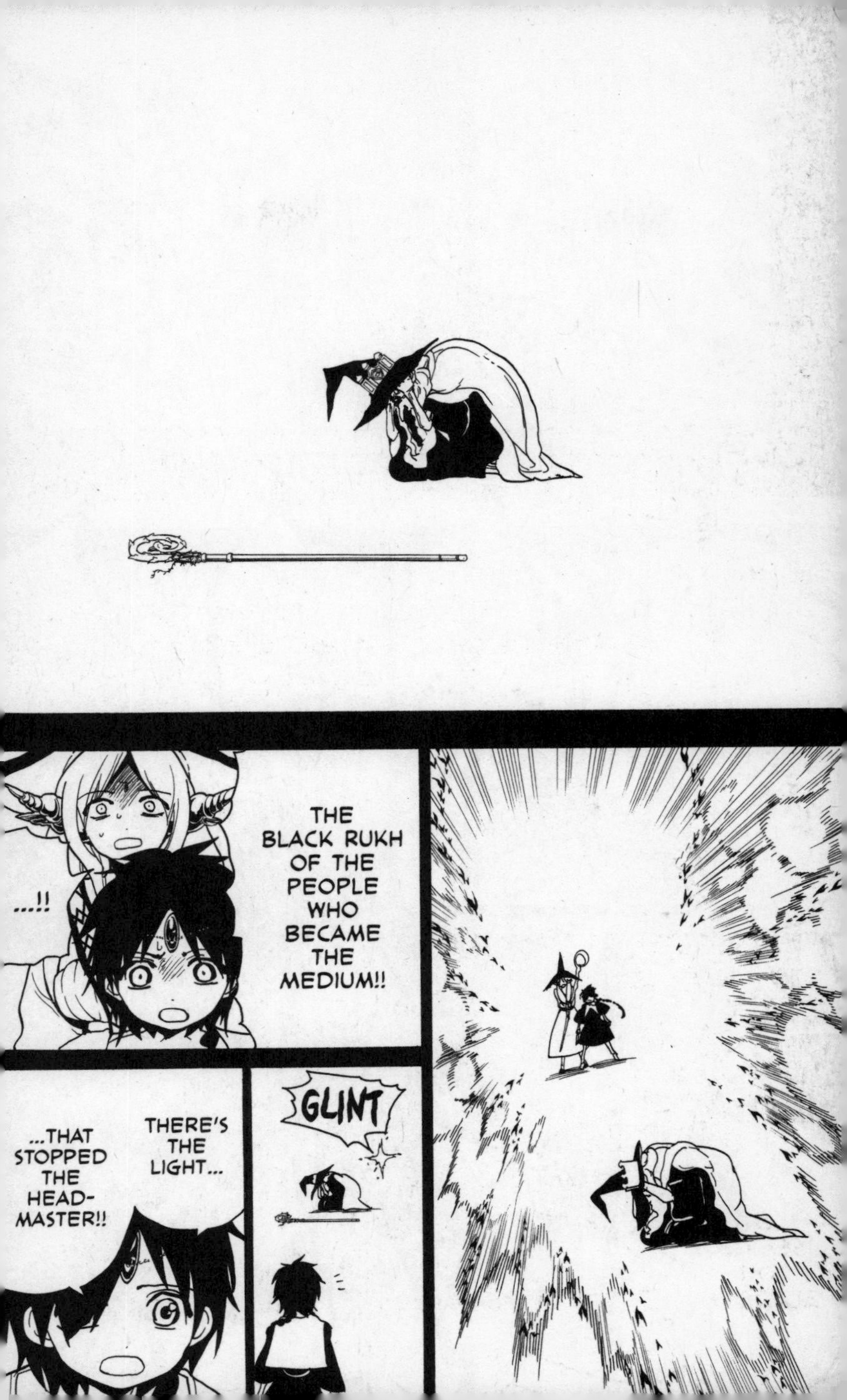
THE BLACK RUKH OF THE PEOPLE WHO BECAME THE MEDIUM!!
...!!
GLINT
THERE'S THE LIGHT...
...THAT STOPPED THE HEAD-MASTER!!

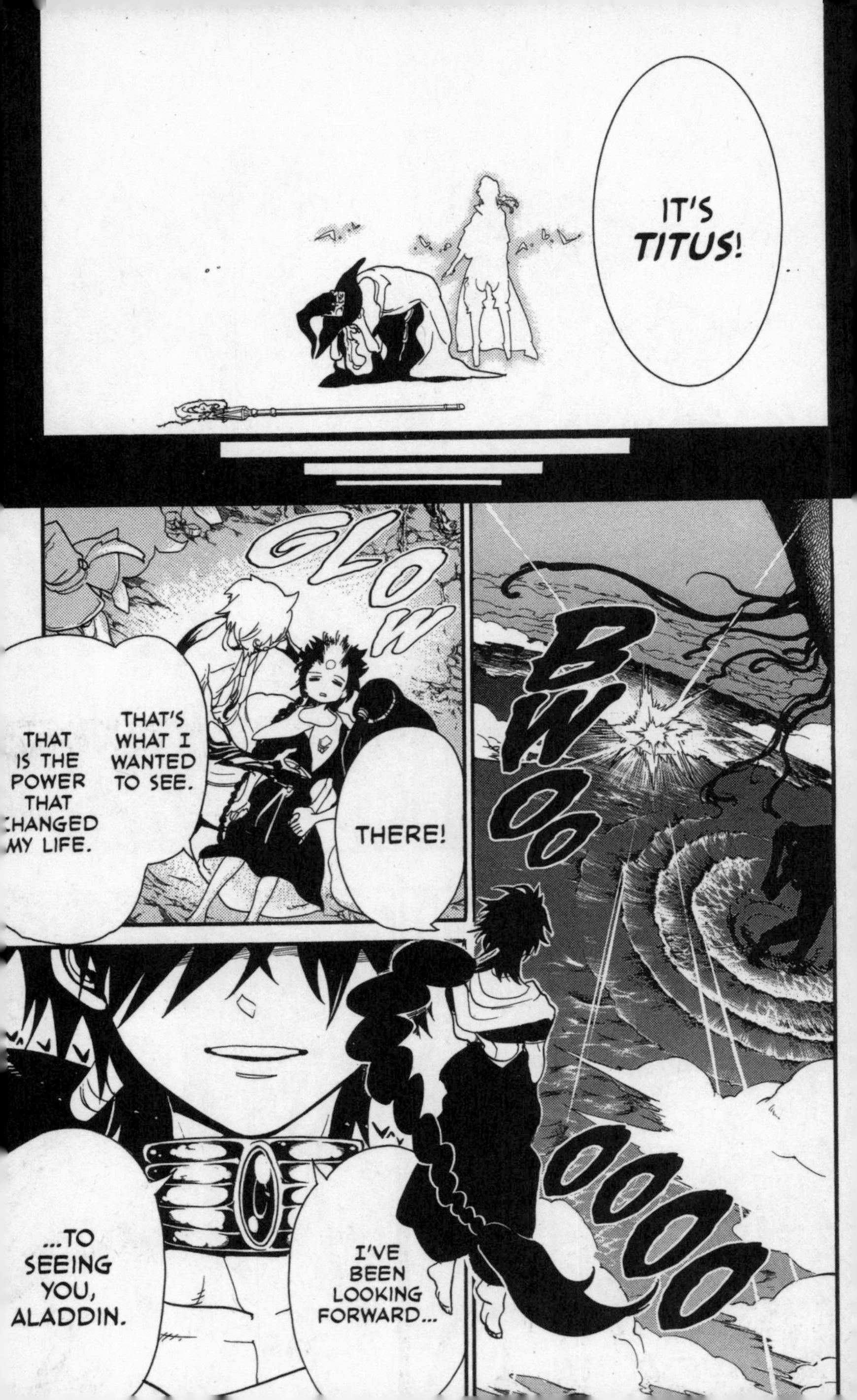

IT'S *TITUS!*
BWOOOOOOOO
GLOW
THERE!
THAT'S WHAT I WANTED TO SEE.
THAT IS THE POWER THAT CHANGED MY LIFE.
I'VE BEEN LOOKING FORWARD...
...TO SEEING YOU, ALADDIN.

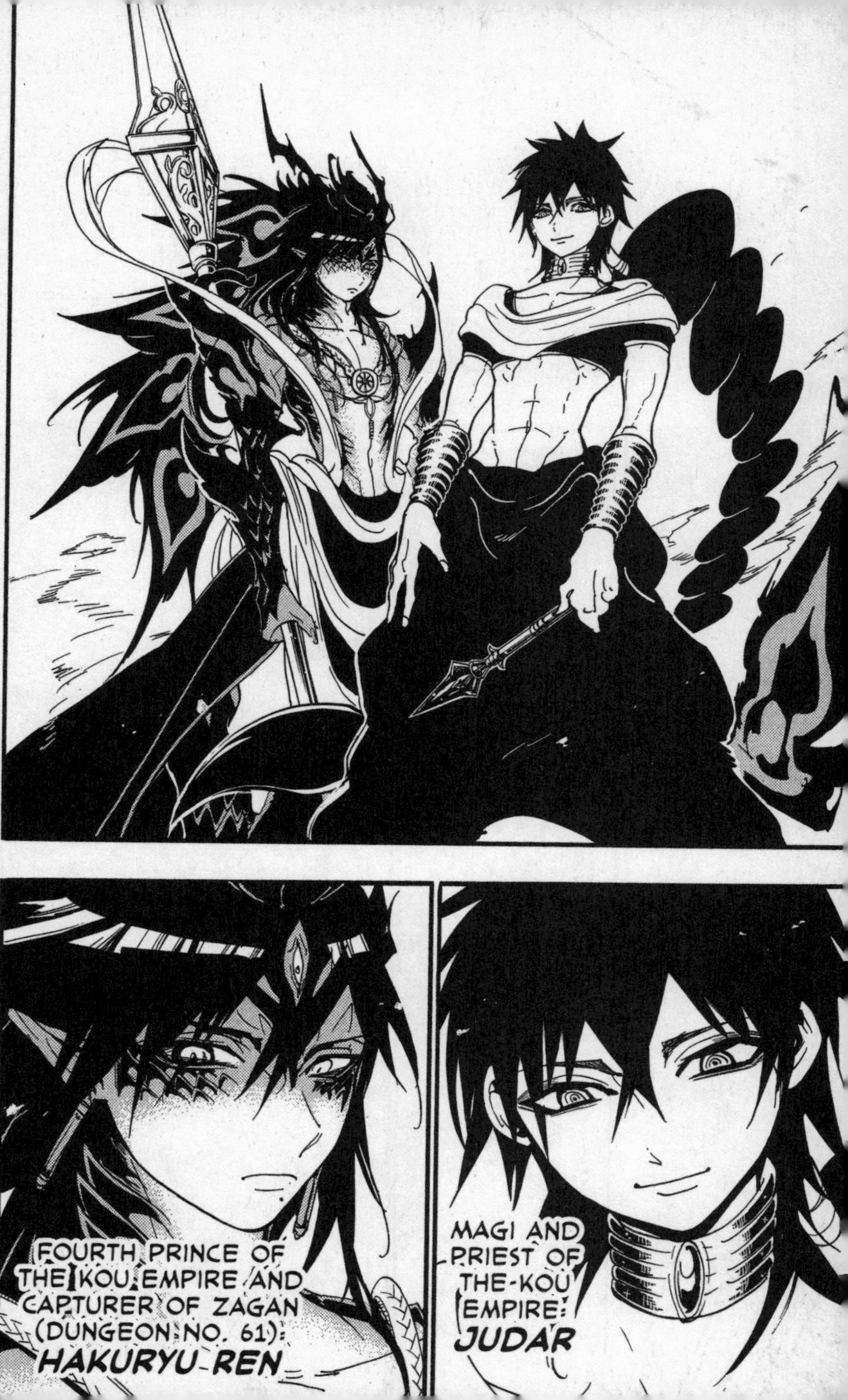
MAGI AND PRIEST OF THE KOU EMPIRE: JUDAR
FOURTH PRINCE OF THE KOU EMPIRE AND CAPTURER OF ZAGAN (DUNGEON NO. 61): HAKURYU REN

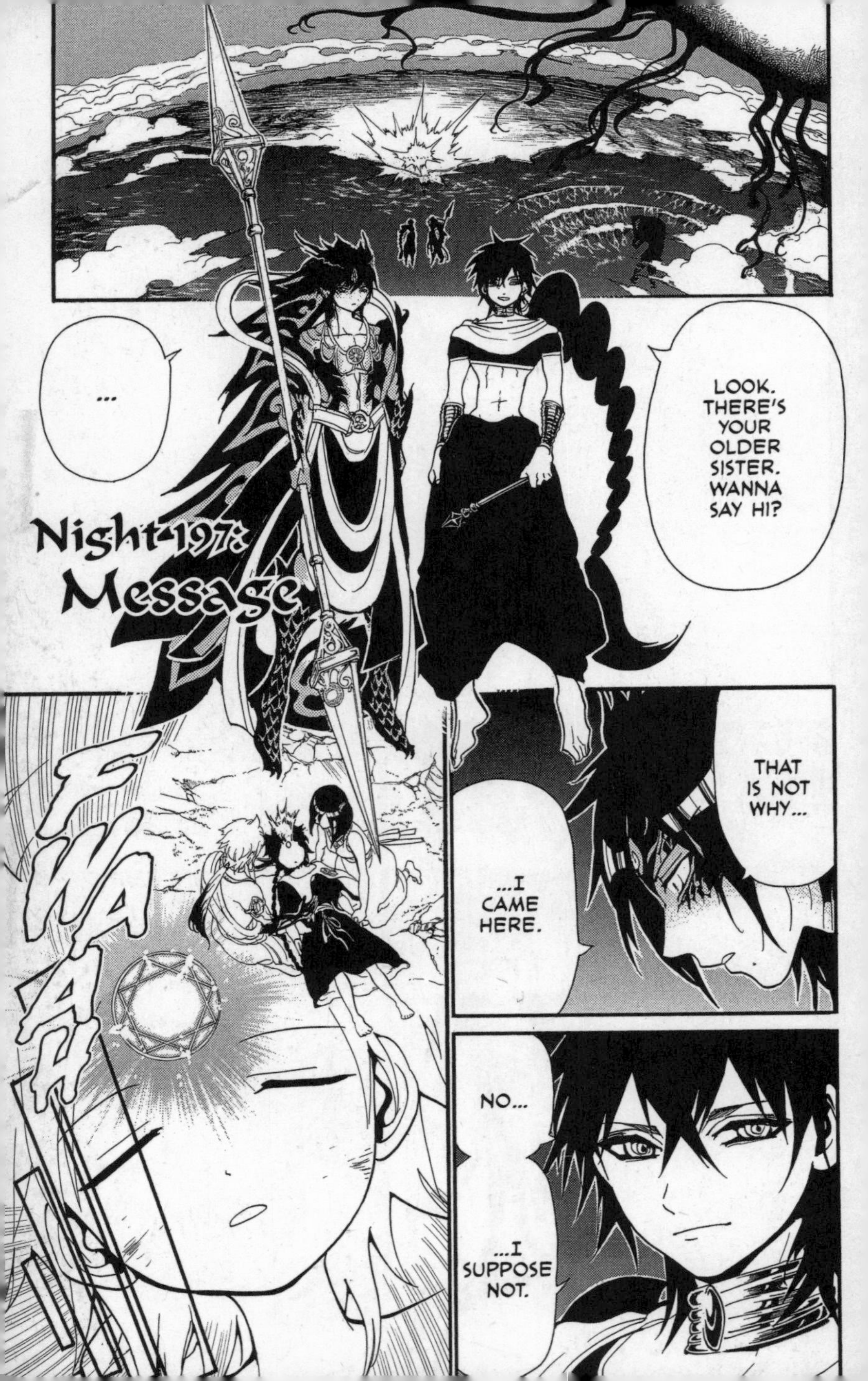
LOOK. THERE'S YOUR OLDER SISTER. WANNA SAY HI?
...
Night 197: Message
THAT IS NOT WHY...
...I CAME HERE.
NO...
...I SUPPOSE NOT.
FWAAH

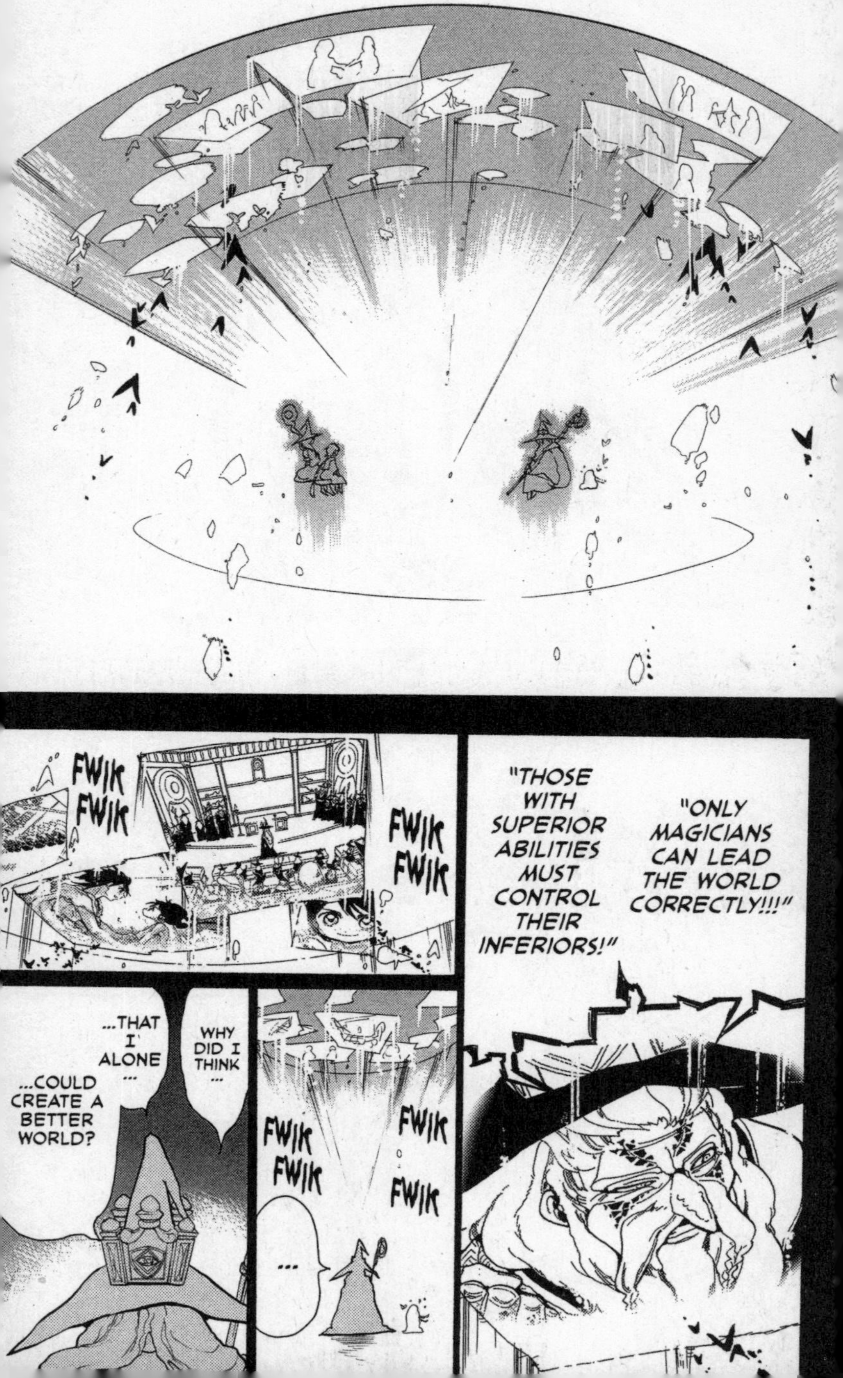
"ONLY MAGICIANS CAN LEAD THE WORLD CORRECTLY!!!"
"THOSE WITH SUPERIOR ABILITIES MUST CONTROL THEIR INFERIORS!"
FWIK FWIK
FWIK FWIK
FWIK
FWIK
FWIK FWIK
...
WHY DID I THINK ...
...THAT I ALONE ...
...COULD CREATE A BETTER WORLD?

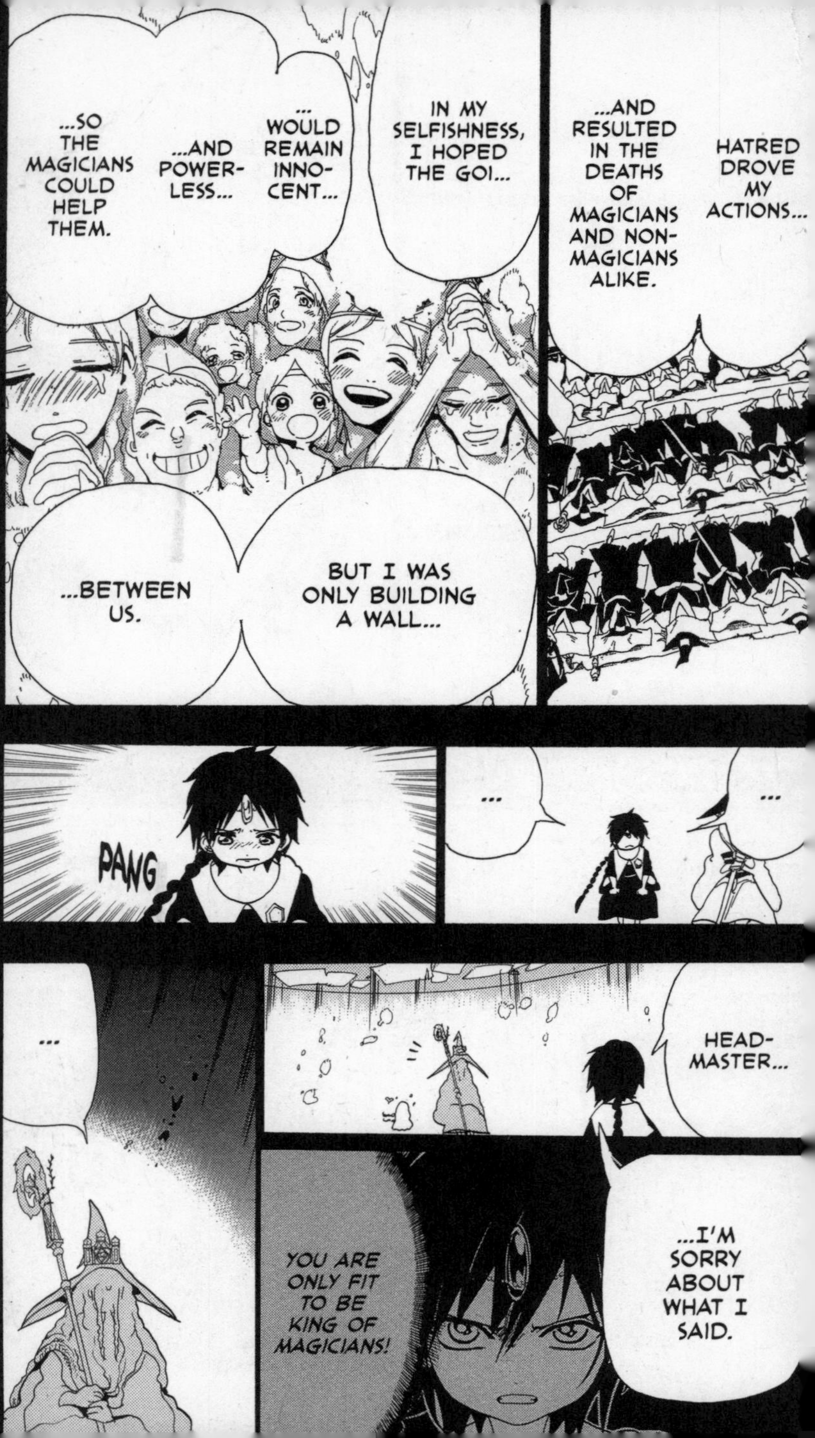
HATRED DROVE MY ACTIONS...
...AND RESULTED IN THE DEATHS OF MAGICIANS AND NON-MAGICIANS ALIKE.
IN MY SELFISHNESS, I HOPED THE GOI...
...WOULD REMAIN INNO-CENT...
...AND POWER-LESS...
...SO THE MAGICIANS COULD HELP THEM.
BUT I WAS ONLY BUILDING A WALL...
...BETWEEN US.
...
...
PANG
HEAD-MASTER...
...I'M SORRY ABOUT WHAT I SAID.
YOU ARE ONLY FIT TO BE KING OF MAGICIANS!
...

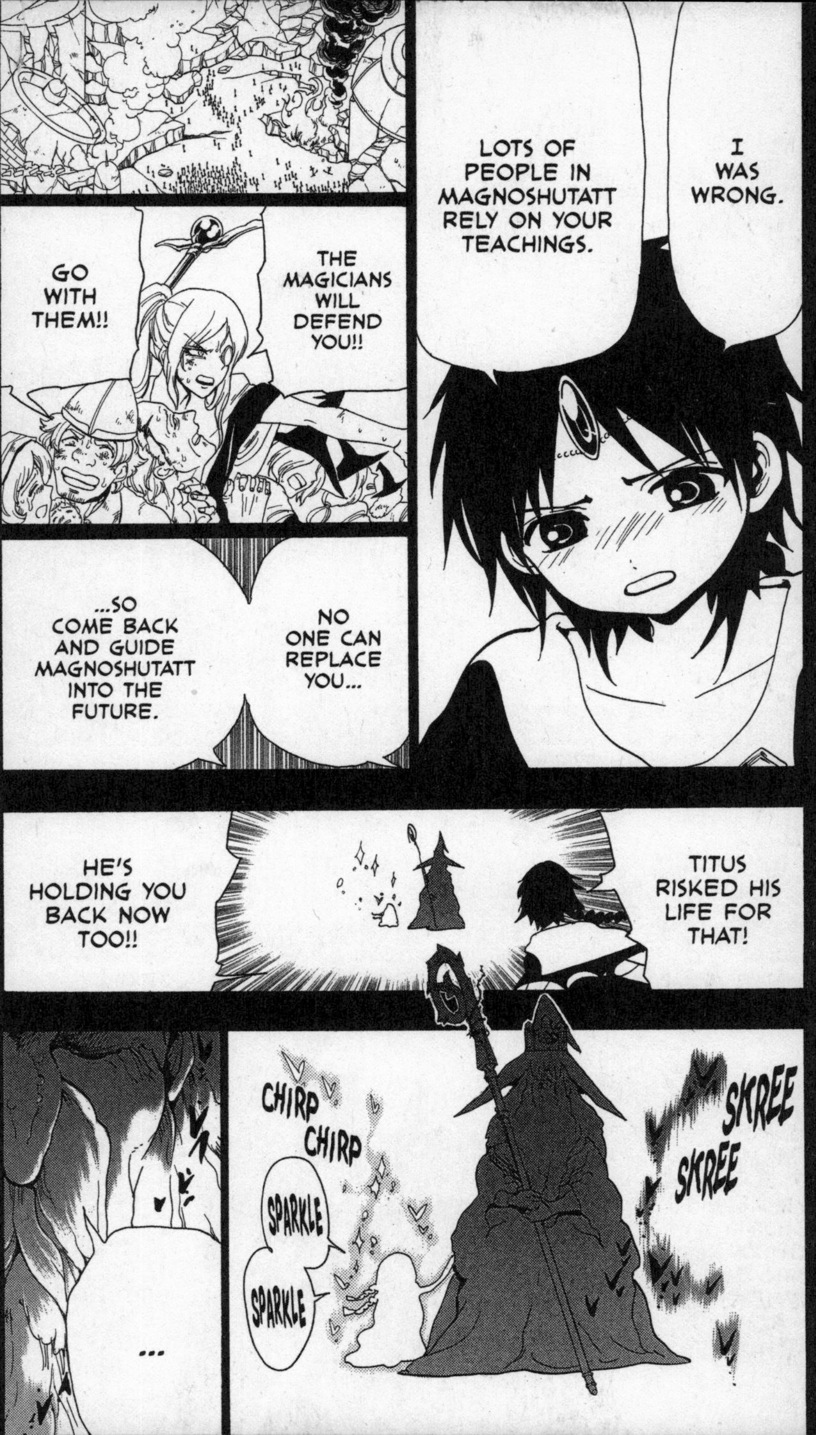

I WAS WRONG.
LOTS OF PEOPLE IN MAGNOSHUTATT RELY ON YOUR TEACHINGS.
THE MAGICIANS WILL DEFEND YOU!!
GO WITH THEM!!
NO ONE CAN REPLACE YOU...
...SO COME BACK AND GUIDE MAGNOSHUTATT INTO THE FUTURE.
TITUS RISKED HIS LIFE FOR THAT!
HE'S HOLDING YOU BACK NOW TOO!!
SKREE
SKREE
CHIRP
CHIRP
SPARKLE
SPARKLE
...

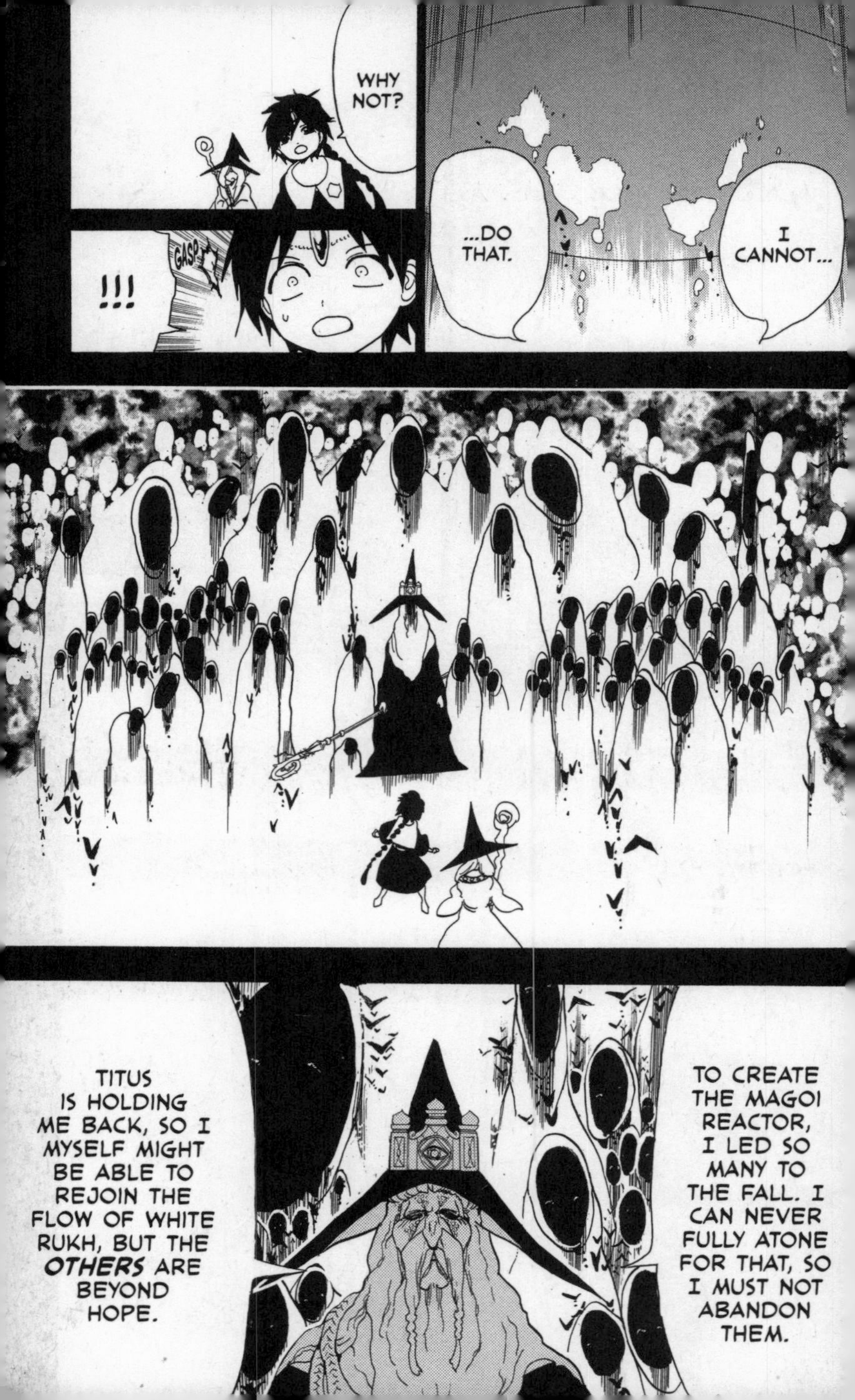
I CANNOT...
...DO THAT.
WHY NOT?
GASP
!!!
TO CREATE THE MAGOI REACTOR, I LED SO MANY TO THE FALL. I CAN NEVER FULLY ATONE FOR THAT, SO I MUST NOT ABANDON THEM.
TITUS IS HOLDING ME BACK, SO I MYSELF MIGHT BE ABLE TO REJOIN THE FLOW OF WHITE RUKH, BUT THE OTHERS ARE BEYOND HOPE.

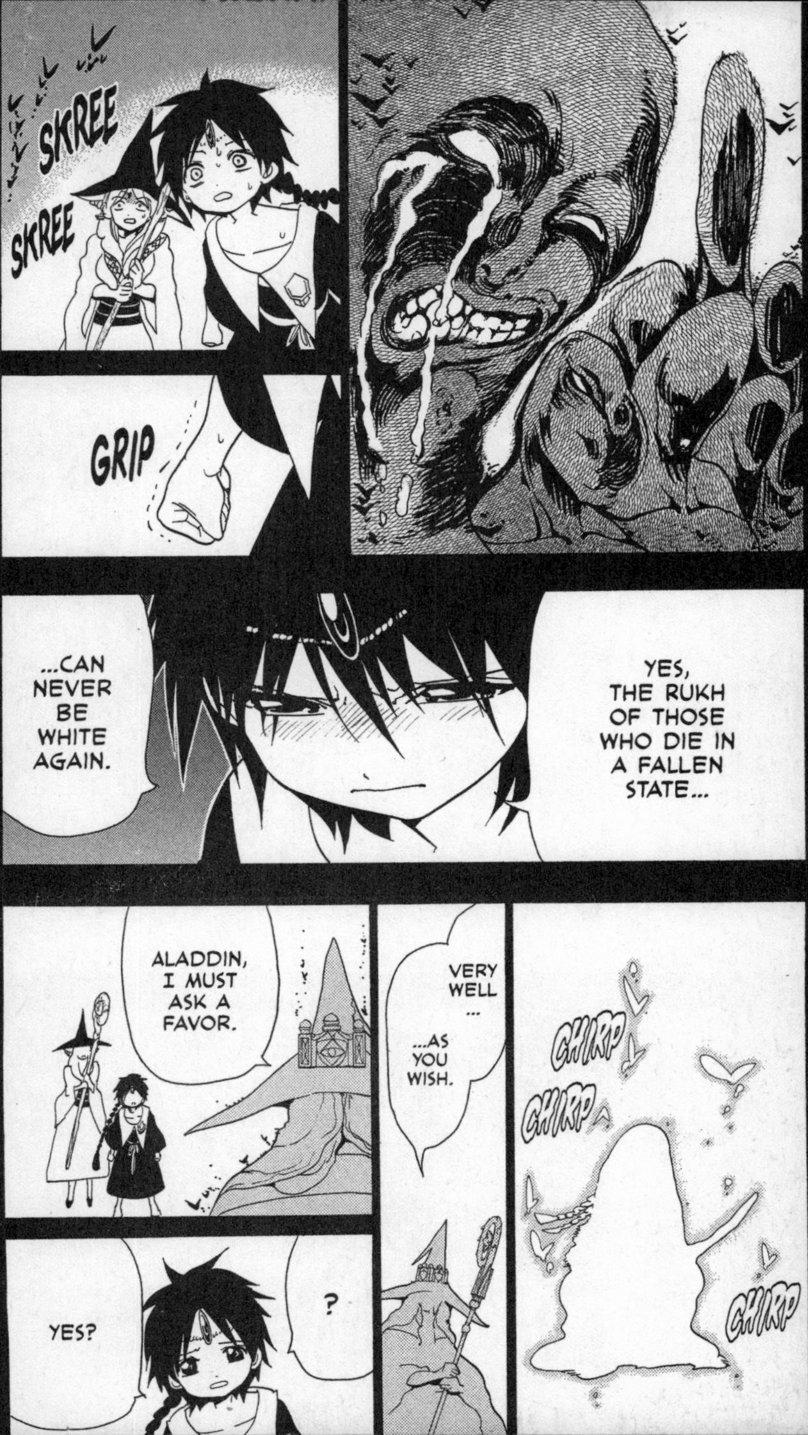
SKREE
SKREE
GRIP
YES, THE RUKH OF THOSE WHO DIE IN A FALLEN STATE...
...CAN NEVER BE WHITE AGAIN.
CHIRP
CHIRP
CHIRP
VERY WELL...
...AS YOU WISH.
ALADDIN, I MUST ASK A FAVOR.
?
YES?

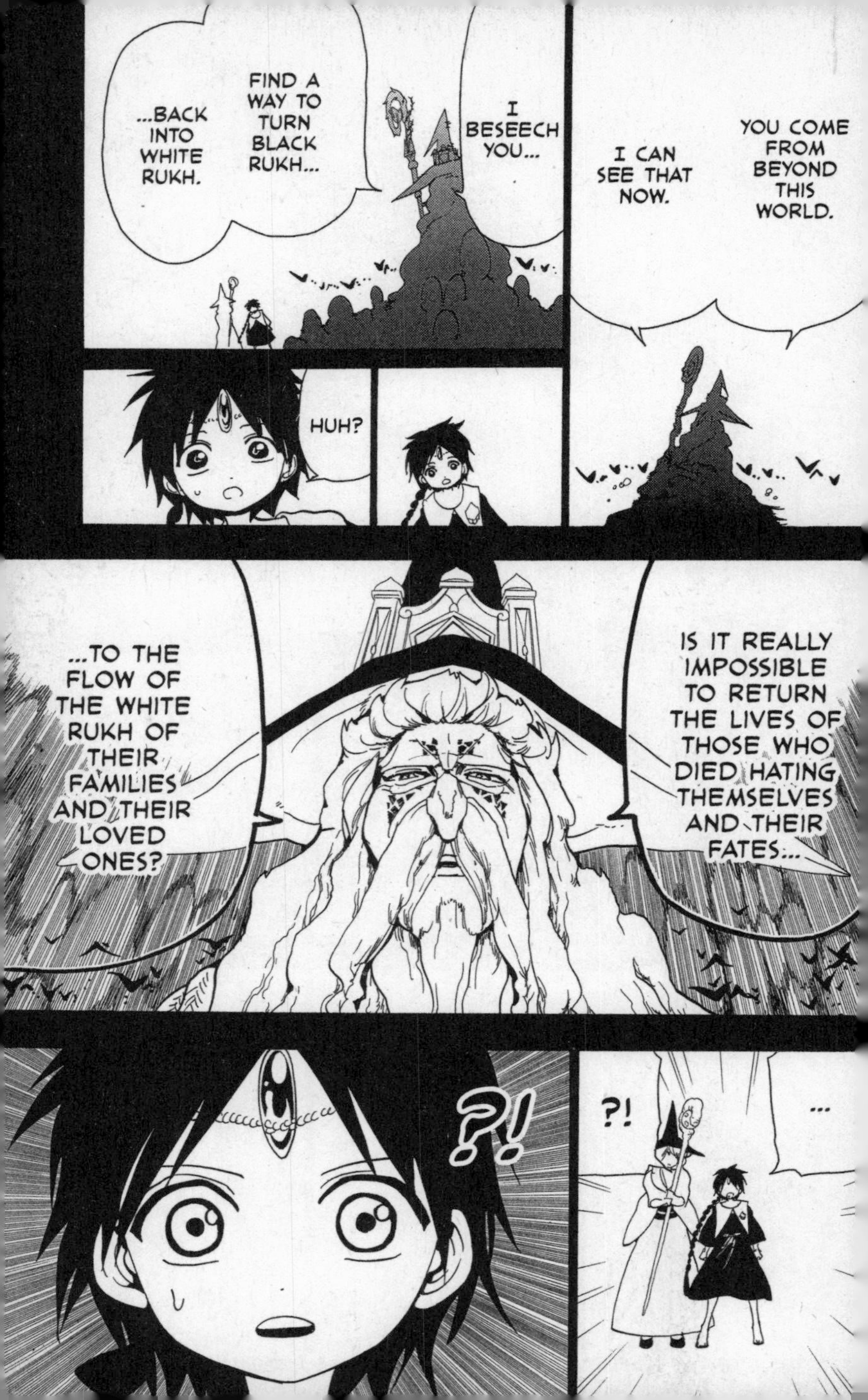
YOU COME FROM BEYOND THIS WORLD.
I CAN SEE THAT NOW.
I BESEECH YOU...
FIND A WAY TO TURN BLACK RUKH...
...BACK INTO WHITE RUKH.
HUH?
IS IT REALLY IMPOSSIBLE TO RETURN THE LIVES OF THOSE WHO DIED HATING THEMSELVES AND THEIR FATES...
...TO THE FLOW OF THE WHITE RUKH OF THEIR FAMILIES AND THEIR LOVED ONES?
...
?!
?!

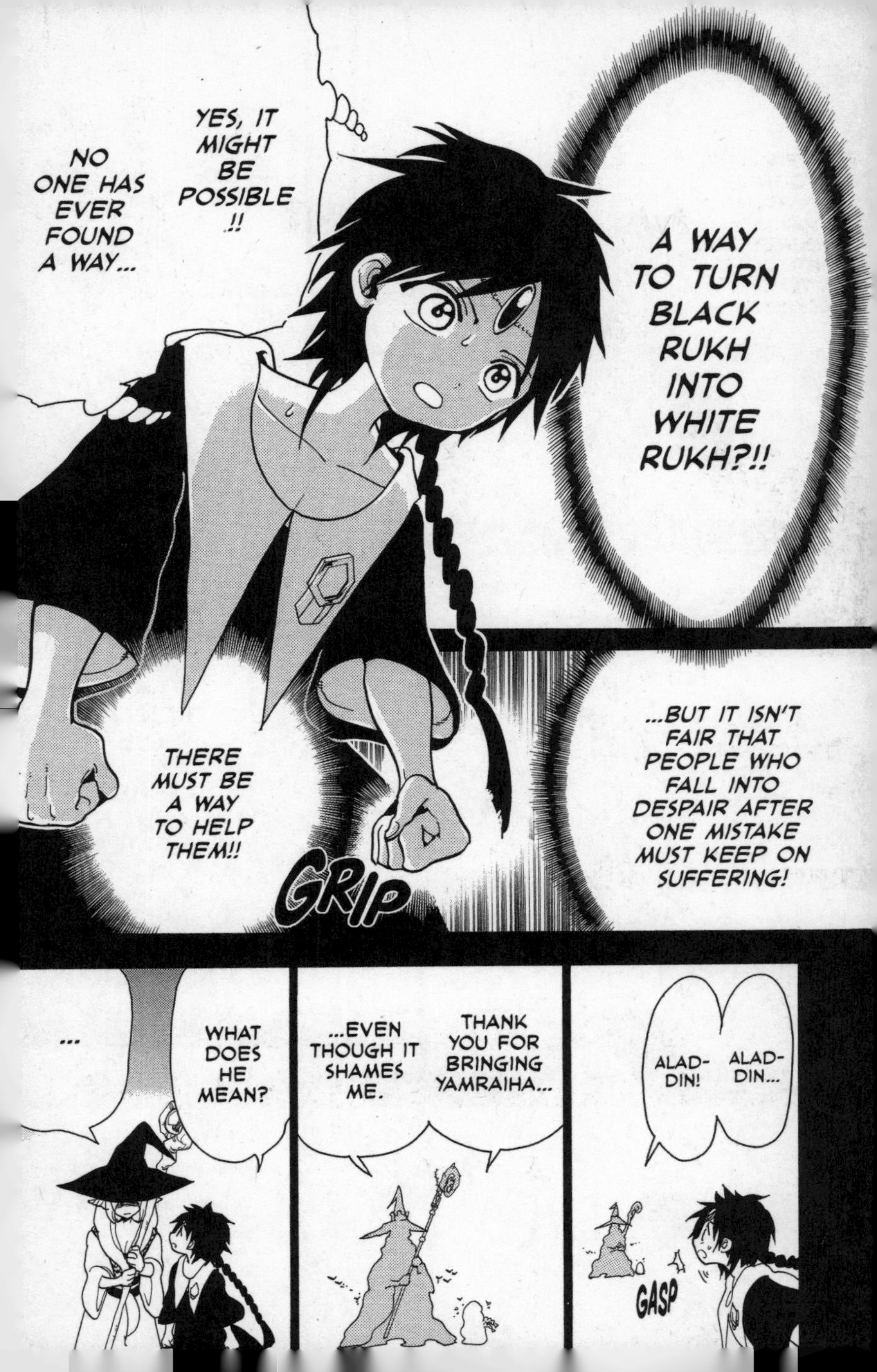
A WAY TO TURN BLACK RUKH INTO WHITE RUKH?!!
YES, IT MIGHT BE POSSIBLE !!
NO ONE HAS EVER FOUND A WAY...
...BUT IT ISN'T FAIR THAT PEOPLE WHO FALL INTO DESPAIR AFTER ONE MISTAKE MUST KEEP ON SUFFERING!
THERE MUST BE A WAY TO HELP THEM!!
GRIP
ALAD-DIN...
ALAD-DIN!
GASP
THANK YOU FOR BRINGING YAMRAIHA...
...EVEN THOUGH IT SHAMES ME.
WHAT DOES HE MEAN?
...

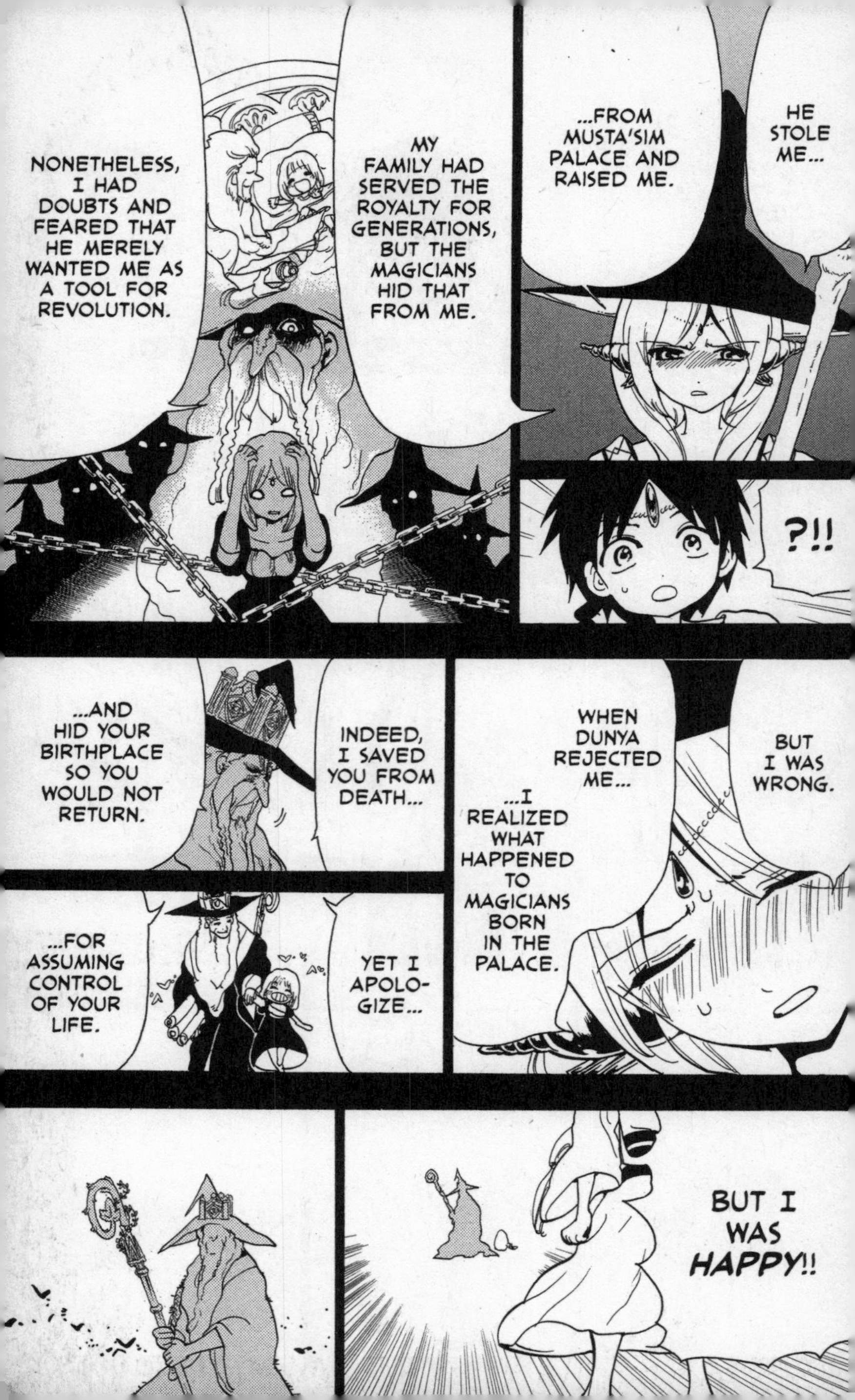
HE STOLE ME...
...FROM MUSTA'SIM PALACE AND RAISED ME.
?!!
MY FAMILY HAD SERVED THE ROYALTY FOR GENERATIONS, BUT THE MAGICIANS HID THAT FROM ME.
NONETHELESS, I HAD DOUBTS AND FEARED THAT HE MERELY WANTED ME AS A TOOL FOR REVOLUTION.
BUT I WAS WRONG.
WHEN DUNYA REJECTED ME...
...I REALIZED WHAT HAPPENED TO MAGICIANS BORN IN THE PALACE.
INDEED, I SAVED YOU FROM DEATH...
...AND HID YOUR BIRTHPLACE SO YOU WOULD NOT RETURN.
YET I APOLOGIZE...
...FOR ASSUMING CONTROL OF YOUR LIFE.
BUT I WAS *HAPPY*!!

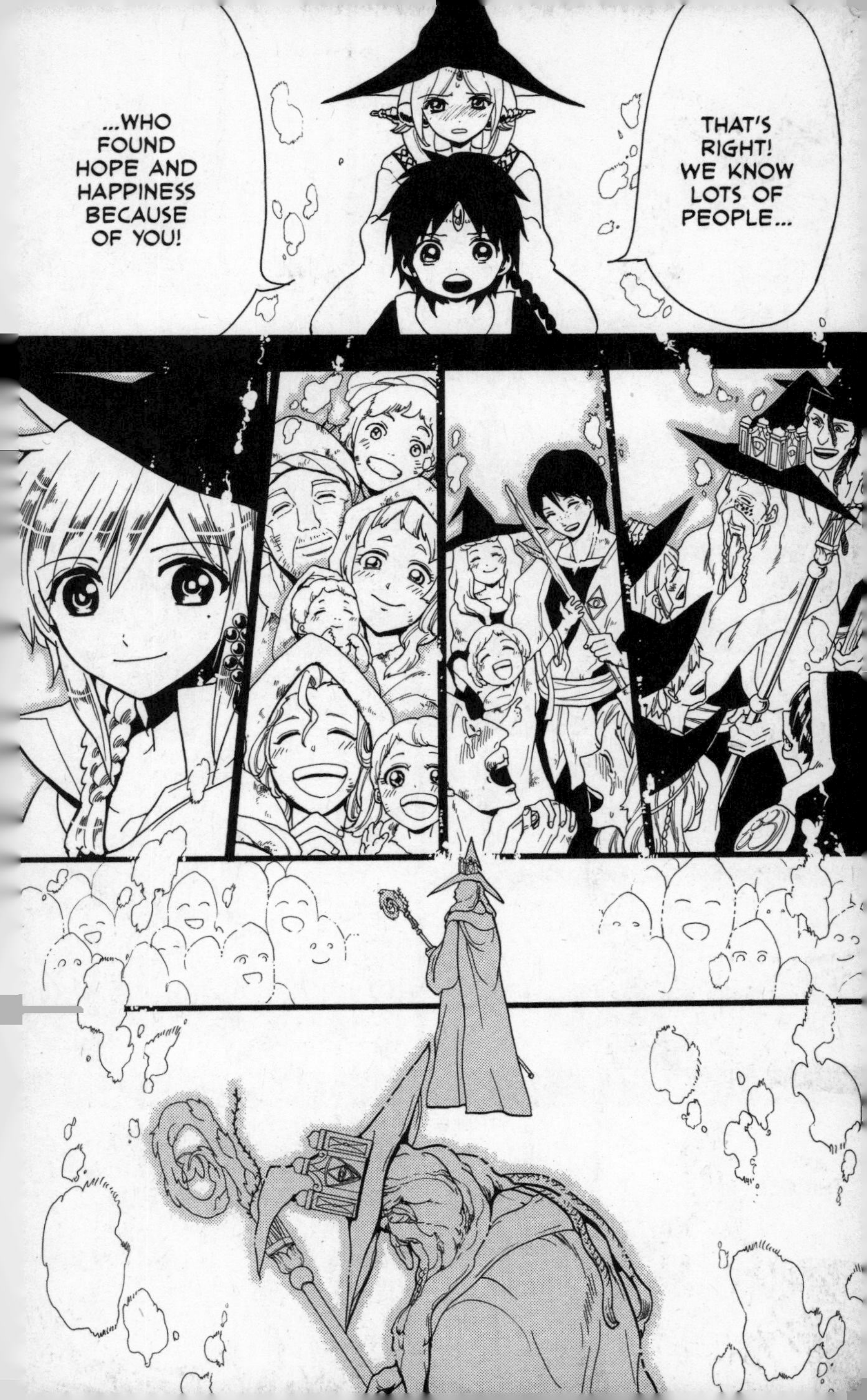
THAT'S RIGHT! WE KNOW LOTS OF PEOPLE...
...WHO FOUND HOPE AND HAPPINESS BECAUSE OF YOU!

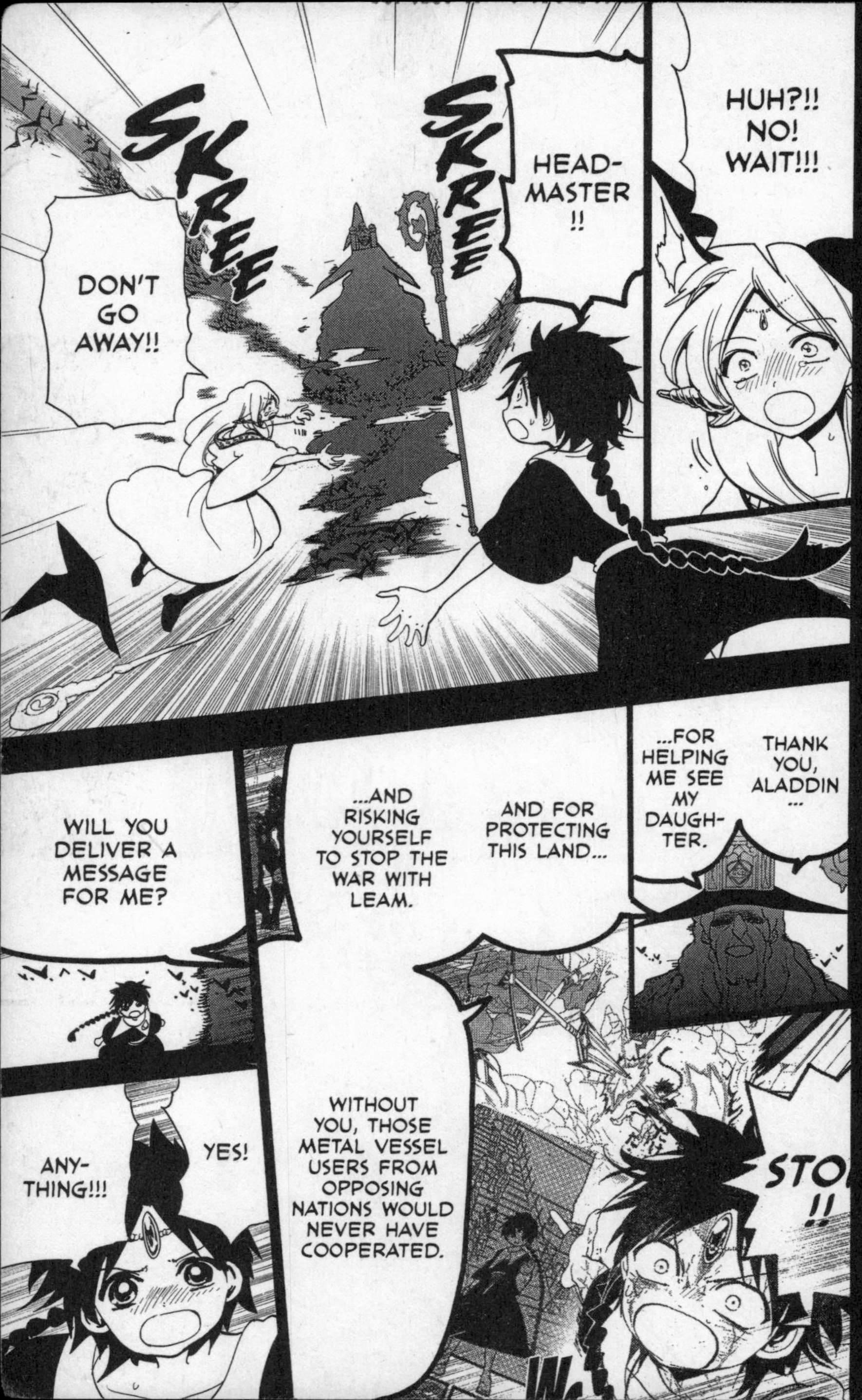
HUH?!! NO! WAIT!!!
HEAD-MASTER !!
SKREE
SKREE
DON'T GO AWAY!!
THANK YOU, ALADDIN ...
...FOR HELPING ME SEE MY DAUGH-TER.
AND FOR PROTECTING THIS LAND...
...AND RISKING YOURSELF TO STOP THE WAR WITH LEAM.
WITHOUT YOU, THOSE METAL VESSEL USERS FROM OPPOSING NATIONS WOULD NEVER HAVE COOPERATED.
STO
!!
WILL YOU DELIVER A MESSAGE FOR ME?
YES!
ANY-THING!!!

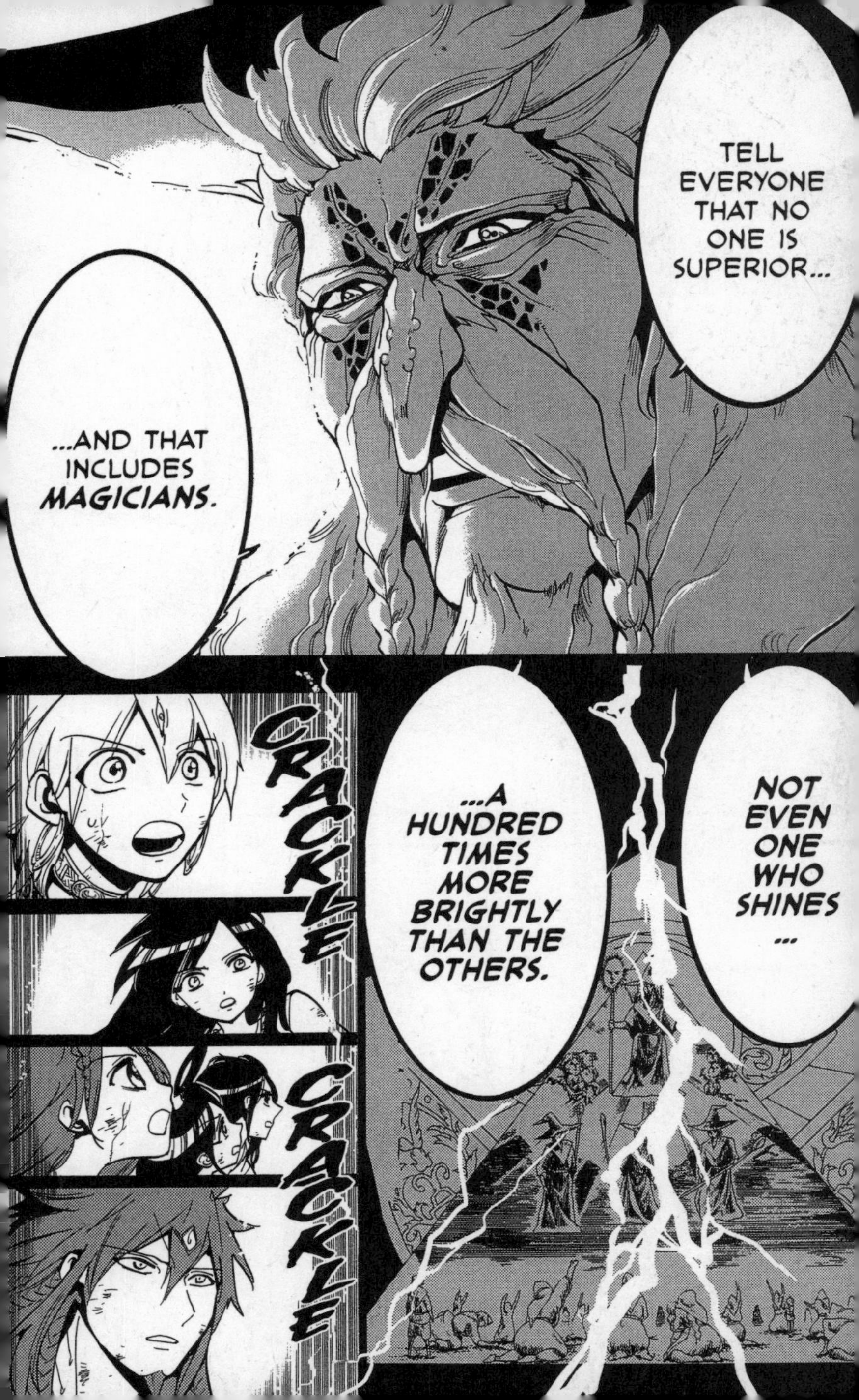
TELL EVERYONE THAT NO ONE IS SUPERIOR...
...AND THAT INCLUDES *MAGICIANS*.
NOT EVEN ONE WHO SHINES ...
...A HUNDRED TIMES MORE BRIGHTLY THAN THE OTHERS.
CRACKLE
CRACKLE

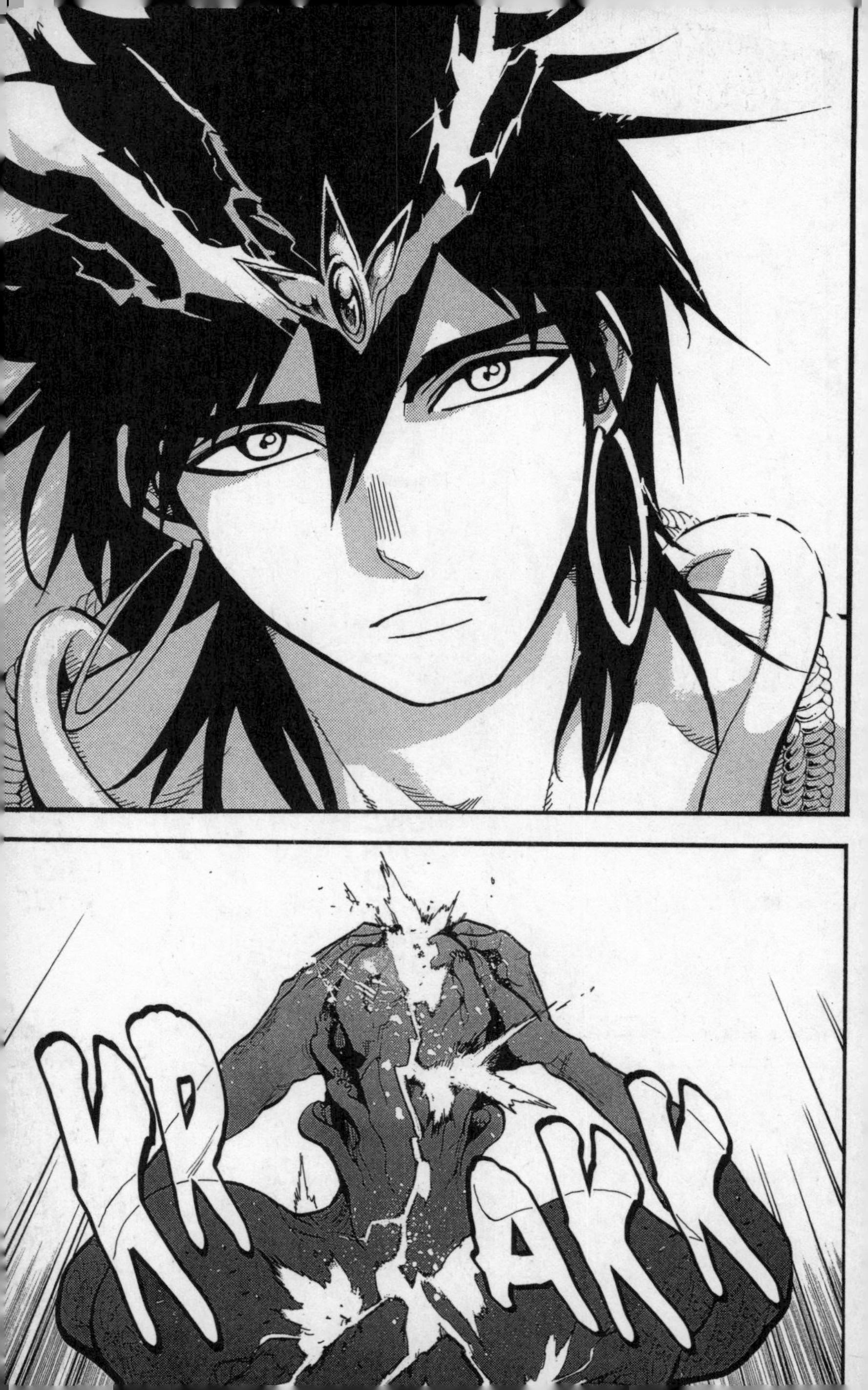
KRAKK

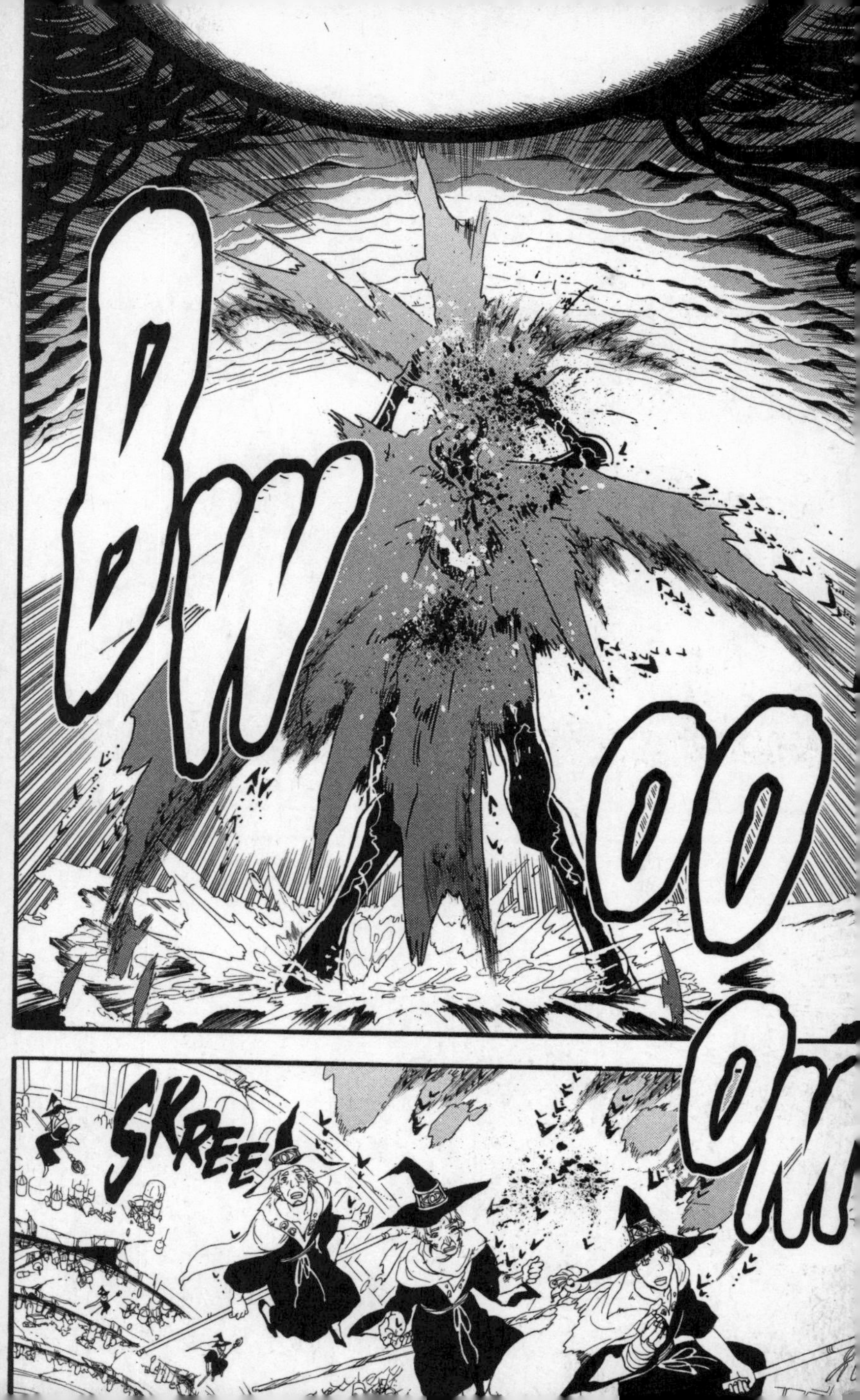
SKREE

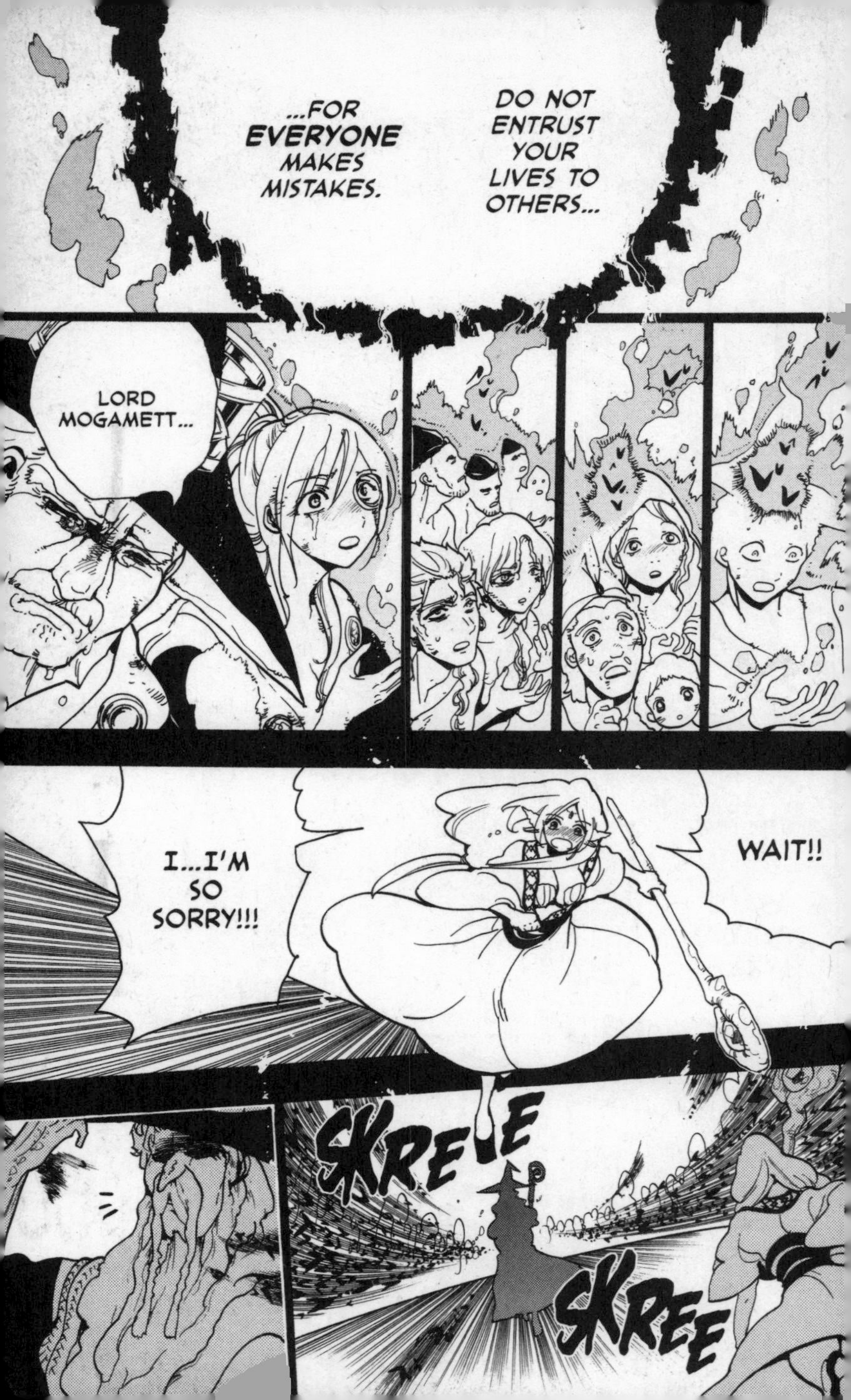
DO NOT ENTRUST YOUR LIVES TO OTHERS...
...FOR EVERYONE MAKES MISTAKES.
LORD MOGAMETT...
WAIT!!
I...I'M SO SORRY!!!
SKREE
SKREE

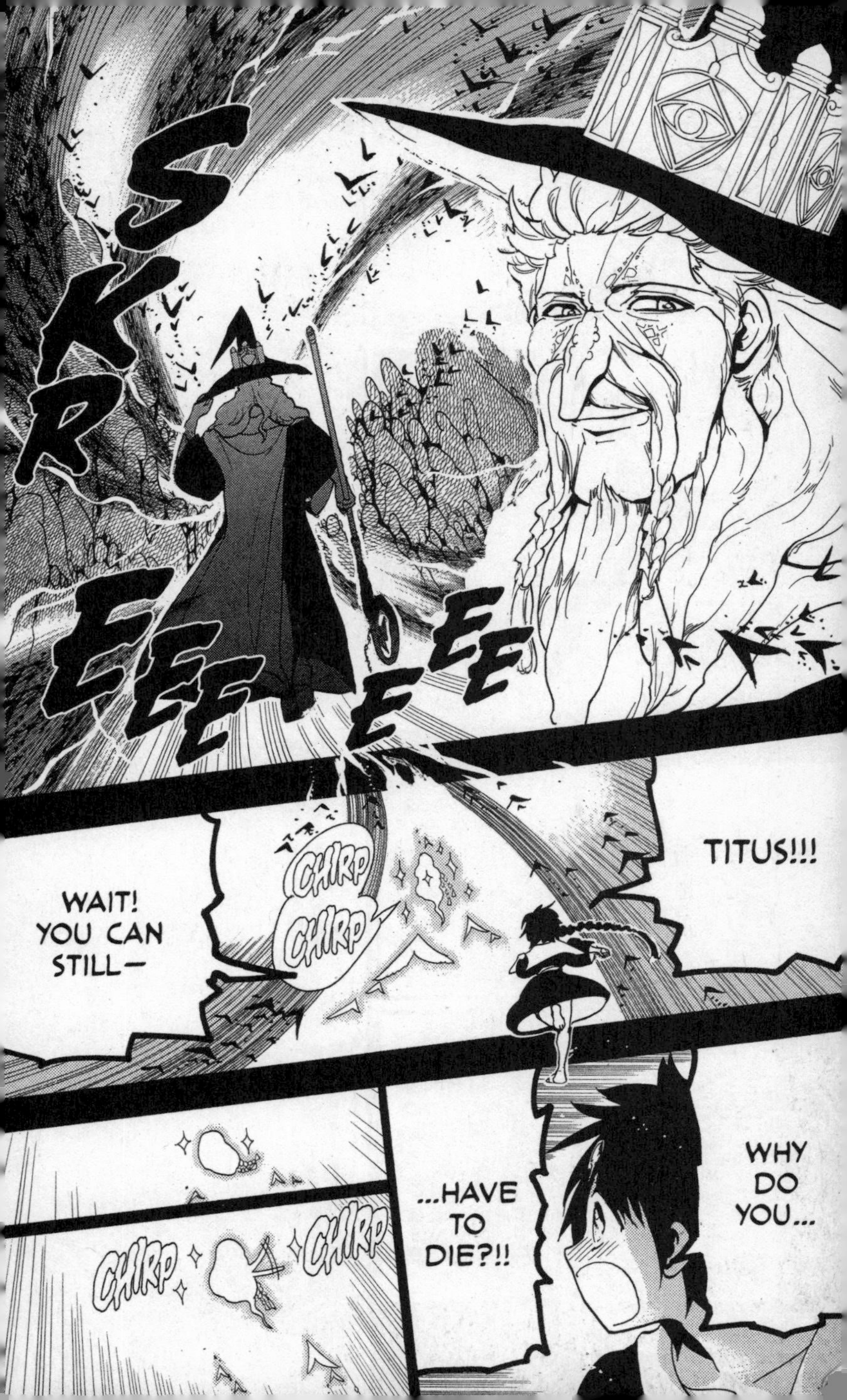
SKREEEEEEE
TITUS!!!
WAIT! YOU CAN STILL—
CHIRP
CHIRP
WHY DO YOU...
...HAVE TO DIE?!!
CHIRP
CHIRP

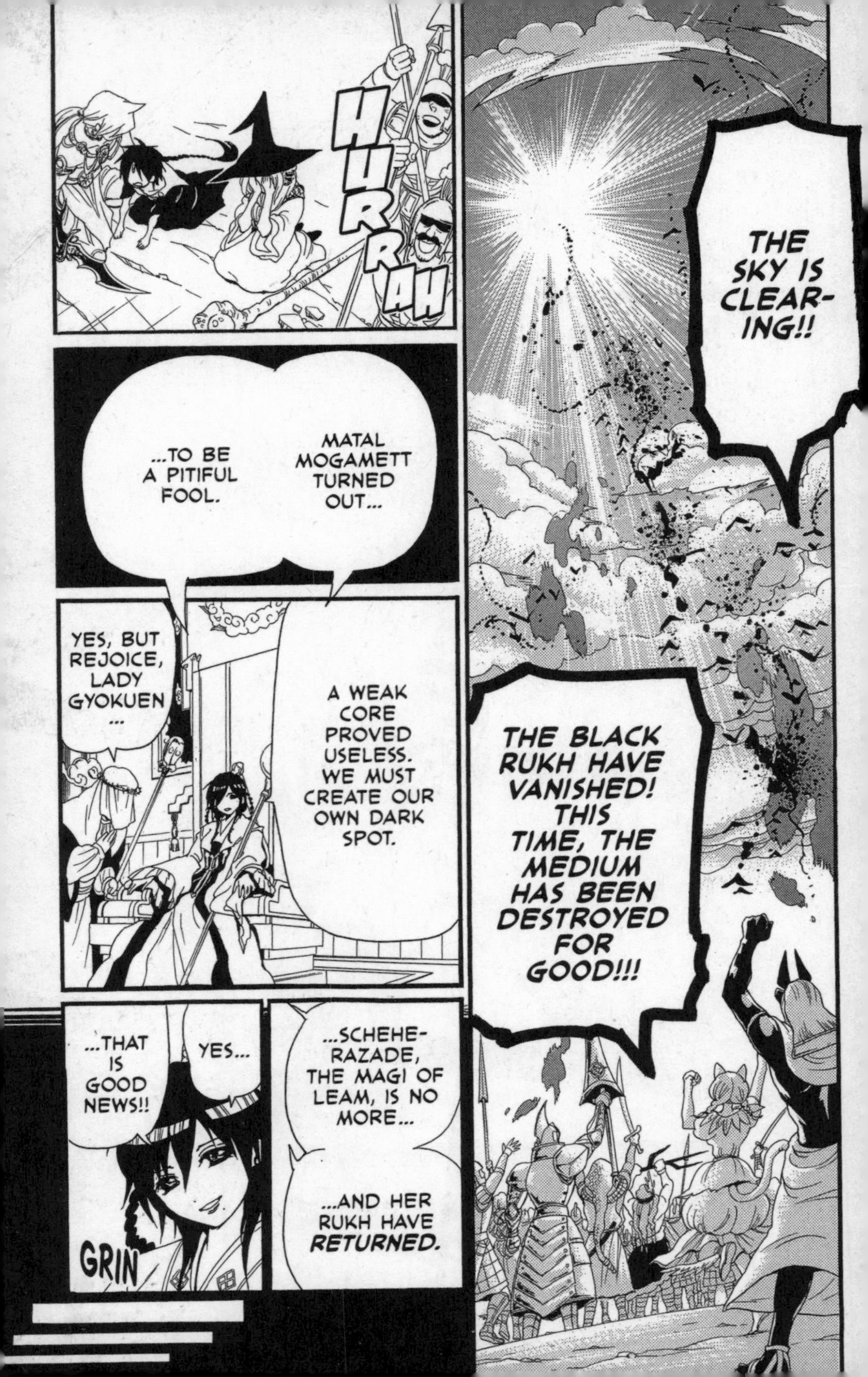
THE SKY IS CLEAR-ING!!
THE BLACK RUKH HAVE VANISHED! THIS TIME, THE MEDIUM HAS BEEN DESTROYED FOR GOOD!!!
HURRAH
MATAL MOGAMETT TURNED OUT...
...TO BE A PITIFUL FOOL.
A WEAK CORE PROVED USELESS. WE MUST CREATE OUR OWN DARK SPOT.
YES, BUT REJOICE, LADY GYOKUEN ...
...SCHEHE-RAZADE, THE MAGI OF LEAM, IS NO MORE...
...AND HER RUKH HAVE *RETURNED.*
YES...
...THAT IS GOOD NEWS!!
GRIN

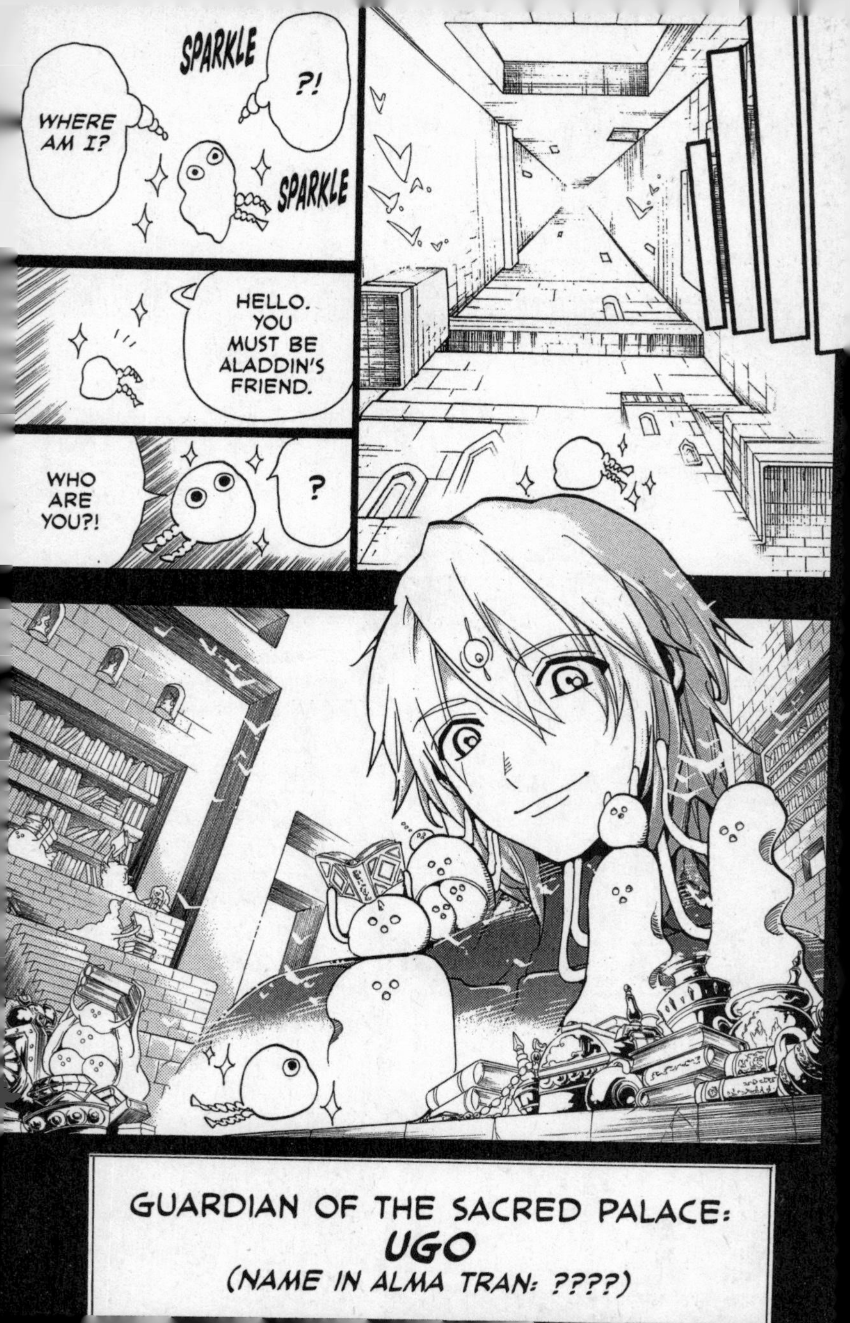
SPARKLE
?!
WHERE AM I?
SPARKLE
HELLO. YOU MUST BE ALADDIN'S FRIEND.
?
WHO ARE YOU?!
GUARDIAN OF THE SACRED PALACE:
UGO
(NAME IN ALMA TRAN: ????)

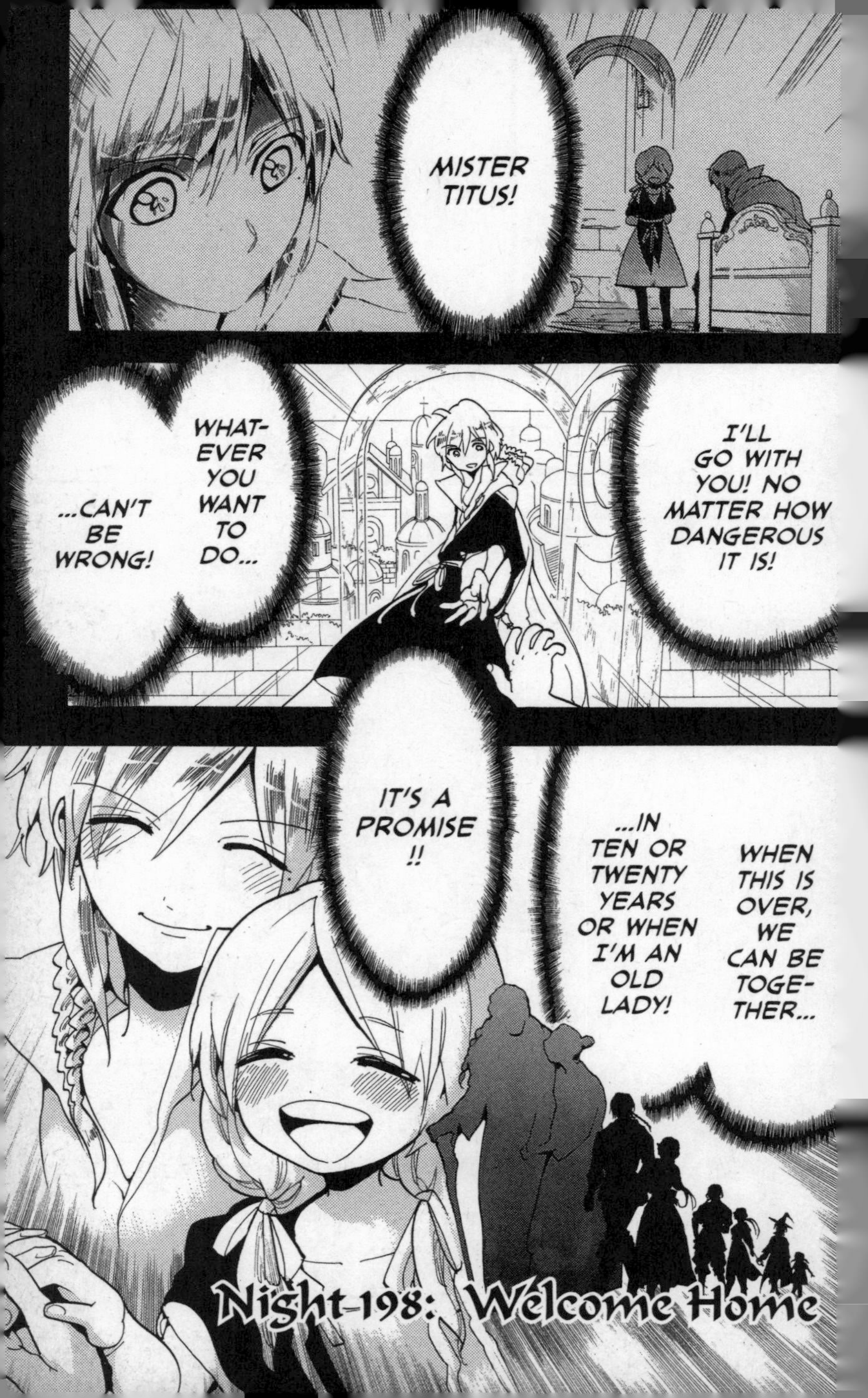
MISTER TITUS!
I'LL GO WITH YOU! NO MATTER HOW DANGEROUS IT IS!
WHAT-EVER YOU WANT TO DO...
...CAN'T BE WRONG!
WHEN THIS IS OVER, WE CAN BE TOGE-THER...
...IN TEN OR TWENTY YEARS OR WHEN I'M AN OLD LADY!
IT'S A PROMISE!!
Night 198: Welcome Home

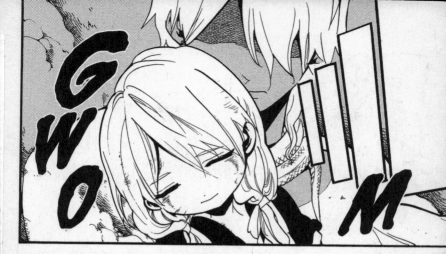

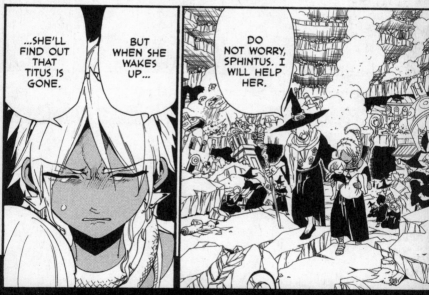

GWOM
DO NOT WORRY, SPHINTUS. I WILL HELP HER.
BUT WHEN SHE WAKES UP...
...SHE'LL FIND OUT THAT TITUS IS GONE.

Night 198: Welcome Home

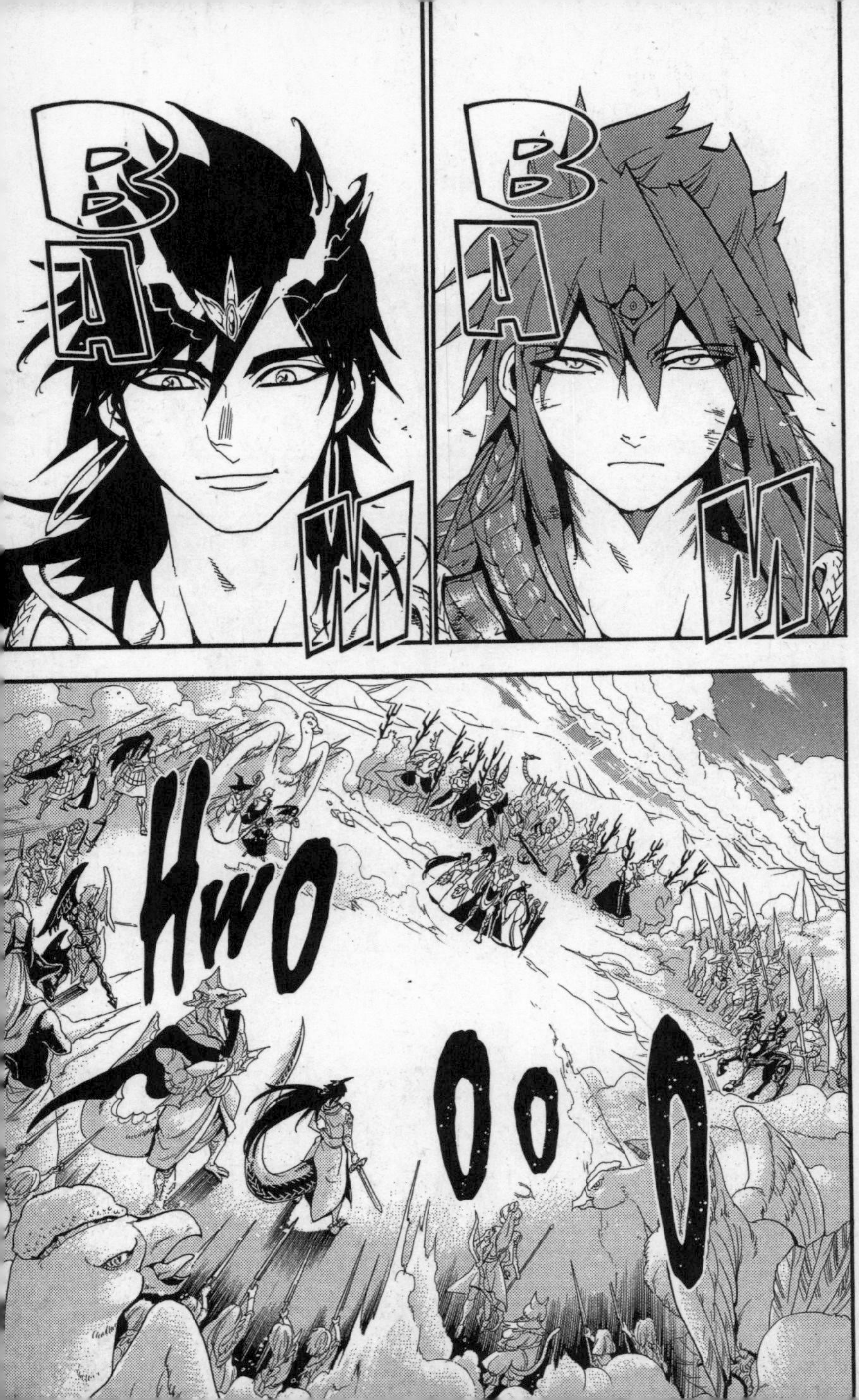
BAAM
BAAM
HWOOOO

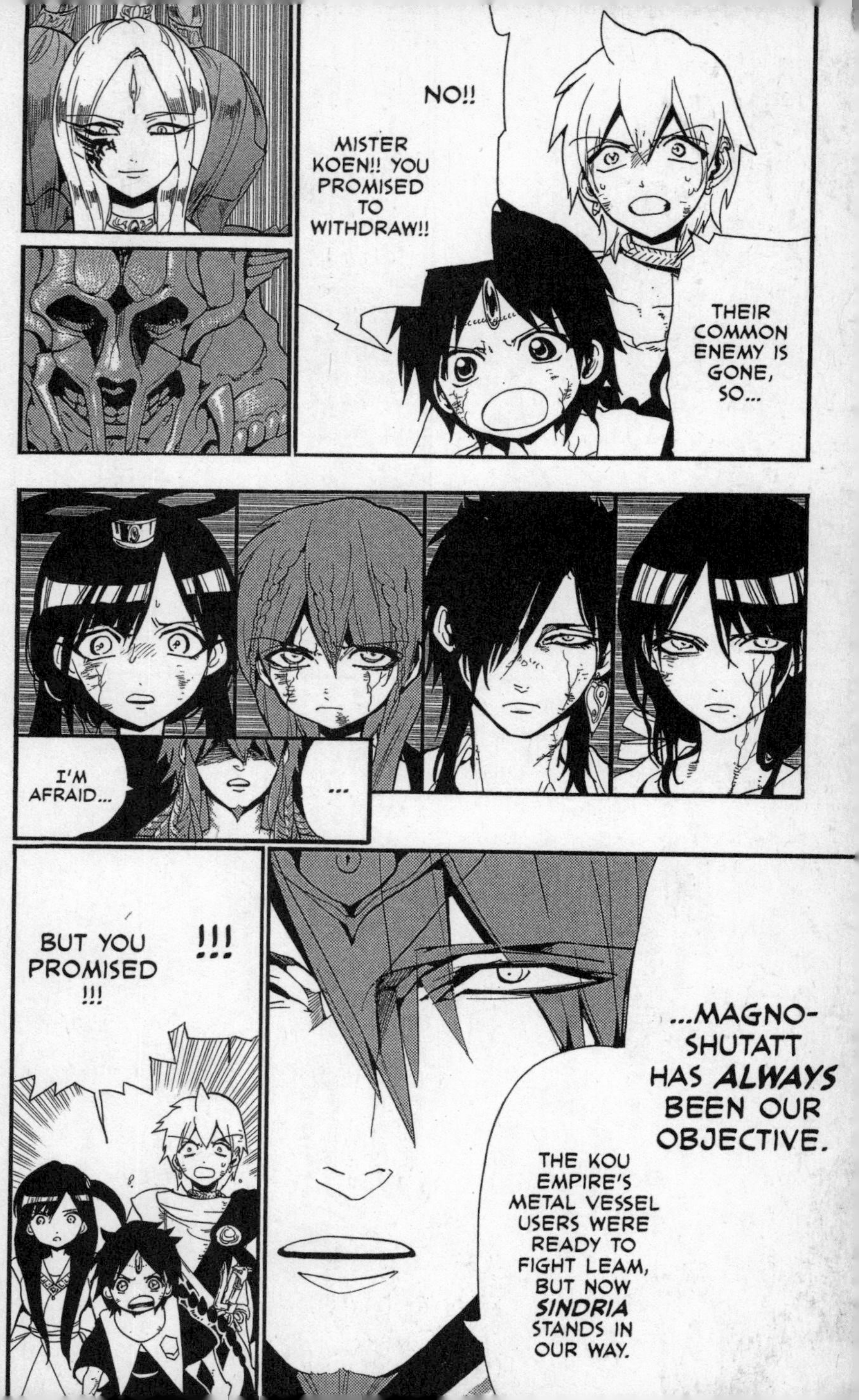

NO!!
MISTER KOEN!! YOU PROMISED TO WITHDRAW!!
THEIR COMMON ENEMY IS GONE, SO...
...
I'M AFRAID...
...MAGNO-SHUTATT HAS ALWAYS BEEN OUR OBJECTIVE.
THE KOU EMPIRE'S METAL VESSEL USERS WERE READY TO FIGHT LEAM, BUT NOW SINDRIA STANDS IN OUR WAY.
!!!
BUT YOU PROMISED !!!

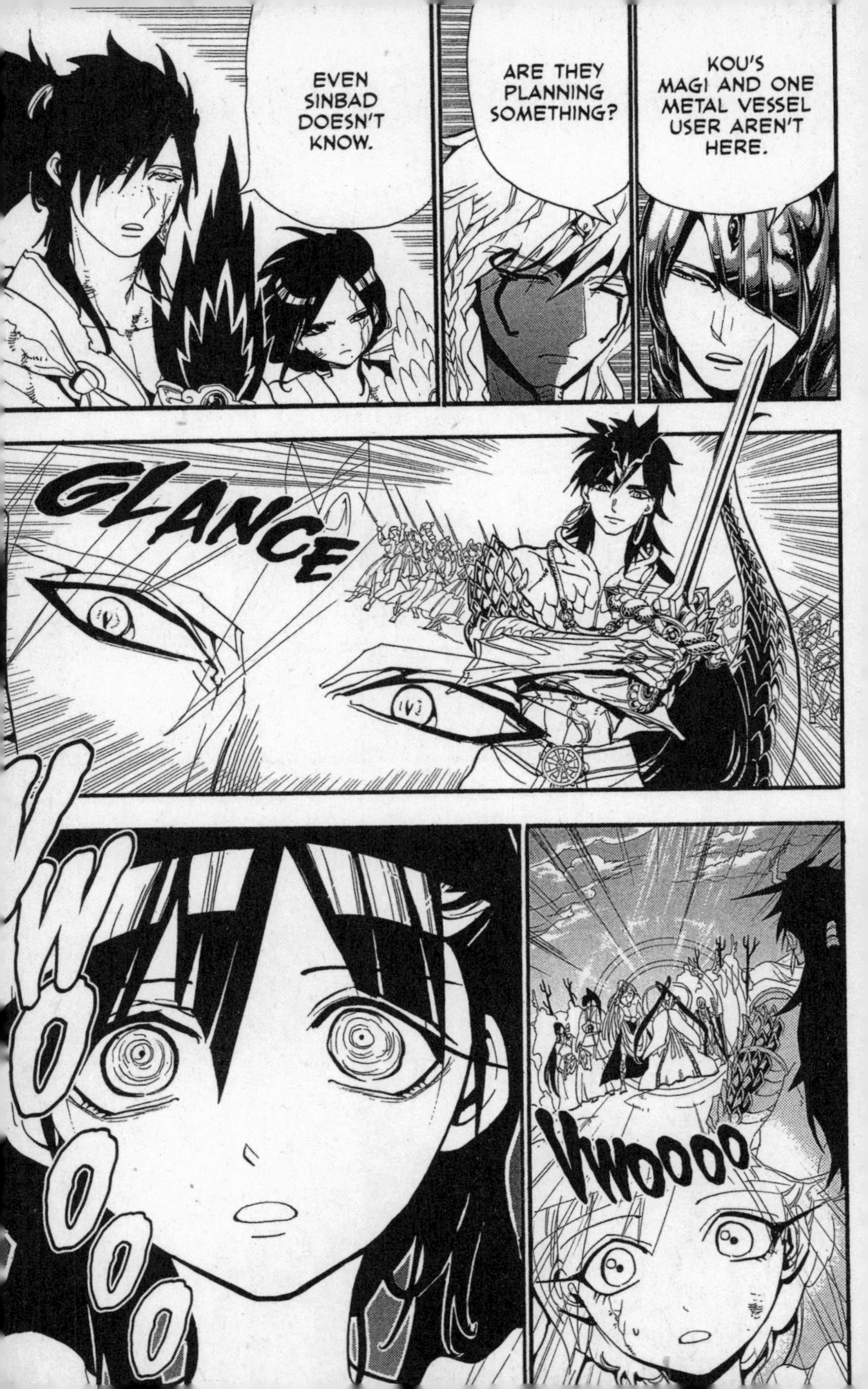

KOU'S MAGI AND ONE METAL VESSEL USER AREN'T HERE.
ARE THEY PLANNING SOMETHING?
EVEN SINBAD DOESN'T KNOW.
GLANCE
VWOOOO

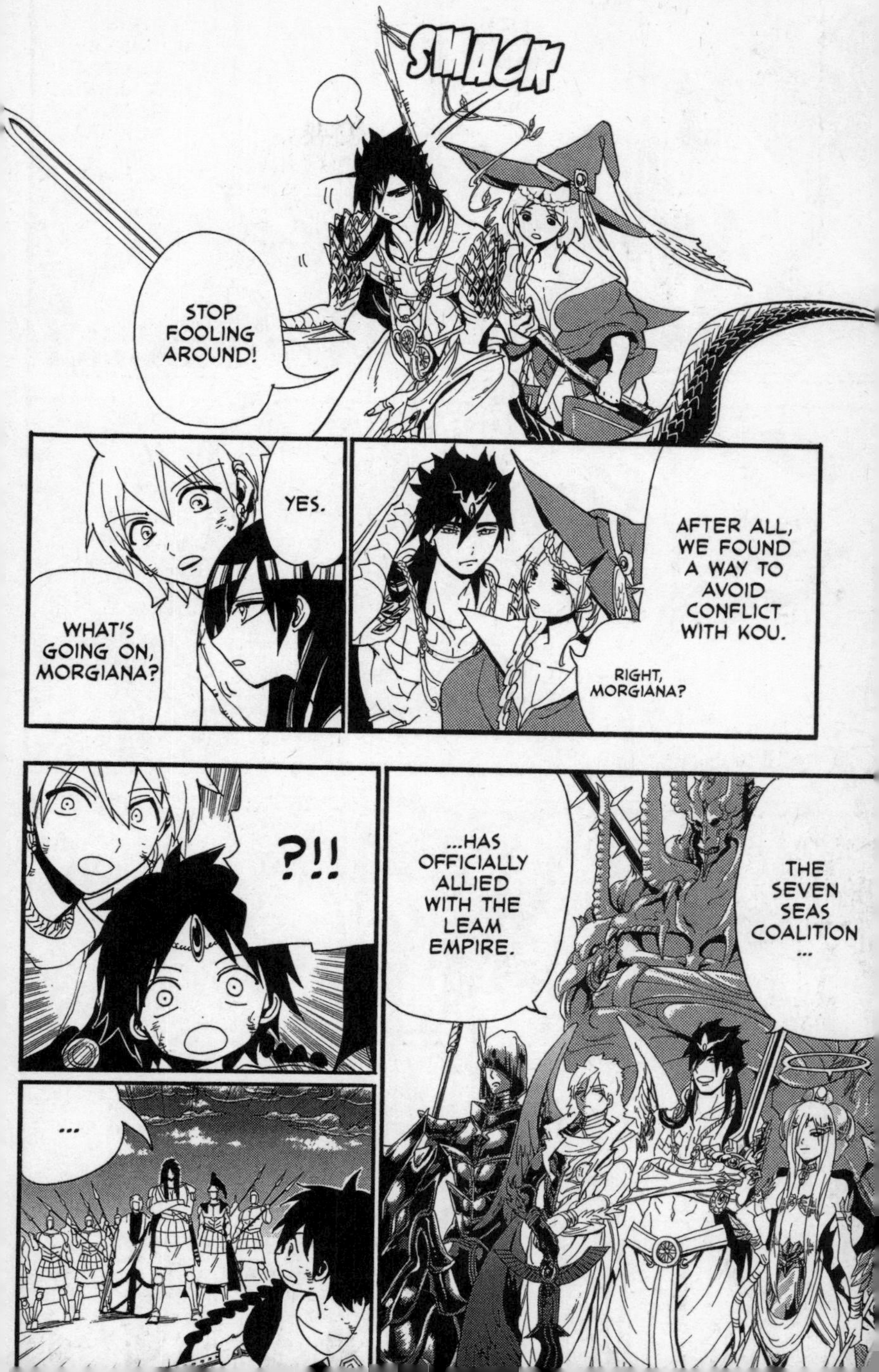
SMACK
STOP FOOLING AROUND!
AFTER ALL, WE FOUND A WAY TO AVOID CONFLICT WITH KOU.
RIGHT, MORGIANA?
YES.
WHAT'S GOING ON, MORGIANA?
THE SEVEN SEAS COALITION ...
...HAS OFFICIALLY ALLIED WITH THE LEAM EMPIRE.
?!!
...

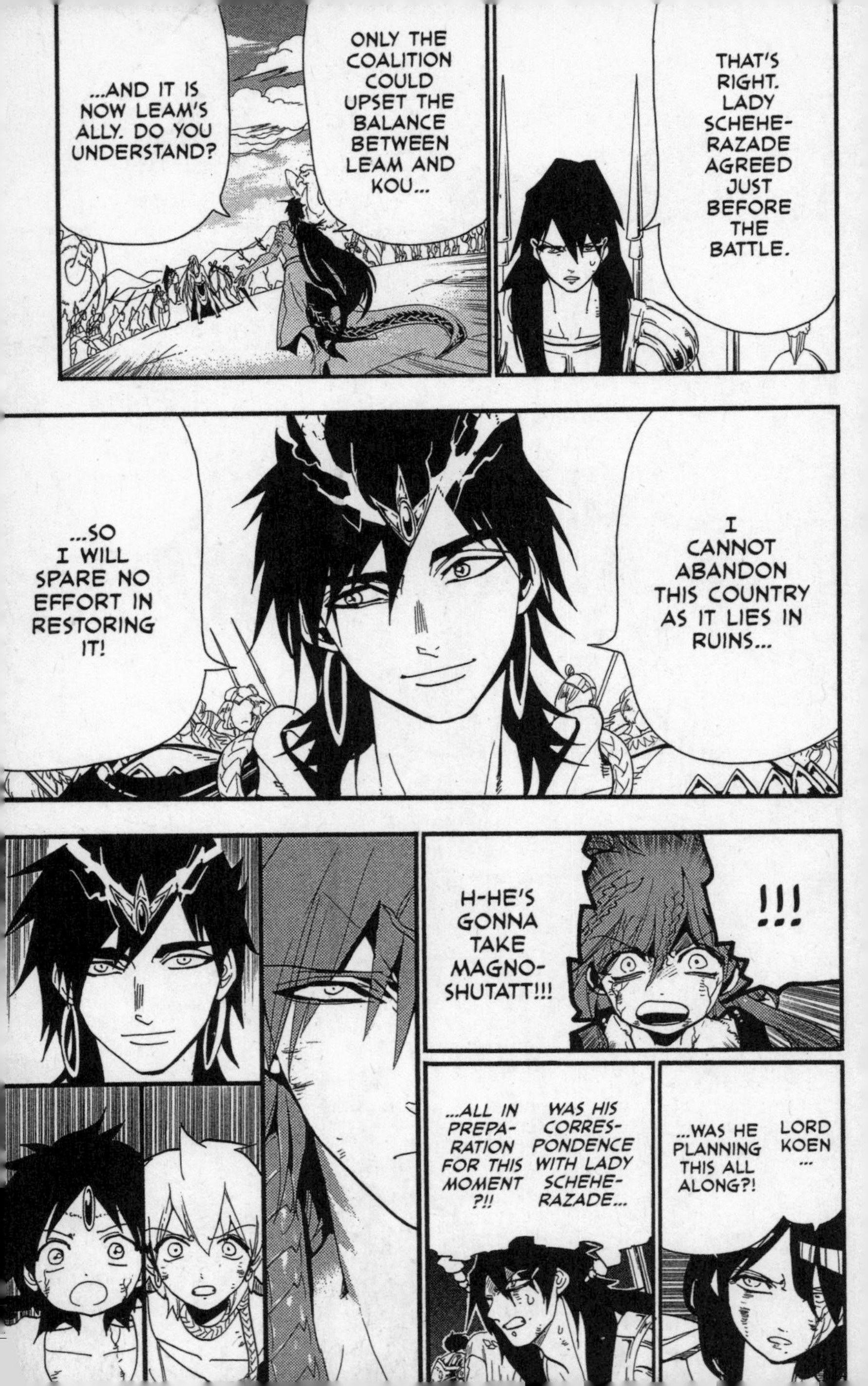
THAT'S RIGHT. LADY SCHEHERAZADE AGREED JUST BEFORE THE BATTLE.
ONLY THE COALITION COULD UPSET THE BALANCE BETWEEN LEAM AND KOU...
...AND IT IS NOW LEAM'S ALLY. DO YOU UNDERSTAND?
I CANNOT ABANDON THIS COUNTRY AS IT LIES IN RUINS...
...SO I WILL SPARE NO EFFORT IN RESTORING IT!
!!!
H-HE'S GONNA TAKE MAGNOSHUTATT!!!
LORD KOEN ...
...WAS HE PLANNING THIS ALL ALONG?!
WAS HIS CORRESPONDENCE WITH LADY SCHEHERAZADE...
...ALL IN PREPARATION FOR THIS MOMENT?!!

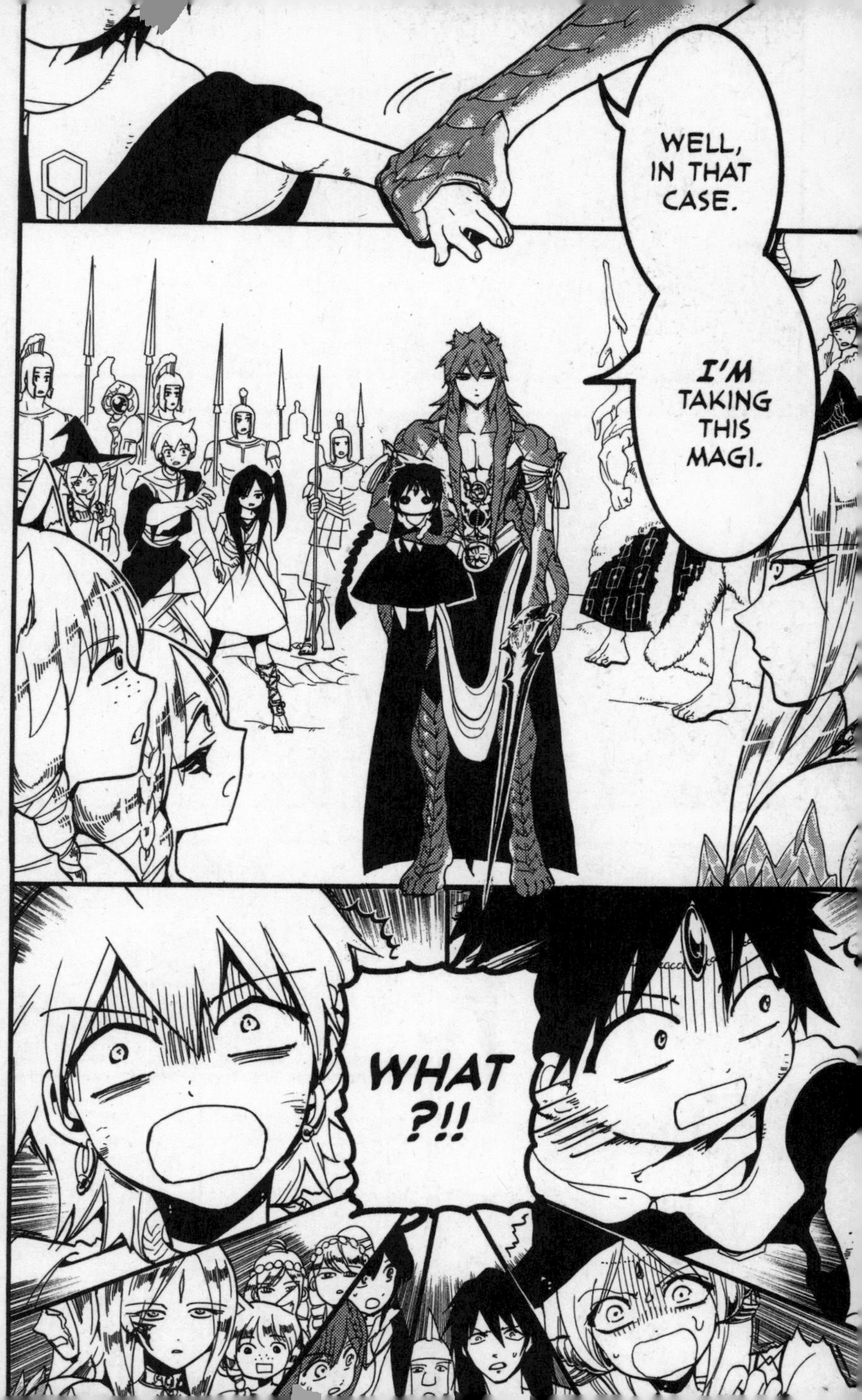
WELL, IN THAT CASE.
I'M TAKING THIS MAGI.
WHAT ?!!

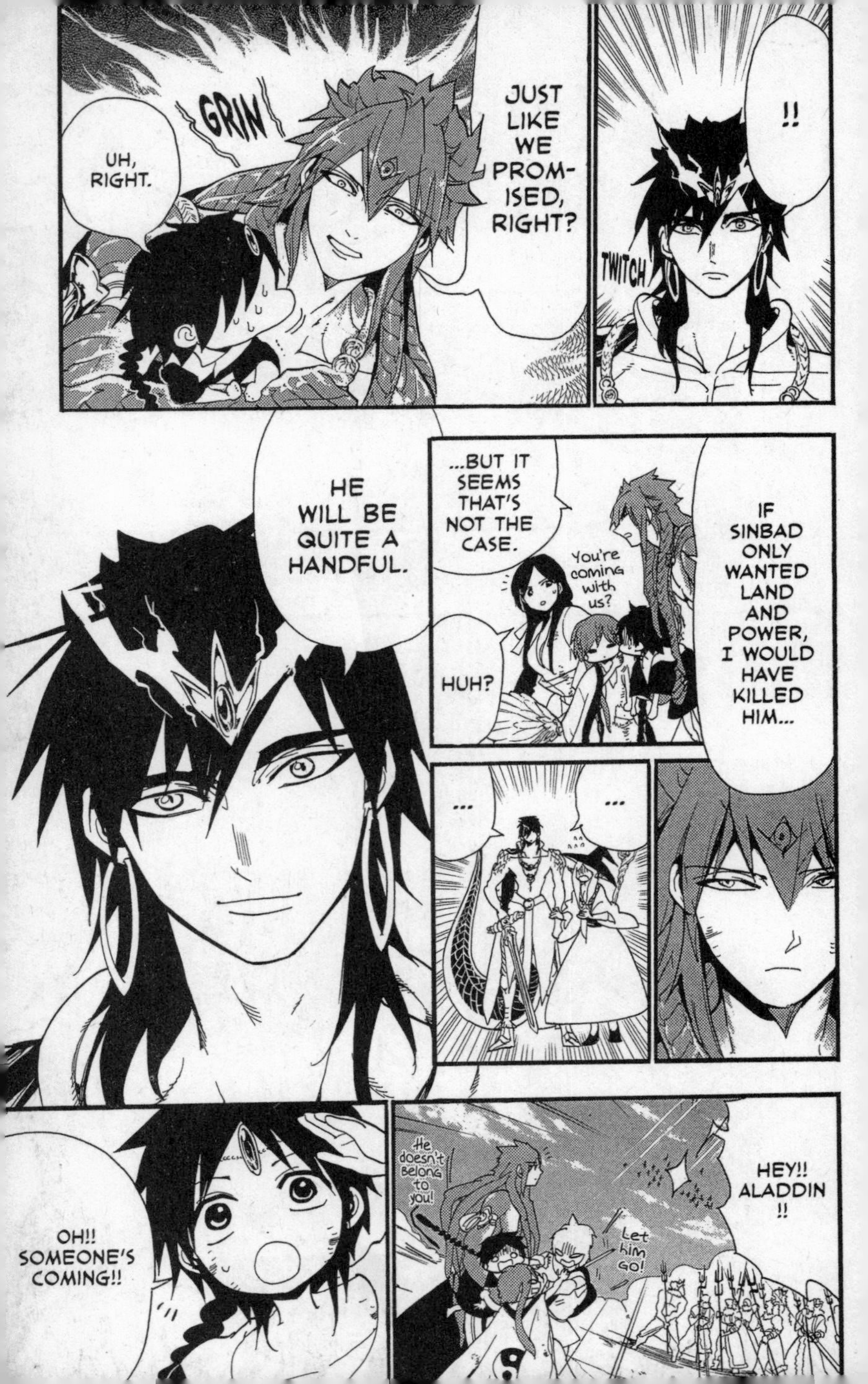
!!
TWITCH
JUST LIKE WE PROMISED, RIGHT?
GRIN
UH, RIGHT.
IF SINBAD ONLY WANTED LAND AND POWER, I WOULD HAVE KILLED HIM...
...BUT IT SEEMS THAT'S NOT THE CASE.
You're coming with us?
HUH?
...
...
HE WILL BE QUITE A HANDFUL.
HEY!! ALADDIN !!
Let him go!
He doesn't belong to you!
OH!! SOMEONE'S COMING!!

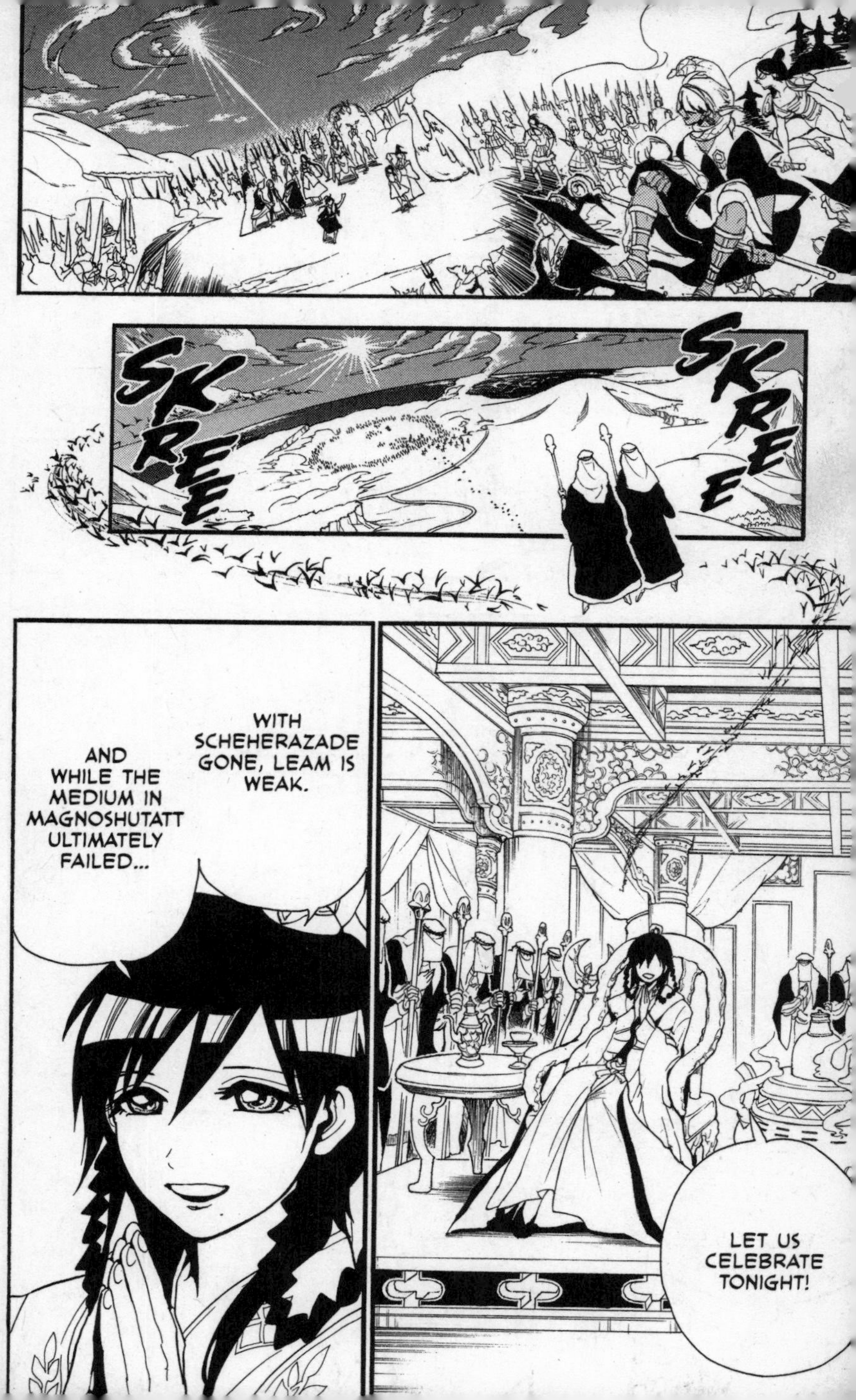
SKREE
SKREE
LET US CELEBRATE TONIGHT!
WITH SCHEHERAZADE GONE, LEAM IS WEAK.
AND WHILE THE MEDIUM IN MAGNOSHUTATT ULTIMATELY FAILED...

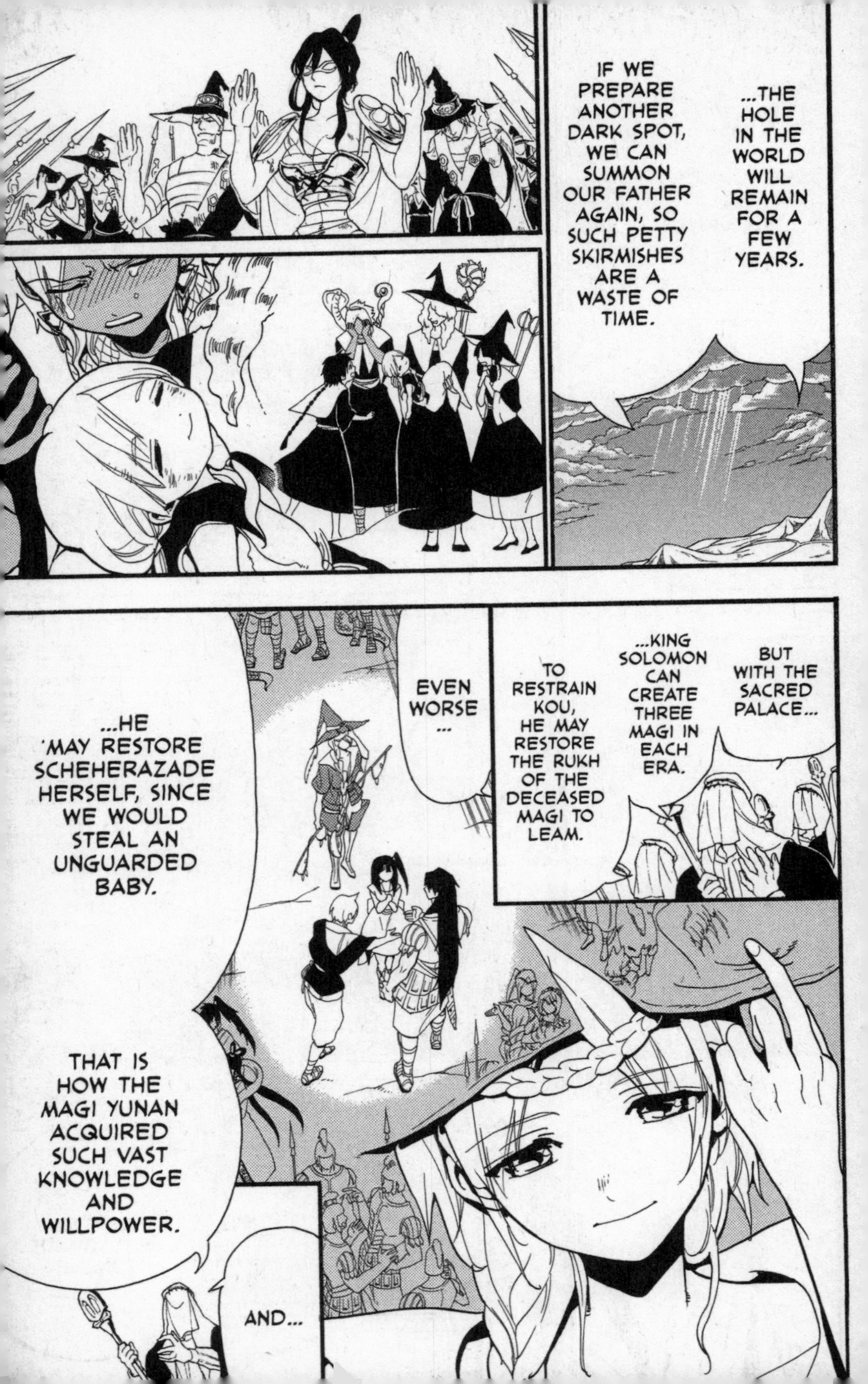
...THE HOLE IN THE WORLD WILL REMAIN FOR A FEW YEARS.
IF WE PREPARE ANOTHER DARK SPOT, WE CAN SUMMON OUR FATHER AGAIN, SO SUCH PETTY SKIRMISHES ARE A WASTE OF TIME.
BUT WITH THE SACRED PALACE...
...KING SOLOMON CAN CREATE THREE MAGI IN EACH ERA.
TO RESTRAIN KOU, HE MAY RESTORE THE RUKH OF THE DECEASED MAGI TO LEAM.
EVEN WORSE...
...HE MAY RESTORE SCHEHERAZADE HERSELF, SINCE WE WOULD STEAL AN UNGUARDED BABY.
THAT IS HOW THE MAGI YUNAN ACQUIRED SUCH VAST KNOWLEDGE AND WILLPOWER.
AND...

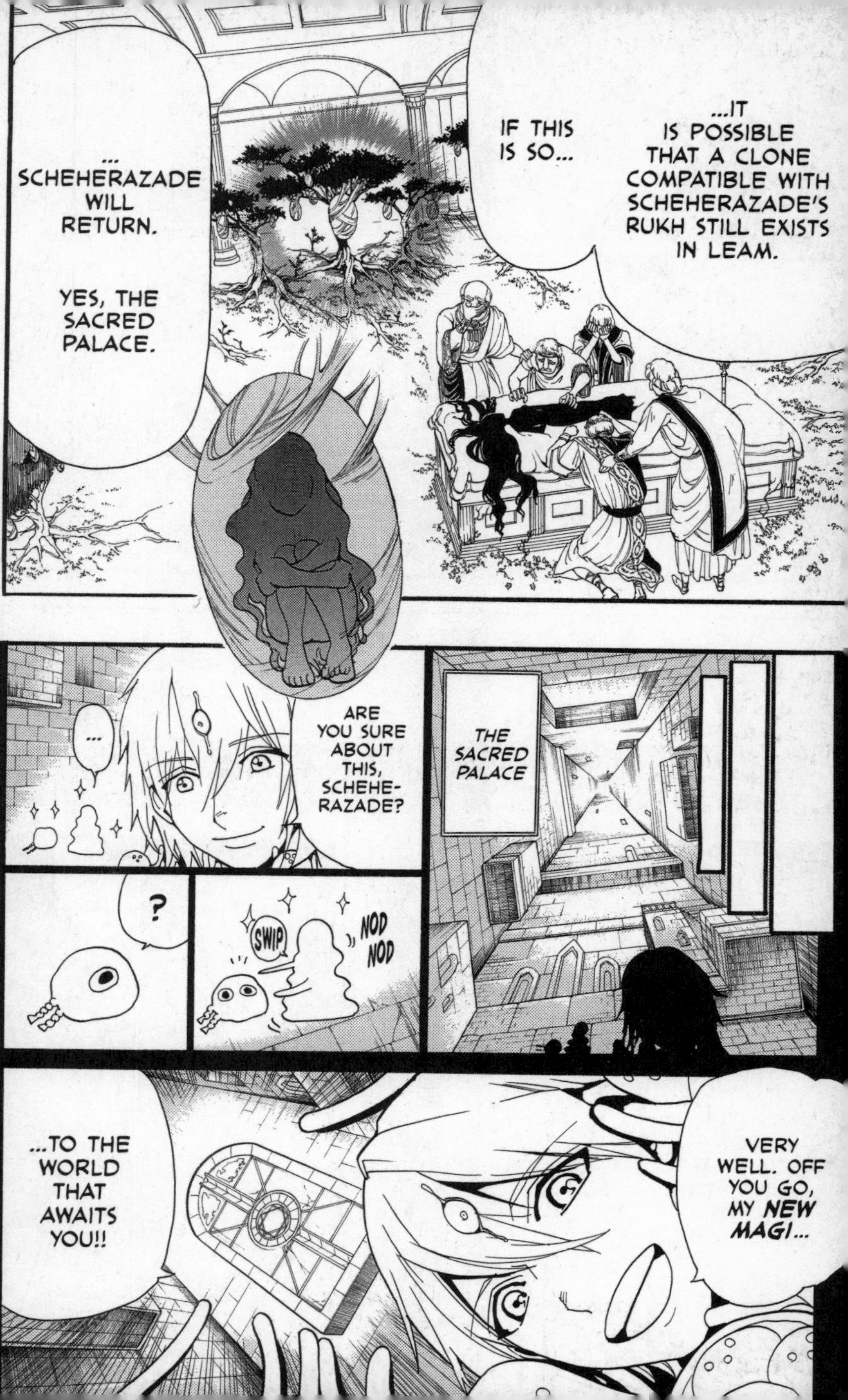
IF THIS IS SO...
...IT IS POSSIBLE THAT A CLONE COMPATIBLE WITH SCHEHERAZADE'S RUKH STILL EXISTS IN LEAM.
...SCHEHERAZADE WILL RETURN.
YES, THE SACRED PALACE.
THE SACRED PALACE
ARE YOU SURE ABOUT THIS, SCHEHE-RAZADE?
...
SWIP
NOD NOD
?
VERY WELL. OFF YOU GO, MY NEW MAGI...
...TO THE WORLD THAT AWAITS YOU!!

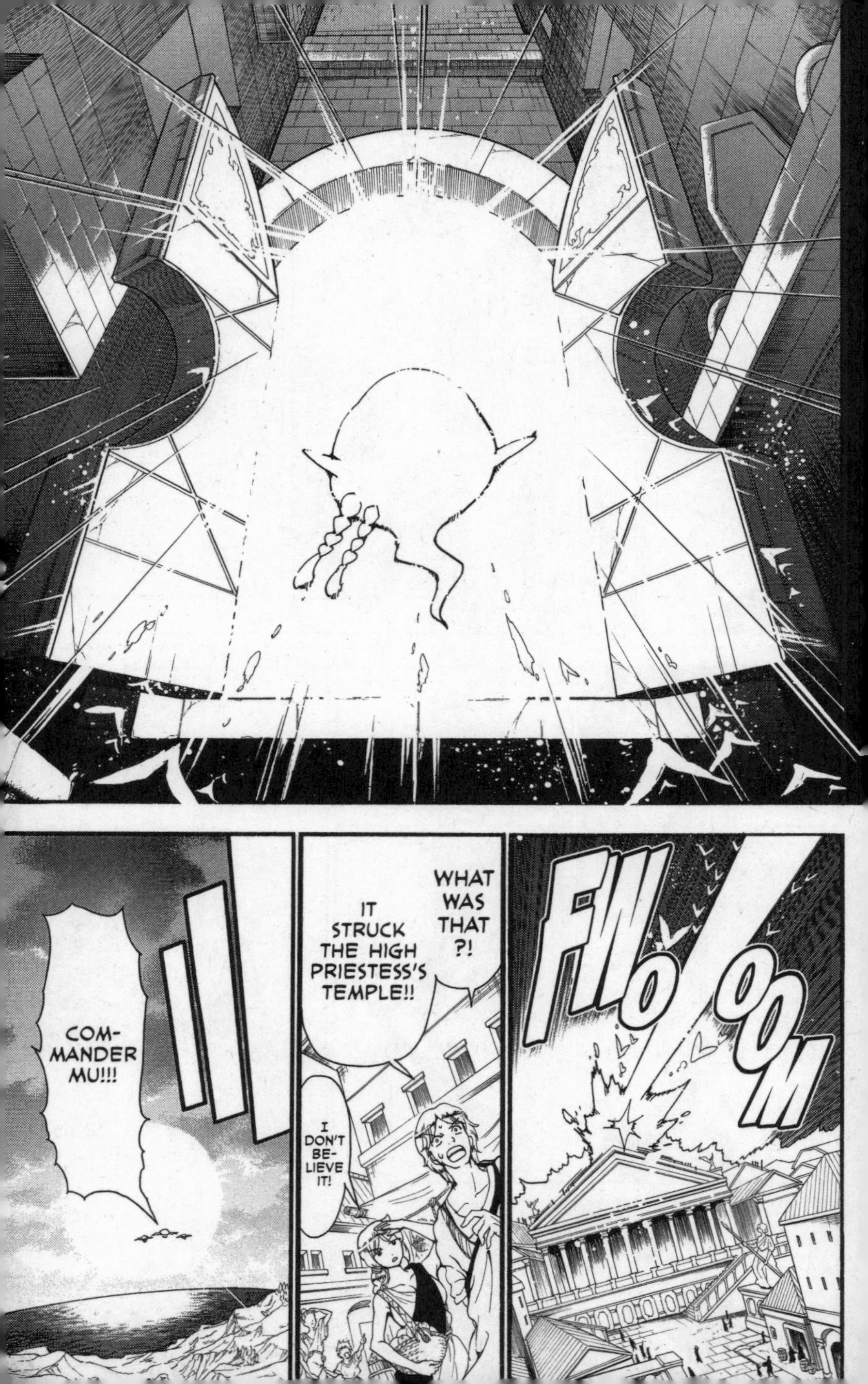
FWOOOM
WHAT WAS THAT?!
IT STRUCK THE HIGH PRIESTESS'S TEMPLE!!
I DON'T BELIEVE IT!
COMMANDER MU!!!

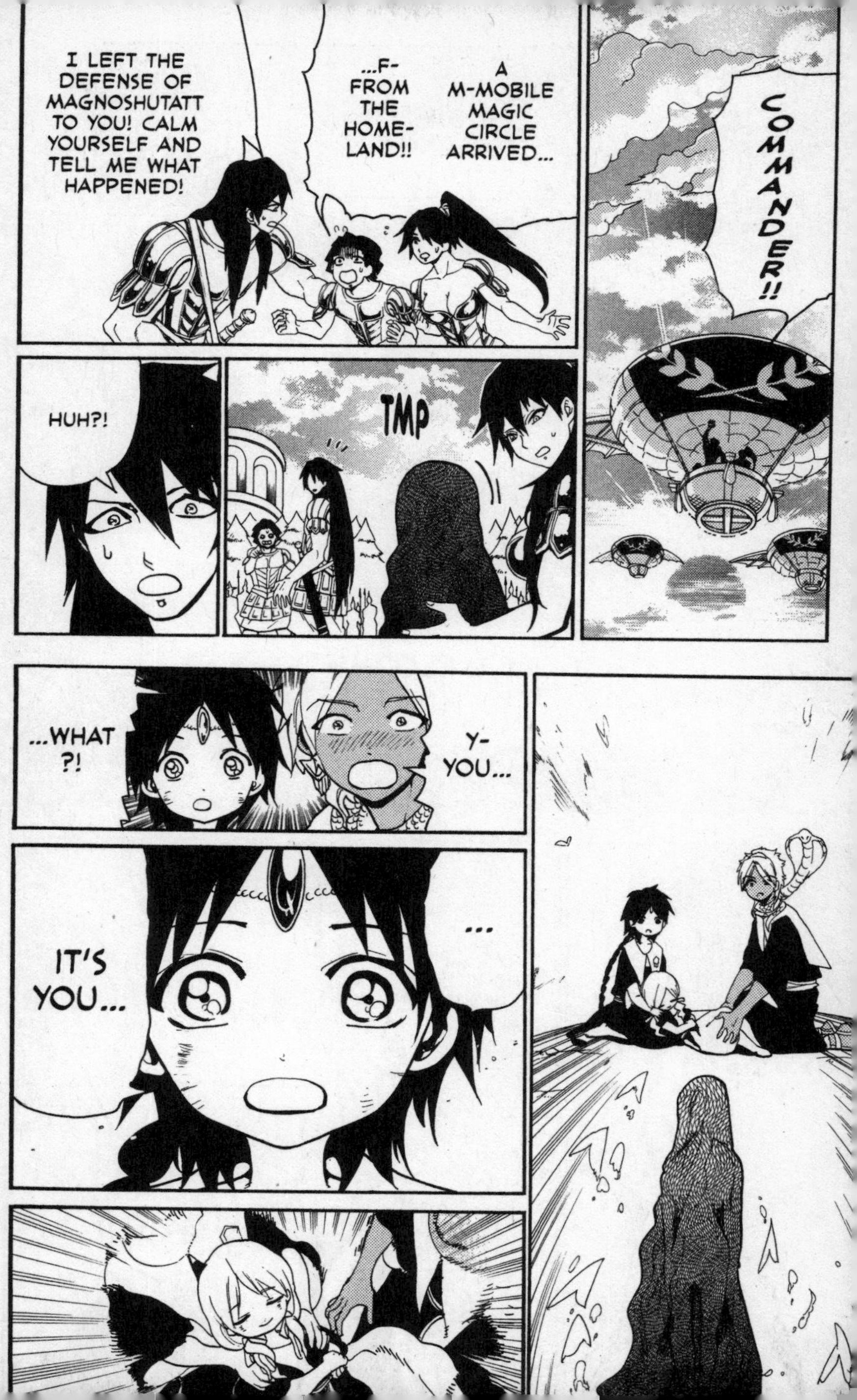
COMMANDER!!
A M-MOBILE MAGIC CIRCLE ARRIVED...
...F- FROM THE HOMELAND!!
I LEFT THE DEFENSE OF MAGNOSHUTATT TO YOU! CALM YOURSELF AND TELL ME WHAT HAPPENED!
TMP
HUH?!
Y- YOU...
...WHAT ?!
...
IT'S YOU...

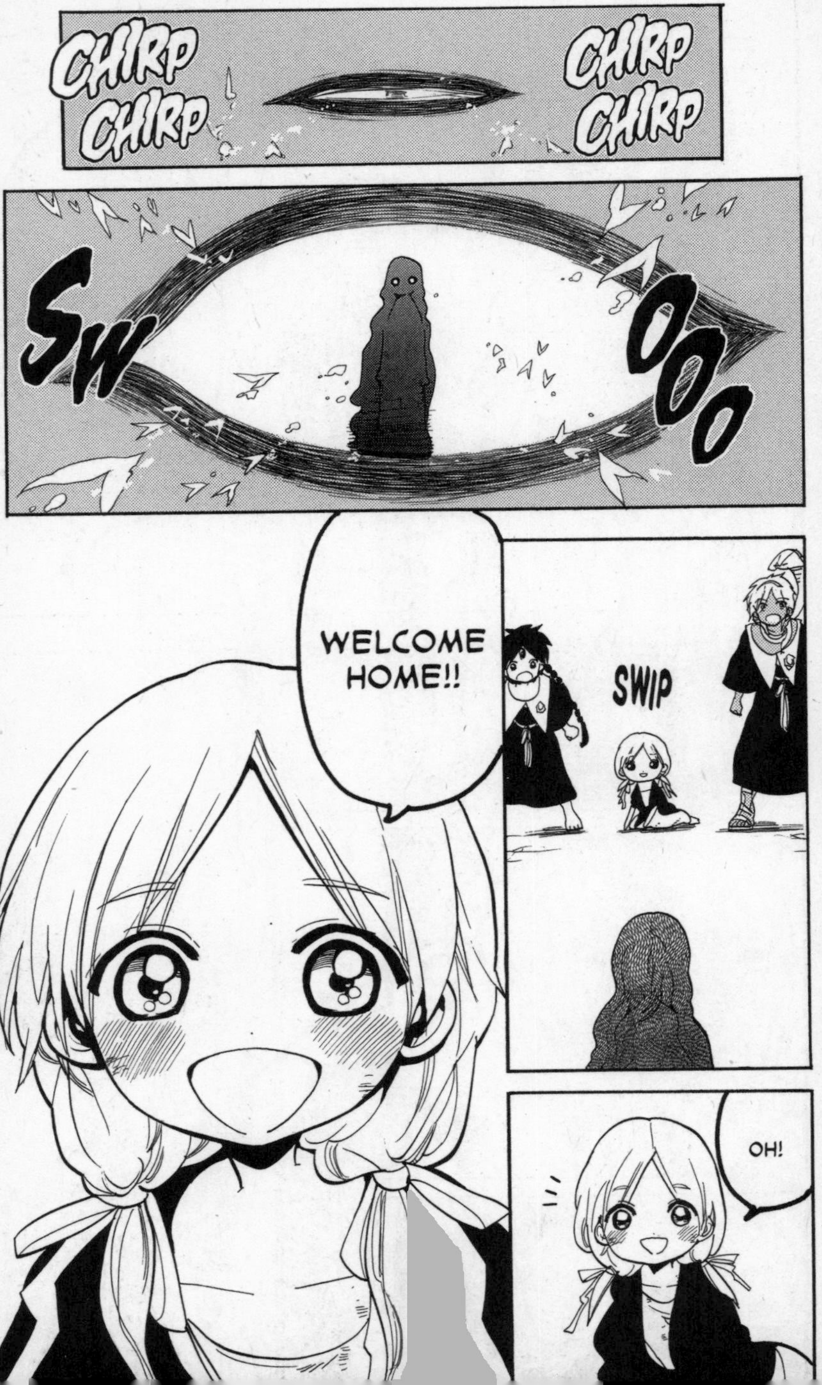
CHIRP CHIRP
CHIRP CHIRP
SWOOO
SWIP
OH!
WELCOME HOME!!

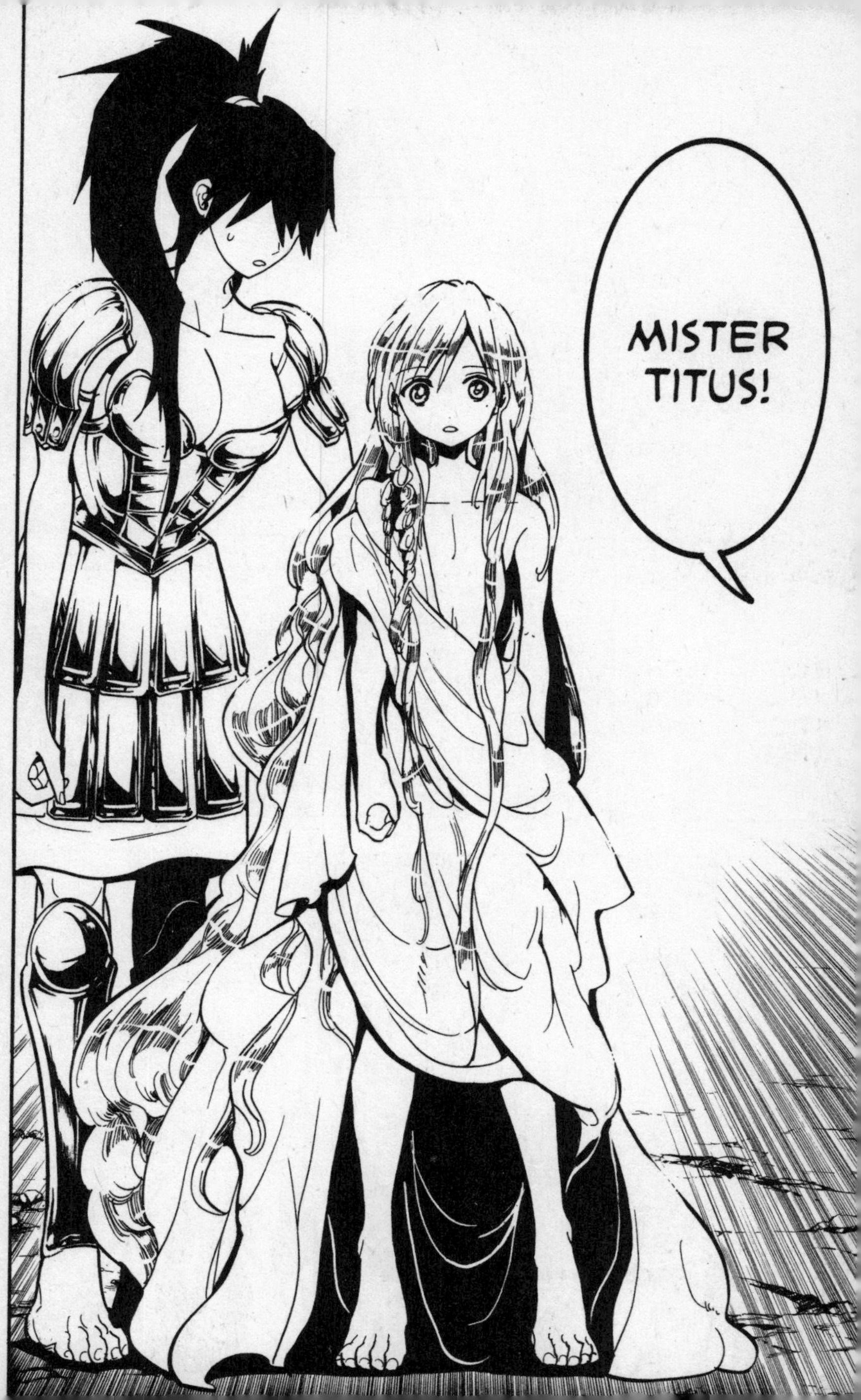
MISTER TITUS!

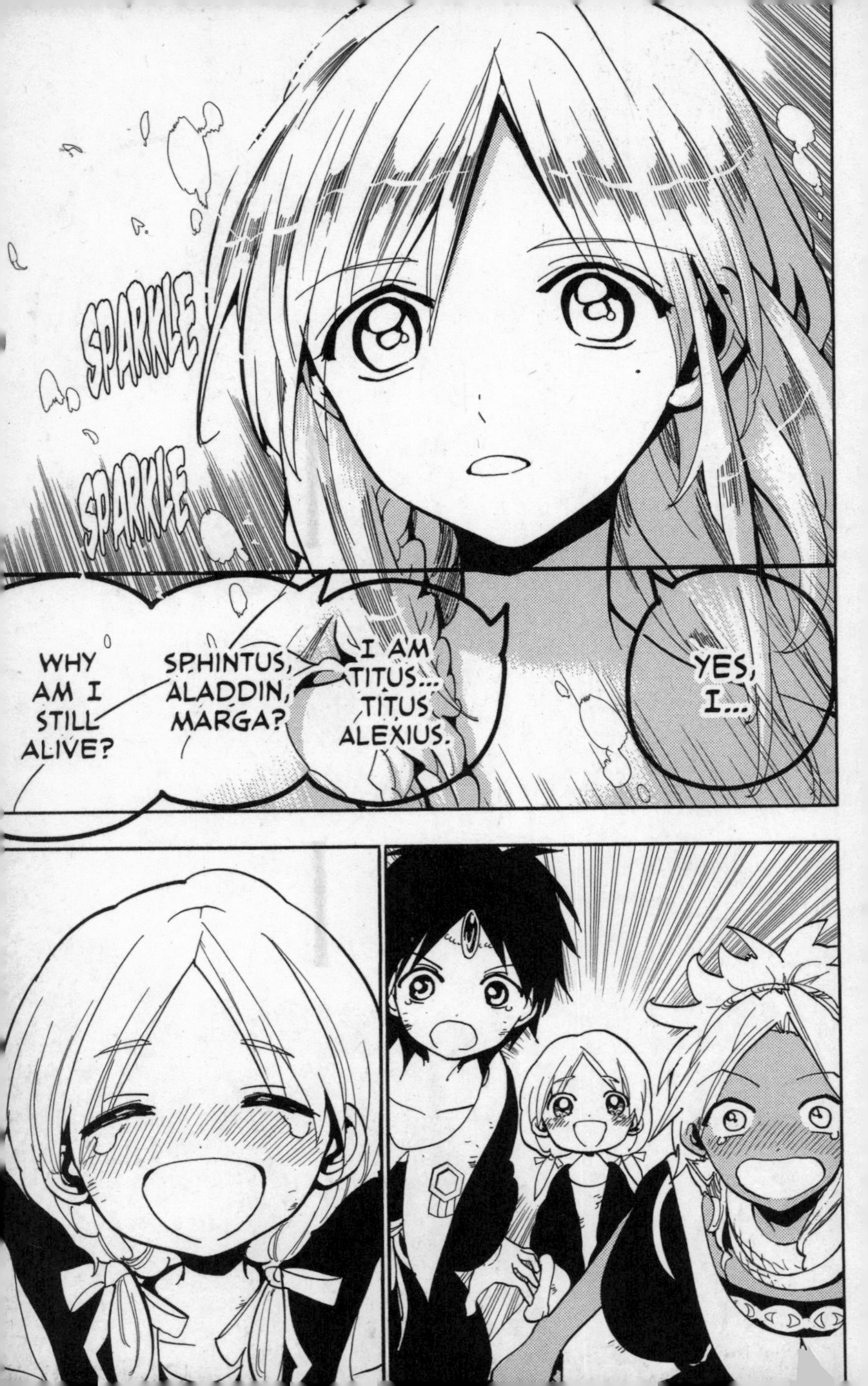
SPARKLE
SPARKLE
YES, I...
I AM TITUS... TITUS ALEXIUS.
SPHINTUS, ALADDIN, MARGA?
WHY AM I STILL ALIVE?

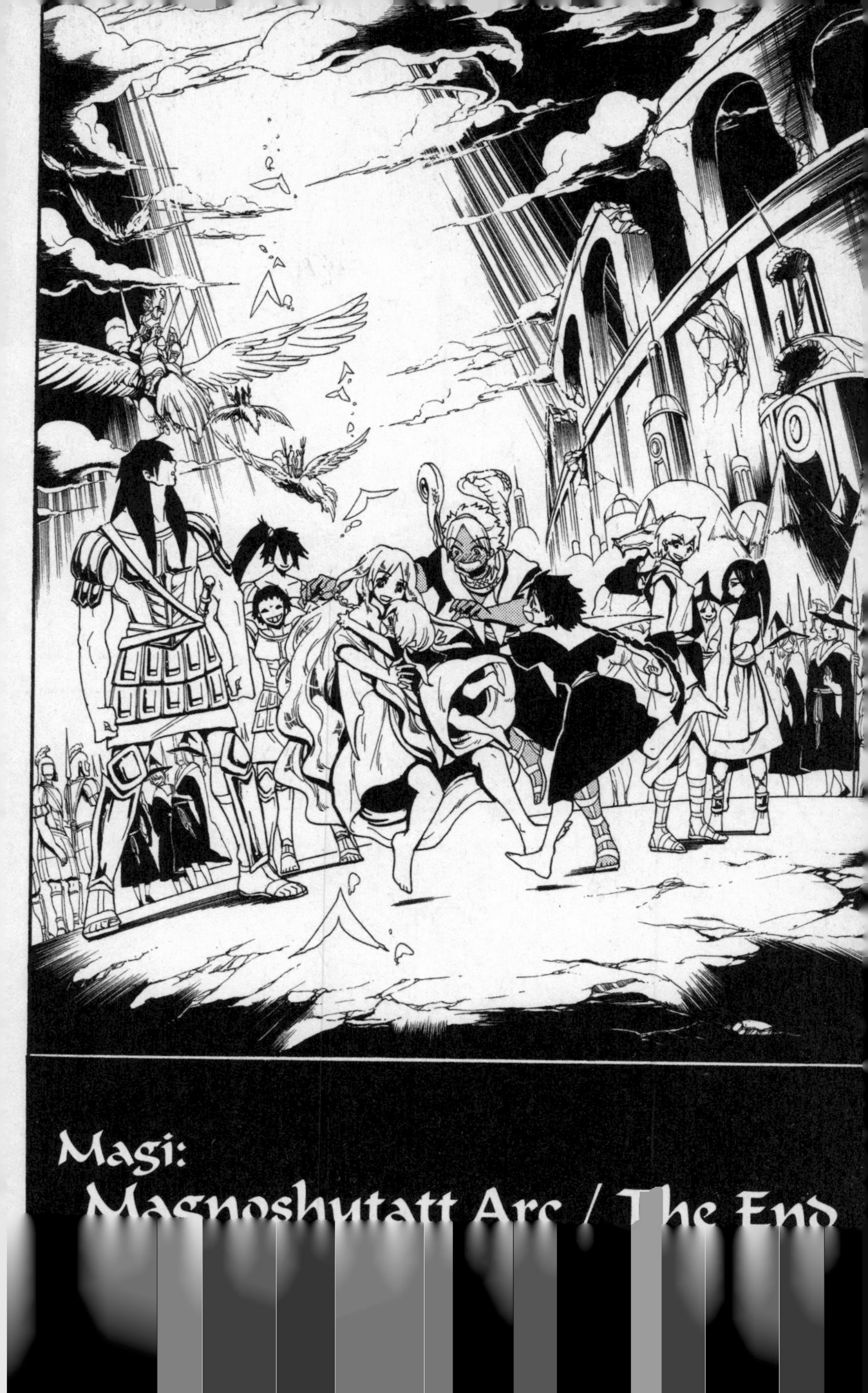

Magi:
Magnoshutatt Arc / The End

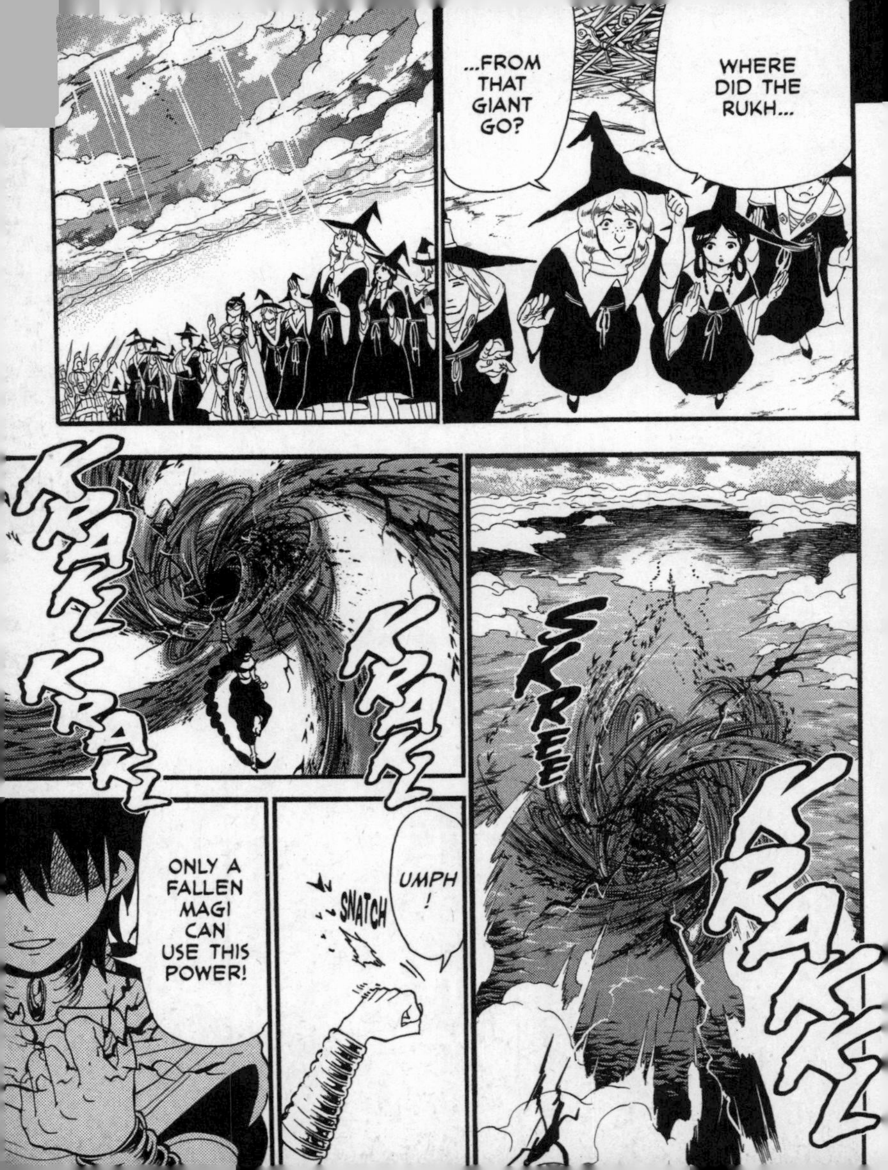
WHERE DID THE RUKH...
...FROM THAT GIANT GO?
SKREE
KRAKL
KRAKL
KRAKL
KRAKL
UMPH!
SNATCH
ONLY A FALLEN MAGI CAN USE THIS POWER!

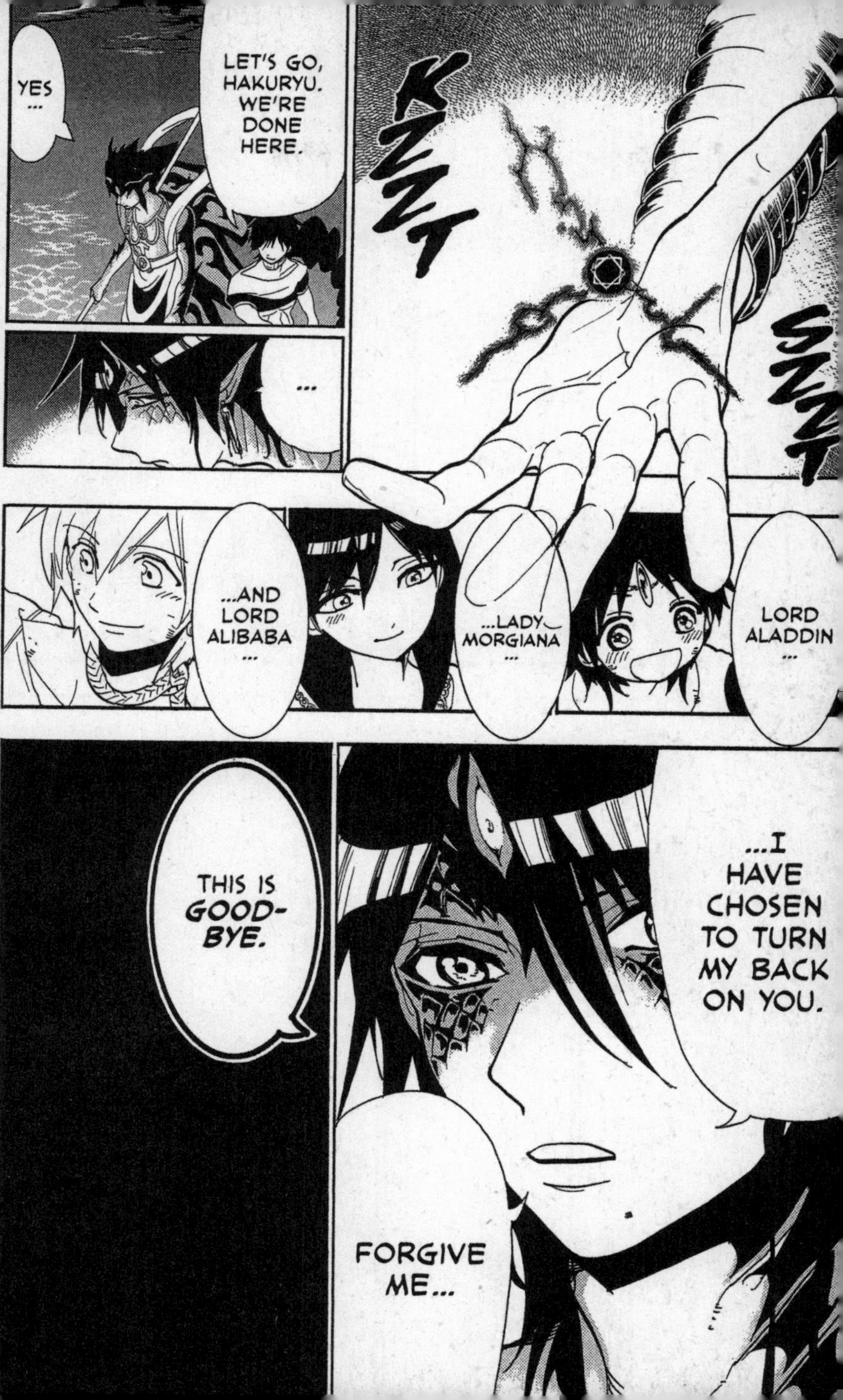
KZZZT
SZZZT
LET'S GO, HAKURYU. WE'RE DONE HERE.
YES...
...
LORD ALADDIN...
...LADY MORGIANA...
...AND LORD ALIBABA...
...I HAVE CHOSEN TO TURN MY BACK ON YOU.
FORGIVE ME...
THIS IS *GOOD-BYE.*

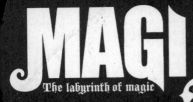

MAGI
The labyrinth of magic
20

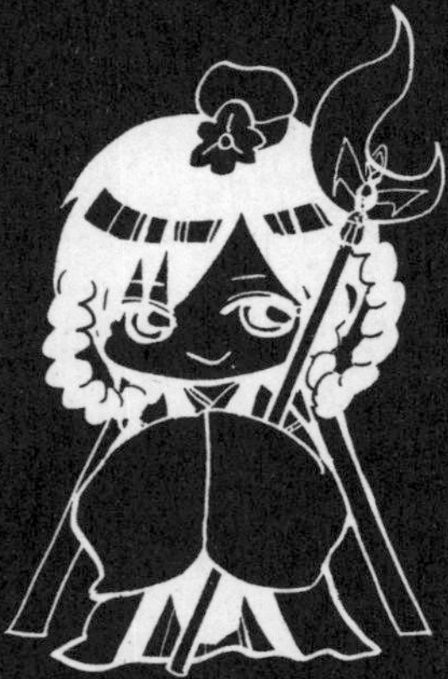

Staff

■ Story & Art

Shinobu Ohtaka

■ Regular Assistants

Hiro Maizima

Yurika Isozaki

Tomo Niiya

Yuiko Akiyama

Megi

Aya Umoto

■ Editor

Kazuaki Ishibashi

■ Sales & Promotion

Yuki Mizusawa

Atsushi Chiku

■ Designer

Yasuo Shimura + Bay Bridge Studio

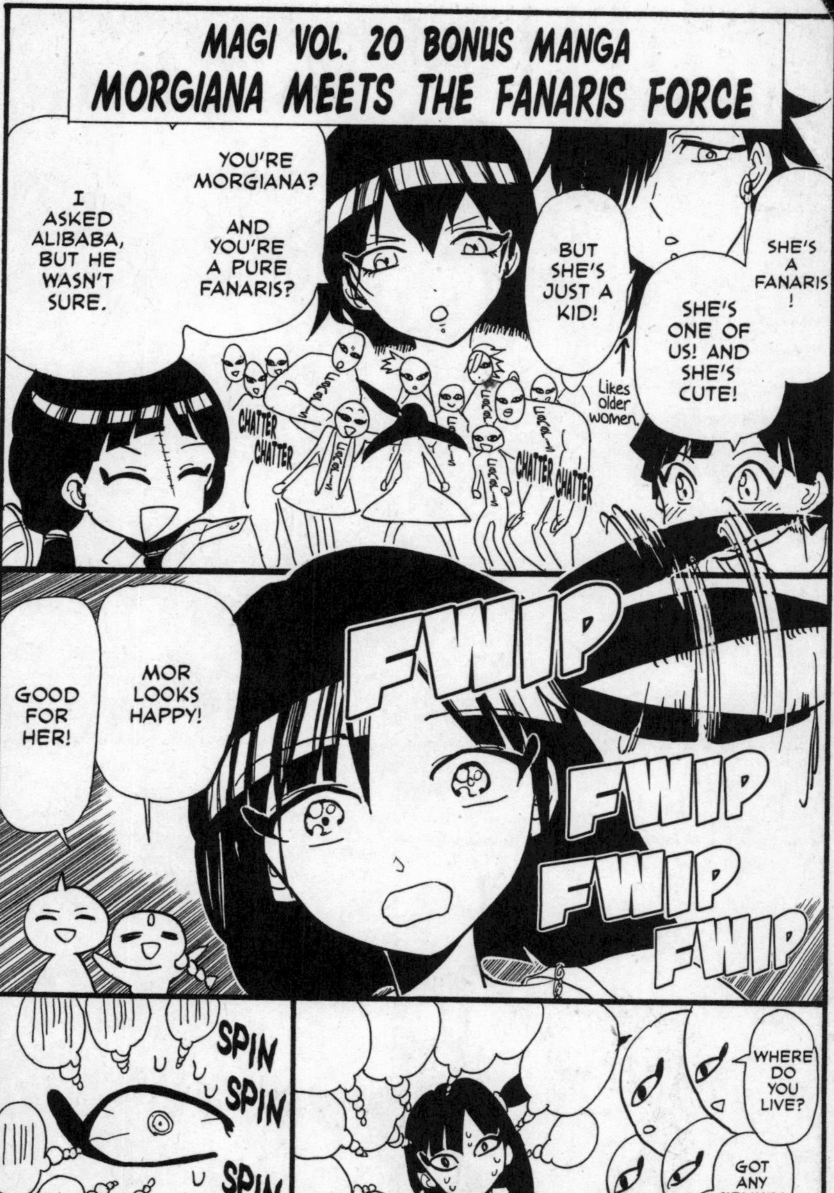
MAGI VOL. 20 BONUS MANGA
MORGIANA MEETS THE FANARIS FORCE
SHE'S A FANARIS!
SHE'S ONE OF US! AND SHE'S CUTE!
BUT SHE'S JUST A KID!
Likes older women.
YOU'RE MORGIANA? AND YOU'RE A PURE FANARIS?
I ASKED ALIBABA, BUT HE WASN'T SURE.
CHATTER CHATTER
CHATTER CHATTER
FWIP
FWIP
FWIP
FWIP
MOR LOOKS HAPPY!
GOOD FOR HER!
WHERE DO YOU LIVE?
GOT ANY SIBLINGS?
SPIN
SPIN
SPIN

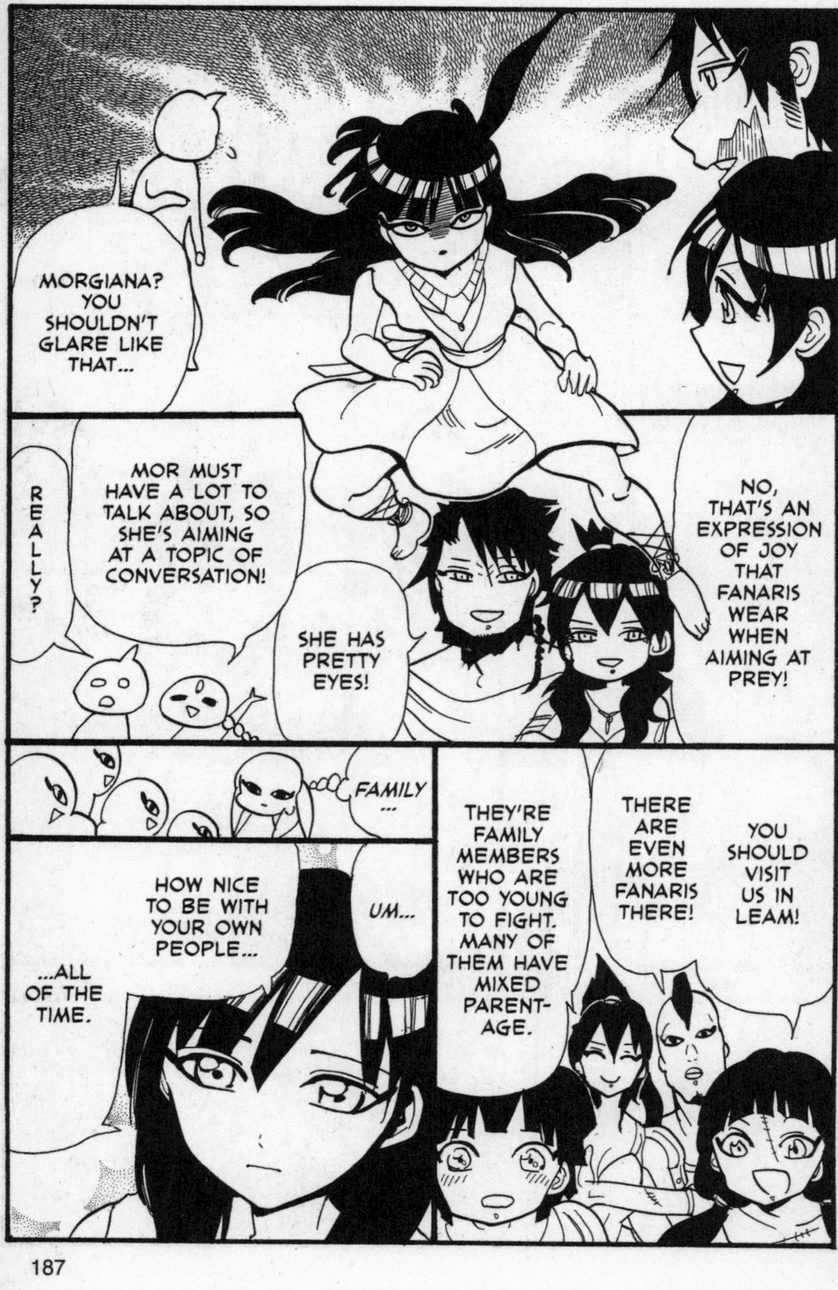
MORGIANA? YOU SHOULDN'T GLARE LIKE THAT...
NO, THAT'S AN EXPRESSION OF JOY THAT FANARIS WEAR WHEN AIMING AT PREY!
SHE HAS PRETTY EYES!
MOR MUST HAVE A LOT TO TALK ABOUT, SO SHE'S AIMING AT A TOPIC OF CONVERSATION!
REALLY?
YOU SHOULD VISIT US IN LEAM!
THERE ARE EVEN MORE FANARIS THERE!
THEY'RE FAMILY MEMBERS WHO ARE TOO YOUNG TO FIGHT. MANY OF THEM HAVE MIXED PARENT-AGE.
FAMILY ...
UM...
HOW NICE TO BE WITH YOUR OWN PEOPLE...
...ALL OF THE TIME.

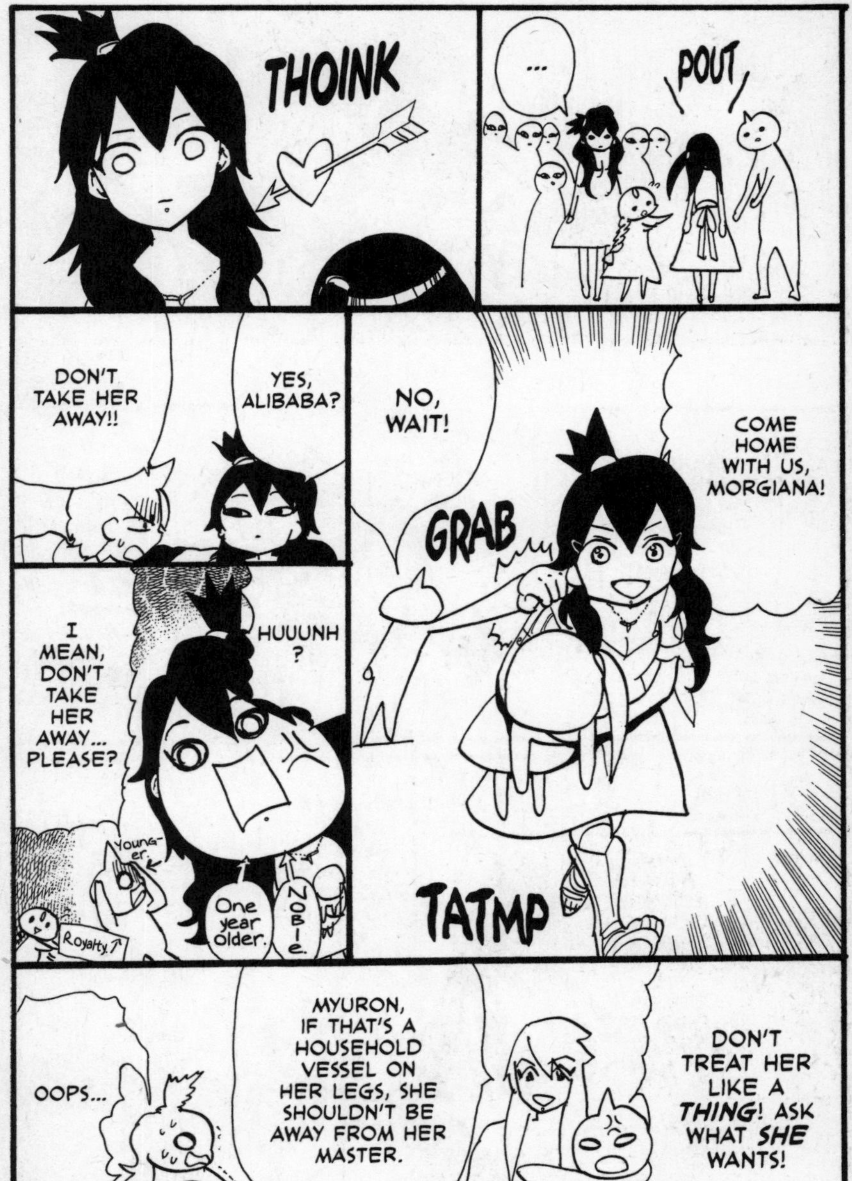
...
POUT
THOINK
COME HOME WITH US, MORGIANA!
NO, WAIT!
GRAB
TATMP
YES, ALIBABA?
DON'T TAKE HER AWAY!!
HUUUNH?
I MEAN, DON'T TAKE HER AWAY... PLEASE?
Younger.
Noble.
One year older.
Royalty.
DON'T TREAT HER LIKE A *THING*! ASK WHAT *SHE* WANTS!
MYURON, IF THAT'S A HOUSEHOLD VESSEL ON HER LEGS, SHE SHOULDN'T BE AWAY FROM HER MASTER.
OOPS...

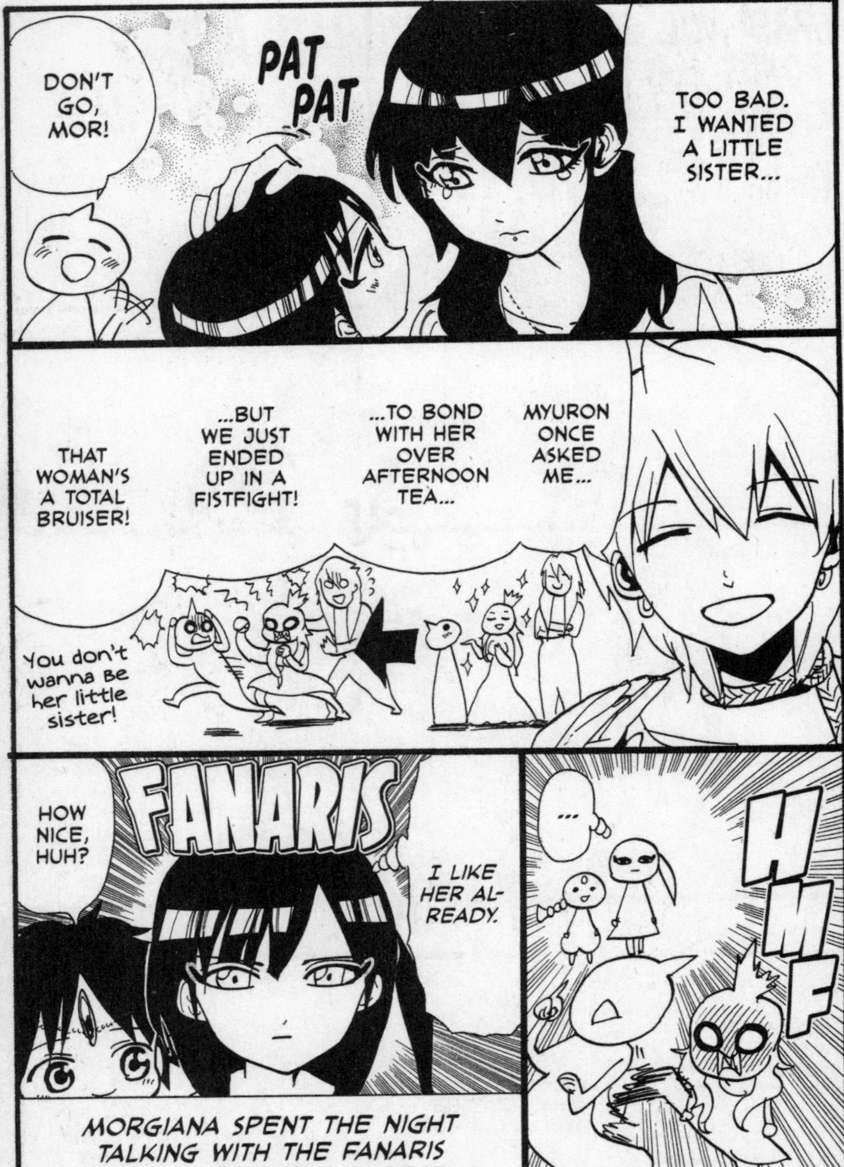
TOO BAD. I WANTED A LITTLE SISTER...
PAT PAT
DON'T GO, MOR!
MYURON ONCE ASKED ME...
...TO BOND WITH HER OVER AFTERNOON TEA...
...BUT WE JUST ENDED UP IN A FISTFIGHT!
THAT WOMAN'S A TOTAL BRUISER!
You don't wanna be her little sister!
HMF
...
I LIKE HER AL-READY.
FANARIS
HOW NICE, HUH?
MORGIANA SPENT THE NIGHT TALKING WITH THE FANARIS FORCE AND HAD A GREAT TIME / THE END

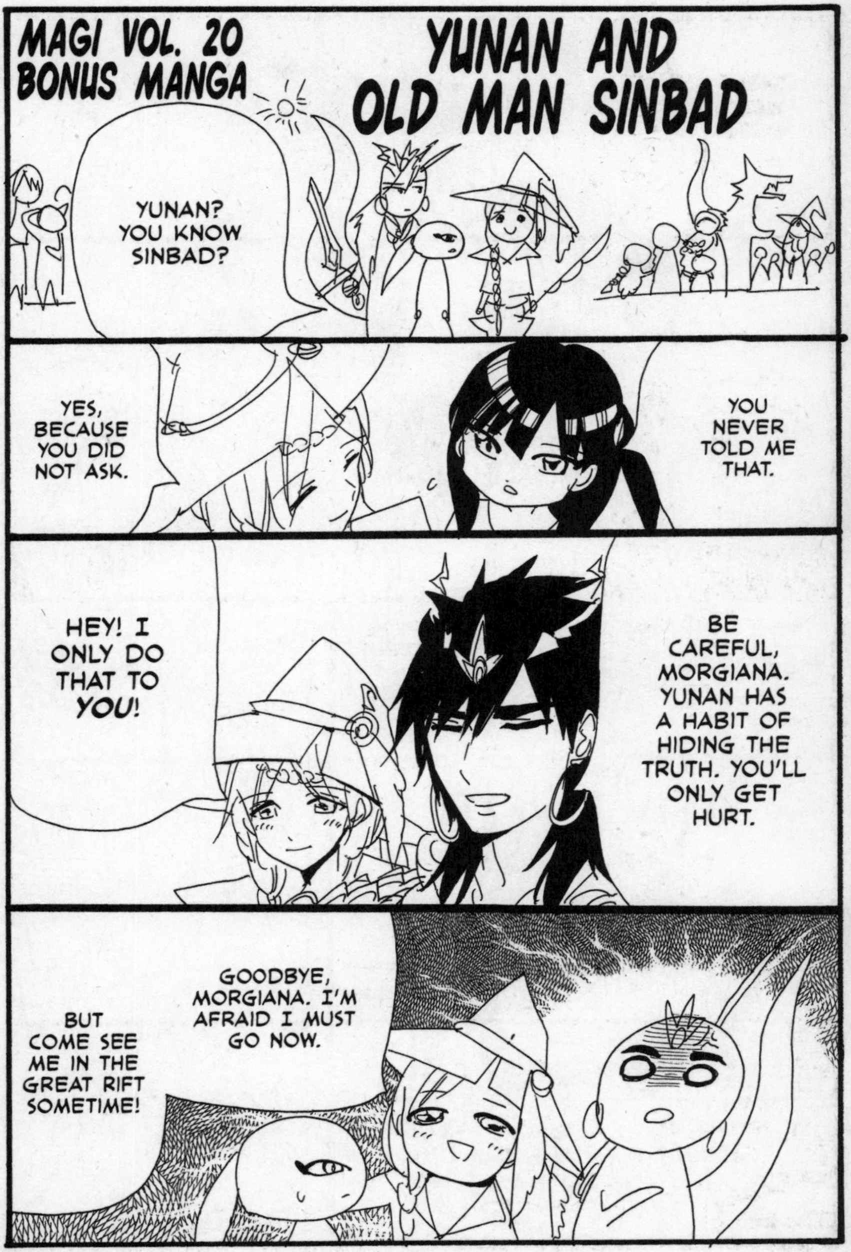
YUNAN AND OLD MAN SINBAD
MAGI VOL. 20 BONUS MANGA
YUNAN? YOU KNOW SINBAD?
YOU NEVER TOLD ME THAT.
YES, BECAUSE YOU DID NOT ASK.
BE CAREFUL, MORGIANA. YUNAN HAS A HABIT OF HIDING THE TRUTH. YOU'LL ONLY GET HURT.
HEY! I ONLY DO THAT TO *YOU*!
GOODBYE, MORGIANA. I'M AFRAID I MUST GO NOW.
BUT COME SEE ME IN THE GREAT RIFT SOMETIME!

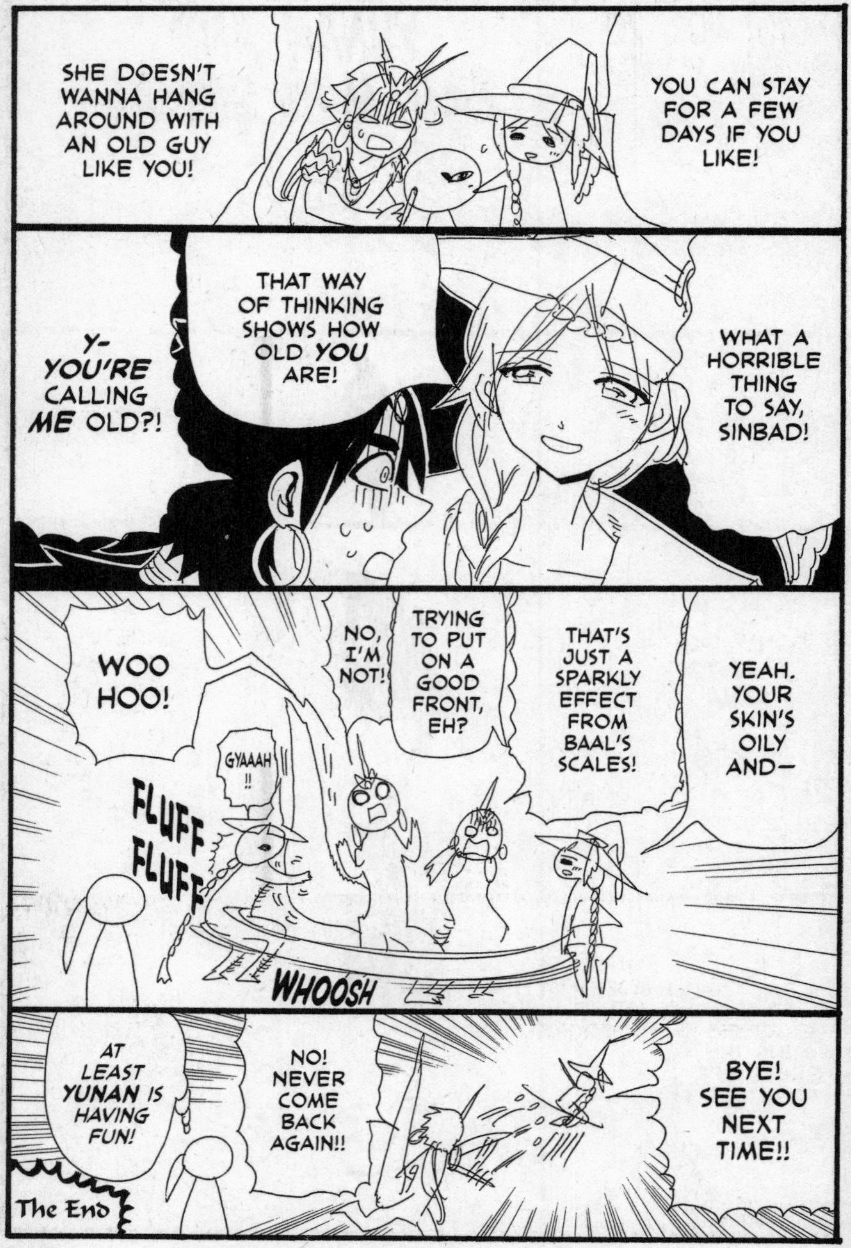
YOU CAN STAY FOR A FEW DAYS IF YOU LIKE!
SHE DOESN'T WANNA HANG AROUND WITH AN OLD GUY LIKE YOU!
WHAT A HORRIBLE THING TO SAY, SINBAD!
THAT WAY OF THINKING SHOWS HOW OLD *YOU* ARE!
Y-*YOU'RE* CALLING *ME* OLD?!
YEAH. YOUR SKIN'S OILY AND—
THAT'S JUST A SPARKLY EFFECT FROM BAAL'S SCALES!
TRYING TO PUT ON A GOOD FRONT, EH?
NO, I'M NOT!
WOO HOO!
GYAAAH!!
FLUFF FLUFF
WHOOSH
BYE! SEE YOU NEXT TIME!!
NO! NEVER COME BACK AGAIN!!
AT LEAST YUNAN IS HAVING FUN!
The End

SHINOBU OHTAKA

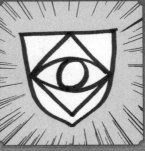

The Magnoshutatt Arc concludes!

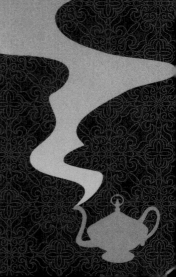

MAGI

Volume 20

Shonen Sunday Edition

Story and Art by
SHINOBU OHTAKA

MAGI Vol.20
by Shinobu OHTAKA
© 2009 Shinobu OHTAKA
All rights reserved.
Original Japanese edition published by SHOGAKUKAN.
English translation rights in the United States of America, Canada, the United Kingdom,
Ireland, Australia and New Zealand arranged with SHOGAKUKAN.

Translation & English Adaptation ◆ John Werry

Touch-up Art & Lettering ◆ Stephen Dutro

Editor ◆ Mike Montesa

Printed in the U.S.A.

Published by VIZ Media, LLC
P.O. Box 77010
San Francisco, CA 94107

10 9 8 7 6 5 4 3 2 1
First printing, October 2016

WWW.SHONENSUNDAY.COM

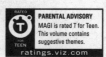
viz
MEDIA

www.viz.com

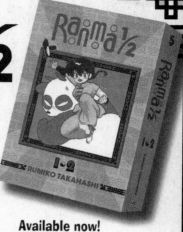

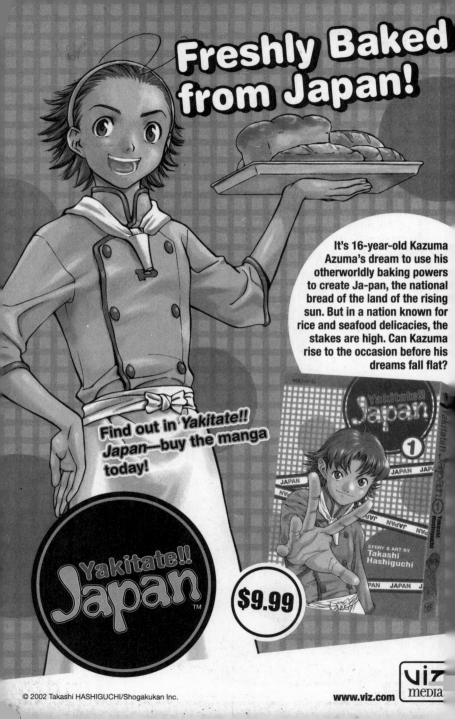

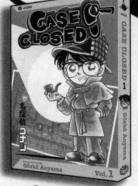

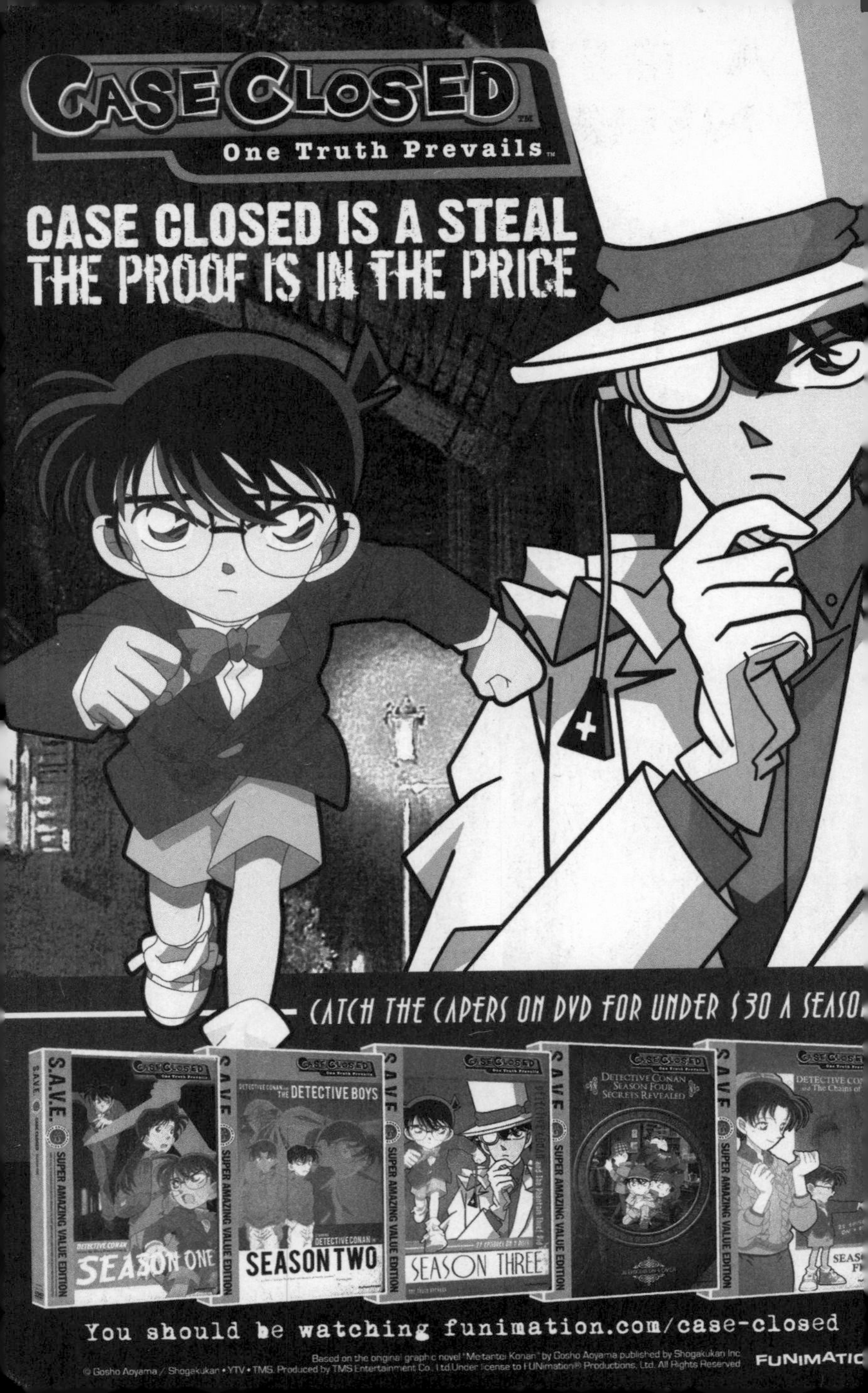

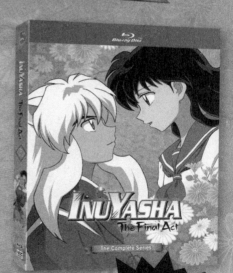

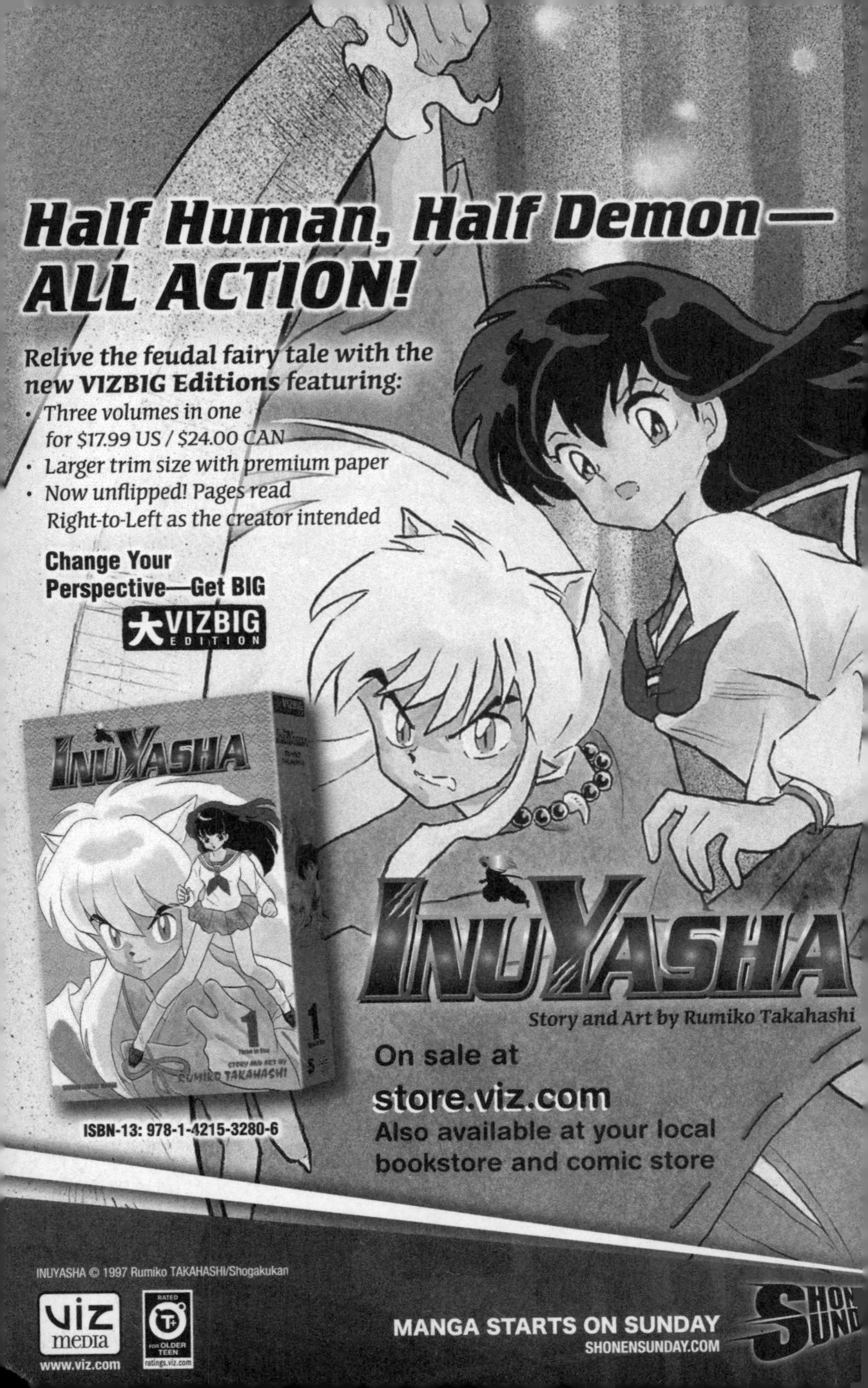
Half Human, Half Demon—
ALL ACTION!
Relive the feudal fairy tale with the new VIZBIG Editions featuring:
• Three volumes in one for $17.99 US / $24.00 CAN
• Larger trim size with premium paper
• Now unflipped! Pages read Right-to-Left as the creator intended
Change Your Perspective—Get BIG
大 VIZBIG EDITION
INUYASHA
1
STORY AND ART BY RUMIKO TAKAHASHI
ISBN-13: 978-1-4215-3280-6
INUYASHA
Story and Art by Rumiko Takahashi
On sale at
store.viz.com
Also available at your local bookstore and comic store
INUYASHA © 1997 Rumiko TAKAHASHI/Shogakukan
viz media
www.viz.com
RATED T+ FOR OLDER TEEN
ratings.viz.com
MANGA STARTS ON SUNDAY
SHONENSUNDAY.COM

You're reading the **WRONG WAY**

MAGI reads from right to left, starting in the upper-right corner. Japanese is read from **right** to **left**, meaning that action, sound effects, and word-balloon order are completely reversed from English order.

1
2
3
4
1
2
5
6
7
8
3
4
9
5
142

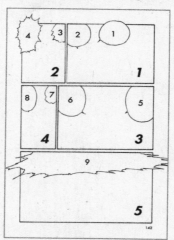

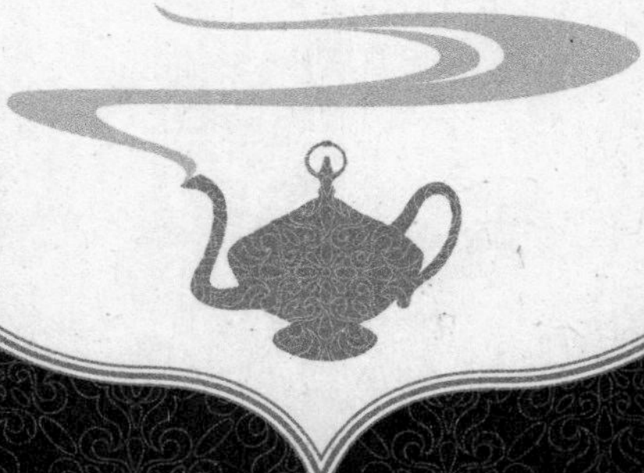